GRACE BREAKING THROUGH

a novel

by

James Clement

GRACE BREAKING THROUGH

a novel
by
James Clement

Published in the United States of America
Published by:
ATC Publishing LLC
160 Lakemont Drive
LaGrange, Georgia 30240

ISBN-13: 978-0-9990607-2-8
ISBN-10: 0-9990607-2-4

TABLE OF CONTENTS

DEDICATION

This novel is lovingly dedicated to my wife, Lily, and my son, Jonathan, both whom I love with all my heart and for whom I will always be grateful.

APPRECIATION

First and foremost, my appreciation goes to the Lord Jesus Christ for all that he has done for me and worked in me. I am also grateful for his grace in allowing this book to be. He is my reason, purpose, and motivation.

Also, I thank my wife and son for their encouragement and support during the writing of this novel and for allowing me to sacrifice the time needed to compose and to revise it.

My appreciation is extended to a few who have taught and mentored me over the years, making a significant impact in my life, either personally in relationship or through their resources. Mike and Sue Bové, who have given of themselves tirelessly to be a ministry of encouragement both to me and to many others over the decades, have been an incredible encouragement to me personally.

I also thank Shayne Russell, who discipled me as a teenager and a new believer in Christ. His investment in me through relationship laid a much-needed foundation for my growth in Christ.

Wayne Jacobsen and Brad Cummings have encouraged me through their publications and The God Journey podcasts presented on www.thegodjourney.com.

I also thank a few friends and acquaintances who read various incarnations or portions of the manuscript for this book. They are: Sue Bové, Susan Randolph, Jim Beebe, James Joransen, Randy Dodd, and Wayne Jacobsen. I am very grateful for their time, input, and encouragement in helping me to make this a better novel.

Finally, I express a special thanks to Jacek Dutkiewicz for his translation. I certainly could not have gotten it right without his invaluable assistance.

CHAPTER 1

HOW DID I BECOME LIKE THIS?

It was a warm, peaceful, summer day. My family and I were enjoying some encouraging fellowship with close friends in a relaxing, inviting setting. That is when I heard the words that I wished I had heard years earlier. Such a message would have spared me from a lot of heartache and despair, if I could have taken it to heart. It revolved around my relationship with God and his marvelous love.

"The problem comes when we let our sins fester without confessing them." The man saying these words was a dear friend and wonderful brother in Christ. He spoke in a gentle, cordial voice with care to the group of us listening. "It really doesn't make any sense *not* to go to Father with our sins. We're already forgiven eternally because of having trusted in Jesus and what he did for us. Therefore, the security of our salvation isn't the concern here. The kind of forgiveness we need spoken of in 1 John 1:9 is for *restored fellowship*. That much is clear in the context of the Apostle John's epistle. When we sin, what we need most is a fresh cleansing and restoration of fellowship with Father. He provides them when we confess our sins to him as that verse assures us. Our confession to him is us remembering and admitting how much we need Jesus every moment of every day. Our sins are evidences of those moments when we've tried to strike out on our own and to act independently of him. And Father doesn't use our prayer time as a chance to browbeat us, so to speak, with shame or guilt."

This had been a long-standing problem of mine, my perspective on taking my sins before God, and at the time I was finally in a frame of mind to understand and to receive God's grace concerning his love and affection toward me. My friend continued speaking.

"By now you're probably persuaded from the Scriptures that he doesn't do that to us. And he always welcomes us back, naturally," the man continued. *"He loves us!* We're his children, and he wants our fellowship with him to be restored even more than we do. So, you see why the enemy wants to discourage us from turning to Jesus when we sin. It's because he knows that we receive restoration and cleansing when we do. That's why he'll feed us negative thoughts about Father when we sin. It's all an attempt to build a barrier or wall between us and Father. He's not called the adversary and deceiver for nothing, you know."

For years the evil one had assailed me with the flaming arrows of negative thoughts about God. It had happened without me even realizing it. All along I had thought that my perceptions about God and my sins were biblical. Eventually they led me into a downward spiral that wounded me spiritually. The perspective that I had conjectured concerning God was deplorable. The thoughts that I was entertaining then would have shocked and alarmed me previously.

> *I don't want anything to do with God! He's not doing anything to solve my problems or to get me out of this spiritual mess I'm Putting him first and trying to live for him didn't do me any good, so why did I ever bother? Nothing that I do pleases him anyway. He doesn't love me anymore, and he's made it pretty clear that he's angry with me. I just wish that he'd leave me alone! I don't need any more of his "help."*

That's how I used to feel at the lowest point in my life. Things had become so bad that all I could see were problems, trials, and difficulties—all with no solutions or hope. There was nothing but darkness, and everything seemed to be against me. To me, God seemed to oppose me more than anyone else.

It grieves me now to think that I once felt that way about Father, but it is presented in all honesty. (Now I sense such a closeness to him and have such an affection for him that I usually refer to him as *Father*.) This just shows how far a believer in Christ can go in his misunderstanding and broken fellowship with God. *Thank you, Jesus, for the work that you performed in my heart then and which you continue to do daily!*

This attitude which I had toward God was appalling and really made no sense. At the time, I was continuously angry, and I couldn't even pinpoint a precise reason as to why. It was a very difficult time for me, lasting over two years. Many were the moments and nights when I stepped back mentally and realized what I had become. During that whole period, I felt as if God were a million miles away from me. I felt so hurt, battered, frustrated, and confused. My heart had grown cold and hard toward God and toward people. Although I felt so distant and closed off from Father, often I would still cry out: *Lord, what has happened to me? How did I become like this? I don't like who I am, and I want to change. I need to change. I can't keep going like this. I'm ruining my life and my family's lives! I just can't be like this for the rest of my life!*

My desperate prayers seemed to have no effect on God at all.

Then, completely unexpectedly, something happened. When it seemed that my life couldn't have become much worse, Father's grace broke through to me. He showered me with his love and compassion in such an effective and unexpected way. It was at that very moment when these words were spoken to me:

"That is just what Father wants: he wants you to run into his arms when you are hurt."

That moment and those simple words shattered my defensive walls and welcomed me into Father's embrace. It was such a heart-changing moment that every time I talk about it, I weep like a little baby. As I've shared my story with many friends and acquaintances, the result is always the same. When I begin to describe that exact moment, the waterworks begin! I can barely get through the retelling of it because of my profuse sobbing. God's grace and love were the only cure for my spiritual hardness, and I'm not ashamed to admit it.

During the worst part of my bitterness, a few Christians tried to encourage me the best that they knew how. In the end they were no help at all. They would tell me, "All things work together for

3

good for those who love God," but at the time, I couldn't see any good in what I was going through. They kept telling me the same, simplistic, trite, Christian sayings like:

"Just trust God. Things will get better."
"You just have to believe."
"You must have some unconfessed sin in your life, hindering his blessings."
"Pray, pray, and then pray some more. And when you don't know what to do, just pray and believe."
"Fast and *pray. That will* really *open the floodgates of heaven."*
"You're just going through your wilderness phase, like the children of Israel. It'll pass in time."
"Maybe this is just God's will for you during this season of your life."
"Just stop being so angry! What's done is done. It's in the past. Get over it!"
"John's problem is that he needs to get over his pity party."

Most of the people who told me or my wife these Christian platitudes thought that they were presenting biblical truths, even though they would have had difficulty finding scriptural proof for them. Even when they quoted the Bible, it was either out of context, completely misunderstood by them, or misapplied to my situation. They didn't even understand my plight to be able to apply their "advice" to my situation. They simply repeated what they had heard or remembered hearing from sermons. Even worse than the advice I received were the cold shoulders and avoidance that I experienced with many whom I had considered my friends. They simply didn't know how to relate to me in that condition.

My real need was not for preaching or spiritual platitudes. After all, I had studied the Bible and presented plenty of sermons and teaching messages to audiences far and wide. I had been a missionary. Any effective biblical counsel for my situation I would have already read about from the Scriptures or presented publicly.

4

Surely it would all be in my files of sermons or even recorded on cassette tape. Shouldn't I know this stuff already? So why was I such a mess spiritually?

A missionary! I was supposed to be above all the indignation and bitterness, all the struggles and doubts, all the spiritual stagnation. I had been ordained and entrusted to carry the gospel of Jesus Christ to people who had never heard it. Missionaries were not supposed to have such struggles and weaknesses, or so I was made to believe. In fact, I understood that they were to be exemplary, showing by their lives how to avoid the pitfalls of sin and counseling others to do the same.

So where did *I* go wrong? What had happened to *me*? This was not what I had chosen to be, "a bitter, washed-up, disgruntled, ex-missionary." No one used those words to my face, but I felt as if some were saying them behind my back. As a teenager in Christ, I would occasionally encounter individuals who professed Jesus and also demonstrated symptoms of bitterness in their lives. They were easily angered, wielding their wrath like a weapon. They were no picnic to be around, and those close to them knew that they had some deeply-seated heart issues which needed the work of God's grace. In my immaturity, I didn't think to pray for them. Instead I would always pray that Father would not allow me to fall into such a snare. *Please, Lord*, I prayed, *don't ever let me become bitter like those people*. Ironically, that's exactly what happened to me some fifteen years into my journey with Jesus.

Jesus Christ came into my heart and life when I was seventeen, growing up in Georgia. I understood then that I was born a sinner and that I needed Jesus. What he had done for me through his sacrifice and resurrection made this relationship with him and my eternal home in heaven both possible and a reality. I became active in a local church and learned about missions. At the age of twenty, I accepted the call to serve in world missions and traveled to Honduras for a brief nine-day tour of mission works supported in part by our congregation.

Just before the trip, I crash-reviewed my college Spanish.

Although it didn't get me very far in a lot of conversations, it was enough to help with many moments while I was there. The American missionaries who were there also helped tremendously as interpreters.

That first experience in Honduras made a life-changing impression on me at various levels. I was greatly moved by the extreme poverty that I witnessed. I was also deeply touched by the precious, humble believers who were mired in poverty and even persecution from their nominal Catholic relatives and countrymen. Nevertheless, they were so in love with Jesus and were excited to live for him. I was mostly impressed and burdened for the national pastors, several of whom had literally lost everything—even being forsaken by their Catholic family members and neighbors—all for the Lord Jesus Christ. Some were from Nicaragua and had fled their homeland amid the civil war there between the Contras and the Sandinistas in the 1980s. I heard testimony after testimony from these pastors about persecution and suffering. One pastor's parents held a mock funeral, saying that since their son had become "evangelical" he was now dead to them. Another related with tears how his brother had been barricaded inside one of the church buildings by Sandinistas, who then burned the building to the ground with the pastor's brother inside. The stories were heartbreaking; yet through all their sufferings, these precious believers in Jesus never considered surrendering to despair or denying Christ as options.

In the wake of meeting these faithful believers, my eyes and heart became opened to the needs of the world, and I felt great shame for my selfish lifestyle as a result. In my spiritual immaturity and selfishness, I had often complained over petty, egotistical concerns as a believer in the States. I had had no thought for others in great need, whether locally or abroad. Simple believers, such as these in Central America and in many other parts of the world, had very little in the way of tangible possessions or even Bible training. Yet they were enduring and even thriving under persecution. For them it was not simply words and photos in a book but a daily reality. What these national pastors lacked in

Bible education, they more than compensated for in character, spiritual commitment, and faithfulness. They simply followed Jesus because he had redeemed them by his great love and grace. Christ and their relationship with him were their motivations to continue. Nothing else mattered in this world to them but him. I returned home from that trip determined to help those pastors. The American missionary couple working there encouraged me to obtain a Bible education at a Christian college which would prepare me to teach and to train the nationals and others for ministry. This became my goal: to get an education in the Bible and missions so that I could return to Honduras and train the up-and-coming national pastors and other Central American believers preparing for full-time ministry.

My desire and goal were to return to Honduras as a full-time missionary. Therefore, I spent a few years earning a degree in missions and spending a couple of summers interning with the same mission organization in Honduras. What I had not expected on my first trip there was meeting a very special girl. During my further trips, Elena and I became friends. Needless to say, due to my desire to serve in Central America and my growing relationship with Elena, I was highly motivated to become proficient in Spanish. I studied on my own and practiced every opportunity I had. Five years after building a friendship with Elena, we married. Some years later we had a son, Nathaniel. Establishing our family and preparing to return to Honduras required a few years; nevertheless, Father's provision for our every need was beyond anything that we could ask or think. The Lord was so wonderful in providing for even the smallest of details. As he provided for our every need right before our eyes, we grew to trust him for things over which I normally would have worried profusely. Yet it seemed that he had orchestrated certain details to win our trust in him. For years to come, the astounding things that he did in those months would encourage us to trust him for greater things without stressing over them.

During that first trip to Honduras, my best friend, Steve, accompanied me due to his own interest in missions. As our group of twenty-one Americans traveled from town to town, meeting the locals, he was burdened for the children. Less than a year later, Steve began his missionary service with this same mission in Honduras while I was still in Bible college. He was a few years older than I and had already earned his Bible college degree. In the two-and-a-half years since our first trip to Honduras, he had also raised his own support, studied Spanish for a year in a language school for missionaries in Costa Rica, and started a Christian school for the mission in his first few months there. He had also entered the mission field as a single missionary, but after two years in the field, he returned to the States to seek a wife.

My family and I finalized the last details for the move, packed all our worldly goods into a shipping container, and flew back to Central America in January of 1999.

We settled not too far from the capital in a town which had no gospel witness, according to what a veteran American missionary in the country had told me. I took that to be Father's direction for us to set up shop there. Elena wanted us to live somewhere much closer to her family, since they were almost four hours away. If I had known what was going to happen, I would have changed my mind and chosen a town which was a lot closer to them.

After settling into a rental home in a new town, we began to execute the ministry plan. The first ministry we began was a Saturday morning Bible club to the neighborhood children ages twelve and under. A neighbor's daughter was instrumental in gathering most of the children that first Saturday, which was around fifty or so. A week or two later, the attendance leveled off to around thirty. Then we began a teen Bible study on Friday evenings. Again, a couple of teens next-door spread the word at the high school, and there were some two dozen or more in attendance that first Friday. We prayed for the townspeople and began to build relationships with them as opportunities arose. Within a year, I started a men's Bible study with just five men and began holding church services with just two other families in a neighbor's home. It was a slow start, but the numbers were encouraging.

8

However, I knew that it was depth and impact that really counted, not numbers, and my prayer was to reach more families and to plant a local assembly.

The town held much opposition for us. The traditional religion had a long-standing history of loyalty from most of the citizens. A couple of cults had been active in the town long before we had arrived, and they had also made quite a bit of headway. Naturally there were some of the typical carnal elements of the world present, luring people of all ages. Since God had given me a heart to reach the teens, and for the longest time it was the main ministry we had, I poured my heart into the teen study and into building relationships with them. Elena quickly built a rapport with the girls, but as the outsider, I had to work diligently and carefully to earn a place in the hearts of the youths. I felt that I wasn't always successful in achieving this goal.

In the teen Bible study, I taught a basic introduction to the Bible, God, and his plan of salvation. We taught at a slow pace to assure that everyone understood the foundational lessons. Each lesson built on the previous ones. The aim of the whole study was to present the gospel clearly so that the teens would understand that they were sinners, yet that they could have a relationship with God through Jesus Christ, who died and was resurrected to provide salvation for them freely. It was essential that they understand that our salvation was by grace, which meant that it was free and apart from any works or effort on our part. If any of them were to misunderstand by thinking that what Jesus did was insufficient and that salvation required some ritual, sacrament, work, or effort on their part or on anyone else's part, then they would have been deceived and would have missed the gospel completely. The language was not a barrier because, due to my various trips and personal studies, I had been fluent in Spanish for ten years by then, and I continued to study and to practice it wholeheartedly. The real issue was any spiritual, religious, and emotional baggage that they might have harbored which would possibly hinder or block their understanding of the gospel of grace. Anything I might do to dishonor myself in their eyes would also make it practically impossible ever to win their trust again. We prayed daily for these teens, and through our monthly update letters we asked our prayer partners to intercede with us for these youths and the unseen spiritual battles being waged in the hearts of individuals.

Almost since the day we had returned to the country, we were confronted with a series of difficulties. Some of them were related to the country and culture. This was unexpected, since I had visited Honduras on many previous trips, even working for two summers there. I had also studied the country and culture as well as taken classes on cross-cultural adaptations and missions at the Christian university from which I graduated. I had felt so much a part of the country and culture that I could immerse myself in it and contemplate and analyze my own native culture unbiased from without. I even married one of the country's own citizens and felt like an honorary citizen myself. Nevertheless, the problems were undeniable.

People treated me differently, like an outsider. Obviously, I was an outsider, but I had not experienced so much rudeness and rejection in all my trips before as when I moved there to live and to work on a more permanent basis. Dealing with store clerks and government agents became a dread due to the hassles and rudeness which confronted me. There were times when a simple drive from one town to another resulted in me being pulled over at a military or police checkpoint. The soldiers or officers would see my American face and apparently thought that they could intimidate me on some trumped-up accusation regarding my passport or vehicle. Predictably, many Americans panicked in such situations and offered them money to smooth over any "infractions." The tactics I had employed with them in previous years no longer had much effect on them, and these encounters were growing more stressful.

There were many hoops I had to jump through just to perform what I expected to be normal interactions in the community. Simple tasks such as renewing my driver's license, paying taxes on a license plate, cashing a check, shopping at a hardware store, and buying groceries became stressful, frustrating ordeals through which I often felt abused and mocked. On one Saturday out of the blue, only two children showed up for the Bible club, not the twenty-six or so I expected. Later that day someone told me that Coca-Cola was sponsoring a promotion that morning at the same time as the Bible club, and the promoters were giving away free products and prizes. Obviously, I didn't know about it, and no one bothered to tell me beforehand. When I was in public, people generally took advantage of me in any number of situations, presumably because I was a "worthless *gringo*." At least that's how I felt that I was being treated. I started to become angry and resentful, and with each negative experience my indignation increased.

Objects seemed to oppose me as well. Whether it was a part on the pickup truck, some hardware or appliance at home, or some gadget or tool I attempted to use, it seemed that everything I touched had something against me and was antagonistic toward me. Physical objects simply didn't comply as they had my whole life before. Nothing worked easily or the first time. And with each incident of objects not working right, I fumed even more.

Elena and I were also experiencing a lot of tension and friction in our marriage. We began to argue with one another and to have conflicts over simple things and decisions of all kinds. It seemed that we couldn't agree on anything. My temper seethed, and many times I lashed out at her both verbally and emotionally. I never harmed her physically, but I couldn't reign in my words and emotions. Admittedly, many days I had caused her to weep. She didn't understand what had happened to me; I didn't understand what had happened to me either. In a sense I was likewise an observer of these changes in my heart and character, watching myself do and say things which seemed so unlike me. Neither Elena nor I liked what I had become, and I didn't know what to do about it. I felt so empty on the inside.

Likewise, my prayers seemed empty. How could I pray when I couldn't control this anger and the things around me that enraged me? I knew all too well the scripture of 1 Peter 3:7 which advises and warns, "Husbands, in the same way, treat your wives with consideration as the weaker partners and show them honor as fellow heirs of the grace of life. In this way nothing will hinder your prayers." Sadly, I lived the fulfillment of the warning in that scripture almost daily during that time. My Bible study and teaching seemed lifeless. There I was trying to reach people with the good news of eternal life in Jesus Christ, yet I felt so numb spiritually. There seemed to be a chasm between me and God, and I sensed that he wasn't pleased with me. I just couldn't figure out how to turn myself around and to get my heart right. Most of the time, God seemed to be distant, callous, and frowning at me.

There was a myriad of other factors, too many to list, which seemed to combine and to work against me. Sleep deprivation was part of my daily existence, and it further fueled my dissatisfaction and rage. I was miserable most of the time, and the irony was that *this was the life that I had chosen and worked so hard to achieve!* Actually, I had dreamed of teaching and training young men for the ministry, so perhaps in that sense it wasn't the exact dream I had imagined all along. Nevertheless, I had talked about living in Honduras, being immersed in the culture, and ministering to the people there for many years. How could I possibly complain about being there? Yet many times I felt so stressed and frazzled that I just wanted some kind of break from it all. It wasn't that I really wanted to leave, but I simply wanted something like a vacation from all the stress, problems, and opposition. My "vacation" never came.

My little son Nathaniel was my ray of sunshine in the midst of my spiritual stagnation. I spent most of the hours in my days with him, feeding him, caring for him, and playing with him. He always had a smile for me, no matter what I felt or was experiencing. While I felt spent spiritually, I always found solace and joy in my moments with him. Many days we would roll his toy cars back and forth across the hard floor, and although for me it became monotonous after half an hour, I delighted to do it because of the time and opportunity I was afforded to spend with my son.

One morning as I fed Nathaniel his cereal, a segment on Sesame

Street in Spanish on TV cut to my heart of hearts. In the show, a six-year-old boy sang about how he loved to spend time with his *papá*. Watching my son give his attention to the music and the depiction of happy moments between that boy and his father, I burst into tears unexpectedly. As I watched, I begged Father to restore my heart. I didn't want Nathaniel to have an angry, bitter dad to raise him. My experiences with my own father and step-father had left deep scars, and for the life of me, I didn't want anything even close to that to happen to little Nathaniel. He was too precious, and he needed a great dad to raise, to nurture, and to mentor him and to be a positive influence on him. Would I be that kind of dad for him? Would he grow up delighting to have me as his father? *Oh, Lord, please change my heart! I need you so desperately!*

Our work continued, despite my spiritual dearth. The youth Bible study, the children's Bible club, the men's Bible study, and the small church services continued weekly. I worked and did what I could to teach and to be a blessing to others, yet due to my hardened heart, I felt as if I were simply going through the motions. Bitterness had stolen my joy.

In the midst of my anger, turmoil, and bitterness is when it happened. After many months of teaching and preparing the soil for the seed of the word, the Friday evening came for me to present the gospel to the teens and to confront them with a decision for Christ. I prayed about it ceaselessly, especially that whole Friday, despite my lack of any sense of a connection with God due to my anger. But my prayers were for them to know the living Christ, our hope of glory, not for me to benefit in any way were any of them to trust him for salvation. On that night I spoke to the teens as plainly and as clearly as I knew how. I stripped the presentation of all emotional and coercive tactics; I didn't want them to respond out of pure emotion or to feel that they had to trust Jesus to please me or their peers or anything like that. In the moment that I gave the invitation, out of the twenty-three teens present that particular night, twenty-two of them responded *en masse*, acknowledging that they were sinners, and trusted Jesus to save them. The only one who did not respond was the youngest and shyest, who probably felt too shy to draw any attention publicly.

Most people would have rejoiced over such a large response, but I was not rejoicing. I was suspicious of what had really happened. I knew that my heart had not been right for a long time, and although I had sincerely prayed for this kind of outcome, I simply couldn't believe it. I *must* have done something wrong to make them react this way. Then again, maybe the gospel is just that easy to understand and that powerful. Whatever good may have happened, it was not because of me, so I took no credit at all for it. In fact, I had feared that my spiritual dearth would negatively affect them as well and that my attempts would cause them to resent Jesus and the gospel. I never fantasized that anything like this would have ever happened.

Thank you, Jesus. But . . . are they really sincere? Did all twenty-two teens just become born again? For their sakes and for your glory, I pray that they did.

The following Friday, I reviewed the gospel with them and made another presentation for a few who had been absent the previous Friday evening; those three or four who heard for the first time then likewise responded by proclaiming their faith in Christ. We had bought Bibles for the teens and gave them to all who trusted Jesus.

At the men's Bible study, I also presented much the same material to them over a few months and eventually appealed to them to trust Jesus Christ as their Savior. One of the five men was already a believer, which I knew. He was there to encourage the others to attend faithfully. One gentleman met with me later and gave me his excuses for not accepting what I presented. I grieved for him, though I knew he was being honest with me. Then one of the men believed, and by his testimony to me the next day, I really believed that he sincerely trusted Jesus.

Okay, Lord. At least there's one I know who I am confident now has eternal life. Thank you for working in spite of me!

◊   ◊   ◊   ◊   ◊

We had just reached a good rhythm with the church services we were holding when that fateful day arrived. It was March 11, 2000, a day I'll never forget. I received a letter in the mail from the IRS informing me that, for the return I had filed the previous year, I owed approximately $20,000 in back taxes and fees. All the support we had received in the months leading up to our departure had been used for moving expenses, plane tickets, residency expenses, and a few teaching tools and ministry resources. I had made the mistake of not paying taxes on any of those monies, trusting in Form 4361, the Application for Exemption From Self-Employment Tax for Use By Ministers. It was a form which I had completed and mailed but from Honduras. The IRS said that they never received it. How on earth would I ever have the means to repay this tax debt? It was a lot more money than the support donations we would receive in a year.

Later that day, I called a friend of ours back in the States who was handling our finances and bank accounts stateside. "You only received half your support this month," came the voice on the phone. I contacted the mission organization and, sure enough, it was true. Not only did we not have the means to pay the $20,000, but we also didn't have enough money to make it to the next month. My heart sank and sank and sank. I couldn't afford to live and to minister on the mission field any longer!

My head was swimming at the thought of all the decisions and consequences facing me. I would have a thousand things to do, none of which I would have otherwise willingly chosen to do. I would have to call the mission president to inform him that we would have to move back to the States. I would have to write to all our supporters to communicate the dreadful news. I would have to plan another move, only this time in reverse, which proved to be much more difficult. Once we arrived back in Georgia, I would have to find a place to stay for a few days while I found a more permanent residence, a job, a vehicle, etc., etc. I would have to start all over again, this time as a "failed missionary."

No one would want anything to do with me ever again. No one would believe the circumstances that led to us moving back. No one would ever want to hear any kind of spiritual teaching or biblical advice from me ever again. I could already hear the comments and criticisms: "Once you fail on the mission field, you're washed-up." "Looks like you'll have to work at Walmart for the rest of your life." "When do you plan to pay back all that support money to the people who scraped and sacrificed just so that you could go waste everybody's time and money in Honduras?" My imagined fears were not kind, and I sensed that I would enter a deep depression, as if the state of bitterness I was already in wasn't depressing enough.

Oh, Lord! What am I going to do! Will I ever laugh again? Will I ever sleep again? Will I ever shake off this shroud of bitterness and anger which seems to permeate my whole being?

We made the hard choices and methodically began to prepare to return to the USA. It took several months to make the preparations to uproot our family and to move back to the States—a course of events which I hadn't dreamed would happen for decades. Meanwhile we hobbled along emotionally, continuing with ministry as usual. I felt so emotionally devastated that what I had dreamed and prepared for during the previous twelve years was coming to such an abrupt and disheartening end. Not only were the beginnings of my dream disintegrating all around me, but I would return home as a failure with no job, no home, no vehicle, no money, a mountain of debt, and no circle of friends to support me either socially or emotionally. I knew that former missionaries who returned from the foreign field so quickly and under such circumstances never fared well, and all their supporters immediately cut ties with them. Therefore, I had all that to expect upon our return.

I didn't know how to appreciate it much at the time, but the Lord brought me a buyer for my Toyota pickup truck. This gentleman was willing to pay me ahead of time for the vehicle and to meet me at the airport to receive it so that we would have a ride to our flight. Normally this would have been unthinkable, but Father was proving again that we could trust him in the details for everything. If only I could have come to my senses and accepted it as that kind of a blessing, then I would have been greatly encouraged. However, because of the attitude that I chose and what I wanted to believe, such was not to be then. My bitterness, though smoldering because of the emotional despair and devastation, was still quite active. The time for encouragement and gratitude would come much later.

We flew home on the day of our eighth wedding anniversary. We had such mixed emotions about everything. Elena was heartbroken again about leaving her family, especially under these depressing circumstances. I was thankful that she had not decided to stay with her parents and to let me deal with all my problems without her. Lesser women would have done exactly that, I knew. In my spiraling despair, I didn't know how to appreciate her for making this sacrifice yet again. Little Nathaniel was oblivious to everything going on around us, being just under two-years-old at the time; he was just happy to ride in a big plane and to be with us.

I wanted relief from the state I was in, and in a sense, I wanted to come home to take a break from the culture, thinking that that was what had inflamed my anger. However, I had never dreamed of coming home like this. I was returning as a failure after only eighteen months of being on the foreign field. Gone forever was my dream of teaching and mentoring young nationals for the ministry in Central America. I had envisioned myself as one day being a seasoned missionary in my fifties and sixties, encouraging, discipling, and counseling young men to reach their own people for Christ. In my imagination, they would view me as a great encouragement and a blessed resource of wisdom and experience; I would rejoice to see the Lord working in their lives to bring many souls into the body of Christ.

None of that would ever happen now. My life had taken a turn for debt and mediocrity. I would be little more than a working stiff, probably having to hold down two or three jobs leading nowhere—all so that I could pay off my enormous tax debt. My hardened heart would probably never enjoy anything in life again or have any sense of purpose.

Where is God in the midst of my whole world crashing down around me? I wondered. *He must have better things to do than to help me. Why would he help me anyway? I certainly don't deserve it.*

These were the kinds of thoughts that I had to console me. Although Father seemed to have turned away from me, scowling at my sinful, spiritual state, he was much closer than I realized. He had been with me and my family every step of the way. I had so much to learn.

CHAPTER 2

"A WASHED-UP, DISGRUNTLED, EX-MISSIONARY"

Father's provision was at every turn, yet I noticed it only super-
ficially; I still didn't appreciate it and let it spur my trust in him to
increase as I could have. In less than a week, we rented a duplex
as a more permanent residence. Also, in those first few days, a
good friend of mine helped me by driving me to an individual's
house to buy a used car. We had enough money from the sale of
the pickup we had in Honduras to use for this purchase. For the
first three months I worked a couple of temp jobs for two different
friends who owned their own businesses. They seemed to want to
help and didn't ask any questions about what had happened in
Honduras and our abrupt return. We were also blessed that Elena
could stay home with Nathaniel to care for him and to teach him
in his prior-to-school education and nurturing years. Having spent
most of every day with Nathaniel for a year-and-a-half, I missed
him dearly while I was at work.

We began attending services again at my home church. This
was where I had trusted Christ and was discipled by the youth
pastor. Here I had proclaimed my acceptance of God's call on my
life for missions. These were the brothers and sisters who had
backed me and ordained me to preach the gospel. Just a short year-
and-a-half prior to that time, my church family had sent us off with
their prayers, blessings, and support, excited to see and to hear
what God would do through us in Central America.

However, things had changed since then at our home church.
What a difference eighteen months had made! In our absence the
congregation had experienced some turmoil. We only heard bits
and pieces after we returned. It was difficult to separate rumor
from fact; however, it was clear that this local body had suffered.
Many of the faithful with whom I had been close and with whom
I had shared so much life in Christ were no longer there. They had
been hurt and moved on elsewhere. A number of new people had

joined, some of them even taking leadership positions and worship team positions. There were many new faces on the platform and quite a few changes in the programs and the look and feel of the way my beloved local congregation used to be. Some of the changes were a direct result and consequence of the questionable and hurtful occurrences which had taken place after the founding pastor retired and we left for Central America.

The new members didn't know us, so we had no history of ministry and relationship with them as we had had with the more long-standing members, many of whom were no longer there. Almost no one knew how to relate to us coming back under such shameful circumstances. There seemed to be a respectable distance between us and the other church family members. At best, things were kept at a minimal cordiality, with plastic smiles, surface questions, and perfunctory handshakes. At worst, a few individuals were rude to us with their silence, unfriendly glares, and avoidance of us, both physically and emotionally. My imagination scrambled to guess what was being said about us.

A couple of weeks later I learned that the "interim" pastor, who took the position after our founding pastor retired, and the board of deacons had met to discuss how to help us or to relate to us. They had learned of our huge tax debt and sudden loss of financial support; they understood that we could no longer afford to stay in Central America. These deacons, the brothers with whom I had served on this board for several years just before we left, decided to continue the church's support to us for a couple of months until we could get settled and earn some steady income. This was a blessing. Beyond this and a few heartfelt conversations and individual prayers with a few of the deacons with whom I was closest, there was nothing else proffered in the way of meeting our practical needs. Since my bitter attitude had me otherwise occupied, I didn't have the clarity of mind to have many expectations of our church family. In my smoldering sludge of bitterness, I had no real sense of receiving much help or encouragement, not having any sense of deserving any. Eventually a few individuals I knew outside the church told me *exactly* what the leaders should have done to reach out to us. This sharing of opinions didn't help me at all.

Soon after that deacons' meeting, the "interim" pastor met with me and basically gave me the trust-God-and-life-goes-on speech. "We don't want to pressure you," he said from behind his office desk, smiling with his reassuring voice. "We understand that you have to get settled and meet the needs of your family. So for now, just do what you have to do. You know, get a job at Walmart or wherever. Do what you have to do to provide for your family. And just try to get yourself and your family back to normal. The Lord will take care of you all."

"Get a job at Walmart?" I thought. *Did he really just say that?*

This advice came from a man several years younger than me. He had been snatched up from an out-of-state congregation where he had only served as youth pastor for a few years. Thanks to the pulpit committee's path-of-least-resistance method for choosing a replacement pastor after the founding pastor retired, he had been selected to lead this sizable membership of around a thousand people. However, if the rumors had any truth to them, he had apparently caused most of the problems which had led to so many people leaving in the months before our return. Then, just three months after our return, he left the church suddenly and quietly.

Although I was back in familiar territory, I was in such a spiritual quagmire that I wasn't getting any spiritual nourishment from any of the services. Everything being taught or preached seemed so simplistic for the simple problems of typical Christians in affluent America. The Sunday school class was bearable, perhaps because it was a small group. It also helped that the man who taught the class of young couples—which had been a class that I started and taught for a couple of years before we left for the foreign field—was also a deacon and a good friend of mine. He was very open, honest, and as encouraging as he could be to me. It seemed that no one at church had had any experience or wisdom relating to how to soothe the bitterness which was hurting me so much. This brother had served in the Viet Nam War, and he

21

compared what I was going through with what he had experienced in the seventies after he came home. "Except that you've returned from spiritual warfare," he told me repeatedly. I sincerely appreciated his comments and encouragement, but I just couldn't compare what I basically did to myself to the horrors of the Viet Nam War which our veterans had endured. During previous years, several veterans from that war whom I knew had recounted to me some of the atrocities that they faced there. I couldn't belittle what they experienced by thinking that my experience compared in any way to what they suffered in that foreign war. However, I did know that if it was truly spiritual warfare like he had said, I must have brought it home with me, because I seemed worse than before. How would it help me to accept that I was in spiritual warfare?

During the Wednesday night services, I simply didn't fit in anywhere. Elena volunteered in the nursery on Wednesdays, so she never struggled with where to go. I, however, faced a real conundrum. The so-called "Wednesday Night Prayer Meeting" was sparsely attended with about thirty to fifty adults on any given Wednesday night. Many more had attended a couple of years before when the founding pastor had taught the class, but all that changed soon after he retired. For one reason or another, mostly because they were all in the middle of their teaching units, the other classes either were not for me or just didn't hold my interest. In my stagnated, spiritual state, I didn't even know what would interest or help me.

Then I began listening to some of the young college kids' conversations. It wasn't really eaves dropping, I thought, because they were just talking together in the pew behind me after the services ended. It was too difficult not to listen. They were so bubbly and jovial, and they really enjoyed each other's company. As it turned out, they were all musically inclined. Six or seven of them had formed a praise band at church called—wait for it—The Praise Band. These young people played and sang as the musical opening to the Wednesday night teen meeting in a separate building called the Teen Center.

22

One Wednesday night I followed the flow of teens from Wednesday night dinner in the dining hall and sneaked into the Teen Center. There were several other adults serving as youth workers, so I must have blended in well. I felt safe, since no one questioned me about what I was doing there. I sat back, hoping for something encouraging. I was not disappointed. The Praise Band was talented, loud, and quite underappreciated by most of the adults in the congregation. They weren't promoting theatrics, stage presence, or themselves; they were simply singing about Jesus and communing with him through song. Anyone listening was welcomed to join their hearts in praise to the one Mediator between God and men, the Lord Jesus Christ. They played some of the then current praise hits heard on Christian radio stations as well as quite a few of their own compositions. After a few weeks, I began to learn the lyrics to their original songs, and I looked forward to attending on Wednesday evenings.

That first night that I sneaked in, I sat next to a teenager who seemed to be attending by himself. I struck up a conversation with him and soon learned that he was present in the meetings against his will. From his vocabulary and comments, I deduced that he was well-versed in philosophy and logic. This teen had a head on his shoulders. Apparently, no one at church had had any idea about how to approach him or how to befriend him—or so I thought at the time. Maybe no other adults had studied college level courses in philosophy and apologetics as I had. At least someone could talk to him and reach out to him, I thought. I asked him a question which must have communicated something to him about how I cared and that I was someone he could talk with about some of the things that interested him.

"Do you believe in absolute truth?" I asked him.

"I'm not sure if it exists," he answered casually.

Through this simple exchange, which didn't solve any world problems, our friendship began. He turned out to be a most interesting person, who was well versed in subjects above his age group. This friendship has lasted now for many years.

After our first three months back, a friend I've had since childhood, who had been a pastor for about seven years by that time, called me. Although he lived and worked in another county, he had heard about my plight and knew that I needed a job. He gave me the name and number of a member in his congregation. He said that he had recommended me for a job to this man, who was hiring for his company, which was a very large corporation. I applied, interviewed, and was hired—all within a week. This was another major blessing of Father's provision. Again, I didn't fully appreciate or understand Father's provision, although I was grateful in my own way.

Elena and I were getting settled into a different kind of life, one without my involvement in any kind of ministry. As I understood it then, in my spiritual condition I didn't deserve any such blessing. This was before I truly understood Father's grace and the work he was continuing to perfect in my life.

In a few months, my rage had settled considerably and leveled off around seething for most of my waking hours. This made me more presentable in public, although an occasional outburst would flare up from time to time. This was usually a result of receiving poor customer service or treatment in stores or on the phone. Elena was embarrassed multiple times by my public misbehavior. Nonetheless, I did seem to be blending in with the rest of the secular culture.

One Saturday in a Christian book store, I rediscovered praise and worship music. In truth, I was curious to hear some of the songs that The Praise Band covered on Wednesday nights at the Teen Center. I realized that I had gotten behind the times with the new Contemporary Christian Music, or CCM, since we had moved to Central America. In the eighteen months that we had been away, a whole new style of praise and worship music and collection of songs had sprung into popularity. Some of those simple melodies of hearts crying out to the Lord for help and encouragement resonated with me, especially the lyrics culled from some of the Psalms. They were a balm to my spirit. Although it didn't necessarily melt any of my bitterness, it did make me realize how far I had drifted. The uplifting music also gave me a glimpse of what I had been missing for so long. I yearned to know intimacy with Jesus as I had before, but how would that ever again be possible?

There was a biography by Melody Green entitled *No Compromise*, which I devoured. Having recently been published at that time, it was about the life and ministry of her husband, Keith Green, a CCM artist with unbelievable talent, heart, and love who had perished in a plane crash back in 1982. His music and message had impacted me during my earliest years as a believer. I was encouraged to read of how the Lord worked in and through him, despite him being just a regular man who loved and served Jesus. Melody Green also detailed her struggle with bitterness over losing her godly husband and little son in the accident. One sentence, located in the epilogue of the book, leapt off the page: "For me, gratitude helped keep bitterness from my door."[1]

Here was another piece of wisdom which I believed somehow must be helpful toward a cure for my spiritual condition, but I just didn't know how to apply it to my life. I simply couldn't fix this problem with rage and bitterness, and God seemed to be of no help to me at all. The only thing I sensed from him was a scowl as he apparently glared at me for my sins, which kept piling up before him.

Seemingly for no particular reason, the new pastor who had replaced the "interim" pastor at my home church of nearly twenty years suddenly called me to see him at his office. He was also younger than both Elena and me, and he had only been in the position officially for a few months. He didn't know me at all, other than what he had heard. He had only joined the church staff as a youth pastor while we were in Central America. I couldn't imagine why he wanted to see me. There was a small note I had completed and torn out of the bulletin requesting prayer for an "unspoken" request. After slipping it into the offering plate, I had forgotten all about it. This new pastor had read the note and thought that he would take this as an opportunity to counsel me and to be a blessing to me.

After a few minutes of conversing in his office about what my need was, I told him a little about my anger and bitterness. He asked a few probing questions, listened quietly, and then made a few remarks. I was as puzzled as he was as to what the specific problem was. Neither of us could understand why returning to my home town with familiar surroundings, customs, and people I cared about and whom I thought cared about me didn't just calm my attitude and fix me right up. He seemed a little frustrated at the brick wall he was facing in me.

Then he paused and picked up a pen and a sheet of church stationary paper. "Let me show you this," he said as he wrote. Immediately, he held up the paper to reveal the words: EVERYTHING THAT HAPPENED IN HONDURAS. "Take this," he said calmly, "and let it represent everything that happened—all the negative stuff—in Honduras."

I accepted the paper and then looked at him. "I want you to ball it up and throw it in the trash can."

I didn't roll my eyes, out of respect, but I was feeling every bit of that reaction on the inside. I complied by balling up the paper and tossing it into a nearby waste bin.

"That's what I want you to do mentally every time you think about one of those moments you had in Honduras, for anything negative you experienced there."

Who would have guessed it? *That was the key!* All I had needed this whole time was for someone to come along and to let me in on this little secret to resolve my mysterious bitterness! I just had to will away the bitterness mentally by "throwing away" those thoughts!

Okay, that's enough sarcasm.

Although I had followed his instruction, I also shook my head on the inside, not on the outside—again out of respect.

This *is his solution?* I thought quietly. *I just need some secular, pop psychology and a gimmicky mental exercise that I can practice on my own?* I had long expected the solution to be something

26

found in the Scriptures involving my relationship with Christ, not something that this new pastor probably conjured up on the spot or read about in some ministry magazine. There's really no telling where this idea originated, but one thing I knew for sure was that it wouldn't do a thing for me. There was no way I was going to try this technique that he suggested.

Before I left his office that day, the pastor prayed for me and then made a one-sided deal with me. He said that whenever he saw me for the next few weeks or so, he would motion with his hand like he was tossing something invisible. That would be his silent way of asking me if I was getting rid of negative thoughts about my past in Central America.

Oh great, I moaned internally. *Now he wants this to be an "accountability issue," so that he can ask me with his secret signal anytime, even in a crowded room, with no one knowing what's happening.*

Over the next week or so, I dreaded seeing him up close for worrying of how I would respond to his "inquiry." It would only be a matter of time and opportunity because my family and I attended every church service, meeting, and activity whenever there was a gathering of any sort. However, with a large membership of roughly six hundred or more in regular attendance, I could probably avoid an encounter with him for a while.

It happened a couple of weeks later, when I least suspected it. A number of people, including me, were walking in opposing directions through a hallway after a Wednesday night service. Someone was following the pastor and in conversation with him about something. The pastor opened a fire door in the hall, noticed me a couple of people behind him, and then motioned to me with his hand, as if he were tossing something invisible.

That's the signal!

I felt a hurried, momentary flush and heard my voice saying quickly, "I'm trying." He quietly nodded, probably suspecting my insincerity, and walked through the doorway with this person, who was still talking with him at his side. For me, this did nothing, other than make me believe that no help for me would come from the church staff.

Lord, will this bitterness never end?

One evening my friend Tom called me on the phone. He was a retired missionary and the person most influential in my desire to enter mission work. I can't remember what the purpose of his call was, but a few minutes into the conversation, the subject changed to that of things that result in angry reactions from people. I commented that some kinds of anger were justified especially when, due to the circumstances, it only made sense.

"All anger is ultimately directed toward God," Tom observed quietly. "We may not realize it, but we blame him for our bad circumstances, our injustices, our frustrations—everything we know that he could change for the better but doesn't. Therefore, our anger is either openly or secretly against him."

That night as I lay in bed, Tom's words smoldered in my heart. They had rambled around in my mind for hours, but now that it was time to sleep, I couldn't rest my mind and heart. Elena was asleep already; her conscience had no reason to wrestle with anything.

Am I really angry at God? I wondered. *Am I blaming him for all the bad things that have happened to me?* Only a fool dared to oppose God, I knew. We obviously weren't on the best of terms at the time, he and I, but did I really dare to accuse him for my negative circumstances—even subconsciously? Likewise, I knew that my anger wasn't just some minor fuming over frustrations. It was some pretty serious, deeply-seated rage.

I thought that God was my friend—or at least that he was supposed to be. Why can't I fix this situation so that things will be better between us? Why can't I just do what I'm supposed to do? I don't want to be angry at God. Tears formed in my eyes and rolled down my face in the dark. *How has all this happened? What am I turning into? What will happen to me if I continue with this anger and bitterness?*

It terrified me to watch what was happening to me and to have these feelings and changes in my heart. It was almost like watching a movie. I saw all the horrible things happening one by one, but like someone shouting at the screen, my efforts and prayers had no effect on what was playing out.

For years I had walked with the Lord, enjoying sweet fellowship with him. As a teen, I had accepted his love, and only a few years later, I joyfully committed myself to the call of missions on my life. I had served in many different capacities in my local congregation, hungering for more opportunities to serve and to be a light to others. I had participated in prayer sessions with other committed believers, praying on my knees with them as we wept and expressed our burdened hearts for the lost. I had attended numerous, weekly Bible studies for years and ultimately pursued a Bachelor's degree in missions at a Christian university. My heart was burdened for the chance to serve the Lord in Central America, reaching the lost for Christ. Ever since my first trip to Honduras when I met the national pastors there, my heart had reached out to them. I longed to teach the Bible to young nationals, preparing them for the ministry in a local Bible school. I had taught Bible studies, Sunday school classes, and preached sermons about Jesus and his love to crowds of people. My life had been presented unto God in the hopes that it would be pleasing unto him. Yet here I was, "a bitter, washed-up, disgruntled, ex-missionary," having returned home in disgrace to start my life and a different career all over again. None of what resulted had been a part of my plans and desires. To say that I was disappointed and heartbroken didn't begin to articulate the devastating blow I had felt to my heart and life.

I don't remember when I fell asleep that evening, but mine was not to be a restful night.

If I had known then what was about to happen, I wouldn't have believed it, even though for so long I had beseeched the Lord for my heart to experience real change. Hope for this change was literally on the horizon, and I was about to experience what for me would be nothing short of a divine breakthrough. God had been at work the whole time during my years of bitterness, and he was about to make himself known to me in a way that I never could have imagined.

[1] p. 373, *No Compromise: The Life Story of Keith Green* by Melody Green and David Hazard; Harvest House Publishers, 2000. Used by permission.

CHAPTER 3

THE BREAKTHROUGH

It had been a grinding workday that second Monday in March of 2001, the year following my disgraceful return from Central America. I trudged through the day feeling numb, apart from some smoldering anger and bitterness which seemed to be my constant companions. They usually crested the surface of my numbed exterior during stressful or unpleasant situations. There seemed to be a shadow of disapproval lingering over me, which I took for God's displeasure at the deplorable spiritual state in which I found myself. I could almost see his arms folded and his scowling look as he viewed me wallowing in my morass of sin and despair. There seemed to be no way out, and I only became steadily worse as the days, weeks, and months passed.

Sometime that afternoon, I saw that there was an e-mail from Tom, my retired missionary friend. He was one of the few and only people who pursued any relationship with me, especially now that I was a "bitter, washed-up, disgruntled ex-missionary, having returned home as a failure." (At least that was how I thought other people considered me.) He asked me to call him when I had a moment. During my lunch break I dialed his number. He and his wife, Sara, wanted to invite us over for coffee and dessert after dinner. "Since you don't drink coffee," he said in a mildly playful tone, remembering my dislike of java, "you're welcome to some tea or hot chocolate." I started to say something into the phone. "But the point is not what you have," he said, clarifying. "We just want to see you and your family."

I had no reason to turn down his offer. Truthfully, I wanted to see Tom and Sara. They were always very encouraging, and I always felt relaxed and uplifted around them. Tom had greatly influenced my decision to go to the mission field. He had always been there for me, providing friendly, biblical counseling to me all along the way. He was kind, gentle, and had a good sense of humor. He was known to say some profound statements applying

31

biblical truth, yet not in a preachy or berating sort of way. Tom didn't play games with other people's feelings or circumstances. He wouldn't repeat the Christian quips to me like others had done.

It was settled then. Immediately, I called my wife and told her about the plans. Elena had always felt the same as I about Tom and Sara, so naturally she was eager to go. In fact, she would even bake a dessert for the occasion. Our son Nathaniel was only two-and-a-half at the time, so he would be happy to be anywhere we were. We had nothing better to do on a Monday night.

That evening, Tom and Sara greeted us as we appeared at their door and entered their home. Tom smiled at our little boy and said something silly to him. Nathaniel giggled and shied away play-fully at the tall man's attention. We settled into the dining room, and each one of us chose a beverage to accompany the homemade brownies that Elena had baked. I was somewhat surprised to see how many flavors of tea they had pulled from their cupboard. Ap-parently inviting over friends was a common occurrence for them.

After we each had a cup or mug of some hot liquid and a dessert, Tom and I casually broke off from the group and found our way to the living room. It was a quaint, wood-framed space with simple yet comfortable furnishings. Photos of their children, grandchil-dren, and many friends of various nationalities from around the world dotted the walls. A few scattered files and ministry or bibli-cal books lay here or there on the desk or book shelves—evidence that they were still actively teaching and ministering in a myriad of capacities, pouring their lives into others.

Tom made small talk with me for a few minutes. I must have looked a little angry as usual, though I was somewhat at rest in the warmth of Tom's reassuring friendship and his inviting home. Elena and Nathaniel were with Sara in the dining room. I didn't feel enraged, but I did feel tired—spiritually more than physically. The folded arms and scowl on my imaginary visage of God remained with me.

Suddenly, Tom turned a corner in the conversation. "I have a question for you." My curiosity was piqued at this sudden shift in gears. "It's a short question—a biblical question."

"Okay," I nodded.

"When you sin, do you find yourself running *toward* Jesus or *away* from him?"

I felt crestfallen at the mention of my sin. I knew there was no sense in pretending to be above sin, and only the foolish and arrogant would attempt to do so.

"Well, I haven't really thought of it like that before." I paused briefly, lowered my gaze, and heard myself say, "I know that when I sin I should confess it—which is what I do—but I really feel like I'm just going through the motions. And I know that no one can deceive God, and since I don't feel sincere about it and I'm just trying to follow 1 John 1:9, it doesn't seem to work. It all seems like I'm in a tailspin or an endless cycle." As I spoke, I could feel my shoulders slumping, and I gradually sank further back into the chair. It was a dry and disheartening yet honest admission. I knew that Tom would not judge me, though I didn't know what good it would do to ask me that question. In my mind, I reviewed the Bible verse I mentioned: "But if we confess our sins, he is faithful and righteous, forgiving us our sins and cleansing us from all unrighteousness."

"Yeah, I do the same thing," Tom said, gazing into the air. His admission surprised me. "You can do it so often that confession becomes just a ritual like anything else, devoid of meaning."

It didn't seem possible that Tom had the same experience in his walk with Jesus as I had had in mine. But neither would he lie about it, just to make me feel at ease. His honesty was refreshing to hear, and I was intrigued, though a bit puzzled.

Then he presented another question. "Do you know what a refuge is?"

I looked up, wanting to hear where this was going. "It's a place of safety, a place to go when you're in danger."

"Yes, that's it exactly," Tom confirmed. "It means safety, security, and rest when you're in danger or trouble. Nowadays it can be a difficult word to describe or define, because most people don't use it often in their daily conversations. I'm sure you know

33

this, but in the land of Israel during the Old Testament, God had established cities of refuge for people who got in trouble. Someone was chopping wood in their field, for example; the ax head slipped off and killed a neighbor standing close by. That person's family would typically seek revenge on the man, even though it was an accident. But if he could make it to one of those cities of refuge, then he would be safe. No harm or vengeance could come to him.

"David, in the Psalms, spoke of God as his *refuge*. In Psalm 46 he said, 'God is our refuge and strength, a very present help in trouble.'* In Psalm 9 David said, 'the LORD is a refuge for the oppressed, a refuge in times of trouble.'* He felt so safe in God's presence that he said to him in Psalm 57, 'in the shadow of thy wings will I make my refuge.'* David also called God his 'defense and refuge in the day of my trouble.'* In Psalm 62 he said, 'In God is my salvation and my glory: the rock of my strength, and my refuge, is in God.'* He also said, 'pour out your heart before him; God is a refuge for us.'*

"Look," he admitted with levity, "I don't remember all the references. But I know that God is our refuge; he's our safe place.

"Sin is damaging to us. It hurts us *and* our relationship with God. It's deceitful, and it messes with our minds and hearts—so much so that we begin to think that *he* is against us, that *he's* punishing us. But according to the Scriptures, that's just not so. When we are battered about by sin, we can come to him and know that we are safe with God, our refuge."

At some point during our conversation, my son was on the floor with some blocks and toys near the edge of the living room. I saw him out of the corner of my eye. Just as Tom was finishing his sentence, Elena, distracted by her conversation with Sara, pulled little Nathaniel up from the floor by his hand, not noticing the proximity of the nearby wall. Nathaniel lost his balance as he was being swooped up, and he swung and struck the wall with his head. When he made contact with the wall, he cried out, and with tears already forming in his eyes, he stretched his arms out to me and ran straight toward me. My heart sank as I saw my little son in pain, though there was no bleeding or visible injury. I caught him up in my arms and began rocking him and caressing him as he wrapped his arms around me. He wasn't hurt badly, but the hit was sudden and unexpected, and he knew at that moment that he needed his daddy.

Tom blinked once or twice, looking carefully to be sure that the boy wasn't seriously hurt. "That," he said calmly, "is just what Father wants: he wants *you* to run into his arms when you are hurt."

In that moment it was almost as if time stood still for me. The words and imagery penetrated my soul and spirit. Suddenly, I understood that *I* was that hurt little boy, whose only thought was that in the midst of his pain his Father's embrace alone would bring comfort and healing. And I *was* hurt—repeatedly and very badly. Yet I didn't run to Father's arms. Why didn't I? Oh, there was that disapproval and distance that I imagined I sensed from him. Yet, as I held my son tightly to my chest and rubbed his little back, I sensed that my heavenly Father—no longer scowling in disapproval with his arms folded—was now beaming with love and affection *for me*, the one who had sinned against him and offended him the most. I was truly accepted and welcomed into his open arms! The picture was so vivid to me: I was both giving love as the father of my son and receiving God's love as a son of my heavenly Father. In my heart, I could see myself run joyfully into his arms as he radiated with a heartfelt smile of affection. There was no longer any fear or shame or doubt or bitterness or anger. Where were they? Only his love and hope and joy and forgiveness and grace remained, having melted away all the pain and misunderstanding, like a wax figurine in the nearby heat of a roaring fire.

Outwardly, in that instant, my tears gushed out like a fountain long forgotten, finally free from a debilitating drought. I wept loudly, and continued for some time, finally realizing that I had allowed sin to deceive me and to thwart me in my relationship with my all-loving Abba. However, I didn't feel scolded for having been so foolish. I felt such a magnificent relief as a heavy burden was lifted from my heart and shouldered onto my Savior and Redeemer. He had liberated me to be a son to my Daddy again!

35

By then, Tom, Sara, and Elena's attention was all on me. Perhaps they perceived that God was doing a long-awaited work in my heart at that moment. I'm not sure what they understood was happening; all I knew was that, at long last, I let God break through the morass of my bitterness. It was the moment when the healing and restoration were impacting my heart. No longer was he the holy God whose only concern was that I had offended him repeatedly and that I would need to do something about it. He was once again the holy, all-loving Father whose heart reached out to his hurting child, whose heart showered his child with love, grace, forgiveness, and healing. All this time, the anger I thought he had aimed at me was actually directed at the sin and deception which had me paralyzed in spiritual pain and misunderstanding. He wasn't offended by my sins, like someone looking for an excuse to cut all ties in a relationship. He was hurt, yes, but he was hurt because of what sin had done to *my* heart. He had grieved and wept right along with me through every painful moment. He had never abandoned me. He had waited patiently for the moment—this moment—when he could peel back the pain and misunderstanding and flood my heart with his love and grace.

For Elena, this moment had been long overdue. She had endured my bitterness and anger for over two years. This may not seem like a very long time, but it was too long for her considering all that she had suffered in life. I could have felt ashamed for having hurt her so, but it didn't occur to me to feel that way at that moment, a reason which will be explained later. Suddenly, I felt so clean and so loved by God. Finally, I was free of the bitterness and restored back into fellowship with Father!

Through my sobs and tears, I could hear Tom reassuring me and encouraging me. "Tears are healing," he said. "Sometimes we need to shed tears to let our hearts be restored and relieved. Father delights to see our hearts heal and turn toward him again.

"Just remember that it's biblical to turn to the Lord when you're hurt," he continued. "What you're doing at this moment is right and needed. James says, 'Draw nigh to God, and he will draw nigh to you.'* In Hebrews 4 we are told, 'Let us therefore come boldly unto the throne of grace that we may obtain mercy, and find grace to help in time of need.'* Now, that word 'boldly' doesn't mean that we approach with an attitude or a chip on our shoulders, like he owes us something. That's just the old King James terminology. It means that we can draw near to him *confidently*, knowing that because of what Jesus did on our behalf we now have rightful access to the Father. Jesus himself said, 'Come unto me all ye that labour and are heavy laden, and I will give you rest. Take my yoke upon you, and learn of me; for I am meek and lowly of heart; and ye shall find rest unto your souls. For my yoke is easy, and my burden is light.'*"

As I held my son, his cries subsided, and he began to feel better. He was quiet now and resting, having had his hurt soothed away by love. I also felt rested, relieved, and at peace. My heavenly Father had demonstrated his love for me, and placing my son as an example and showing me through my own love for Nathaniel was the best way to touch my heart. *Is this what it's like for Father to love us?* I wondered silently.

"Thank you," I whispered, as my tears subsided.

"Remember," Tom said with a quiet smile as he put his hand on my shoulder, "always run to Jesus, even when it doesn't make sense."

Without him saying it, I understood later that Tom had been praying for me fervently for at least the better part of a year, ever since I returned from Central America. His approach was not to come across as braggadocious, saying, "Hey, John, I've been praying for you." Instead, he did what was needed by interceding on my behalf, perhaps knowing that any mention of the fact might detract me from what Father was quietly orchestrating behind the scenes in my heart.

On the way home that evening, Elena was mostly quiet. Occasionally she broke the silence with a question about what I experienced and how I felt. I answered her questions as best as I could, apologizing for my years of bitterness and anger. It was rarely fun living with me that whole time. This we both knew.

"I'm so sorry, Elena," I stated blankly yet somewhat

devastatingly as I drove through the night. "I've been so angry and mean to you and difficult to live with."

She began sobbing in the darkness. The heartfelt touch which I received was encouraging her as well.

Fresh tears rolled down my cheeks. I was deeply grieved at the person I had been for so long, and I didn't want to be that way anymore. Because of what Jesus had worked in me that evening, he had freed me with truth, and I no longer saw any reason for that bitterness to remain. My soul now delighted in Jesus, and I was so elated and thankful just to know him and to have him in my heart and life.

My elation and ecstasy lasted for days. I had no qualms, fears, or doubts between my Father and me. I don't claim that I was sinless during that period, but my heart delighted in him, and my spirit enjoyed a continual praise fest of ecstasy as my thoughts focused perpetually on my Jesus. It felt like becoming born again all over again. The only difference was that this time I truly had the understanding of what he had done for me and knew how to appreciate better what he meant to me. As people at church began noticing the changes in me, they said that it was my "spiritual honeymoon." I no longer "walked under a cloud," someone said. What I demonstrated didn't seem forced or faked, as if I were putting on some act for appearance's sake. I merely rejoiced in Jesus and expressed thanks to him continuously. It seemed as easy and as unpremeditated as breathing. I had no pretensions, as far as I knew my own heart. I didn't judge or look down on others either. I simply enjoyed him and my walk with him, as imperfect as it was. As I encountered believers who could seemingly appreciate what I had experienced and even some who looked puzzled by my testimony, I shared with them what had happened and how the Lord broke through my bitterness with his grace and love, taking it all away. I could never recount that moment without sobbing profusely. It was such a moment filled with his love and grace! I was free from all the bitterness and anger, and I was spiritually alive! I had to tell others. How could I possibly not want the same for them?

After hearing the news of what happened to me, the new pastor at our church even invited us over for dinner with his family that week. We all talked and fellowshipped around knowing Jesus, giving testimonies of praise and rejoicing in knowing him. There was no mention of the throw-away-the-negative-thoughts therapy which the pastor had counseled me to use. By that time, I had forgotten all about it. I viewed all my relationships with new eyes and a fresh perspective of life and Father. It was sheer bliss!

My coworkers, who didn't have any kind of relationship with God as far as I knew, seemed a little perplexed at this sudden difference. They hadn't exactly liked me before, perhaps because I had seemed moody and judgmental due to all my bitterness. Now that I was better instead of bitter, they seemed a little more stand-offish, but for different reasons. Maybe all my joy and gratitude were viewed as somewhat of a threat to them. I had shared with them in previous months some of the stories about us living in Honduras as missionaries. I left out the "preachy" parts so as not to offend them. Therefore, they had already known that I had been in some form of ministry. But it was probably easier for them to view me as the "washed-up, disgruntled ex-missionary" than it was to see so much joy emanating from me.

With the passing of the days and weeks, my gratitude expanded as the reality sank in that Father had freed me from a prison of my own making. I would no longer be that bitter, angry person I had become. My heart and life were being transformed for the better for both me and my family. Finally, I was free from the grip of bitterness and anger. *Thank you, Jesus!*

The events of that night at Tom and Sara's house when Father's grace and love broke through to me were so unexpected. As I reflected on what had happened, I realized that it was very personal and intended for me individually. Who else has had such an experience? There was no way for me to know. Whereas the particulars of my history of bitterness varied from what others have experienced, the specifics of his grace breaking through to me would also be very personal and individual to me. Nevertheless, as the Great Communicator and the Inventor of languages and of

39

communication itself, God is more than apt to reach anyone through any means of his choosing. In the midst of my circumstances, he reached me through the one person in this world who is the dearest and the most precious to me—my son. Likewise, he made his love and grace toward me crystal clear in that moment so that I would not miss out or misunderstand. Since he did that for me, I am persuaded that he does the same for others, perhaps reaching out to individuals every day and intersecting their lives through the person or thing dearest to them. Therefore, for everyone struggling with bitterness, brokenness, disappointment, shame, arrogance, unforgiveness, addiction, or whatever the spiritual problem may be, there is always hope in our Lord Jesus Christ. That is why, as believers in Christ, we can pray for his working with hope and expectancy. We cannot underestimate what he may be doing in the details of our lives to break through to us with his love and grace. We become aware of this only as we are open and attentive to his dealings with us in the details of our lives.

In the months ahead, Father would demonstrate his grace and love toward me time and again. He would also teach me that there was more to be done and that he was only beginning to perfect the good work he had begun in me. His purpose was not merely to shower me just once with his love and grace and then send me on my merry way. He would be intimately involved in my spiritual growth and in the process of making me more like Jesus than I had previously realized. There was so much for me to learn, and God himself would disciple me.

Much of what had resulted in my bitter spiritual condition was a body of misunderstandings about Christ, the Scriptures, and his relationship with me. All those misconceptions and wrong beliefs I had concerning him would soon begin to be replaced by biblical truths which I had either not previously learned or not fully understood. This adventure, as I would soon understand, was only beginning.

*KJV

CHAPTER 4

ON THE MOUNTAINTOP

A couple of days after our visit with Tom and Sara, I received another call from Tom inviting me to join him and a few other ministry-type brothers as they climbed Stone Mountain and enjoyed a picnic together. It was a fellowship that they enjoyed together usually once a month, or sometimes less frequently if familial responsibilities or ministry commitments crowded out the opportunity. I would certainly be delighted to join them. Spending a Saturday morning in the fresh outdoors fellowshipping with other brothers who loved Jesus and were on similar journeys would be wonderful!

That Saturday I met Tom in the parking lot beneath the behemoth of granite known as Stone Mountain. It's literally a mountain-sized outcropping of granite with a carving of three Confederate leaders on the front face. Three dimensional visages of Jefferson Davis, Robert E. Lee, and Thomas J. "Stonewall" Jackson were depicted as mounted on horses and holding their hats over their hearts. The mountain had been developed long ago as a state park. Every summer evening through Labor Day there is a laser and fireworks show presented on and above the carving face. It is a popular attraction for both tourists and locals alike.

Tom introduced me to the other men who joined us for the fellowship: an author of Christian fiction and part-time missionary named Walter, a seminary professor named Greg, and a former associate pastor named Bob.

After we exchanged introductions and greetings, we turned to the mountain and sized up the challenging climb before us. Walter motioned to the mountain and observed in a feigned serious tone, "It's a big mountain, the only one in Atlanta. But most people here take it for *granite*."

Tom put his hand on Walter's shoulder and then spoke, leaning toward me. "Yeah, he really said that. Walter's one of *those* guys."

41

"Puns can be a form of art, you know," Walter said with a playful, incredulous look.

"Maybe *good* puns," inserted Bob jovially. "If you think of any, write them down for us, would you?" A few chuckles were shared among the group.

With that, we started the climb up a trail on the back side of the mountain, which was not nearly as steep as I had imagined. Having never climbed Stone Mountain before, I thought that we might have a lot of vertical steps, like the climbs I experienced on mountains in Central America. It was a relief to me to see that this was mostly smooth stone with only a moderately steep angle. We were a little winded in a few places, but we didn't stop too many times to catch our breaths. The air was crisp and pleasantly warm for one of the last days of winter. The sun shone brightly despite the scattered cumulonimbus clouds slowly sailing above us. Along the stone-slab path the sparse, short pine trees provided only a minimum of negligible shade. Consequently, I was thankful for my sunglasses and baseball cap, which protected me from a fair amount of the ultraviolet rays. With the pale hues of gray stone as the surface and an array of flat boulders scattered where we walked, this was unlike any other mountain I had climbed. We saw little to no soil from the path we followed.

As we ascended the mountain, quite a number of people passed us from time to time descending the mountain. They all seemed relaxed and content. "You see?" Greg posited. "It will be a lot easier on the way back." Smiling at his observation, I adjusted the small backpack I carried on my shoulder.

We proceeded to climb with little fanfare or event. Other than pointing out some interesting sights as differing vistas came within view or sharing a few exchanges of small talk, we made little conversation on the way up. Having reached a level area with boulders the right size for sitting, we considered it to be the top of the mountain and settled in for lunch.

The view was magnificent! With my recent transformation in spirit and attitude, I could truly appreciate the vista of God's Creation before me. I removed my sunglasses briefly to absorb the sights, immediately blinking hard for a moment in the bright, natural light. The forest of pines and other trees below continued for miles toward the horizon, with ever paler shades of green as they faded into the distance. Pearl-colored clouds skated lazily above their shadow partners on the landscape below. Along with the clear, blue water of the lake and river which meandered around the mountain, a symphony of greens, blues, and grays, visible only at such altitudes, painted a breathtaking patchwork quilt as far as the eye could see. The few scatterings of visible buildings, as well as the city of Atlanta to the west, seemed so small and distant to the beauty of Creation surrounding us. Gazing at all this wonder from the edge of the mountain, we seemed to be poised in a balcony box anchored between the beauty of the sky and that of the landscape below. The bright, welcoming sun and the exhilarating breeze accented this scintillating view. This was to be the backdrop for our lunchtime fellowship!

Walter led the prayer of thanksgiving before we partook of the assorted sandwiches, snacks, and canned and bottled drinks which we each brought and shared. As the conversation began and participation was shared, I was impressed by what I noticed with these men. They were all a decade or more older than I was, since I was only in my mid-thirties at that time. Yet I was amazed with how equally they treated one another. There was no "pecking order," so to speak, no condescending remarks or belittling due to another's lack of age, lack of experience, limited perspective, or particular background. In many ways, Tom outranked them all in age, wisdom, and experience, but he never seemed to come across that way. This had been my experience with him as well, so that didn't surprise me about him. He was content to converse with each man and learn from him. Each man regarded the others as equal brothers in Christ, and they accepted me in the same way with no reservations. Their joyful camaraderie was refreshingly different from the way of the world. How much fellowship I had missed with brothers like these due to my period of bitterness! Such an uplifting fellowship might have shortened my dismal years of anger and misunderstanding. However, I had been too self-absorbed to reach out for help or encouragement then.

"So, John," Tom interjected and paused, turning the conversation toward me, "I understand you've had an interesting few days. What's something you would like to share with us from this week?"

The question was anticipated, and I had so much to share from what I had learned and experienced recently. I not only wanted to encourage others; I also hoped to glean from the combined wisdom of these brothers in the Lord.

I opened my mouth, thinking that I was ready to speak, but I uttered nothing. An awkward smile dawned on my countenance. "Where do I start?" I finally said with a chuckle.

"I usually find that the beginning is always a great place to start," said Walter affably.

"No, it's okay," I replied, perceiving his levity. "It would just take too long to sum up over two years of wrong thinking and behaving. I guess the easiest way to summarize is to say that I let problems get the best of me and allowed bitterness to creep into my life while I was on the mission field with my family. Circumstances resulted in us coming home, and my bitterness worsened." I glanced at Tom. "God broke through my aggressive and hardened heart Monday night and showed me that I had him all wrong for most of my life."

"In what sense did you have Father wrong?" pursued Greg.

"While I was ministering in Honduras—or at least trying to minister—I taught about the attributes of God to a group of teenagers in a home Bible study in my garage. My wife and I reached out to those teens. We were relating to them and sharing the Scriptures with them for the purpose of evangelism and with the expectation of eventually leading them through discipleship and church planting. Practically all were nominally Catholic, so they had familiarity with religion and tradition and the like, but they didn't have any real relationship with God. The more we got to know them and to talk with them and to participate in their lives, the more we understood that they really had no idea who Father or Jesus were. It was the same situation with the small group men's

Bible study that I taught."

"What did you do under those circumstances?" asked Bob.

"Well, I thought that they needed to see from the Bible what God is really like, that he's not just some good luck charm you can pull out of your sock drawer whenever you need him to get you out of whatever trouble you're in and then forget about him and go back to living any way you please."

"That's what the teenagers were doing?" asked Tom.

"In a sense they were. It seems like most of the country is doing that, because so many of them are nominally religious people with no reality of Christ in their hearts and lives. But it's not a planned strategy; they simply don't know any other way to live or to consider God, especially with all the wrong teaching that they've absorbed. So, I started a Bible study with these teens, first giving them some general information about the Bible and its nature. Then I turned to God's attributes to help them to get to know its Author."

"And which attributes did you teach them?" Greg asked.

I sighed a little sheepishly. "Well, it sounds cruel and twisted now, but I wanted to slam them with their sins and lost spiritual condition, so the first attribute was his holiness. Then I taught them about his righteousness and justice. It was all so that they could understand about their sinfulness and their need for salvation."

"I bet *that* went over well," chuckled Walter with good-humored sarcasm.

"I was hoping and praying that it would."

"What happened?"

"It didn't work. At least it didn't work on them. In fact, I didn't really notice any difference in them at all. You know—me showing them from the Scriptures that God is holy, righteous, just, and the Judge of all sin." My voice lowered somewhat. "Each week the meeting would end, and they'd pick up with their lives the same place they'd left them at the door."

"So, it was all academic?" questioned Greg.

"Probably. It didn't seem to faze them at all, but it really did a number on me. I would think about God and these intimidating attributes throughout the day and each week. And I started fearing him, because, you know, I'm not *any* of those things apart from him. I mean, I would sin and then think, 'God's so holy and righteous. How can I do this to him?' So of course, I would confess my sins," I said, looking again at Tom, "but it was all just a ritual. I did it out of fear of being out of fellowship with him and being under his indignation. And God is omniscient—he's all knowing—so no one can hide anything from him. So, my prayer of confession went something like this: 'Lord, what I just did was sin. I know that I should be sorry for it and turn away from it, but I don't really seem to be sorry. And I keep doing the same things over and over.' So, it was just a frustrating cycle with no resolution and no end."

"You didn't sense the forgiveness and cleansing," Bob stated.

"Exactly. I was just stuck because I didn't seem to be doing it right, and God didn't seem to be accepting my prayer or even listening. And I didn't realize that my view of him had changed."

"What do you mean?" Bob asked.

"I started imagining God as scowling at me with disapproval and looming over me with his arms folded. The problem, I thought, was that I didn't deal with my sins like I was supposed to do. So, he seemed to be saying, 'When you get this right, I'll help you. Until then, don't bother.'"

"I see," Walter added. "You thought Father wanted *you* to clean up your act *before* he entered the picture."

"Well, yeah, that's what I thought confession was."

"It sounds like it was a walk of *self-effort* focused on you instead of a walk of *grace* depending on God's work *in* you."

"Right, exactly." This was crystallized in my understanding just as Walter was explaining it.

"You didn't realize," offered Tom, "that *he* is responsible for cleaning you up, not you yourself."

I nodded in agreement.

"It's like a little boy whose dad buys him a new pair of shoes," Tom continued. "His dad lovingly tells him, 'Now enjoy the shoes, but don't get them muddy.' But what's the first thing he does?"

"He jumps in the mud puddles," I answered.

"Yes! He splashes and jumps and plays in the mud puddles. And when he comes home, he goes to his dad, crying and showing him his filthy, muddy shoes. But you know what? His dad bends down and lovingly washes off the mud from those shoes and cleans up his son. The boy admits that he did wrong; he doesn't hide it from his dad. But *the father* is the one who cleans the boy. He knows that his little son can't do that. You see? It's like David's prayer in Psalm 51 after he had committed sin. He prayed, asking Father, 'Wash me thoroughly from mine iniquity, and cleanse me from my sin.'* Further in the same psalm he said, 'Create in me a clean heart, O God; and renew a right spirit within me.'* A verse or two later he said, 'Restore unto me the joy of thy salvation; and uphold me with thy free spirit.'* He asked Father to do the work of cleaning him up and healing his heart because he knew that he wasn't capable of doing it. It's a job that only the Holy Spirit can do."

"Wow, Tom! You're right," I said quietly, awed at the realization and implications.

"A lot of believers," Walter began, "view God or the Scriptures as a coach before the big game. He gives the team a rousing pep talk—a motivational talk—reminding them of what they've learned and practiced. He raises the bar of his expectations and then says, 'Now, let's go out there and win this one!' But God's not like that at all. This life in Jesus is not about learning principles or rules or even the Ten Commandments so that we can head out by ourselves and attempt to walk in righteousness." He motioned with his palms up. "It simply can't be done."

"And that certainly leads to a lot of frustration," Greg added. "It's not that Father thought it would be *best* to grace us with his Holy Spirit to *help* us live this life. It's that he knew that without him living inside us to empower us with his grace and himself to provide all the necessary resources and to live his life through us that it would be *impossible* for us to live the Christian life. We simply can't do it in our own 'strength', which is fleshly weakness.

47

Therefore, it's not just the *best* way; it's the *only* way to be Christlike. We have this intimate relationship of dependence on him to live through us. Just as Jesus said in John 15, 'apart from me you can accomplish nothing.' Therefore, the only things we do with any eternal value are achieved by Christ living through us. Paul said in Philippians 4:13, 'I am able to do all things through the one who strengthens me,' by whom he meant Christ who strengthened him. Living this way isn't a natural ability, of course; it's something that only Jesus can do, and he does it by living his life through us. However, we must yield to him for it to happen. It's what Paul called 'dying to self.' Giving up our own agenda, our own desires—that's what it means."

"You're right, Brother Greg," said Walter. "Jesus didn't die just to give us a list of rules or expectations to follow. He came so that we might have *life—abundant* life—*his* life in us. When we serve someone who's difficult to get along with, it is Christ serving through us by the Holy Spirit in us. When we love the unlovely, it's him loving them through us. When we forgive others or do any of those things demonstrating the fruit of the Spirit, it's Jesus being himself through us. When we abide in Christ as he taught in John 15, then we yield ourselves to him, allowing his life to live through us. It's seldom easy surrendering control of our lives moment by moment and yielding to him. Nevertheless, when we grow to trust that he knows best how to live this life in Christ and that he wants to live his life through us, avoiding a lot of pain and heartache for us, then it becomes pretty clear that his way is the best way to live."

"It all sounds so freeing!" I observed joyfully. "So, what do we say about things like the Ten Commandments and all the laws and things in the Bible that people think we are supposed to follow? I know that the Ten Commandments were for Israel, but a lot of Christians think that they are for us to obey today as well."

There was a pause in the conversation. I wasn't sure who was going to respond to my question, but in the moment, there seemed to be no volunteers. For the life of me, I didn't understand why. Perhaps these brothers had discussed this topic before and they were waiting for one of them to jump in with both feet. After a few seconds, it was Greg who spoke.

"Well, that's where it gets interesting," he replied with a somewhat awkward smile. Then he looked around at the others in the group. "You all feel free to jump in here whenever you want."

"Oh no," protested Tom jokingly. "You're doing fine so far."

"Go for it, Bro!" added Walter.

"Well," Greg continued, quickly stroking his chin once, "see if this makes sense." He began to motion with his hands at this point. "God called his people Israel out of Egypt and into the desert and presented them with the Law—the Ten Commandments. It's basically what Bible scholars call the Mosaic Covenant. There are really some 613 individual commandments presented throughout the Books of the Law which are based on the original ten. It's packed with all the minutia of daily life: everything from the types of lambs suitable for sacrifice and the kinds of cloth allowed to use in clothing to dietary laws and what to do if you find one of your neighbor's animals wandering off his property. The nation of Israel hears the Law—every last detail—and says, 'We will obey all the LORD has commanded us.' Of course, they meant well, or seemed to, but there was really no way they were going to obey all those commands perfectly. And Father knew that. He really designed the Law to teach them a very important lesson: that it would be impossible for them to keep all 613 laws."

"Huh?" I was a little stunned. "*That* was the Law's purpose? He gave it to them to show them that they *couldn't* keep it?"

"*Now* you've done it," jabbed Walter, slapping his knees. "His mind is blown, and *you'll* have to put all the pieces back together."

"Okay, now, John. Follow me here for a minute," Greg said, shifting his seat on a boulder. "Remember in Acts 15 when the apostles and church elders met to discuss whether the new believers from among the Gentiles should have the Law of Moses enforced on them?"

"Right, the Jerusalem Council."

"That's it. You'll remember that Peter stood up and basically said to the council, 'Look, guys, this whole keeping-the-law thing is a burden that neither we nor our ancestors have been able to bear.

49

We believe we are saved by the grace of Jesus just like these Gentile believers are, not by keeping the law.'"

"Is that a literal translation from the Greek?" Walter inquired facetiously.

Greg nodded, halfway rolling his eyes. "Somewhat. That's the gist of it at least. Then James chimed in by telling them that reaching the Gentile nations was a fulfillment of prophecy. He told them that they just needed to give the new believers a few cultural guidelines which would help the Jews and Gentiles to get along better socially. The whole council then agreed. Peter and James got it. They understood that the real purpose of the Law—in addition to pointing out sin as Romans 3:20 states—was to teach mankind that he can't keep it, that he needs divine help—that is, that he needs the life of the Divine living through him to keep it. It wasn't a way to earn salvation."

"The Law really just points out what sin is," I said, thinking aloud.

Bob contributed to the point. "*And* it highlights our need for Jesus. It effectively points us to him, as Paul teaches in Galatians 2 and 3."

"Sin is seen in a different light now," continued Greg. "It goes beyond breaking a commandment; it's living our lives and acting independently of Jesus." Greg kept his gaze on me, pausing for a moment to let this new definition sink into my comprehension.

"Oh . . . oh! I get it now! Wow! That's pretty deep." I sat back a little, contemplating what this meant. "So, sin is more than just a list of bad deeds we do; it's a habit and a lifestyle which excludes Christ."

"It is that, but there's more to it. It means that even the good things we do without him are wrong because they are done in the ability of the flesh. That's a definition of sin that addresses act, motive, and enablement."

"Man! That really changes our whole perspective on sin and confessing it."

"It does, doesn't it? So, when I don't yield to Jesus in me, when I don't abide in Christ, I'm giving into temptation more easily."

50

"And you know what, John?" Bob said with a tone of compassion. "I think a better mindset of confessing sins to Father is to view it as admitting that what you did was wrong and that it happened because of not relying on Jesus. In that prayer of confession, you're reminded of how you really need him living through you more than you realize. Like you say, he knows everything; he knows your heart. So instead of trying to feel sorry or repentant and falling into that introspective trap, just focus on him. Talk to him about your weakness in those areas of temptation, knowing that he already forgave you nearly two thousand years ago, and that he loves you more than you can imagine. He didn't design prayer and confession as a 'gotcha' sort of thing to shame you. He uses it as a way for us to share our hearts with him so that he can clean us up—just like the dad did for his son with the muddy shoes."

I could sense the moisture forming in my eyes. "He's so loving," I said, almost whispering. "Why does he do it? Why does he love us so? I mean, just think about it: he becomes human, puts up with so much doubt and mistrust from people on earth, endures the cross, suffers and dies for us, resurrects to give us his new life, comes to live within us, and becomes involved with us in all the details of our lives. Even when we don't trust him, and we turn away from him, he still loves us with all he is. He still wants to serve us and to do things for us by living his life through us. Why does he still love us, even when we won't let him have his way?" The air was silent for a moment. Perhaps each one of us was giving quiet praise and gratitude to Jesus in that moment.

"God *is* love," someone finally said. It was Tom's voice this time. "It is his nature and arguably his greatest attribute."

"Is that one you taught the teens?" asked Walter.

Still delighting in the love of God, I noticed that the question was for me. "Oh, well, yes. But it was only after teaching the scary-sounding ones first, and, even then, it was more of an encyclopedic teaching."

A cordial chuckle was shared among us all.

"Some of Father's attributes," offered Walter, "may *seem*

scary—*if* we don't know him and relate to him in a frame of grace."

"*Another* truth I learned the hard way. Even so, that's what almost scared me the other day—God's love, I mean."

"The love of God *scared* you?" inquired Bob. "What do you mean?"

"Well, Tom told me to run to Jesus always, even when it doesn't make sense. I went home that night so relieved and refreshed. I was just floating with joy and thanksgiving! But the next day, I wondered why God would still want me and love me, even after all I had done to turn away from him and to distrust him and to have such negative thoughts about him. It just didn't make sense. He loves me at my worst, even as a believer who should know better than to give into sin, bitterness, and the 'introspective trap.'" I nodded to Bob with a grin. "That's a good term for it, Bob. But if he loves me after all that and even when I still can't get this walking-with-Jesus right, then when would he *not* want me to run to him?

"Because I used to think: 'Yeah, God loves everyone, but he probably doesn't pursue it with the same passion and intensity for some people as those who just don't care about him.' Kind of like certain undesirable relatives at a family reunion. The head of the family can announce to the crowd that he welcomes and loves everyone present, but the ones who avoid him, annoy him, and create messes get less of his attention and affection.

"Anyway, back to what I was saying." I get so wordy sometimes. "When would he *not* want me to run to him? I was a little panicked, so I started searching the Bible for different exhortations to seek God and examples in stories where people were encouraged to seek him."

"What did you discover?" Bob asked.

I couldn't answer him at first, blinking back the urge to break down in tears. At that moment, I was getting more and more misty eyed. Yet I just *had* to get this out!

"I was so awestruck!" I reached into my small bag and pulled out a few sheets of paper on which I had written some verses from my research. "You probably all know these. I'm sure that none of this is new for any of you."

"No, by all means: Share with us," Greg said encouragingly.

"Okay. Here goes." I read aloud some of the Bible verses I had written. "Jesus said in Matthew 11: 'Come to me, all you who are weary and burdened, and I will give you rest. Take my yoke on you and learn from me, because I am gentle and humble in heart, and you will find rest for your souls. For my yoke is easy to bear, and my load is not hard to carry.'

"And Hebrews 4, which is written to Jewish believers who were being pressured and tempted to fall back to Judaism because of persecution, talks about Jesus being our sympathetic high priest. It says, 'Therefore let us confidently approach the throne of grace to receive mercy and find grace whenever we need help.' When we face strong temptations, he encourages us to come to him for his mercy and grace.

"In Psalm 145, 'The LORD is near all who cry out to him, all who cry out to him sincerely.'

"Jesus gave another invitation in John 7 where it says, 'On the last day of the feast, the greatest day, Jesus stood up and shouted out, "If anyone is thirsty, let him come to me, and let the one who believes in me drink. Just as the scripture says, 'From within him will flow rivers of living water.'"'

"And just before this happened, in John 6, Jesus said some things that offended the crowd. Therefore, many of those so-called 'disciples' turned away and left him. 'So Jesus said to the twelve, "You don't want to go away too, do you?" Simon Peter answered him, "Lord, to whom would we go? You have the words of eternal life. We have come to believe and to know that you are the Holy One of God."'" I looked up from my notes and glanced at each one of them. "Peter's like, 'It doesn't make sense, Lord, but we know that you're the only one for us. We have no other options, because no one else even comes close to comparing with you.'

"I have a list of some other verses that talk about God drawing near to us if we draw near to him; Jesus not sending away all who come to him; God letting all who seek him to find him, never forsaking us, and not rejecting a repentant heart, and so on. I've searched and searched all through the Scriptures, and I just can't find *any* verse or example where God *doesn't* want us to come to him.

"As it turns out, Father is my hiding place, my refuge, my shield, and my hope, besides being my Redeemer, my Savior, my Lord, and the Lover of my soul. I mean," I said quietly, half-shrugging my shoulders, "Jesus means *everything*. In him are all the treasures of wisdom and knowledge. He's the source of all grace—even grace upon grace. He's everything his Father is. I just can't find *any* reason for not running to him, even when it doesn't make sense, even when I don't understand, even when I'm at my worst. I don't know why, and I don't understand it, but he just loves me and wants me to be close to him."

"It's very freeing, isn't it?" Walter's smile dawned ever brighter on his face.

"Yeah," I admitted. "I don't understand his love for me—or for anyone for that matter—but I'm all too aware of my own sins and weaknesses, so I just don't know why he would want me."

"He did *create* you."

I pondered Walter's reply for a moment. "That's true. But then again, he created everyone."

"He is the Creator and Author of all life," inserted Greg. "He loves you as his child, through both creation and adoption through the new birth."

Bob let out a sigh and held a reflective gaze in his eyes. "You know, as a parent I have learned a lot about my relationship with Jesus. With six children of my own, most of whom are now grown and a couple have even started their own families, I guess you could say that he had a lot to teach me." He chuckled after he ended that sentence. "You may find the same to be true being a father to your son as your relationship with him grows. I know that for me, as Father gave us each child and brought a new son or daughter into our family, our hearts expanded more and more. My wife, Linda, and I have shed some tears, had some hurts and heartaches, but we have also learned a lot about love: our love for each one of our children, Father's love for each one of them as his children, and

54

his love for us individually as his children. I can't say that I fully understand his love for me, but being a parent has given me a glimpse of understanding his love for us from his perspective."

Tom nodded respectfully to Bob. "That was very well said, Brother. There's a lot of truth in that."

"Thank you, Brother," replied Bob. "It's just a little of what Father has taught me. He is the Great Teacher."

"So, John," interjected Greg, "getting back to the original topic: You had all these thoughts about Father being holy, righteous, and just, and you felt unworthy in his sight because of your sins."

"Right. I imagined that Father was looking down on me disapprovingly. The God I pictured would say things like: '*When you fix your attitude, then we'll talk.*' I had unconsciously rewritten my views of him to create this false theology of God."

"Praise the Lord that he corrected your thinking about him," Greg replied. "Most people don't even recognize their false theology and wrong beliefs or opinions about Father. What was your false theology?"

I released a sigh at the remembrance of what I used to think concerning Father. "It went something like this: God is holy, righteous, and just; and you are not, despite all your attempts. When you sin, you have to make things right. Confess your sin but be sincere about it. Repent, which means turn away from it and don't ever commit the sin again. Make restitution and restore what you did wrong. And once you're clean, then God will restore you back into fellowship."

"Goodness, Brother John!" exclaimed Walter. "That's a lot of expectations, hard work, and self-effort to have to fulfill! That kind of thinking would discourage *anyone* from going to Father."

"Yeah," I snickered halfheartedly, "you're right."

"And how does your view of him now make a difference?" inquired Greg.

"Well, he's everything to me now," I replied, sensing a glow on my face. "I know that it's not about me or my performance. It's about him and what he did for me and what he continues to do for me each moment of each day. And I know that he loves me beyond

55

what I can fathom—though I still don't know why. But that's okay. I'm just so thankful and overjoyed and relieved. And I sense a great peace between us. It makes me love him so much more!"

"That's a blessing," said Tom sincerely. "That is wonderful to hear you say that." His smile was encouraging.

"But I've also learned that the phrase '*run* to Christ' is a great way to put it. At least for me it is. You see, I'm so introspective and analytical that if I were just to start casually *walking* to Christ, so to speak, to confess my sins, then I would have too much time and start thinking too much about what I did and how unworthy I am. The whole vicious cycle/endless loop thing would start all over again."

"It's that 'introspective trap,'" interjected Bob.

I smiled brightly. "Yes, that 'introspective trap.' And it *is* a trap. So as soon as I sin, I have to 'run' to him immediately, leaning on his help and grace."

"So, what happened on Monday that changed your thinking about Father?" asked Walter.

I looked sheepishly at Walter, then at Tom, then at the ground. The emotion was rising in my heart, and I could feel it on my face. "I . . . I don't even know . . . if I can tell it all without . . . crying through the whole thing."

"That's okay," Walter replied contentedly. "The important thing is that Father touched your heart and changed your life and thinking."

"Yeah," I said, with a tremor in my voice. "He even demonstrated his love further to me through the one closest to my heart—my son Nathaniel." My voice broke as I spoke his name. This little boy had become my whole world since the moment he was born. It's funny how I never had to ponder why I loved him; I simply did. Now I understood a little better why Father loved me, and I accepted his love humbly and gratefully.

"So . . . I'll try . . . because it is important. And Father will receive the praise." I took a deep breath and exhaled slowly. "Tom invited us over for coffee and dessert, so we went to his house Monday evening. I was just stewing in my bitterness—not that I was angry at Tom or anyone else. It's just that indignation had become my *modus operandi* for so long. He asked me if when I sinned I found myself running toward Christ or away from him." I paused. "It seemed like such a simple yet profound question. I told him how I went through the motions of confessing my sins, trying to follow 1 John 1:9, but that it only led to confusion, despair, shame, and more distance between me and Jesus. He explained to me about God being a refuge, and he quoted a few verses from the Psalms. And that's when . . . my son . . . hit his head." The tremor in my voice and the tears in my eyes grew. "He was hurting, so . . . he . . . he." That's when I lost control. The sobbing began anew. I was reliving the whole moment. "He ran into my arms," I said between loud sobs. "And Tom said . . . that that's what . . . Father wanted . . . *me* to do . . . when I'm hurt." I stopped and wiped away some of the tears.

"Amen, Brother," someone said.

"Praise you, Jesus!" said another.

I couldn't speak any more at that moment. The memory and emotion were all so fresh and vibrant. Father had spoken to me in such an effective and profound way, and it would leave me changed forever. The small circle of brothers in Christ remained silent, one or two were praying or whispering praises to our Lord as the tears streamed anew down my face. They gave me the time I needed. They could tell that this was a deep and important work that Father was even then still continuing in me.

After a while, Bob broke the silence with a low chorus of "Hallelujah." One by one, we each joined in, lifting our voices and spirits in song. After the song, he offered a prayer of thanksgiving for what Father had done in me. I was humbled, uplifted, and filled with even more gratitude. *How could this get any better?* I wondered. *Will it be like this in heaven with us all praising and focusing our hearts and love on Jesus?*

We exchanged embraces and contact information. These were definitely the kind of brothers I wanted to meet with again and grow with in this journey. Then we collected what little gear we had brought with us, gathered any trash, and began to make our way toward the path and down the mountain.

After reaching the bottom, we took a break in the facilities. I used the time to call Elena to check on her and to let her know that I would be home soon. That was the age before cell phones were so commonplace and affordable.

"Honey," she said urgently on the other end of the line, "where have you been?"

"I've been on the mountaintop," I replied, not realizing the double meaning implied from the statement until after I said it. "Why? What's wrong?"

"Your pager has been going off for over an hour. Ron has been trying to contact you, but I didn't know how to reach you." It was my boss from work.

"What could he want on a Saturday?"

"I don't know, but you better call him now."

My heart began to slump. "Okay," I replied with a sigh. "I will."

When I ended my call with Elena, I then called my boss. He was irritated that I hadn't answered my pager. "I don't need you now," he snapped. "I needed you to come in over an hour ago to take care of something. When you didn't call me back, I called Carol. She came in and took care of it." He was very displeased. I apologized, but it only seemed to make things worse.

I hung up the phone and headed home. The rest of the weekend was not as encouraging as the mountaintop meeting, and it was then that I sensed that the "spiritual honeymoon" had ended. Nevertheless, it had been an unbelievable four-and-a-half days. The emotional high may have subsided for the time being, but Jesus continued being faithful as always, as I was to see in the coming weeks and months.

The things that Father had shown me and the grace and love he had worked in me would prepare me for other moments which I could never have foreseen. He would teach me more and expand my understanding of his transforming love and grace. Some significant questions which I had carried with me for most of my life

58

would soon be answered. These were questions concerning God's love and sovereignty in a fallen world, which seemed to reflect very little of Father's grace and love. Father would also use the Scriptures and this expanding fellowship of brothers in Christ to teach me how to walk with Jesus and to abide in him. After being a believer for seventeen years, studying the Scriptures, praying, and being active in a local body for as many years, graduating from Bible college, and even serving on the mission field in full time ministry, I was about to learn that there was much more for me to learn. Some lessons would include teachings which I had heard and believed most of my life that I would have to unlearn.

*KJV

CHAPTER 5

FATHER'S GIFT OF FREE WILL

The days and weeks continued, seemingly with little change in one sense: my circumstances remained the same. My job, finances, housing, and relationships showed no sign of any noteworthy change. The pallor of bitterness, however, which had hung over me for the previous two years had dissipated. I felt as if I had been given a new perspective and fresh insight concerning the daily situations which confronted me. The doubts, worries, and indignation which had hounded me for so long were not to be found. Instead I sensed a calming peace take hold of me, along with ample doses of Father's love and grace for living each moment. And oh, the joy and gratitude! Repeatedly throughout my days I found myself silently thanking Jesus for practically everything and praising him just for who he is. His joy, peace, love, mercy, grace—all the things that I had read about so many times in the Scriptures—were permeating my heart and life. Elena and I were growing closer again, and I noticed that she was enjoying the changes evident in me and this new way that I related to her. Existing conflicts between us simply fell by the wayside in light of our growing gratitude, grace, and love.

Things at work remained basically the same, though my change in attitude made all the difference for me. My coworkers still didn't say anything directly to me about what they had to have noticed as a difference in me. However, I had not earned the right to be heard among them. There seemed to be a constant, invisible strain between me and my boss, Ron. We didn't cross paths often, but when we did he appeared very serious and displeased with me. The quality and quantity of my work had improved in some ways, so it didn't make sense to me. He even claimed to be a Christian, yet apart from his church service attendance, it wasn't evident in his life. However, Ron was on his own journey, and it wasn't my place to judge him.

61

◊   ◊   ◊   ◊   ◊

About a week or two later, the brothers with whom I had climbed Stone Mountain planned a potluck fellowship at Bob's house. They invited my family and me. It was to be a time for all of us with our spouses and children to share a meal, to get acquaintted, and to talk about our walk with Jesus. This kind of fellowship and sharing, I was about to learn, was quite common in Tom and Sara's various circles of friends. It was something that I really craved now since I had been freed from my bitterness. But just like that fateful evening at Tom and Sara's house, I had no real idea of what encouragement I would receive from this gathering of believers.

We parked in the driveway outside Bob and Linda's house. Elena and I piled out of the car with little Nathaniel, a covered dish, and a gallon of sweet tea in hand. I was more than a little curious to meet the wives of these brothers who had encouraged me so. Perhaps the relational dynamics among these couples would give me a glimpse of what Elena and I could anticipate as we grew closer in our marriage, maturing in the seasons of life.

Upon entering the house, we were greeted warmly by Bob and his wife Linda. Then we were introduced to Walter and his wife Cindy and to Greg and his wife Kathy. The other wives were particularly warm and friendly toward Elena, and this made us both feel welcomed and at ease. The children, I learned, ranged in age from five to nineteen. Our little Nathaniel wasn't quite three at the time, but the other children, I would soon observe, would include him in their activities. I couldn't remember which children were whose, but as the evening progressed, I managed to learn a few of the names. Tom and Sara arrived a couple of minutes after us.

After a few minutes of arranging the different dishes on the kitchen counter and exchanging greetings and a few jovial remarks, we were led in prayer by Bob in giving thanks for the food, those present, this opportunity to share their home, and the joy and freedom we have in Christ. It was brief and touching. Once the closing "amen" was said, Walter immediately followed up with:

62

"Bob, you forgot to pray for all the missionaries." He was using his high-pitched, facetious voice in a mocking gesture.

Bob shook his head, grinning. "Brother, we pray for missionaries at other times. You can pray for them whenever you want. Right now, it looks like these youngun's are ready to eat."

I didn't know what to think of Walter's feigned complaint, but it seemed to be a joke of sorts. Perhaps the answer would be revealed later.

The mealtime was simple. It was somewhat like a family reunion. We formed a line as families with us parents preparing plates for our small children. The large, main table in the dining room was joined with a smaller table on one end. A third table for overflow was positioned nearby. Not all the chairs matched, but no one seemed to mind or even notice. The meal itself was delicious and had such variety, being a potluck with no apparent menu.

The discussion around the tables was interesting and inviting. There was no evidence of any cliques in this fellowship of about seventeen or more people. Everyone seemed to converse, to laugh, and to share with different individuals among both the adults and children alike. Elena and I were new to this group, though we both had known Tom and Sara for years, yet we were casually drawn into various conversations as the meal progressed. We felt comfortably a part of them as if we had all known each other for most of our lives. The other wives were so taken with Elena. She shared a few of her intriguing tales of growing up in poverty in Honduras, the cultural differences between our two countries, and the hilarious episodes of her early years of living in the United States and learning English. Once they learned of her culinary skills and crotchet work, they began to ask her about some of her favorite recipes and crotchet projects. Elena was shining socially and making friends quickly, which she never ceased to have a knack for doing. It warmed my heart to see her enjoying the time with these brothers and sisters in Christ.

After the meal, we continued some of our conversations begun at the table. Eventually we made our way to the great room, into which the dining room opened. We adults took our seats in an uneven circle of sofas and recliners. A few of us even sat on the floor. The children went as a group out to the back patio and back-yard. Bob and Linda's youngest two were the oldest children in the group, and they assured us that they would watch over Nathaniel. He happily paraded along with the big kids out the back door.

Our conversations flowed back and forth from present family activities to current concerns in our changing society to some of the heartbreaking stories in the news. Once a few observations were made about the school shootings which had been making headlines for some time by then, we settled on this topic for a while. The sideline conversations quickly drew to a close as we all turned out attention to some of the details of these horrific tragedies.

Then I made an observation which I intended as a question. "I guess I just don't understand why Father would let something like that happen."

"Why he 'would *let* it happen'?" Bob asked, looking a bit puz-zled.

"Well, you know," I explained slowly. "Since he's all-loving and all-powerful, it seems like he could have done something to prevent it so that there wouldn't be so much suffering."

Bob stared into the distance, pensively. "Hmm. Your question is based on the presupposition that Father is somehow *responsible* for all the pain and suffering in the world: that either he *causes* it or he *allows* it to happen."

A sense of sorrow struck me then. "Oh . . . well . . . I didn't mean to assign any *blame* to Father." *Is that really what I'm doing, Father? I had no intention of doing so.*

"That's okay, John," Bob said reassuringly. "It's an honest question and one that everyone asks sooner or later."

Greg leaned forward, rubbing his wrists. "That's a question which sages and scholars have wrestled with for millennia, so you're in good company." He smiled warmly toward me. I felt at ease.

"Bob," he continued, turning his attention, "what's the verdict in the God's-sovereignty-versus-man's-free-will debate?"

"Well, you and I and some of the others have had this discussion before," he said warmly.

"You got me," Greg admitted, thrusting his hands outward. "I'm baiting you."

"How about if we ask some other folks to see what they understand from our past discussion?"

"Sounds great." He looked around the room. "Any takers?"

Cindy, Walter's wife, suddenly had a revelatory look on her face. "Oh! I remember this discussion very well! It had a significant impact on me at the time, one which has encouraged me ever since."

Walter's face lit up like a Christmas tree with a dazzling display of multicolored, blinking lights. "Well, this is news to me, Darlin'. Do tell!"

Cindy was not disenchanted by his playfulness. She eyed him just as playfully.

"Honey Bunch, *that* hasn't worked on me for over twenty-two years, and it certainly isn't going to work on me now."

Several of us snickered at her comeback. It was obviously all in fun.

"As I was saying," Cindy proceeded, with a motion of her hand, "we had our own little discussion about this very issue some time ago, and it really was a comfort to me." Her attention darted back and forth, sometimes on me or Elena, sometimes on someone else in the group. "First, we have to orient ourselves to the heart of Father concerning his longings, desires, and will for his Creation. And we have to remember that he is always motivated by love for his Creation and those he created. After all, love is his most significant attribute."

"Man, I sure did learn *that* one the hard way," I inserted with a knowing look at the men.

"As the Creator, Father spoke into existence the universe—or rather he did so through Jesus, since everything was made through him. After creating the stars and planets, the oceans and mountains, the birds and other animals—all the wildlife—after he

65

created it all, it came down to his crowning achievement—his masterpiece, if you will. He created mankind in his own image. This one was different from animals and insects. Human beings were created last and best in the very image of the Divine."

"What exactly does that mean about being created in God's image?" I asked. I had read the opinions and interpretations of various Bible scholars, but I was curious to know what this group's perspective on it was.

Greg stepped up to the plate. "This is one of those lengthy discussions," he said cordially. "We'd be happy to converse with you about it sometime in greater detail, John, but for the moment you may want a more condensed version."

"Sure, that's fine."

"Being created in God's image includes many facets. Mankind is triune in his nature as a spirit being with a soul and inhabiting a physical body in a similar—yet not exact—way that God is the Trinity of Father, Son, and Holy Spirit."

"Greg," interrupted his wife Kathy, "please, Honey. You're going to bore some of us to tears if you give us the seminary definition."

"Not to worry," he assured her. "The rest is in simple terms." He scooted closer to the edge of his chair and began enumerating on his fingers. "Mankind, as a creature created in God's image and after his likeness, has some very special qualities. He is creative like God; he has imagination like God; he has individuality, personality, and temperament. He has been given authority to have mastery over the Creation and its resources as stewards under God. He is also a social being who desires fellow-ship with other social beings. Significantly, he was also given meaning and purpose in life and morality. These are all exalted gifts which we do not share with the animal kingdom since they are not created in God's image. Therefore, man was given an exalted nature, not much less than that of angels and the heavenly host. Yet there was another quality given to humanity which was perhaps the greatest gift given to him at his creation."

"Free will?" I suggested.

Greg straightened his back suddenly and grinned. "Bingo! *Free will!* We were given the ability to make choices. Another triune quality of mankind is our having a mind, will, and emotions. We have the capacity to think, to reason, to rationalize; to choose, acting upon our reasoning and understanding; and to feel emotions, to sense compassion, anger, sadness, joy, contentment, etc."

"May I add something?" asked Bob.

"Of course, Bob. In fact, you may have the next segment."

"Thank you, Brother." Bob turned his attention toward me.

"The use of our will can be erroneously influenced and guided by our thoughts and emotions. Therefore, the focus of our minds and the content of our emotions at any given time can hold a powerful sway over our will. In other words, if we're not carefully yielded to the Holy Spirit's guidance, our thoughts and feelings can strongly influence our choices. No doubt you've seen people make decisions based purely on emotions, turning a blind eye to reason, wisdom, and the clear counsel of the Scriptures. Conversely, you've also seen or heard of other individuals who chose a certain course of immoral actions because their hearts and minds were focused on a particular mindset or anticipated outcome."

"You mean like religious people doing wicked things because they think that they're right or somehow doing God's will?" I offered.

"Exactly! Oh, throughout history, and even today, there have been so many wrongs committed in the name of Jesus. And it's mostly because people had filled their minds with the wrong kind of thinking, following after their flesh. Hence, free will is a great gift and a powerful tool. It can be influenced and used for good or evil."

"That's very true," Greg stated, nodding in agreement. "We know that the Bible teaches us how to walk or to live by the Spirit. We can exercise our free will to meditate on the Scriptures, thereby renewing our minds with Father's thoughts. We can likewise choose to yield ourselves to Father as we grow in Christ and walk with him. Gradually our emotions will become more aligned with his heart and will. Granted, it won't mean that our emotions will

67

always be perfectly attuned with what he wants them to be, but they will keep us out of many pitfalls. With our minds being renewed by the Bible, our emotions will more easily follow his heart and our volition can more easily and more often choose his agenda over our own selfish desires."

"That's a great way to exercise our will," observed Walter. "As we live by the Spirit, our triune nature of mind, will, and emotions is yielded unto Jesus. Galatians 5 tells us that we'll walk or live in one of two ways: either by the Spirit or by the flesh. And I know from personal experience," he said, shaking his head and blinking his eyes rapidly, "that the former is a whole lot better than the latter."

"As long as . . . ?" Greg asked with raised eyebrows. He seemed to expect Walter to complete his sentence.

"As long as we depend on Father's grace to enable us," Walter added. "Walking with him is not a self-made, performance-based achievement. We depend on Jesus for *all* things, not on our weak flesh."

"Amen, Brother Walter," said Tom, beaming.

"Free will is a wonderful gift," averred Bob. "It's a *powerful* gift, given to us by Father. With it we can make such marvelous decisions to help and to encourage one another. We can use this God-given ability to choose to seek Father in prayer and to act upon a course of action, considering the wisdom, direction, and resources he has set before us, thereby determining what needs to be done. This is true for every given situation, not just the big choices.

"Now, the point is that Father gave us this precious gift of a free will. He created us as free beings with the ability to make choices freely. We are free to choose; however, whether we make poor choices or wise choices, the consequences are not divorced from our choices. Therefore, we choose our consequences by the choices we make, whether they only affect us or others as well. This brings up an important point about what happened in the garden in Eden." He looked around at the others. "Does anyone else want to contribute some of what they remember from our discussion at this point about the fall of mankind in Genesis 3?"

No one seemed too shy to speak in this group, seeing as they really did encourage one another to participate. This was very refreshing to me to see how they welcomed one another's involvement. It felt so open, free, and uninhibited.

After a few seconds of silence and several people looking at Sara, she seemed to overact at rolling her eyes playfully. "Oh, all right. If you insist." She giggled, as did a few others. Then she spoke.

"We talked before about how in the garden the first man and woman were equipped with everything they needed before they even had a need. Father provided fruit-bearing trees before people were even created, before their stomachs and appetites existed. He provided oxygen for them before he even created them with lungs and bodies that required oxygen. He provided myriads of animals and wildlife before tasking Adam with the job of naming them, which tapped into his intellectual ability and creativity—and so on and so forth. He provided the fellowship of his presence for their spiritual needs and the fellowship of each other for their social needs. He also provided a moral choice for them in the middle of the garden in that he provided the tree of life and the tree of knowledge. The tree of knowledge, of course, was the tree of the knowledge of good and evil. Father provided all these trees in this grove just bursting with luscious fruits of all kinds, along with these two special trees in the middle of the garden."

Sara leaned forward toward Walter. "We haven't heard from you in a while, so *tag, you're* it." She tapped him on the shoulder.

Walter grinned a silly grin as he glanced back at her. "I should have known you'd pick me when the story turned to eating." More snickers ensued.

"Well, I tell you, I think I would have had a field day with all those fruits." He licked his lips and rubbed his belly slowly, closing his eyes. "Man, I can just taste them all: cantaloupes and mangoes and strawberries and kiwis and bananas and pears—"

"—Focus, Walter," Tom reminded him gently and good-humoredly. "Focus on the two trees."

69

Walter shook his head as if regaining consciousness from a fond dream. "Right, right! The two trees!

"Along with those two trees, Father gave them a warning. Well, it was more than a warning. It was a command and a promise too. 'You can eat any of these fruits,' he said. 'Eat all you want and as many as you want.'"

"There he goes embellishing!" interjected Greg, sounding facetiously exasperated.

"Back off me, Bro," Walter said jovially. "I haven't had dessert yet." Greg's countenance was friendly.

"As I was saying, they could eat any of the fruits except for that one, the fruit from the tree of the knowledge of good and evil, because Father told Adam that if they ate of that tree, then they'd surely die on that very day. Yet it was a *spiritual* death on that day and a *physical* death many years later.

"As I'm sure you know already, Brother John, death signifies separation. Physical death is when the spirit leaves the body. Spiritual death, which Adam and Eve experienced when they first sinned, is a separation or loss of spiritual life and of relationship with God. It's literally the death of the spirit within a person. All descendants of Adam are born spiritually dead, being born according to Adam's nature. No doubt you'll remember that Romans 5:15 teaches this very thing, where Paul says, 'the many died through the transgression of the one man.' That's the spiritual death which was passed on to us all. The book of Revelation speaks of a 'second death,' that of eternal separation from God in the lake of fire, which follows physical death for those who are not in Christ."

"That spiritual death," inserted Greg, "was passed to all Adam's descendants. That's why every one of us was born a sinner, because of our spiritual heritage—or should I say the spiritual death—passed on to us from Adam."

"We here have talked before," said Bob, "about the need of all people for the Lord Jesus Christ due to their condemnation as born sinners. One of the consequences of the first sin was that this depravity passed to all Adam's descendants. Some people take offense to this doctrine from Romans 5, as if they couldn't possibly

be sinners or depraved because of their social status, their up-
bringing, or perhaps their good deeds. So many folks think that
they're 'good enough' to go to heaven because they don't commit
any 'big sins' or maybe because they keep most of the Ten
Commandments."

"They don't realize," added Linda, "that their condemnation is
not due to the sins they commit but due to their inherited sin nature.
That's what condemns us all."

"That's right, Linda," continued Bob. "Despite what most
people think, the Bible teaches that we all need Jesus to be able to
enter heaven because of the sin nature we received from Adam. In
reference to Adam's first sinful act in the garden in Eden, Romans
5:18 states that 'condemnation for all people came through one
transgression.'

I nodded slowly, having studied these grave truths for many
years. "Yes, this is all very familiar."

Walter directed the conversation back to his earlier comments.
"Let's turn back to the garden. Regarding death of any kind—be
it physical, spiritual, or eternal—Adam and Eve didn't really have
any experience with death, since at the time of their temptation
they had never seen anything die, neither plants nor animals. Consequently, they didn't fully comprehend the implications of death
or separation."

"However," Cindy interrupted, "they should have known that it
was something they needed to avoid. They should have just trusted
you-know-who."

"*Whom*," Walter corrected.

"God, of course," she answered with a serious look.

"No, Darlin'. I mean that it's, 'they should have just trusted you-
know-*whom*.'"

"*Writers!*" Cindy said with feigned exasperation. "What can
you do with them?"

"Now, Darlin', you know that I'm a grammar geek," he stated
casually.

"Anyway," he continued, jokingly rolling his eyes, "back to the
story. You're right, Darlin'. They should have trusted God enough

71

to know that he was their Creator and loving Father and that he had given them this lush environment with every provision they could possibly need or want. Their only experiences proved him to be loving, giving, kind, wise, and perfect. There was no reason for them to think that he would be holding out on them about anything."

"But instead they listened to the snake," Cindy inserted excitedly, shaking her head slowly with her eyebrows lowered. "What in all their experience of naming the animals made them think that a snake was trustworthy or that it should even be capable of intelligent speech?"

"That's true. They should have asked God: 'Hey, Dad, are the snakes supposed to talk? None of the other animals do, but there's one here that does, and you won't believe what he told us.' Laugh if you want, but they should have really questioned what was happening." Walter held out his palms upward, mimicking a balancing scale. "Hmm. Let's see: listen to a snake who isn't supposed to have the gift of intelligent speech and which we only just met or go by what we know about Father and trust him." His hands bobbed up and down like a seesaw or balancing scale would move. "Aw!" he exclaimed in a silly way, tossing his hands up. "We'll go with the talking snake!"

The performance was hilarious! I wasn't necessarily comfortable making light of biblical passages like this, but it helped to communicate some of the finer points I hadn't pondered. I secretly hoped that it wasn't disrespectful to the Scriptures while I enjoyed the humor nonetheless.

"You know what happened, right, John?" Cindy continued with her wide-eyed expression. *"They listened to the snake!* He made it sound like God was keeping something from them: *'He's lying! You won't die. Eat this fruit and you'll become like God, knowing good and evil.'* But y'see? *They already were like God* since they were created in his image and likeness. At least they were as much like God as possible for their limitations, what with their free will, creativity, mind, emotions, and freedom. Even in Psalm 8:4 and 5 David said, 'Of what importance is mankind that you should pay attention to them, and make them almost like the heavenly beings?' But the enemy didn't tell them about the loss, sin, separation, spiritual death, broken fellowship, guilt, and shame that they would experience."

"You got it, Darlin'," returned Walter. "Instead of asking Father about this weird statement from a talking snake, they chose to act independently of God and to trust in their own judgment. They used his gift of free will against Father and against themselves."

"Wow!" I shuddered. "When you think of it in those terms, it really does show how foolish and rebellious their decision was."

Bob flashed a knowing smile. "Imagine that you give your children this wonderful, beautiful gift only to have them use it to hurt you, others, and themselves. In a sense, Linda and I have been there as parents. When one of our children rebelled for a time, people would look down on us, criticizing us and saying that we must have done something wrong in raising the child. However, when you read Genesis 3, you realize that even the most perfect parent—our heavenly Father—had rebellious children. And he did everything in love and with holiness."

Cindy's expression became wide-eyed again as she spoke. "And you know what Father—the perfect Parent—did for his rebellious children? Long before the foundation of the world, he *knew* that they were going to exercise their free will to sin and to rebel against him. Yet he lovingly gave them the gift of free will anyway. And he didn't even try to snatch it back from them once they sinned."

"I think I see it now," I said, pondering out loud. "God determined to make a way to redeem humanity back from their terrible decision—back before any of it happened. God had already decided that the plan of redemption would become a reality before Adam and Eve, before the garden, even before the universe was created."

"That's right," Tom agreed. "That's why Jesus was 'the Lamb slain from the foundation of the world,'* as Revelation 13 tells us. As a loving Father, God wanted his children to have free will just

73

like the angels. Mankind would not be a race of robots pro-grammed to love God. Instead they would be allowed the freedom to choose on their own to love him or not. And while seeing into the future and knowing that they would abuse his gift of free will, he also determined to provide for their salvation."

The pieces of the puzzle were fitting together. It was like shining a bright light into a dark room. I was awed at the real-ization.

I sat back in my chair, not having realized that I had been creeping toward the edge during the discussion. "Let's see if I have this right. Because of Father's love for us, he gave us a free will even though he knew that we would abuse it to sin against him, ourselves, and each other. And because he knew that we would do that, he also planned to redeem us by sending Jesus to bear our sin on the cross, to break its power in our lives, and to quicken us alive spiritually, providing us with a new nature and his spiritual life that's new and eternal."

"Mmm-hmm," replied Tom. "You've got it so far."

"But," I continued with a tremor in my voice, "How does *he* benefit? I mean, what does *Father* get out of all this?"

"That's an astute question." Tom tapped his finger on his chin. "Anyone?" he asked, looking around the room.

Greg let out a heartfelt sigh. "Well, at a great personal sacrifice to God himself, he receives love from those who truly love him by choice and not by obligation, coercion, or programming."

"But so much pain and suffering . . . heartache and tragedy. Why's all that necessary?"

Bob lightly patted my shoulder. "You know, John, I don't think it's best to think of it all in terms of being 'necessary.' It might be more helpful to think of it as simply the way mankind has played it all out given his choices and depravity, which he also chose. Some things like probabilities, possibilities, and all the 'what if' questions are just too big for us to understand fully. However, I can say that, as a father myself, I can sort of understand God's position of wanting his children to love him freely and not by force. I know that his heart's desire is for everyone to know him. I also

74

know that *he* knows that not everyone will choose to love him.

"Maybe it would help to picture the analogy of a young fellow looking for a potential wife. He has a heart full of love, and he longs to share it with just the right girl. Maybe he's one of those romantic boys who fantasizes for years what it will be like when he finds the one for him: what their courtship and wedding will be like, how they will share their love, their dreams, their life together, their hopes for the future, and how they will one day raise a family. Anyway, let's say that this fellow starts searching for a potential bride. Would he want someone who felt forced or obligated to marry him and to perform the 'duties' and 'obligations' of a wife like an indentured servant? Would he want something like an arranged marriage or a mail order bride? Of course not. He doesn't want some ulterior motive on her part spoiling the love relationship, nor does he want someone with an emotionless commitment of simply going through the motions of marriage. He would want a girl who would have a mutual love for him and choose to marry him because she wants to, not because she has to or because she fears what might happen to her if she didn't."

As Bob spoke, I gazed at Elena and squeezed her hand. Her eyes sparkled at me, and she dazzled me with that smile that first won me over many years ago. A smile brightened my face, and my heart soared.

Bob grinned and rubbed his chin. "I see you've had some experience in that department."

"I sure have," I answered cheerfully. Then a thought struck me.

"So, when we see so much suffering in the world, like the Jewish Holocaust, school shootings, child abuse, and mass murders, it's not really Father causing or allowing any of it, is it?"

"When you view it from a biblical perspective, it's really people abusing the power of their free will against others and themselves."

"And if Father were to step in to intervene and to stop those tragedies before they happened . . ." I wasn't sure how to finish the sentence.

"Then free will would be no more," added Bob. "Or rather, it never would have existed to begin with. It would have all been a

75

deceitful scheme—just some talk about free will with a lot of smoke and mirrors to keep up appearances. And we know that Father is not like that at all.

"But there may be many other reasons he doesn't intervene as well. We must also remember that there are the many-faceted works which Father labors toward all individuals, 'behind the scenes' so to speak, as he gently persuades them. And in God's sovereignty, his plan will not be thwarted or interrupted by us or our expectations of him or the way we want our lives to be. You know how people sometimes say, 'If God really loved me, then he would do so-and-so.' Or, 'If there were a God, then he would do this and that, or he wouldn't allow this or that.' Father *does* love each and every individual in the world, but he doesn't play the game of living up to our expectations just to prove something to us. We can't manipulate him like that."

This new perspective was sinking into my understanding. Bob continued as I listened quietly.

"Know that Father faithfully loves you through every painful moment of your life. Understand that he bears the pain along with you. After mankind abused Father's gift of free will, God made the ultimate sacrifice, bearing the sin of all humanity by suffering a cruel crucifixion nearly two thousand years ago. In doing so, Jesus reconciled the world unto Father, resolving our sin which separated us from him, giving us eternal spiritual life, sealing us with his Holy Spirit of promise, and taking away our sense of unworthiness. Therefore, he has made the way possible to restore our relationship with him and to make us new creations in his Son. Each one of us may exercise our free will to love and to follow him—if we so choose. You see, even when he knows what's best for us, he still leaves the choice to us. He doesn't pressure us or coerce us, even for us to choose what's best for us."

Bob must have seen something like a puzzled or questioning look on my face then, because he added: "It's okay for us to misunderstand Father. We may sometimes suffer the consequences by doing so—especially if we make some crucial decisions or actions based on those misunderstandings. Nevertheless, he doesn't love us any less or feel disappointed in us when we misunderstand him. People have been misunderstanding Father and misinterpreting his actions and work since the garden in Eden. All throughout the Bible he's had his heart's desire and plan for mankind—for both nations and individuals. Yet he is misunderstood time and time again."

"And it's funny," Walter added, "but you never read anything in the Bible about God wringing his hands or pacing back and forth with worry about being misunderstood. Misunderstandings happen, and he knows that they will beforehand because he knows each one of us better than we know ourselves. But it's okay when we misunderstand him. He still loves us with an unconditional love."

"And you know what, brothers and sisters?" Tom began. "As each individual enters the world with their free will, sin nature, and inclination to misunderstand Father and a lot of what happens to them in life, his love never changes for them. He continues to love each and every one of us. Now, he is grieved when people choose to hurt themselves and others through their poor, foolish, sinful choices, but his love for them all never waivers one bit. It is a paradox for the ages: an all-sovereign God and a free-willed humanity together in the same universe. From our perspective, the two may seem contradictory. I don't pretend to understand it all fully myself. Yet I am persuaded beyond a shadow of a doubt that Father's love for me and for everyone else is sincere, absolute, and unfaltering—despite whatever circumstances or feelings may present to me otherwise."

"You've really knocked a home run there, Brother Tom," commended Bob. "Any understanding of Father and his presence in the midst of a fallen humanity and Creation must be firmly grounded in an unwavering conviction that he truly does love us— no matter what our emotions, our circumstances, or anything else may try to convince us to believe otherwise."

"Amen to that," said Greg. "There are many voices out there attempting to dissuade us of the fact of Jesus' love for us. It's easy to surf the wave of his love and sing his praises when things are going well for us and for our loved ones. But when tragedy hits, our trust in Father's love could potentially take a beating."

He looked empathetically at his wife Kathy and gently wrapped his arm around her. She already looked misty-eyed as if she knew what he was about to say.

"Kathy and I have had some heartaches of our own. We bore the loss of our first three babies to miscarriage in the early years of our marriage." He smiled through the tears now forming in his eyes. "It was so hard to go through. We experienced the whole gamut of emotions like most couples, even fearing any further pregnancies."

He paused to look at Kathy once more. His voice began to break as he spoke again. "Then we were blessed with little Katie . . . and she has brought such joy to our lives. Sure, we questioned Father about her CHD—her congenital heart defect. Who wouldn't? We weren't some kind of super-spiritual believers immune to such doubts and misunderstandings. But it all came back to his love for us and Katie and those three little blessings awaiting us in heaven."

"And our little Katie isn't so little anymore," added Kathy with a sniffle and a chuckle. She began to wipe the tears from her eyes. "You know, through the years as I've been by her side, helping her through every trauma, every surgery, and every recovery in her precious, little life, I have learned so much about Father and his love for us all. He's blessed me and taught me so much through her. Early on, we set our gaze on Jesus and stayed in the Scriptures. And that sure foundation of his love for us through the trials and the hard times—through anything that life throws our way—his love for us has never faltered, and I don't think we've ever really questioned it since then."

As the couple held each other tightly and quietly, Tom spoke what he had observed.

"Kathy and Greg, I've known you both since years before those trying times, and I can testify to the fact that Jesus has sustained you three through those years and more. It has been a blessing and encouragement to me and to my family to see Christ in you all and

78

living through you no matter what came your way."

This was amazing to me to hear that veteran missionaries like Tom and Sara, who were spiritual giants from my perspective, would be so edified by the example of others. I had heard many of the stories of their ministry experience with a primitive tribe in Malaysia. They have always stood out in my mind as the humblest and most Christlike people I've ever known. It's not that I admired them in the sense of putting them on any kind of pedestal or accrediting them with doing magnificent works for God, for it was Christ living in and through them doing the works. By that time, I had known them for fourteen years, and I knew that any sort of praise or complements were the last thing that they would have desired. They were great encouragements to me through the examples of their lives, their ministries, and their walk with Jesus. I was humbly grateful to know them and to call them not only my brother and sister in Christ but also my friends. As far as I knew, they had never had their names in lights anywhere. They were not well-published or well-received in ministry circles or in the media as "influential Christian leaders." Nevertheless, they were servants of God who humbly and—by their own admission—imperfectly walked with their Lord. It made me wonder how many other Toms and Saras there were whom Father had placed throughout the world, far from the spotlight, so that they might be an encouragement to the few and the several.

"I'm sure we can all testify to Father's steadfast love for us in the midst of the most difficult circumstances of our lives," Linda offered quietly. "And through those hard times, we learn to depend on him and to trust him a little more. He has proven himself to us in so many ways. It's not because of who we are or anything that we've done to earn his love. No one could ever be deserving of Father's love. His love is showered upon us freely. He just loves us; that's who he is. That's his grace. It's that simple."

"You're right, Linda," concurred Cindy. "He doesn't know how to relate to us in any other way but by love. Even when he disciplines us, it's all in love. As Psalm 145:17 teaches us, 'The LORD is just in all his actions, and exhibits love in all he does.'"

79

This thought hit me squarely. *Naturally he relates to us out of love! How else would a perfect Being who exudes perfect love relate to anyone?* And that verse! It used to be one of my favorites that I cherished and clung to in my youth whenever things happened which I didn't understand. Somehow, I had forgotten all about it since my heart had turned bitter. I guess that I became disillusioned about Father and that verse when things didn't go my way. *But he exhibits love in* all *that he does, whether I realize it or not,* I mused silently. *Plainly, the fault could never have been with Father; it had always been with me and my tainted perspective. The problem was my view of him in my life, not with God himself.* I had been so wrong about Father for so long. But now he was lovingly correcting this wrong view I had had of him. He did so without any scowling or scolding. He corrected me out of love! My heart soared again, delighted to gain another glimpse of his love for me.

Aloud I said to the group: "How could I have misunderstood his approach—his way of relating to me?"

"It happens to us all, Brother," Walter affirmed. My glance around the room was met with nodding heads. Even without knowing everyone's story, I was certain that each one had learned similar lessons as mine, sometimes even the hard way.

"I sort of wish that I could take back those years of misunderstanding. So much of my life would have been so much better."

"Now, remember, John," Bob said gently, "it was Father who taught you his grace in and through those difficult circumstances. Do you think that you would have learned these lessons to the same depth of understanding and appreciation if you had just read about them in a book or learned them in a classroom or heard them in a sermon?"

"Well, that's true," I thought aloud. "I don't think the truths of God's grace and love would have impacted me the same way. But I wouldn't wish my experience on anyone."

"Oh, certainly not," he agreed. "However, it just goes to show how Father can take the worst things in our lives and transform them into something precious. It's what the Psalms and other passages refer to as Father turning our mourning into dancing or our grief into joy."

"Perhaps given enough time and opportunity, I would have fallen into the same pit eventually whether it was on the mission field or here in the States."

"Hey, Brother," Bob said in a low but cordial voice, "you might be overworking those analytical and introspective skills of yours."

My somber facial expression broke. "You're right. But they're probably not so much skills as detriments."

"There's a place for that in the body of Christ," he said reassuringly. "We just have to submit everything to Jesus' lordship and not let our particular skillset thwart what the Spirit wants to accomplish in us for our growth and his glory."

"So, getting back to the topic of God's unfailing love," Walter began, changing gears, "no matter what may happen, we can still be sure of Father's love for us and not interpret his actions toward us through the lens of suffering as his abandoning us."

"I see that now," I acknowledged. "You know, it's one thing to quote the verses that say he'll never leave nor forsake us. It's another thing to stand firm on the truth of his love for us when everything's falling apart, or at least when it seems like it is."

"Agreed, Brother John. Paul knew that well, which is why he expressed it in Romans 8:28 the way he did, saying that nothing shall separate us from God's love, be it life, death, anything in the present, anything in the future, height, depth, or anything else in Creation. That list of his was meant to be all inclusive of everything. It was his way of saying 'no matter what you can think of, it won't stop God's love for us.'"

Greg contributed to the point. "And, like we discussed earlier, most of that suffering comes from other people or even from us ourselves. You know what Proverbs 19:3 teaches: 'A person's folly subverts his way, and his heart rages against the LORD.' It's that kind of thing. Father gets the blame for a lot of suffering in the world due to our limited perspective and knowledge, our misunderstandings of our circumstances."

"What about natural disasters?" I wondered aloud.

"Earthquakes, hurricanes, floods—that sort of thing. Doesn't God control the weather and Creation?" I looked around the room, eager to hear who would answer this one.

"That's another excellent question," Tom stated after taking a sip of his coffee. I had almost forgotten that he was in on the discussion. He seemed to be allowing a lot of opportunities for others to participate.

"The Scriptures teach that he is sovereign over his Creation, and examples abound of how he interacts through the weather and other aspects of Creation. But remember that it's an arena of both God's sovereignty and man's free will. Many of our actions seem to influence climate change and the weather, what with the pollution and the waste we generate and how, as a society, we mismanage the resources of Father's Creation. Now, I'm no scientist, but from some of the things I've read, I would say that's a fair possibility. Maybe some of the science behind it is plausible."

"So, there's not a definitive answer then?"

"Perhaps there's not a completely satisfying answer. We are, after all, attempting with our finite minds to understand the infinite God. We can learn much from the Bible, but it's not always going to answer everything to our satisfaction. That's not really its purpose, after all. It's the story of the unveiling of God's glory amid his loving pursuit of humanity by his grace as he works the redemption of mankind in a fallen world. It's not a book to answer all our curiosities."

"You mean questions about aliens, time travel, ESP, and Big Foot?" It was Walter again, using his factitious tone of voice. "I've searched the Scriptures for decades looking for those kinds of answers."

Tom's response was immediate and bore a pleasant smile. "Walter, if you find those kinds of answers, you could write a book detailing your findings and make a lot of money." He chuckled and took another sip of his coffee.

"Okay," Walter continued. "But what if there are some hidden, biblical codes to crack which predict future events or spell out the fastest growing stocks or winning lottery ticket numbers. You know, some secret algorithms decipherable from the Greek letters or Hebrew words."

Tom continued to smile. "Those are not the kinds of 'secrets' present in the Holy Scriptures. No, the Bible isn't given to us for any of those purposes. It's not Father's nature to deceive us with obscure truths or 'hidden secrets' only decipherable to a few who 'crack the codes.' But it is invaluable for getting to know him and seeing some of the things which he has done throughout some parts of history in his romance with mankind."

Walter lifted the facade and matched Tom's smile. "I was just leading you on, Brother Tom, to see what you'd say."

"That's what I suspected."

"Don't worry, Tom, you and I are on the same page," he assured Tom, adding, "pun intended."

Greg bowed his head in mock disgust. "Aw! There he goes again!"

Tom turned to me once more. "John, before the air becomes permeated with puns, let me state the point I was trying to make. When we see bad things happening in the world, it's probably best not to jump to conclusions and to declare that some natural disaster or other calamity is God's judgment on an individual, people group, or nation. This also coincides with an earlier point about our frequent misunderstandings of Father and his actions. We're simply not in the position to discern accurately everything that he does or doesn't do or allows or doesn't allow. However, we can be persuaded, as was Paul, that Father's love for us is genuine and steadfast."

"Thanks, Tom," I responded, smiling. "I've also heard people blame Father for making them sick or giving them cancer, diabetes, cardiac disease or some other poor health issues. And I don't mean to make light of people's suffering, but it just makes me wonder about Father's role in all this."

"What do you think about it, John?" he inquired plainly.

I thought for a second before replying. "Well, I can't really imagine Father giving people diseases and illnesses. That doesn't seem to be in keeping with his nature."

83

"In light of our discussion here tonight, John," probed Walter, "how do you think we should view those cases—biblically speaking?"

"From the Scriptures, it's clear that Father is all-loving and sovereign, while mankind has a free will, even though he's fallen. I would have to say that, since so many of those health issues are the consequences of our poor dietary choices and lifestyles, it must be that many people have those kinds of illnesses and even others due to their freewill choices."

"That would cover a number of those cases," he replied, nodding. "Then there are other health issues which are influenced by their genetics. Those may well be the results of their ancestors' poor choices. Either way, they are consequently the byproducts of mankind's choices, not Father's."

"Walter," called Greg, "if I may, I'd like to add something along these lines."

"Be my guest, Brother," he replied, motioning to the floor before him.

"John, when it comes to nutrition, there is enough research and data to demonstrate that for all our knowledge, technologies, medicines, and gadgets, we're not necessarily getting healthier as a humanity. In fact, we tend to make poor choices based on our senses: what appeals to our senses of sight, smell, sound, taste, and touch. I've known people who have fallen ill due to eating foods that were not the best for them, whether they were aware of it or not. For years they didn't realize that their diet, lack of exercise, and other environmental factors were detrimental to their health until it was too late or perhaps never at all. All these elements involve choices of the will, not Father's design. There's a good bit of science showing that the right kinds of foods have some curative properties, which is more in line with Father's desire to provide what we need to maintain good health."

Walter piped up, sounding a little sarcastic. "This is starting to sound like an infomercial for the right nutrition and healthy choices." He cocked his head toward Greg. "Brother, are you say-ing that we need to form healthy eating habits, to exercise daily, to wear sunblock, and to stay away from smoke, junk foods, and other foods that are harmful to us?"

Greg beamed contentedly. "You might say that I am. By the way, I'm not presenting any kind of diagnosis for anyone. I'm simply trying to make the point that in this fallen world marred by sin, we and other free-willed individuals play a very active role in our sufferings due to the bad choices that we or others make. Therefore, let's not be too quick to point a finger at Father for all the negative circumstances in our lives."

I had to pause for a moment to think through that one. "I think that you're right, Brother Greg. When I reflect on so many pains and problems that I've experienced in my life thus far, they all seem to be the results of choices that I or others have made, impacting my life detrimentally."

"Whether it's detrimental or not, we know from scriptures like Genesis 50:20, Romans 8:28, and James 1:17, among others, that God can work good despite the choices that we or others make."

Kathy nodded approvingly at his side. "We can testify to that," she said with a smile. "Father has blessed us in our lives, no matter what we've experienced. Even with all the health issues that Katie has had in her little life, we've seen Father's blessings and have come to know his wonderful grace and fathomless love for her and for us."

"Amen," said Tom softly.

A gentle hush fell over the room as we contemplated the implications of this discussion.

Elena gently cleared her throat and stopped in the middle of the blanket she had begun crocheting just that evening. "May I say something?" she asked quietly.

"Yes, Elena," answered Tom, "by all means."

Her countenance displayed a warm and timid smile as she spoke. "Well, I've been listening to this whole discussion about God's love, and it's very wonderful to learn about his love for us all. I keep hearing you all say that Father has *unconditional* love and *steadfast* love and *genuine* love and *unfailing* love and so on.

"My parents showed me love as I was a little girl growing up in our little house in Honduras. We lived in poor conditions with a dirt floor, no electricity, and no running water inside. For some years, we didn't have much to eat besides tortillas and salt, and some years there were a few days when we didn't eat at all. You see, my dad didn't make very much money as a carpenter, raising a family with five daughters. None of us girls had shoes until we were ten years old. We were poor, but we didn't realize we were poor because we were loved by our parents. And I always knew that my mother and father loved me. They used that word, 'love'— well, the Spanish word, *amar.*

"I never thought of love as being anything less than uncon- ditional, steadfast, genuine, and unfailing—all the things you said about God's love. It was only when I came to this country and saw how people related to one another that they would say things like, 'so-and-so doesn't love her anymore,' or 'they fell out of love.' To me, there is only one kind of love—and that is the kind that is unconditional, unfailing, and so on. If it isn't all those things, then it's something else besides love. It isn't true love at all."

Tom nodded slowly. "That was a wonderful observation, Elena. Thank you for sharing that with us. It's true that our cul- ture has created different things which masquerade as love, which are not really love at all. They may be love of self, but they aren't love for others. Love *is* unconditional and unfailing, otherwise it isn't love. It can never be conditional or failing or temporary. The difficulty with the word 'love' is that it has come to have so many negative connotations in our culture that, when we speak of Father's love, we have to use these extra words to remind our- selves that his love is the real thing—not that counterfeit that we see so often in society, which claims to be love."

At that moment, the glass door to the patio slid open, and in came the children, giggling and talking loudly. My son Nathaniel was there, being led by the hand by Charis, one of Bob and Linda's daughters. He was smiling so happily, enjoying being with the big kids.

Having heard a piece of the story of Greg and Kathy's daugh- ter, I searched the small crowd for little Katie. She wasn't little at all, and she was quite content and confident. By the looks of her, I thought that she was about fourteen-years-old. I couldn't imagine the sufferings that Katie had experienced in her young life and through which her parents had agonized along with her. However, as I had heard earlier, Father's love permeated every moment, making every experience a learning one concerning Father's love for them. Children are truly a blessing from the Lord!

On the way home that evening, I reflected with Elena about some of the things I had learned from the potluck fellowship. The realization that I had been the cause of many of my problems and stresses had made a significant impact in my spiritual comprehension. Father's love for me is genuine, I realized. In fact, it is the only way he relates to us all. *Thank you, Jesus, for your love for me!*

I had misunderstood Father and his workings in my life for decades. However, after that night, I *definitely* wanted to know him more and to understand his ways much better. His grace and the understanding of it were becoming sweeter and more precious to me. My desire to learn more of his grace would soon come to fruition. A brief road trip with my best friend would soon afford me the opportunity.

*KJV

CHAPTER 6

GRACE UPON GRACE

Steve called me about a month after the potluck fellowship to invite me to join him on a Saturday morning road trip. He was planning to run an errand across town to pick up a washer and a dryer which another couple was donating to his mom. Since his dad had recently passed away, Steve and his wife had moved from Texas to the north side of Atlanta to live closer to his mom and to care for her. This had also brought him closer to me, even though we lived on opposite sides of the metro area. Any opportunity to spend time with Steve was always welcomed. Life was always more fun and adventuresome with him.

"Hola, Juan. ¿Cómo estás, Hermano?" came the voice over the phone. I would have recognized his voice anywhere, even in Spanish.

"Bien, gracias a Dios. ¿Y tú, Hermano? ¿Qué tal estás?

We always began our phone conversations in Spanish for at least a couple of minutes. It was sort of a game with us, as each one attempted to say something goofy to make the other crack up with laughter.

Ours is a friendship which encompasses practically every facet of life, while having the depth of fellowship by which we can share our most intimate thoughts, joys, and sorrows apart from any judging. It feels ever fresh. We know each other about as well as two individuals possibly can in this life, apart from any self-serving agendas or negative attitudes. We have always been able to discuss life issues, to pray together, and to laugh together, sharpening each other as iron sharpens iron. We have encouraged one another in our walks with Jesus throughout our decades of friendship. Everyone needs a friend like Steve.

Steve is a few years older than me, so he had served as a missionary in my wife's home town a few years before I could finish college, marry, and return to serve full-time. By then he had left, returning to the States to find a wife. Those were our it's-better-to-marry-than-to-burn years, as we referred to them, after which we finally became serious (or borderline desperate) about seeking the wife Father had for each of us. "'A man's gotta do what a man's gotta do,'" Steve would sing, "'but he doesn't have to do it alone.'"[1] He's also that kind of goofy friend. In the midst of all the circumstances and scenarios we have encountered in life, humor has always played an important part of our walk and friendship.

On the Saturday in question, I parked outside his house and knocked on the door. Steve opened the door almost immediately. "How ya doin', Brother?" he said in his deep, loud, and facetious voice with a weird and almost creepy grin.

"Doin' great, Flamen'!" Then we gave each other a hug while patting each other's back loudly.

This may need some explanation. As in some close friendships, Steve and I have a repertoire of quirky inside jokes, one-liners, song references, and character voices which we use in each other's presence whether the moment calls for them or not. The deep, loud voice of greeting hearkened back to a former coworker of his at a factory many years before. The friendly gentleman always made an effort to express his warm salutations above the din of the noisy equipment surrounding them. Something about his manner of greeting struck us as being hilarious, so we used it predictably.

Steve's nickname became *Flamen'* after an outing long ago with our singles' Sunday School class in which he shared about his encounter with a "flaming evangelist." The term referred to one of those fire-and-brimstone preachers who attempt to "scare" people into a relationship with Jesus by frightening them with sermons about hell. Although we found humor in this, it was truly sad to think that there were so-called "ministers" in the world who still practiced that philosophy. Nevertheless, despite the dark reality of the reference of this abuse of the gospel (if what they preached could even be called the gospel) parading around in the name of Jesus, the nickname stuck with him. To me, he has always been "Flamen'" ever since then.

"How are Elena and Nathaniel?" he asked, grabbing a travel bag from the dining room table and scooping up his keys in the same motion.

"They're doing well. When I left, Nathaniel was eating break-fast."

"Well that's good," he announced, nodding repeatedly with a half-mocking expression of one of his character portrayals. "You ready to go?"

"Ready as you are. Hey, where's Aby?" I suspected that his wife was not home since she didn't appear at the door to greet me.

"She's having brunch with her sisters."

"Hey! Then it's just brother to brother today, huh?"

"That's right." It was a distinct yet similar character voice this time. "Brother to brother!" Steve sang this a few times in differ-ent pitches as we exited, and he locked the door. He had sung bari-tone in a gospel quartet for many years in addition to many solos and duets in our home church before he left for the mission field. Singing has always been a passion of his. In fact, his enjoyment of music and singing had transpired to me very early in our friend-ship.

We climbed into his pickup, strapped on the seat belts, and backed out of the driveway. Seconds later, we were heading down the road and out of the neighborhood toward the expressway.

"Let's skip the music session for now," Steve offered, turning off the stereo, "and do some catching up."

"Okay, great!"

"So, how've you been, Brother?" His countenance was warm and welcoming.

I opened my eyes a little wider. "I've been doing great, Steve. Father has just filled my heart with joy and peace and gratitude. And it hasn't grown old. Admittedly, I've had some moments that were not all hallelujah choruses, and I don't mean to imply that I've been sinless during this whole time. But the bitterness is just gone, and any anger is pretty rare and nothing like before. I think that, because of the way that Father has changed my heart, attitude, and perspective, his grace and love have really diffused practically all anger. Even now when I sense some anger, it isn't a seething rage fest like before. It's just some annoyance or mild sense of frustration. It's not something that lingers and sets up shop."

"Hey, Bro, that's great to hear!" he said enthusiastically. "Maybe you could teach me a few things about anger."

My smile betrayed my surprise at his statement. "Well, I don't think I'm anyone to teach anything concerning anger. I believe that it's just hard to be angry now that I know how much Jesus loves me. I mean, I've heard about what he did for us on the cross and in his resurrection almost my whole life. I've memorized Bible verses and sung songs about his love too. But having that confidence of his open arms for me to run to when I'm hurt, lonely, afraid, or misunderstood—it's just too easy to run to Jesus instead of becoming angry."

"Has he given you something to replace the anger?"

I thought for a second: *Something to replace the anger?* "It has to be his love, grace, peace, joy—and gratitude."

"Good night! That's a lot of great replacements!"

"Flamen', I never would have imagined it, but I'm so *grateful* for things. And it's kind of crazy because I was a missionary to Central America, so I've been to some of the poorest places imaginable. I mean, I lived in a town with neighbors who had almost nothing. Why, I've even visited the homes of people so poor that all they lived in was a bare spot in a dirt road with some branches bound together and some discarded plastic over the bundles for a roof. Even the displaced survivors of Hurricane Mitch to this day *still* live in little plastic matchbox-huts provided by some governmental program. And they live in such squalor conditions with just the clothes on their backs." I felt my eyes begin to swell with tears.

"I know, Bro," he said empathetically. "I've seen it too. Some of those situations we saw together. They're just . . . devastating."

"But . . . why wasn't I grateful *before*? Especially witnessing all that poverty and suffering. I mean, I *thought* I was grateful back then. If anyone had asked me back then, I would have said that I was and not have perceived it as a lie. I felt in my heart that I was grateful—even though I was going through all that anger."

"Hmm. Good question," said Steve pensively. Maybe it's because anger produces a complaining spirit. It's really hard to be thankful and to complain at the same time."

That made sense. Another light turned on for me. "You're right, Flamen'. There must be a verse in Psalms or Proverbs that addresses that."

"Yeah, we'll have to look that one up when we get a chance."

"You know, I also think that Father has been doing a deep cleansing in my heart. And I think he's been drawing me out of this bitterness for some time now."

"How so?"

"Well, I remember a few months before that Monday night when he broke through my wall of bitterness that I heard a lyric in a song on the radio. I forget the name of the song, but the line was, 'And I will open up my heart And let the Healer set me free.'²"

"Mmm!" he uttered. "That's powerful!"

"Yeah, isn't it? It made me think that, for me to get over the bitterness, I had to *let* Father get rid of it for me. I had to *choose* to yield to him."

"That makes sense. He does the work of sanctification in making us more like Christ. What did you do then?"

"Well, at the time I still didn't know what to do, but it just seemed like a work that God would have to do instead of me. I just figured that I had to *yield* to him in order for him to do it."

"So, it wasn't so much a ritual or act as it was a surrendering."

"Yeah, that's a good word for it."

"Man, this is great!" Steve beamed brightly. He really enjoyed exploring Father's ways like this. It was encouraging to both of us to see how Father was working in our hearts, even when we had no notion of him doing so in the moment.

"Yeah. I also think that Father was using praise music to soften me a little so that it would be easier to break through my bitterness. That music got me perusing the Psalms a few times. I especially enjoy music with the kind of lyrics that I can pray to Father. It makes it easier for me to focus on him and to exalt him in my spirit.

"One of the things that really encouraged me about all this—which I only realized after he broke through my bitterness that night—is that Father had not forgotten about me or been discouraged with me. He was still doing a work in my heart and life to complete what he had begun in me seventeen years ago."

Steve grinned excitedly. "His love is really awesome, isn't it? The Psalms and some great praise music—especially songs that quote the Psalms. Those are really heartwarming."

"Yeah, they're very therapeutic. And all this—it's like a dream come true. I didn't grow up with my earthly father, so for me to learn in a new way that God is my all-loving, heavenly Father and to be persuaded that he loves me through the circumstances and trials of my life, it's really rejuvenating. He really lifts my spirit and draws me closer to him."

Then I remembered something that I wanted to discuss with him.

"Flamen', you remember that I told you how I searched the Bible, looking up verses about when and how we should run to Christ?"

"I sure do."

"Well, during that same search I also saw verses about his grace. And I realized that I didn't know much about God's grace, except for Ephesians 2:8 and 9 and a few other well-known verses. But most of those relate to salvation. And then I thought that it was really bizarre that in all my years of hearing sermons, studying the Bible, and even attending Bible college with college level courses on the Bible and missions, that through all that there was very little teaching on the grace of God. At least there was very little *depth* of teaching, even though the word was mentioned a lot."

"Hey, yeah." It seemed to dawn on Steve just then. "We preach grace to the lost, and then, once they come to Christ, we preach law to them to control them."

"I realized that I only knew that grace was 'unmerited favor' and 'God's Riches At Christ's Expense.' But other than reciting a few verses or trite Sunday school phrases, I had no understanding of what grace really is."

"So whadya do?"

"I happened to be in the church library one day, and I noticed a couple of books about grace. There was one called *Transforming Grace* by Jerry Bridges. I checked it out and read it."

"Oh, yeah," he said reflecting on a memory. "I read that some years ago. That *is* a great book about grace!"

"Yeah, it is. It showed me from the Scriptures that grace is more than God's gift of unmerited favor at salvation. It's also the power or ability Father bestows on us to live the Christian life each day."

"And it's a gift that's totally undeserved," added Steve. "He gives it to all who are in Christ."

"That's true. I looked up some other books about the grace of God and read a few of those as well. I wanted to learn all that I could so as to be well-grounded in my understanding of this important truth."

"What other books have you read?"

"I read three books by Steve McVey entitled *Grace Walk*, *Grace Rules*, and a new one called *Grace Land*. Their teachings on grace are so liberating!"

"Yeah, I know what you mean about grace being so freeing. But I don't think I've read those books." His right eyebrow arched in thought.

"You can borrow my copies."

"Hey," he said, suddenly grinning, "thanks, Brother!"

"You're welcome. Just be sure to give them back."

He gave me his wincing, furrowed-brow look then.

"Watch the road, Flamen'!" I said, gesturing ahead of us.

Steve gripped the steering wheel firmly at 10:00 and 2:00 with determination.

"Another little project I started," I continued, "and haven't finished yet is rereading the New Testament and jotting down all the observations I notice about grace—not just passages which mention words like 'grace' or 'favor,' but even verses which depict it or demonstrate it in different ways."

"Now *that's* a great idea."

"It has really helped me to see the whole New Testament and many passages in a different light. It's been an amazing learning experience, so much so that I encourage everyone I can to do that."

"All right, then. I'll find the time to do that."

"Do it, Flamen'. It has shined the light on some of the legalistic residue in my own life. And if it's one thing I don't want in my relationship with Father it's to have any legalism in my walk with or understanding of him."

"I don't blame you there. As soon as I realized that Father is all about his grace enabling us to walk in him and sustaining us when we fail, the legalism I had walked in for so many years just lost its appeal and its seeming power."

"I've experienced that too, which really surprised me. I thought that I had been inoculated against legalism through all the things that you shared with me about *your* experiences."

"You're welcome, Brother," he offered with a factitious, glaring glance.

"Even though there was a mixed culture of legalism and grace in Bible college, I really thought before I went there that I could spot it a mile away and was armed to deal with it."

"It still shows up today in some corners of Christianity—or 'churchianity' as some call it. When you're a new believer in Christ and excited about his life and eager to serve him, following a system of rules to try to please Father just seems right. Those in authority tell you that in order to please Father you have to conform to a list of rules—things like what you can and can't wear, which activities you can and can't participate in, which places you can and can't go to, and so on. After a few years of that, you get burned out on all the rule-keeping, realizing that you just can't do it. That's when you fall exhausted into Father's arms and long for his rest spoken about in Hebrews 4."

There it was again!

"Yeah, it's just like these friends of Tom's told me. The children of Israel thought that they could keep the Law, and they had to learn the hard way that they couldn't. As believers in the body of Christ, we run pretty much the same cycle."

"Yes," Steve replied, shifting gears and changing into another voice characterization, *"'it's a vicious cycle!'"*

I smiled at his humor; then I pondered for a moment. "But the truth is, we're *already* pleasing to Father because of what Jesus did on our behalf. His righteousness was put on our account so that we *don't* have to perform to please Father or to earn some type of blessing. And his nature is love, so he already loves us more than we can imagine."

"Amen to that, Brother. He's definitely not holding out on us, dangling some carrot called 'Acceptance and Approval' just beyond our reach."

I turned to face Steve as he continued looking ahead to drive. "We teach these truths, more or less, in a lot of the local congregations and Christian schools, but then we live like they aren't true. I wonder why our tendency is to practice and to promote legalism despite what we profess. Why can't we—the body of Christ—just teach the truths about Father's grace, enter into his rest, and yield to and depend on Christ to live his life through us instead of trying to *perform* for him all the time? I mean, why is legalism so attractive? Why does it seem to be our default way of relating to Father? Flamen', I've missed out on so much trying to live for him instead of letting him live through me. And it hasn't been all it's cracked up to be."

Steve blinked and thought about it for a second, paying attention to the road and the traffic all the while.

"It's just man's nature. He likes to control his circumstances, environment, relationships, and future. Man feels more comfortable when he can control things. If he can control God by his actions, then he thinks *he's* in control, not some mysterious Deity he can't perceive with his senses. As strange as it is, God seems safer to some people when they think that they can control him.

"Besides that, for some churches or denominations, it's *all* about control. They want to control their membership, so they teach that pleasing God means following a list of rules. It can get

97

pretty messy and embarrassing dealing with all those outward sins—especially any kind of sexual misbehavior."

"The flesh does tend to resist any kind of rules or attempts to control it," I commented. "That outward pressure to conform to man-made rules only leads to fleshly indulgence, just like Colossians 2:16-23 warns."

"That is does. But the harm done by such attempts to control people goes beyond merely the outward. If the leadership can convince the congregation that grace has its limits—that we can forfeit our salvation by our sinful behavior—then there's that internal motivation of fear to keep people in line. That's why some denominations teach that we can lose our salvation if we commit certain sins. People tend to believe it because, y'know, the church leaders teach and preach it, and they can string together a few Bible verses which seem to back it up, so 'it must be true.' Ultimately, it confuses people and makes them misunderstand grace and their relationship with Christ."

"That is tragic," I replied. "Then some of them no longer trust in Christ to keep them saved by what he did, but they begin trusting in their good behavior to keep them saved."

"Which, oddly enough, still makes it seem like we're in control, affecting the outcome from our actions, even though it's in a negative way.

"There's also another catch. A lot of local congregations teach and promote that pleasing God also means serving in various capacities in the church." Steve bobbled his head slowly just thinking about it. "Brother, in one church I used to attend, I was involved in so many ministries and outreaches and served on so many committees—it was pathetic! I was 'working for God' practically every day or night of the week. And Sunday was *not* a day of rest for me. Aw, no! With all the pre-service prayer sessions, choir rehearsals, Sunday school classes, worship services, children's church ministry, bus ministry, afternoon visitations at prisons and nursing homes, committee meetings, evening classes and services—it wiped me out! After all," he began in his baritone, announcer-voice characterization, "we were created for good works, Brother. That means we have to serve 'til we drop in the local church. And if we're not doing all these works, then we must not be saved."

"Yeah, that's a tiresome routine," I commented with a look of frustration. "Elena and I know friends who are wearing themselves thin in their local congregations with all their ministry obligations. They work full-time jobs forty hours or more a week and then spend practically all their spare time serving in ministries for different groups in their church. They do everything, like serving in the nursery, singing in the choir, cooking and cleaning in the kitchen for Wednesday night meals, serving the widows and elderly, going on visitation, and helping out in the youth department. They're so busy 'serving Jesus' that we rarely ever see them. In fact, it seems that they rarely get to relax and to have any quality family time at all. Their busyness is even worse than what Elena and I did before we moved to Honduras. But you know, church used to be a lot simpler, Flamen'. What do you think happened?"

"That's a great question." At this point his eyebrow arched again. "In the first century, the church started out small. It looks like the bigger things grew, the more work and 'ministry' were required. Pastors had to marshal the troops and motivate them to do more for Jesus, because the *pastors* can't do it all."

I made a guess as to where he was leading with this. "So they pleaded Acts 6 and said that they needed to spend their time in prayer and in the ministry of the word. That way others would have to step in and do the majority of the work of the ministry."

"Some of them justify it that way, but I'm not so sure that was right even for the early church in Acts 6—or for the church today."

"What do you mean?"

"I mean that just because they found an example of that in the Bible where the apostles used that as an excuse, it doesn't make it right."

"*'An excuse?'* But these are the apostles we're talking about."

"Right, and at that time the disciples were increasing in number, which was a great thing. The problem in Acts 6 was that the Jewish widows from the Greek culture were not receiving the distribution of food like the more traditional Jewish widows were. Did you notice how they handled the problem?"

If it was a quiz Steve was giving me, then I felt up to the challenge. "They decided to have the disciples appoint seven godly men to distribute the food."

"Exactly! They set a system or program in place to let *other people* be responsible for meeting the need."

Suddenly, another light turned on for me. "And how many times have you heard Acts 6 presented as evidence for having deacons in church? Yet the word 'deacon' doesn't appear at all in that passage."

"Uh-huh," he said nodding, as his face brightened. "You're catching on now, Brother. The Twelve wanted *others* to run a program, even though that's not how Jesus discipled them to handle ministry problems. Remember what he always did?"

I blinked a couple of times, trying to remember. "Well, let's see. I guess he just knew how to make the best decisions, being God."

"Certainly, because being God he knew everything. But he also taught by example. Think about what he did, for example, just *before* he chose the twelve disciples near the beginning of his public ministry."

That detail I did remember reading about. "Oh, I see. He spent all night in prayer just before that."

"That's it, Brother! Fellowship with his Father meant everything. And he was demonstrating to those watching that communion with Father is the means for getting his mind and knowing his will. Remember how he prayed for the disciples in the upper room in John 17? He also prayed fervently that same night on the Mount of Olives before he was arrested, tried, and crucified. He was teaching us all the importance of communing with Father, especially before making important decisions or taking big steps. So now think of all the 'sanctified decisions' pastors and ministry leaders have made simply by assessing a particular situation and coming up with a solution—sometimes on the spot—like in a 'church business meeting' or a counseling session."

"Hmm. You're right, Steve. Those fast calls may make them *look* wise or godly, but they don't always turn out to be the greatest decisions."

"Maybe they want to pull a Solomon and appear to be full of godly wisdom. Maybe they want to show off their problem-solving skills. We'll never know for sure. However, some of those quick decisions can result in the worst consequences. There's really no substitute for seeking Father's face before making decisions that affect our lives and the lives of others. The apostles made an unguided decision early in the opening chapters of Acts when they decided on their own that they needed to choose a replacement for Judas Iscariot."

"That's right! They did something like voting with a lottery."

"And you know how *godly* voting is," he said in a sarcastic-sounding character voice. "Imagine the apostles voting on the will of God—and then leaving the final result to a casting of lots!"

"And the lucky winner is . . . Matthias! No doubt he must've been a great guy since he followed Jesus and was respected by the apostles, but he's someone you never again read anything about."

"Yep. In fact, Luke seems to show that while the apostles chose Matthias, God chose Paul on the road to Damascus in Acts 9. And if you follow Luke's narrative closely right after those seven were appointed in Acts 6, you'll notice that two of them—Stephen and Philip—sort of took center stage for a while instead of the Twelve."

"Hey, yeah! The others really seemed to miss the boat on that one."

"Maybe if they had sought the Lord in prayer about the neglect of those widows, Father would have shown them a much better way of handling it instead of organizing some programmed solution."

"You're right, Flamen'. And maybe then they would have realized that the body's neglect of those widows was a symptom of a bigger relational problem."

"That's what I'm thinking too. But y'know, most people today would say, 'Why pray about it? The answer is simple: just get some people to serve them the food. You don't have to pray about every little detail in life.'"

"Maybe not," I acknowledged, "but it seems like it sure helps for a lot of stuff."

"We don't have to do tons of praying about God's will when it's clearly presented in the Scriptures," he said as he merged into another lane. "We never have to ask, 'Lord, should I lie or tell the truth? Should I steal or work for a living?' Those kinds of questions are clearly addressed in the Bible."

"That's true. Most people pray about things like which job to take, whom to pursue as a potential spouse, which city to live in, and other such personal decisions."

"But challenging situations," continued Steve, "like widows missing out on food provisions aren't so cut and dried as moral issues. It sounds like there was some prejudice or favoritism going on among those believers. It was a symptom of some heart issues among the body which at that time had suddenly become a mix of different cultures of Jewish believers, even before Gentiles were included. Those two groups had been divided for some time due to their preferences of language and adoptive culture. It's the kind of people problem through which Father can use prayer to bring heart issues to light and also to direct us in ways we never would've imagined. Prayer is not always just about seeking an answer or guidance. Sometimes he uses it to give us a better understanding of people and situations. You just never know how he's working behind the scenes in people's hearts while we only see things with our limited perspective."

"Wow, Flamen'! I hadn't thought of prayer as being useful in those ways."

"There's also the issue about the apostles practicing as authorities telling the other believers what to do. They were just 'too important' to wait tables."

"That didn't exactly demonstrate the spirit of servanthood that Jesus taught them, did it?"

"The first shall be leaders, and the last shall wait tables." That was a sarcastic misquote not found in the Scriptures. It's one brand of Steve's humor.

"What was it that Jesus told them, Flamen'? Something like, 'the rulers of the Gentiles lord it over them, and those in high positions use their authority over them. It must not be this way among you! Instead whoever wants to be great among you must be your servant, and whoever wants to be first among you must be your slave.' Do you remember the reference for that?"

"Hmm. Yeah, that's from Matthew 20." He released a sigh. "The body of Christ is no place for lording authority over people, that's for sure. It's too bad most people don't like the idea of being a slave. It's a hard thing to do because it involves dying to self, surrendering one's will to Jesus. The feel-good 'gospel' has people thinking they're going to be 'showered with prosperity' and that they'll 'inherit the earth.' Books about dying to self or being a slave of Christ just don't sell too well in the Christian book stores."

"You're right, Flamen'. Surrendering my will is not always the most fun," I admitted, "but Jesus leads us by his example and teaches us along the way."

"Speaking of slaves, the word for 'slave' used in that passage—the Greek word *doulos*—is really interesting in its simplicity. In first century Greco-Roman society, it simply spoke of a slave who was bound for life. It's the same word Paul used when he referred to himself as 'a slave of Christ Jesus' in some of his epistles. We're truly not our own; we're 'bought at a price,' like he said in 1 Corinthians 6."

"You know, Steve, before this change in me, I was somewhat hesitant to think of being any kind of slave for Father. But I see now that it's so much easier to accept the fact and relax in him when we get the biblical perspective and understand how much he really loves us. Knowing that he loves me makes it easier for me to surrender my will to him."

"He really is the love of our lives. He chose us, and we chose him. It's God's sovereignty and man's free will meeting together."

This was another connection to my discussion with the fellowship group: the topic of man's free will. This time it related to the usage of a particular Greek word. On one hand, it showed

103

me that Father allowed us to choose him—or not to choose him—of our own free will. On the other hand, he purchased us at the cross of Calvary, which ironically resulted in liberation from the enslavement of sin to allow us to walk in the freedom of Christ Jesus.

"Okay, Flamen'. Speaking of 'slaves', here's something I wanted to discuss with you: In one of Jesus' parables, he presented some amazing insights into the heart of his Father."

"Wait a minute, Brother," he said, shifting into fourth to reach the top of an incline on the highway. "Are you *shifting* gears on me?" His expression mocked seriousness with a raised eyebrow.

That pun was too obvious. I had to top him.

"You might say I'm *turning a corner*."

"All right, Brother," he replied with a grin and a chuckle. "What you got to share?"

I licked my lips and cleared my throat. "This particular parable paints a picture of Father's heart toward us as overflowing with grace and love."

"And I can probably guess which one you're talking about."

"Which one?"

"The father and his two sons from Luke 15?"

"That's it. I've been reflecting on it lately since I started looking for grace throughout the New Testament."

"Yeah, I don't think that one has the word grace in it. But it definitely demonstrates the grace of God."

"It really does. As you know, most people refer to it as the parable of the prodigal son."

"'*Prodigal*'—another word not stated in the text."

"Right again. Anyway, this has become my favorite story that Jesus told. It really communicates the heart of his Father, even though the father in the narrative says very little."

"His actions communicate more than his speech—another trait of our heavenly Father."

"You probably have more insights on the passage than I do. I just wanted to share this with you as an encouragement, a reminder, and as a help for me think it through as well. You make

104

a good sounding board."

"Thanks, Brother. But don't sell yourself short. Maybe Father wants to show me something in our conversation about it that I haven't realized before. I'm open to be taught however he wants to teach me and through whomever and by whatever means."

That comment stayed with me. As the Master Teacher, God can truly use anyone and any circumstances to teach us. Why wouldn't I be open to learn from him by whatever means or through whomever he chooses to teach me? This was a truth that would help me for years to come.

"Okay. First of all, you'll remember that Jesus told the parable to encourage the people who were following him and fellowshipping with him and also as sort of a rebuke to the Pharisees and experts in the Law for their judgmental attitudes against those followers."

"There were many 'undesirables' from the perspective of the religious crowd following Christ—people like tax collectors, adulterers, and all kinds of 'sinners.' Got it."

"Yes," I agreed. "The self-righteous Pharisees and Law experts were complaining that Jesus was welcoming and eating with the so-called 'sinners.' He told a three-fold parable of one lost sheep out of one hundred, one lost coin out of ten, and one lost son out of two."

"And each segment ended with tremendous joy over the lost object of affection being found."

"The self-righteous crowd," I observed, "should have recognized that these were repentant hearts drawing near to Jesus, and they should have rejoiced with him just as the angels in heaven rejoice over every person who trusts him for salvation."

"In an ideal world, that's what they would have done, but they were rejecting Christ themselves. They neither welcomed him as the Messiah nor realized that they were sinners and needed salvation. It's just like some people today who are missing out on his love and grace."

I reflected for a moment, remembering my own bout with bitterness. That's the way I now thought of myself in my years of

105

bitterness before Father broke through my self-erected wall of indignation. I was still a believer in Jesus during those years, and I knew that heaven was my home. However, I was so bitter and disillusioned about life. I really had little desire for anything to do with my Savior, since I only seemed to fail him constantly with my lifelong dreams, my relationships, and everything else that mattered in my life. It's so strange and sad to me now, looking back on those years and my heart attitude then. The time I had wasted and the way I had made my family suffer needlessly were inexcusable. My son was so young that he wouldn't remember any of my behavior and attitude; that was a gift to him from Father. Elena, however, had to bear every moment of my fury and doubt-based actions. She would have a hard time forgetting those years and all the adverse moments that they contained. Nevertheless, in time Father would bless her in ways I couldn't have imagined. He would restore those years that the locusts had eaten, and she would grow in grace from the aftermath of the experience. After all, Elena is a child of his also, and he loves her with all his heart.

"You okay, Bro?" Steve's question brought me back to the present.

"Uh—yeah. I'm just thinking about how faithless I was to Father for those years." I felt a tremor in my heart.

"Hey, John, he freed you from all that, Brother," Steve said, smiling. "And Father didn't change during your time of bitterness. He's always faithful to us even when we're faithless to him. Remember 2 Timothy 2:13? 'If we are unfaithful, he remains faithful, since he cannot deny himself.' The truth is, you've always been lavished in his love; it's just that you didn't always recognize it and walk in it."

"That's what I've come to realize, Steve. Father didn't love me any less during those years, and he doesn't love me any more now that he's taken away the bitterness. His love has been the one constant throughout my whole life. Perfect love from a perfect, all-loving Being has been his gift to me every moment of my existence. I simply wasn't aware of it throughout my years of bitterness.

106

"It's just like the father in this parable. His younger son asks for his inheritance, so the father divides his possessions between his two boys and gives this son his portion. Yet he knew his son well enough to know that it was not for godly purposes that he wanted the money. He granted his request out of love—infinite, perfect love. Then the son left his father and entered a society without him."

"Man, the dad must have been heartbroken! He had no assurance that he'd ever see his boy again. And he probably figured that he would get into trouble with all that money."

"But, Steve, he did it out of love for his son. He allowed him the freedom to choose as he wished. And he honored his son's wishes. It's Father's gift of free will which he granted us in the garden in Eden."

Steve sat up straighter. "Hey, Bro, you're right! I haven't made that connection before." Deep reflection showed on his face. "In the garden, the choice was to eat from the tree of life or from the tree of the knowledge of good and evil. In this parable the choice was to stay in fellowship with the father or to forsake him for a world without his fellowship. Good night! That is deep!"

"It's powerful. But then life is often about the choices we make, and some are a lot bigger or have bigger consequences than we realize at the time. That's one of the life lessons I had to learn the hard way.

"But let's get back to the narrative. We see that the father loved both his sons throughout the whole parable: *before* the son asked for his inheritance, *while* he asked for it, *when* he left home with it, *the whole time* he was gone and had no contact with his dad, and *when* he returned home in shame. Even when the older son complained about his brother's return and the fact that he'd never been given even a small party with his friends, the father still loved the older son as well. The whole story is *permeated* with the father's undeserved love. That's love—God's completely undeserved love. And that's the grace of God."

"Man, it's awesome!" exclaimed Steve. "I guess most of us could say that we've all had our moments when we wanted to dabble in the world to see what it was like without Father. Then we saw how destitute and wounded it made us, and we longed to be with him again."

"In a sense, both sons knew their father and had a measure of fellowship with him at the beginning of the parable. But in a sense, neither son had a closeness of relationship with him as much as their dad wanted."

"You're right. At least the younger son eventually gained that closeness and deep fellowship with him after he returned—so *he* represented the tax collectors and 'sinners' in the audience. The older son didn't have that special relationship with his father at *any* time in the story, so *he* represents the Pharisees and Law experts listening to Jesus at that moment."

"Hmm. We could say," I added slowly, thinking through what Steve had just said, "that the narrative was a wake-up call to the self-righteous crowd. It's like Jesus was saying to those judgmental folks, 'You're being jealous just like the older son! Recognize that you're not being treated unfairly. In fact, you're being loved just as much. Rejoice with me that your lost brothers and sisters are turning to me and turn your hearts toward me as well.'"

Steve's expression changed from contemplative to serious. "The younger son wasted his inheritance and truly was left with nothing materially. Everything he would receive from then on would be a gift of grace—not just the ring, robe, sandals, and celebration. And the older son still had his inheritance intact, since his father had said, 'everything that belongs to me is yours.' He should have been encouraged to see how his father loved and forgave, but he was too concerned with his desire for justice and punishment. He realized that he would have to support his brother with part of his own inheritance."

"Yeah, most of us haven't looked at it that way. I guess he didn't realize the depths of despair that his brother had experienced."

"Hmm. We tend to forget that, due to its very nature and the consequences that follow it, sin provides its own punishment. Sin and its consequences are so damaging that we don't need any extra from Father. There's a portrait of God's mercy there as well."

"Which brings us back to the father's heart in the story," I continued. "He was so compassionate, and he longed for his son to be with him again and to have that intimate fellowship with him. He must have known when his son asked for the inheritance that he was in for a series of hardships. He probably guessed the end result from the beginning and hoped and prayed that his son would return one day. He likely knew that his son's sinful adventure would led him to brokenness."

"Yeah, that's why the father saw him from a long way off," said Steve. "He was hoping to see him come back home."

"The younger son only returned when he had reached the absolute rock bottom."

"I know, Bro. Imagine what Jesus' audience felt when they heard that the rebellious son was so destitute that he could only get a job feeding pigs—about the most unclean animals to the Jews. Then he became so hungry that the pig slop looked appetizing to him. Yuck!"

"But those circumstances *did* allow for him to come to his senses and to realize how good his father's servants had it back home. That's why he prepared a speech of reconciliation to present to his father and started on the journey home."

Steve picked up the story. "I can just picture it: his dad is looking down the road each day and throughout the day, hoping and waiting to see his son appear. There's no telling how long he had to wait: perhaps months, a year, or even many years."

"And his love never wavered or faltered one bit," I noted. "He continued to love both his sons, both the rebellious one who forsook him and the ungrateful, bitter one who worked with him."

"Good night! That's right!" Steve exclaimed. "The older son basically said that he had slaved away for his dad for many years without having even a small party with his friends. So just like the Pharisees, he wasn't grateful either for all his father had done for him. He was just as disappointed with his father as the Jewish religious leaders must have been with God in that day."

"They were bitter instead of grateful, just like you said, Flamen'."

"Man, that helps us to put that story into sharper perspective."

"Father loves the pious, religious crowd just as much as the rebellious and the repentant. He loves us all and wants that close fellowship with all of us."

"Hmm. I know that we benefit from the fellowship with him because we are the recipients of his grace and love and all spiritual blessings that Father showers upon us. The only thing he seems to get out of the relationship is the sheer joy of it. If you think about it, we can give him our praise and gratitude, but even if it were perfect and consistent, it still wouldn't be enough for the Almighty. How could it possibly be enough to an infinite, perfect Being?"

This brought to mind something Bob had said.

"You know, I think it's kind of like it is for any parent who truly loves his or her child. To have that love reciprocated freely without any coercion or ulterior motives is a true delight."

Images of my son came to mind, many in which he beamed his precious smile to me, hugged me, and told me, "I love you, Daddy!" Again, I was lost in the moment of sentimental remembrance. "It's the kind of thing I feel as a dad to little Nathaniel," I heard myself say aloud.

Then I remembered that parenthood was often a sensitive topic for Steve. Even after seven years of marriage, he and Aby had not yet been able to have children.

As long as I've known Steve, he's always had a great heart for children. In the local congregations in which he had been involved, he had organized and participated in various kinds of children's ministries and activities just for them. He especially had a soft spot for the nine- to twelve-year-old age group. They particularly seemed to share some of his same childlike qualities of wonder, playfulness, and a zest for life. As a missionary in Honduras, he had helped found a grammar school and then a high school as part of the mission with which he worked. Through a mission sponsorship program already in place, he had even facilitated in his short time there the sponsoring of hundreds of children to get an education. His love for children had truly blossomed on the mission field. One of his anticipated joys of marriage was to

110

have his own children and to share in the delight of raising them with Aby, who also had a great love for children and desired her own. It was her main motivation for becoming a school teacher. However, up to that time there had been no pregnancies, and they were sometimes saddened by the emptiness they felt. I could only empathize with them to a limited extent since Elena and I had not been blessed with Nathaniel until six years into our marriage.

I glanced beside me at Steve. He was quiet, seemingly all-attentive to the traffic as he merged into another lane.

"Sorry, Brother," I said softly.

My apology seemed lifeless. With all the joy I experienced with my son Nathaniel, I so much wanted Steve and Aby to share in the delight of having children of their own. However, I knew that there were difficult moments like this for them almost every day. That's why Elena and I prayed for them and their desire to raise their own family.

"Nah, it's all right," he replied, shrugging it off. "We'll just keep waiting to see what Father has in store for us. Which reminds me that we should reach our destination in a couple of miles."

"You know, I think the greatest part of the story for me personally," I said, referring back to the parable, "is when the father sees his son and runs to greet him. You know how the men of that day wore those long clothes, like robes and tunics. They weren't made for running."

"I read somewhere," commented Steve, "that even in work clothes, for a man to run in that day and in that culture, he would have to pull up and hold the folds of his clothes, exposing his legs, so that he would have the freedom of movement to run."

"So, it was potentially embarrassing," I deduced.

"Surely it was. But love doesn't worry about feeling embar-rassed. That father's only concern was to lessen his son's shame and pain, and the only way he knew to do that was to reach him as fast as possible."

"That reminds me of that song by Benny Hester, 'When God Ran.'"

"Yeah, that's a great song. It makes me want to praise Jesus and

111

walk with him closer whenever I hear it."

"Hmm, me too. And you know, it's just like Father to go beyond whatever is necessary to love us. Whether it's running in public in an embarrassing way, becoming an infant and being born in an animal feeding trough to unlikely parents, or suffering and dying a cruel fate in a Roman form of execution, he always does what's needed."

"Amen, Bro! There's nothing he wouldn't do to sacrifice for us so that he could share that intimate fellowship with us for all eternity."

The thought was staggering. "Wow, Flamen'! What amazing love Jesus has for us!"

"And you know," he added, "the son didn't get to finish his prepared speech before his father interrupted him by calling for the servants to bring on the gifts."

"His father had so much love that he wanted his son to be showered with love and grace, instead of the shame he was feeling."

"That is an important truth: He takes away our shame and replaces it with his love and grace. Huh," he said, and I could tell that the wheels were turning in his understanding. "Y'know, that's exactly what he did with Zacchaeus too. And the Samaritan woman at the well . . . and Bartimaeus . . . and the woman caught in adultery . . . and the man in John 9 who was born blind." Steve cocked his head in my direction. "Shall I keep going?"

"I don't know if we have that kind of time," I said, chuckling. "When you think about it in *that* light, Jesus seemed to spend a lot of time with individuals *throughout his whole ministry* removing their shame. I remember seeing each encounter as a showering of grace upon grace, but I've never really noticed before that he graciously took away each individual's shame. But, Flamen', that's exactly what he did—among other things to bless them and to forgive them."

"Well, Brother, he did come to bear our sins on the cross, breaking the power of sin in our lives, restoring our relationship with Father, and bringing us eternal, spiritual life. Removing our shame, or the sense of it, helps to restore that relationship. May-

112

be in Jesus' interactions with people as he loved them, removing their shame was the most sensible thing for perfect love to do."

It was a humbling and glorious truth: Jesus *did* come to remove our shame, as well as to deal with our sin and to provide salvation for us. As he suffered and died publicly before Father and the whole world, Christ did everything necessary for us. He knew that, in our condition of spiritual death and depravity, we could never have done anything to help ourselves. Love is always about removing the sense of shame, not delighting in it or heaping on more. My heart soared anew with joy and gratitude toward my all-worthy Father and Savior.

"Thank you, Jesus!" I said aloud.

"Amen, Brother! Thank you, Lord Jesus!" Steve reveled in these truths along with me. "'Amazing love! How can it be That Thou, my God, shouldst die for me?'" he sang loudly in that baritone voice of his. "Man, what boundless love and grace! He removed all our shame and continues blessing us beyond what we can contain!"

The smiles and delight that shone on our countenances that day endured.

We soon reached the house of the fellow believing family who had contacted Steve about donating a washer and a dryer to his mom. Steve introduced us, and we spent a few moments sharing in the joy and growth Father was working in each of our lives at that time. This adventure wasn't merely an errand to run. It was also an encouraging time to fellowship and to share Father's grace from the Bible, both in the car as we headed both directions and at the home of these believers. These people I had not met before weren't strangers; because we shared the same Father, they were family.

It was a day full of Father's blessings, and I was rejoicing in the walk with Jesus that the Holy Spirit was teaching me. This is what I had longed for and missed so much; this is what my heart had needed for so long. *Thank you, Jesus!*

While my walk with Jesus was uplifting, some of these new

teachings I would learn would arrive as rude awakenings. Apparently, there was a strain of paganism in my heart which I didn't know existed. That would definitely need to be addressed by the teachings and ministry of the Holy Spirit.

[1] "I Just Can't Make It By Myself," Gloria Gaither, J.D. Miller, Suzanne Jennings, William J. Gaither. Copyright © 1986 Hanna Street Music (BMI) Songs Of Promise (BMI) Townsend And Warbucks Music (ASCAP) (adm. at CapitolCMGPublishing.com) All rights reserved. Used by permission.
[2] "I Could Sing Of Your Love Forever (Over the Mountains . . .)," Martin Smith. Copyright © 1994 Curious? Music UK (PRS) (adm. in the US and Canada at CapitolCMGPublishing.com). All rights reserved. Used by permission.
[3] "And Can It Be That I Should Gain," Charles Wesley, 1738, Public Domain.

CHAPTER 7

TO GRATITUDE AND LOVE FROM SHAME AND FEAR

My life was undeniably much better than it was before. Father's work of grace in my heart was growing and teaching me to deny some particularly troubling sins. The bitterness was not to be found. In its place were peace, gratitude, joy, and love. I was neither perfect in my walk with Jesus nor sinless for an entire day at a stretch; but these were not goals for which I endeavored. As a result of my conversations with Tom and others, I was learning not to set myself up for any major disappointments in my spiritual walk.

My immediate aim was simple: I simply wanted to know Christ better and to enjoy my relationship with him more than ever. With the recent softening of my heart by the Holy Spirit, there was a calmness and joy in my soul. I still encountered the problems of daily life in a fallen world and sinful, self-based society. However, I now had a closeness with Jesus which availed me of all the spiritual resources in him necessary to live the life of faith. These were the spiritual blessings that I had received in Christ as soon as he entered my heart and life when I was seventeen, I realized. *Why had it taken so long for me to appropriate them into my life?* I wondered. Bob's warning then came to mind about the "introspective trap." Maybe it was one of those questions that would neither have, using Tom's words, "a satisfying answer" nor accomplish anything beneficial in my life. All the "why" and "what if" questions did seem to distract me from my relationship with Father in the present. Therefore, I decided not to dwell on them.

One of the unexpected observations I couldn't help but notice was that some of the most encouraging and refreshing experiences of my new walk were born out of the simplest moments of fellowship with other believers who were not complicated in their approach to loving Jesus. A few friends were some I had known for years, like Tom, Sara, and Steve. Others were new friends such as Bob, Walter, Greg, and their respective wives. The fellowship we shared was seldom shallow, being filled with mere talk about sports, politics, entertainment, or other such topics. In my relationships with these fellow believers as we met and crossed paths from time to time, an openness to share and to discuss things that Christ was working in each other's lives became apparent. It was the joyful exchange of encouragement and edification as each one of us expressed what Father was doing in our lives, both blessings and our personal failures. Such sharing was often intertwined with a few scripture verses or biblical concepts to demonstrate what we were learning individually. This kind of fellowship was nurtured in an atmosphere of acceptance, love, and grace. Without anyone airing out their "dirty laundry," so to speak, it appeared that each of us understood the importance of listening attentively to see what Father would have us to contribute to our conversations. I didn't perceive any judgmental or negative moods in these simple gatherings. Spiritually speaking, they were like a balm to my emotional wounds and cold water to my previously parched spirit.

As I began to recognize the value of our fellowships together, I looked forward to such social gatherings with great anticipation and expectancy. I kept in mind what Steve had said about being open to learn from Father through any vessel and any means by which he would choose to teach me. My heart had been hardened and closed for too long. Now that it had been soothed by Father's grace and opened by his love, I had no intention of missing anything else he would want to show me. At least this was the desire of my heart, though in reality I knew that being imperfect I would on occasion completely miss some opportunities and perhaps even spoil parts of the process of what Father wanted to communicate to me. Nevertheless, I chose not to let such moments discourage me from enjoying his process of perfecting his work in me. Therefore, I practiced running to Christ through prayer throughout each day in order to avoid the introspective trap.

With Jesus as my constant companion, talking to him about anything and everything on a moment-to-moment basis was easy. Paul's exhortation to "pray without ceasing" became more meaningful to me in this way. No longer was I merely beseeching Father's help just a few times during the day and only in time of need. I was mostly directing my thoughts toward him much like a child who enjoys the company of his or her parent and simply expresses thoughts freely, knowing that they will be heard and appreciated without any rejection, scolding, or impatience. Whereas before my thoughts in general were introspective and directed towards myself, now they were more open like conversational prayers presented to Father. Although I refer to these as "conversations" I don't mean to imply that I heard an audible voice from Father. I simply mean to indicate that I knew that he was listening, and in time, as events and circumstances were unfolded, the threads of different prayers were joined, resolved, or otherwise referenced in my daily walk with Christ. For me, prayer was seldom spending hours in a secret place away from everyone and everything. I would simply talk with Father anywhere and at any time about different elements in my day, be they people I crossed paths with, challenges and assignments at work, prayer concerns brought to my attention, or hopes and dreams for my family, loved ones, and our future. All these "conversational prayers" were interspersed with thanksgiving, silent praises, songs, and even confessions.

By now I was learning to run to Christ to confess my sins without the dread and despair which used to accompany such moments. And my days were pleasant, despite some of the challenges, frustrations, and failures which before would have distracted me from Jesus. As I mentioned before, it was not a perfect or sinless walk with Father, but it was a growing one in which I became better acquainted with him and enjoyed and appreciated his presence. When I sinned, confession was more immediate and joyful, for I knew that I was approaching the one who alone could clean me and restore my fellowship with him, apart from any scowls or scolding. How I had missed out on this kind of Christian walk for so long! *Thank you, Jesus!*

Since my outlook had changed for the better, I desired to feed my heart and mind with the kinds of thoughts which would edify me in my new walk with Christ. This would help to combat some of the negativity my mind had festered on for those two years, as I could start replacing those negative thoughts with positive ones and hopefully curtail some of the introspective traps. I began memorizing scripture verses which would encourage and remind me to run to Christ. They were the ones I had referenced to the brothers on Stone Mountain. There were other scriptures I encountered in rereading the New Testament which demonstrated "grace moments" as I had mentioned to Steve. While I re-examined and memorized these different scriptures about Father's grace and running to Christ, they came alive anew for me. I now saw them as describing and displaying Father's gracious and loving heart toward me and all people. They were reintegrated into my theology of Father and his heart of grace, love, and compassion for me. Memorizing them afforded me the convenience of meditating on them throughout the day. This became a delight, ruminating on scriptures which reminded me of Father and his unfathomable love for me. I didn't hide in some prayer closet or sit in a yoga position with my eyes closed. I simply went about my day, and as I reviewed the scriptures I had memorized, I sometimes saw or heard things which seemed to highlight what I was meditating. For example, at times I saw a child in the grocery store being played with or cared for by a parent, and I was reminded of a verse about Father's care and affection for me and how I am his child in his sight. At other times I would see a sunset, rain, or beautiful scenery in Creation that reminded me of Bible verses about Father's beauty, creativity, or sovereignty.

Music had been a significant part of my spiritual growing up years as a teenager and young adult; naturally I wanted to find songs which somehow lined up with Father's recent teachings to me of his grace and love. For most of my Christian life, I had listened to the music of Keith Green and Michael Card, two Christian artists whose songs had nurtured my spirit in various ways. I continued to listen to their work, enjoying their hearts and the scriptural truths they presented in song. The new praise and worship music at the time which I had heard in the Christian book store that day became some of the encouraging music I delighted to hear and to accompany singing. Admittedly, most of the accompaniment was while driving in the car. There was a "Wow" Worship series of different colored CDs, with which I also became familiar. This series introduced me to some amazing songs like "Breathe" and "Hungry (Falling On My Knees)" sung by Kathryn Scott, as well as "Agnus Dei," "Lord Reign in Me," and "Open the Eyes of My Heart." A few classic favorites also encouraged me, such as the ones Steve and I mentioned in the car that day. There were also "He Will Carry You" by Scott Wesley Brown, which was based on Matthew 11:28, and songs based on the Psalms by The Maranatha Singers from the seventies and eighties.

Just when I was beginning to sense disappointment that there seemed to be no songs dealing with anything close to the bitterness issues I had had, there was a new song at that time by Erin O'Donnell. It was entitled "No Place So Far" and was based on Romans 8:28. It seemed to hit close to the mark, as if coming out of nowhere. Although it didn't directly mention bitterness, it did describe some of the sinful drifting and misunderstanding of Father like I had experienced, as well as the hope and grace of there being no place so far that we could evade Father's persistent love. I was surprised at how this song resonated with me.

Spiritually, there were significant changes in my life. The new outlook, the prayer throughout the day, the meditation on specific scriptures, and the musical soundtrack of grace, praise, and gratitude all combined to make my walk with Jesus much more enjoyable. Elena was enjoying these changes in me and my rejuvenated walk with Jesus; I was finally fun to be around. My road trip with Steve had also yielded so much spiritual encouragement that I just had to share with her the highlights of our conversation. Some of the same evidences of Father's grace were showing up in her life as well, which was both a humbling and gratifying experience for me. Our hearts were growing warm and close to one another again! *Thank you, Jesus!*

A couple of weeks after my road trip with Steve, my family and

I spent part of a Saturday visiting a local mall for some light shopping. Mostly it was an excuse to break away from the duplex we rented for a while and to enjoy being where people frequented, since we didn't buy anything due to our limited funds. We brought along a collapsible stroller for convenience in case little Nathaniel wanted to rest or to nap.

As we were admiring some items from the entrance of a store, I felt someone bump against my shoulder and arm. When I turned around, I saw Walter with a silly grin suddenly stepping backward. "Well, look who's here, Darlin'!" He wore an expression of pretend shock. "It's Brother John, his wife Elena, and their little boy Nathaniel! Imagine bumping into them here!"

Cindy half rolled her eyes and waved him off with her hand.

"Oh, stop it, Walter. People don't fall for that anymore." Then she smiled quickly at my wife and said, "Hi, Elena! How are you?" They exchanged a hug and began chatting, leaving Walter and me on our own.

My countenance brightened to see someone I knew. "Hi, Walter! It's great to see you! What brings you out here?"

"Oh, you know," he said, motioning toward his wife, "my darlin' wanted to do some shopping, so I had to *drag myself away* from my responsibilities at home to come here with her."

"You didn't bring Lynette and the boys?" I inquired.

"No. They're with their grandparents today and are probably having more fun than should be legal." He glanced at Elena and Cindy, noticing how quickly they became engrossed in full conversational mode as if they had known each other for years. "You know what this means, Brother?" he said, nodding as he motioned to the ladies. "It means that we'll be here for a while, so we better get comfortable."

We enjoyed some casual conversation, and after a few minutes it was decided that we all would have lunch together at the food court. The perimeter of the mall's food court was bordered with a dozen or more fast food restaurants. Some offered selections that were a little healthier than others. Each restaurant was unique from the others in the cuisine and menu items available. After we surveyed the choices with a quick glance around the open area, Walter commented on the scene. "It's a smorgasbord of choices!" he assessed with a grin.

We each decided what we wanted, waited in our respective lines to order, and then met back at one of only several vacant tables in the center of the food court. Walter led in giving thanks to Father for the meal, ending with: "And bless all the missionaries working so hard to share you with others and to make your gospel known. In Jesus' name, Amen." It reminded me of a question I had had since the potluck fellowship at Bob and Linda's house. A moment after we began our meal, I presented the question to Walter.

"Hey, I have a question for you, Walter."

"Sure thing. What's up?"

"That night at Bob and Linda's house, what was the joke about Bob forgetting to pray for all the missionaries?"

"See?" Cindy chided, laying aside her plastic fork and darting her eyes toward her husband. "I told you it would be misunderstood."

"Now, Darlin'," Walter answered almost whining, "it'll be okay. I'll explain it to them right now." Then he looked at me while mixing and chopping his food with his plastic fork and knife, speaking in a relaxed manner. "It's sort of a running joke I have with the brothers about how some people use prayer wrongly. Many seem to think that it's a ritual that has to have all the T's crossed and I's dotted."

"Oh, really?"

"Yeah, some people get all bent out of shape about their prayers having to include certain elements and catch phrases every time they speak to Father."

"So, what is it about praying particularly for missionaries?"

"It's just that when some people pray in a gathering of believers, often times there's someone who wants to correct the one leading in prayer, saying, 'You forgot to pray for the missionaries' or 'Aunt Mabel' or 'Cousin Fred' or 'the church building committee' or 'people serving our country,' and so on."

"Which isn't to say," interjected Cindy, motioning with her fork in her hand, "that there's anything wrong with interceding on behalf of those folks, because it's always a good thing to pray for others."

"Yes, Darlin', I was just going to say that." He sounded a bit condescending while his smiling eyes danced around for a second.

Their playfulness was encouraging, for there was no mean-spiritedness at all in their exchanges. Some of their knowing glances at each other were, no doubt, full of meaning for a couple who had been married and family together for decades. They were quite comfortable with each other, so much so that their banter was multilayered and well-played. Not everyone would have picked up on this. As we met with them socially over several months, I learned how to interpret their remarks to one another and found the humor in it. Elena thought that their playfulness in this way was "cute."

Walter glanced up at me occasionally as he prepared to eat. "I sometimes like to jab a little at the brothers whenever one of them prays in our group. It's just a reminder that prayer isn't something that we only do in public—as if we had to mention all our petitions only during those times."

"Of course, we *do* pray for missionaries," Cindy continued, "most of whom are friends of ours still on the field full-time. And when we travel in Europe for ministry purposes, well that just makes it all the more significant."

I pondered their comments about prayer for a moment. "Prayer is really just talking to Father, right?"

Walter nodded convincingly as he swallowed what he had been chewing.

"You got it, Brother! He just wants us to seek him and to talk to him openly and honestly like we would do to anyone else. He wants us to choose him to be the integral basis and fragrance of our lives. That's why prayer shouldn't be difficult at all. There's none of this." Walter stood up, shut his eyes, raised his right hand high into the air, and assumed a solemn tone of voice. "Our most gracious heavenly Father, we come before thee humbly once again to beseech thee on behalf of our dear brother John."

122

Cindy quickly pulled him back down to his seat. "Walter, stop! I'm sure they get the point!" Walter's stunt and volume drew the gaze and snickers of a few onlookers for a moment.

He chuckled lightheartedly. "Sometimes we can complicate prayer with certain expectations—either ours for ourselves or for others or even the expectations which we imagine others have of us."

"Since prayer is fellowship with Father," Cindy reasoned, "we can talk to him about anything, y'know." She winked at Nathaniel and caressed his arm, adding, "Hey, Cutie!" Nathaniel smiled up at her while Elena handed him a sippy cup.

"That's true, Darlin'. Yet sometimes we can make it seem like a foreign exercise in the absurd when we cloak it in all the trappings of 'thees' and 'thous' and peculiar vocabulary which are not a part of our everyday conversation. A certain mindset out of character with the whole nature of prayer can sometimes accompany prayers crafted in such antiquated or unusual vocabulary. Besides, our 'little recorders' are usually around listening and mis-interpreting most of what we say and do." Walter nodded toward Nathaniel, who was being fed by Elena at that moment from his own plate. "Children are the best recorders, but they're also the worst interpreters. We can sometimes project a wrong image of Father by how they hear us speak to him in our prayers and how they notice us relate to him in our daily lives."

"That's something I don't want to do to my son," I answered soberly, looking at Nathaniel. "What do you advise?"

"Just be real to him about your relationship with Father. It's as simple as that. Be who you already are, without any facade or pretense in prayer or relating to Father."

"Y'know," Cindy offered, "this reminds me of the early years of our work in Europe. Father showed us that we had a fair amount of paganism in our relationship with him—that is, as far as what we imposed on him in how we related to him."

"'Paganism'? What do you mean?" This I had to hear.

Cindy looked at Walter, who picked up where she left off.

"You know how typical pagans are all about 'appeasing the

deities' so that they will have success in hunting, plenty of rains for the crops, and protection from evil spirits, storms, accidents, and whatever else?"

"I just know what I've read and heard."

"Okay. At some point it dawned on us that we seemed to be treating Father in much the same way without even realizing it. For example, we used to pray before every meal religiously and use repetitive, rote religious jargon as we prayed aloud. It was as if we feared that we would die of food poisoning or choking if we didn't bow our heads and offer up a formal prayer of thanksgiving for the food before we took even one bite. It was prayer as being obligation-based instead of grace-based. We also felt the need or duty to offer up whatever petitions were in mind at the time."

"Okay. So, what changed?"

"Now we don't feel compelled to bow our heads before every meal. We don't even feel guilty about not doing so. Don't get me wrong, Brother. We still pray aloud sometimes, especially if we are with others. It helps to look collectively to Father at the beginning of our time together when we're in a group. It kind of facilitates focusing our hearts on him together. But honestly, there is no biblical exhortation stating or implying that we must bow our heads before every meal and offer up a prayer to express our thanks. Gratitude is an attitude, and that is what the New Testament teaches us. Passages like Ephesians 5:20, Colossians 3:17, and 1 Thessalonians 5:18 exhort us to give thanks always to God the Father in all things and to pray with an attitude of thanksgiving. That would seem to include more times throughout the day than just before meals."

"Oh, I see. It's really an attitude or heart motive rather than the outward appearance of physically bowing, closing the eyes, and praying."

"You got it, Chief! It's *being* rather than *doing*. Having a thankful heart is possible either with or without bowing the head."

"And conversely," Cindy added, "you can also bow your head and go through the motions without being thankful."

"You're right, Cindy," I agreed. "It's something I did a lot of during my bitter years. Well, honestly, it happened many times even before my bitterness."

"But," said Walter, "you probably felt like you had done your 'Christian duty' by bowing before every meal and offering up 'the sacrificial prayer of thanksgiving' before consuming what Father had provided for you. Am I right?"

"Uh, yeah," I replied smiling, "I guess you hit the head on *that* nail. It quickly became more of a habit than a heartfelt expression toward Father."

"We've done the same thing, Brother John, believe me—and for most of our Christian lives. But Father showed us that he looks on the heart, not on the outward expression or position of our bodies while praying. The freedom we have in Christ under the New Covenant truly freed us from the outward forms of the Old Covenant."

"So, do we just stop praying because we have all this freedom not to do so?"

Walter swallowed what he was chewing and wiped his mouth with a napkin. "No, it doesn't mean that that's the path we take. We don't use our freedom as a cloak for a rebellious heart. The truth is, we're really just trying to peel away the layers and to re-cognize our heart motives. Or rather, we're yielding to the Holy Spirit to have *his* way with us, shining the light on what's not so much like Jesus in us, then letting him work on that. Being open to him facilitates his job of rooting out any paganistic, legalistic or fleshly residue we may still have in our relationship with Jesus. There may be a lot more than we realize, so it may take some time."

Cindy put down her fork and stepped up to the plate. "We still thank Jesus for the food; we just don't want to make a show of it like the self-righteous crowd in the New Testament times did. Y'know how Jesus scolded the Pharisees for praying in public just to be thought of by others as 'more righteous' than they."

I chewed more slowly as I processed where this line of reasoning was going; then I swallowed. "So, we're not *really* saying that we *don't* thank him for the food, right?"

"Right," answered Walter. "We just don't want talking to him

125

to become a lifeless ritual or trite habit just for show. We really don't want *anything* in our lives to become any kind of ritual. And again, when we're in a group—like today—we have no qualms about joining together with brothers and sisters in Christ to express our thanks openly and audibly. Either way, we are always grateful for his provision, and in our hearts, we communicate that to Father. In fact, I'd say that since we're more used to giving thanks silently before meals without the whole head-bowing ordeal on a regular basis," he glanced at Cindy, "that now I usually think more about how thankful I am to him for the food with every bite throughout the meal, instead of just giving a token thanks at the beginning and immediately forgetting to be grateful. Wouldn't you say so, Darlin'?"

"I sure would, Honey Bunch. Our gratitude usually begins long before we eat in anticipation of a meal as well." This time she smiled at Elena. Then she looked and spoke to both of us. "We've been in some impoverished situations ourselves—both in our mission work in Europe and here in the States. That's why it really hits home with us how Father provides for all our needs, not just for food and drink, but for our health, our finances, and other needs too. With all that we've seen and experienced, how could we possibly take it all for granted and not be grateful to Father?"

"This makes a lot of sense to me," I said. "I remember one time many years ago when I was a new believer on my lunch break at work. After sitting down and bowing my head to pray, I realized that I had forgotten my fork. I had to go to a room down the hall to get it. When I returned, my coworkers were there and had just sat down for lunch. Since they hadn't seen me when I prayed earlier, I was more than a little perplexed, wondering if I should pray again just so that they would see that I wasn't some hypocritical believer who doesn't live what he says he believes."

"Uh-huh," Walter said, grinning playfully. "What did you do?"

"I wasn't sure what to do, but eventually I bowed my head and prayed again just to keep my witness intact." As I heard myself say that last phrase aloud, I realized how ridiculous it sounded.

Walter looked at Cindy and then leaned forward, still grinning.

126

"Brother, I'm pretty sure that Father knew your heart at that moment. He understood that you were grateful to him without you bowing again just to be seen by others. Surely what your co-workers thought of you in that moment would not have determined their place in eternity. Besides, Father can easily iron out any such misunderstandings from people's limited perceptions whenever and if he ever wants. But don't sweat it. We've all been there and done that too."

"So, it wasn't a big deal?"

"Not unless you let that bad feeling have its way with you. If you're like us, you've probably had times when you bowed before a meal in public and felt good about 'proclaiming your witness to the world,' as some people say."

A shy smile came over me. "Yes, I have."

"You'll probably find that, as you walk with Jesus, relating to him as a child to his father will be very liberating and will free you from a lot of self-consciousness, which can tend to be more self-serving than God-honoring. Just for fun, let's consider prayer in this light. Think about when you give something to little Nathaniel there, and he thanks you. How does it make you feel?"

My spirit lifted a little more at the thought of learning something from my son. I gazed at Nathaniel as I spoke.

"It warms my heart. It lets me know that I've made a connection with my son and that he's learning to be thankful."

"That's wonderful! And that will grow even more significant to you the older he becomes as you relate to him over the years. Now, just imagine if Nathaniel were to receive something from you, and, instead of looking up with a smile and thanking you, he were to bow his head and say, 'Oh gracious Daddy, I thank thee for thy kindness in giving this to me, thine humble servant.'"

Elena and I chortled at the thought.

"It would seem a little absurd, wouldn't it, Brother? After all, it's not the words or the ritual or anything other than him being grateful in relationship with you that really matters at that moment, wouldn't you say?"

"You're right, Walter. You know, this really makes sense; it makes biblical sense. I've had a heart full of such gratitude these last couple of months, and I know the outward show is not what Father wants."

"Right, because that would be more like paganism. What's that verse in Psalm 51? David said, 'Certainly you do not want a sacrifice, or else I would offer it; you do not desire a burnt sacrifice. The "sacrifices" God desires are a humble attitude—O God, a humble and repentant heart you will not reject.' And that was coming from a man after God's own heart under the Old Covenant with its ritual sacrifices. God had revealed to David that something better was behind all those outward forms. You see, Father's more interested in our heart motives and attitudes than in our head-bowing and recitation aloud."

"That's a wonderful psalm, Honey Bunch," Cindy interjected. "And what you quoted are verses sixteen and seventeen."

"My darlin's a virtual walking Bible!" Walter continued enjoying his meal.

I sat back a little, remembering a few moments in my past.

"I've had times when a brother was talking to me before a meal—going on with some long story—and in the middle, someone announced that we would bow for prayer to give thanks. The brother stopped in mid-sentence just long enough to pause for the person to lead in prayer, and as soon as he heard 'amen,' he picked right up where he left off. It's like he didn't even participate in talking silently to Father with the rest of us. The prayer was just an interruption to him."

Cindy and Walter laughed lightly.

"That kind of thing does happen," Walter assured me. "But we're really just focusing on our relationship with Father *individually* through all this. Those public prayer moments aren't really for us to look at others and think, 'Is *he* bowing his head and giving thanks? Is he *really* thankful?' Or, 'Is *she* bowing her head and giving thanks? Is she *really* thankful?' No, it's not for me to focus on others or to judge them for what they may or may not be doing in their hearts. Rather it's for me as an individual child of Father to focus on *my* heart before him and ask, 'Father, is this just

128

a go-through-the-motions kind of thing for me that I do without any sincerity in it, or am I really grateful for your gracious gifts?' In those moments when he shows me that it's the latter, it's a signal that I need to let him do some work in me.

"And you know, Brother? Despite what we may or may not seem to be doing in all this conversation about being genuinely thankful to Father for the food he gives us, we're not trying to change what y'all do as you walk with Jesus. That's between just y'all and him. We're simply sharing with you what Father has shown us as an answer to your earlier question. Because, you know," he said, smiling playfully, "you seem like a brother who wants to steer clear of legalism, selfishness, and a paganistic mindset so as to bask in this freedom we have in Christ."

The mention of freedom again was exhilarating. I let out a sigh and sat up a little straighter.

"You're right about me, Brother Walter. I *do* want to enjoy my walk with Christ and to get to know him better than ever before. And while some may be content to do the ritualistic giving of thanks, I want to be closer to him than any rule or the expectations of men can attempt to regulate or to manipulate me in my walk with him."

Nathaniel looked up at me and smiled. I returned the smile, stroking his back and giving him a quick kiss on the cheek. "My precious boy!"

"That's great, John." As he spoke, Walter scooped up a forkful of whatever Chinese dish he was consuming. "Because for me, when I take a bite of this delicious food. *Mmm!* I'm thanking Jesus with every bite. *Thank you, Jesus!*"

Elena and I laughed at his demonstration.

"There's so much I've been learning recently," I said, shaking my head incredulously, "it just doesn't stop. Father is helping and guiding me to rethink a lot of beliefs and perspectives that I thought I had already nailed down since Bible college."

Walter grinned cordially. "If we do this walk of faith as it was intended, then we'll never stop learning. This is a good thing, because Father has so much for us to know, and he's always teaching us, one way or another."

"We just have to be teachable," added Cindy, motioning with her fork, "and to watch for those moments when class is in session."

"I hope I don't miss out on anything," I said in a low voice.

"Oh, don't worry," Walter said plainly. "You *will* miss out—on quite a few occasions."

My facial expression must have looked shocked and startled. "Wait—what?"

"I'm just saying that you will miss it sometimes. Maybe you'll even miss it a lot of times. You are human, after all."

"But . . . I don't want to miss *anything* Father would teach me."

Walter's eyes brightened, and he leaned a little closer to me. "Think of it this way, Brother. You're Nathaniel's dad. Does he always understand everything you say to him and teach him?"

I thought for a moment. "Well, I suppose not. He's not even three yet."

"That's fair enough. But, does he know that you love him?"

I looked at Nathaniel, who was chewing at that moment, and our eyes met. He lit up with a big smile and giggled. I smiled back and reached down to give him a hug, whispering my love to him. Then I returned to my seat and replied to Walter. "I believe he really does."

"For his current age and level of comprehension, what could be more important than that in your relationship with him?"

Once again, my son and my relationship with him were the crux of Father's lesson for me. What a wonderful way for the Holy Spirit to reach my heart! I remembered Steve's comment about being open to learn from Father according to whatever method or medium he chose.

"That's amazing! You're right, Walter. To understand my love and Elena's love for him truly is the most important thing he needs to comprehend at this point in his life."

"He's learned this very early, so for him it will be easier to accept it and to walk in it. Even though years from now he won't recall most of these moments when you've cared for him, played

130

with him, and expressed your love and affection to him, he won't have a load of scarred memories from his early years of times when he thought you didn't love him. Those negative thoughts and emotions coursing through the synapses of the brain can have a long-lasting, emotional impact, especially in a child's early years."

At this point, Walter's voice became lower and softer. "There was a time not long ago when you had forgotten Father's love for you. Or maybe you had not been totally convinced of it since the beginning. Be that as it may, he did get through to you recently, didn't he?"

I nodded contentedly.

"In our relationship with Father, it's not really up to us to understand every time and to be open to him constantly. Try as we might, we're not always battin' a thousand. We're imperfect and fragile. As the psalmist said, 'For he knows what we are made of; he realizes we are made of clay.'

"But just as the burden of the relationship between you and little Nathaniel is on *you* to get through to *him*, so it is on *Father* to get through to *you*. After all, he's the one maturing you and conforming you to Jesus' image, not you yourself. And sure, from time to time you'll miss out on what he's teaching you. But that's okay because he's always patient, and he'll keep communicating to you and teaching you at your level, over and over, until eventually you get it. He does that with me too. In fact, he does that with us all."

At that moment, I put my hand near Nathaniel's and let him wrap his tiny hand around my fingers. I looked from him to Elena, who was smiling and taking in the whole discussion.

"He's such a blessing," I said slowly, my heart exulting in my love for my son and for my Father. "I just don't deserve him or any of this. I mean, think of all the people who *don't* understand Father's love for them." Suddenly, I was grieved for some of those I knew who came to mind.

Walter leaned back, holding his chin and looking pensive. "He truly loves us all, but not everyone grasps it. Usually it's because of some past hurts we've received or disappointed expectations we've had of him."

"How his heart must break for those who don't accept his love for them!" I observed.

"We can only imagine how deeply he yearns for them. He's like the father in Jesus' parable of the father and his two sons. He rejoices for the younger son who finally understands and accepts his love, yet at the same time he grieves for the older son who misunderstands his actions and may never come to the realization of his father's love for him as well. It's why we carry the message of Father's love to those who don't know him. In our relationship with Father, we long for them to know him as we do because he has given us some of his heart for them. Hence, we go and share Christ with them."

Suddenly I wished I were still in Honduras, loving, teaching, and reaching the people there who needed Jesus so much. However, I also longed to have been a better missionary, not the bitter, angry mess that I was then.

"I wish I were still in Honduras," I said sadly. "It took so much effort and planning and so many resources to get us there. Then the circumstances changed, and we didn't have the means to stay." I looked at Elena. "And my sweetheart had to leave her family again to come back to the States with me. It's such a shame."

Walter placed his hand on my shoulder. "John, any feelings of shame you may sense didn't come from Father. That's not a tactic that the Holy Spirit uses."

His reassurance was uplifting. The shift in the conversation also reminded me about my conversation with Steve.

"My friend Steve and I were talking about this a little."

"About shame?"

"Yes," I said, nodding. "It seems like one of the goals Jesus had in ministering to individuals was to remove their shame."

"That's true. Hey, Brother, that's wonderful that you see that!"

"Praise the Lord!" offered Cindy with a smile.

I smiled, glancing at Elena. "Yes. Yes, it is great. Thank you, Jesus!"

"So, what did you two realize about this important truth?" asked Walter.

"Let me think," I said, trying to review the conversation we had had about it. "Oh, now I remember. We were discussing this same parable about the father and his two sons. By the way, there's got to be a better name for that than the parable of the prodigal son. It sounds like it's focusing on a negative, and it uses a Latin word that's not even in the original narrative."

"You could call it the parable of the gracious father, if you prefer."

"That sounds perfect! That really highlights the point of the narrative.

"Anyway, Steve and I realized that near the end of the parable, the father ran to his younger son because he could tell by his appearance that he had already suffered greatly, and he didn't want him to feel another minute of shame. That's why he ran to him, which meant that he had to lift up his robe or whatever clothing he was wearing to free his legs for running. Back in that day and culture, it was an especially embarrassing thing for a grown man to do."

"Right," Walter said, tracking along with me.

"And we realized that the love and affection of the father meant that he wanted to replace the sense of shame his son felt with an abundance of love, acceptance, and grace."

Walter's smile reflected contentment and joy. "Father has taught you something very important and very encouraging, John."

"Yes, he has. After my conversation with Steve, I started looking up some of these different encounters Jesus had with individuals in the Gospels. In everyone that I examined, he took away their shame and ministered grace to them."

"What are some of the examples you found?"

"Okay. Zacchaeus, from Luke 19, was one of the first ones I considered. He was a social outcast among the Jews since he was a chief tax collector. Yet Jesus announced publicly that he was going to visit his home that day he was in Jericho. As Zacchaeus got to know Jesus, the man's heart changed. He said that he would give half of his possessions to the poor and pay back four times whatever he had cheated from people. That's when Jesus said,

'Today salvation has come to this household, because he too is a son of Abraham! For the Son of Man came to seek and to save the lost.' Jesus removed the social disgrace and shame from him by honoring his home with a visit and transforming his heart and life with his grace for salvation."

Walter and Cindy nodded slowly with bright expressions. "Zacchaeus is a wonderful example of what Jesus can do in a person's heart and life," observed Walter. "Who else is a notable example?"

"Well, the Samaritan woman is another good example of an outcast being accepted and sought by Jesus. He went to a public place, the town well, where he knew she would cross paths with him. He spoke directly yet compassionately to her. And she, in turn, told the people in town to come and to listen to him. As a result, Jesus stayed in Samaria for two days, and many Samaritans in that town believed in him. From then on, she was no longer the woman who had had many ex-husbands and who was living with a man to whom she wasn't married. She then became known as the woman with a new heart who introduced Samaria to Jesus."

"She was no longer defined by her failures and weaknesses," commented Walter. "She made a great missionary, didn't she? Who else stands out to you?"

"There's the example of Jesus healing ten lepers all at once in Luke 17." Reflecting on each grace account, I felt like I was on a roll. "Their shame was taken away when they were healed, having been outcasts in society due to their disease. When they went to the priest to be declared cleansed of their leprosy and to offer a sacrifice according to the Law of Moses, their healing was also a sign to the Pharisees as to Jesus' messianic claims. For generations the Pharisees had debated why there were all these instructions and procedures in the Law about what to do when a leper was healed, even though in their history no Jew had ever before been healed of leprosy. And they had pretty much concluded that the healing of leprosy would likely be something that the coming Messiah would do, since it wouldn't have been included in the Torah unless there would be people healed of leprosy at some point in time. It served as an occasion on which Jesus used the language of the Pharisees by healing ten lepers simultaneously in fulfillment of the Law. It sent a loud and clear message to them that he was their Messiah, fulfilling all those prophecies. Maybe one healed leper could have been hidden from sight or explained away somehow. But it was impossible to deny the healing of *ten* lepers."

"That's some great insight, John. Did you read about Jesus removing shame from anyone who was already a believer?"

"Yes, and it was Simon Peter, of all people. After Jesus' resurrection, he met with Peter and some of the others on the shore of the Sea of Tiberias in John 21. Peter must have felt like the biggest failure, since he had three times denied knowing Christ the night before he was crucified. Being a fisherman for most of his life, he may have felt that he was undeserving of anything better than returning to that trade. Therefore, he told some of the disciples that he was going fishing. Several of them went with him. Jesus used the miraculous catch of fish to grab Peter's attention. It was just like what he did with the first miraculous catch in Luke 5 when he called Peter to follow him. In front of the other disciples present, Jesus had Peter answer three times that he loved him. Then he gave him the assignment to feed his sheep and to follow him. Jesus took away the shame that Peter had felt and sort of reinstated his call to ministry."

"You see that Jesus didn't try to make him feel any shame for his sins, right?"

"You're right," I agreed, pushing a last bit of food with my fork on the plate. "That's *exactly* what he did. He had already forgiven him, and Peter had not lost his faith in Jesus anyway—even though he was obviously wrong in denying Jesus. I guess it's more like he lost his courage under the circumstances."

"We can be sure that things like shame, condemnation, and guilt are not tools that Father uses with us. The way Jesus related to Peter is a prime example of this. Also, Romans 8:1 states that, 'There is therefore now no condemnation for those who are in Christ Jesus.' You see, originally mankind had no shame or consciousness of sin because he had no sin. You'll remember that

Genesis 2 says that Adam and Eve 'were both naked, but they were not ashamed.' Giving into temptation and sinning is what brought shame, guilt, and condemnation into our human experience, along with a host of other spiritual problems. The enemy deceived us into allowing both sin and its accompanying shame into our lives, thereby really distancing us from Father. The sin killed us spiritually and separated us from God; the shame made us feel unworthy of him—his grace, love, and forgiveness. When Christ did his work of salvation on the cross, he resolved our sin problem, breaking the power of it in our lives. Since shame is a spiritual consequence of sin, making us feel distanced from Father, he dealt with that as well. Therefore, when we have any sense of guilt or shame, we can be sure that it's not from Father. Its origin can only be from the enemy, society at large which is greatly influenced by the enemy, and even from our own flesh."

This truth was so wonderful! In Christ, we are free from guilt and shame! My spirit was ready to soar with delight, but I still had a nagging question.

"What about conviction of sin? Doesn't the Holy Spirit make us feel bad when he convicts us for sins we commit?"

"That's an astute question," he replied, nodding. "The ministry of the Holy Spirit in the life of a believer is not one in which he uses shame and guilt to motivate us, though. That's a misperception on our part, which again is often fueled by a sinful society, our own flesh, and the enemy and his minions. Remember that there is a difference between someone pointing out to us that something we do is sin, which is what the Spirit does, and some-one shaming and guilting us for our sin, which is what those three are notorious for doing. Besides, you'll remember that part of the Spirit's ministry in us and to us is to provide us with the grace necessary to overcome sin, not to condemn us for having done it. Darlin'," he said sweetly to Cindy, "will you share with them Titus 2:11 and 12 please?"

"It's one of my favorite passages," she said, in a perky voice. "Here goes: 'For the grace of God has appeared, bringing salvation to all people. It trains us to reject godless ways and worldly desires and to live self-controlled, upright, and godly lives in the present age."

"Thank you, Darlin'. We see from that passage that Father's grace is what he uses both to redeem us and to disciple us in his righteous ways, changing our hearts as we grow in him. There are other scriptures which talk about him relating to us out of love, kindness, and other wonderful qualities. On the other hand, those godless three—the world, the flesh, and the enemy—are infamous for heaping shame and condemnation on us. Meanwhile, Father heaps his grace and love on us. He's always working to make us like Jesus, and he doesn't use guilt, shame, or condemnation to motivate us to be like his Son. Those things only make us feel unworthy of him, adding to the problem and driving us farther away from intimacy with Father. In that regard, it wouldn't make any sense if he were to use those on us. That's one of the things Jesus came to do—restore our relationship with Father."

The truth was penetrating my understanding like sunbeams piercing through the clouds. My spirit again exulted in my all-loving Father. He affectionately and tenderly had been providing everything I needed to walk with him and to enjoy him amid a fallen and imperfect world.

"Walter . . . it just seems too good to be true! What great love Father has for us!"

Elena spoke softly, having absorbed all that had been said. "You know, I can see how shame is often used against people to make them do what they may not want to do. And I understand what you mean about it not coming from Father but from other people, our own flesh, and the enemy. Thanks for sharing that, Walter."

"You're very welcome, Elena," Walter replied. "Father has been our Teacher and Guide all through this journey with Jesus. It really helps to understand that individuals within the society at large can fall for the trap of shaming. Having been victims of it like the rest of us, some of them easily learn to wield it skillfully like a weapon. People of all walks use it, whether it's in schools, the work place, religion, politics, or even in parenting and marriage, it's sad to say. Yet shame is a poor motivator, because it promotes insincerity and fleshly works in those who perform out of shame motivation. Plus, it shows weakness on the part of those appropriating it, speaking volumes about those who use it against others. These are just a few of the reasons why Father doesn't use it. Then there's the fact that he doesn't need or desire to relate to us based on our shame but based on his grace. He blesses us with his love and grace, persuading us gently and winning us over to the fact that he only and always does what's best for us. Since we know that he has given us a free will to decide, he leaves the choice to us."

"Don't forget to mention, Honey Bunch," inserted Cindy, "that the Bible reveals that people who attempt to wield shame against us are really being coerced by the enemy for his purposes."

Walter raised his eyebrows toward her in agreement.

"You're right, Darlin'. How could I forget? Ephesians 6 tells us, 'For our struggle is not against flesh and blood, but against the rulers, against the powers, against the world rulers of this darkness, against the spiritual forces of evil in the heavens. For this reason, take up the full armor of God so that you may be able to stand your ground on the evil day, and having done everything, to stand.'"

"So, when people try to shame me or those I love," I replied, thinking out loud, "it really indicates that they have been victims of the same tactic sometime in the past and that they are now victims being used by the enemy on the wrong side of spiritual warfare."

Walter paused for a second in thought. "Yeah, that's one way to put it, Brother."

"I wonder," I said pensively. "I wonder if my anger and bitterness resulted from the shame and condemnation I felt from how far short I had come as a believer and a missionary. Maybe that was especially true, since back then I was focusing so exclusively on Father's holiness, righteousness, and justice apart from his love, grace, and mercy."

Walter gazed up above his forehead for a moment, considering

138

the possibility of what I surmised. "You know, that may very well be what happened in your case. Shame and anger *do* have a working relationship, in a manner of speaking."

"I know that shame tactics have been a part of my past, but I don't want them ever to be a part of my future." Again, I looked at Elena and Nathaniel. "I don't want to wield shame as a weapon against those I love, nor do I want to lash out at them with my anger. Walter, how do I prevent that from ever happening again?"

Walter finished a bite and set down his fork. "John, there are no promises that we'll never again commit any particular sin in this life. Now, I know that you realize this, since we've already mentioned that we fail from time to time as imperfect human beings. But there are some truths that can encourage you in your walk concerning this.

"As with any sin, Christ has already broken its power through his work on the cross and in his resurrection. In him we are free from sin and its power, as Romans 6 through 8 teach. Whether it's a lifestyle of wielding shame, an abusive addiction, or any other sin from our past, we can trust that Jesus has freed us from it just as the Scriptures proclaim. Nevertheless, let me give you some preliminary information which may be of help to you.

"Recognize that while we have Father's grace and love, which are the only effective antidotes for sin, we also have to contend with our flesh. It's a pretty good guess that the enemy would like nothing better than for you to have a time of grace, rejoicing in your victory, only so that you'll gradually gain a false sense of confidence in yourself. During all that smooth sailing you'd probably run to Christ a little less and begin to feel independent from God. That would lead you to start walking apart from Christ. Not noticing that this is happening would be the deception in it all. The deceiver would likely want to see you set up like this just to watch you tumble down and crash, expecting to discourage you from the work that Christ began in your heart and also plotting to make you think that Father's grace doesn't work. He wants to do everything he can to use discouragement and despair to lead us all away from dependence on Jesus. So, be wary of the enemy's

139

devices; lean on Jesus and his grace. Remember to 'run to Christ' daily—practically as often as you breathe.

"Furthermore, it's of greatest importance to remember that this life in Jesus isn't at all about your effort or work. It's about his work and what he accomplishes in and through you. Philippians 2:13 tells us that 'the one bringing forth in you both the desire and the effort—for the sake of his good pleasure—is God.' Even when we are desiring and working and doing the things that we do in relating to Father, it's really him doing it in us, to us, and through us.

"With all this in mind, again, it's best to run to Christ, and even that is something we can only do by his grace. Walk in Jesus' presence and remain open and honest with him at all times. Yield to the Spirit and allow him to do the work within you. And in those moments when you stray from him—and believe me, Brother, it will happen sooner or later, even a number of times—just run back to him as soon as you realize it. He's with you always, and he's ready to take you back into fellowship with him. Also, as you commune with Jesus, remember that this life in Christ is not about learning rote prayers to recite like magical incantations. This means that there are no specific catch phrases to use in your prayers. Just talk to him about what happened, confessing your sins like we talked about on Stone Mountain, and know that he doesn't shame you or guilt you in any way. He understands better than we do how detrimental those tactics are in our relationship with him. He truly rejoices to have you return to him just like the younger son in the parable of the gracious father. Obviously, you don't have to stray as far as did the younger son in Jesus' narrative. But even if you do, Father's love and grace are always there for you. That's just one of many reasons why it's so much better than a paganistic way of relating to God."

He ended his remarks with a knowing look at both Elena and me. Cindy also gave us both a cordial smile of acceptance.

"Thanks so much, Walter," I replied gratefully. "This is all so very uplifting and spiritually invigorating! Okay, so that reminds me of what I wanted to ask you about the paganism discussion from earlier. How do believers sometimes relate to Jesus as pagans? That seems like a strong term to use for Christians, and it would probably offend a lot of people."

Walter glanced at Cindy with a sneaky grin. They seemed to be privy to some secret. Then he looked back at me.

"You see, John, what we have with Father is a special relationship based on grace. It's a grace-based relationship, not a merit-based relationship. Since the fall of man in the garden, practically all other relationships are merit-based, or at least they start out that way. Some are redeemed through our grace-based relationship with Christ. Friendships can be transformed and be-come grace-based if they are founded in Jesus and dependent on him. Marriage is another one of those that we all want to be grace-based as well, and it can be by Father's grace.

"In a grace-based relationship, love, kindness, thankfulness, and so on, are all given freely. There's no sense of meriting or earning anything from either party. In a merit-based relationship, people keep score and remember what favors were done for whom. They invest in said 'favors' anticipating a future payback. So, there's no room for grace or love—except maybe love for self, which really sounds like an oxymoron. It's the heart attitude which says, 'I'm doing this for God so that he will do—*fill in the blank*—for me.' Ultimately, it's an attempt to control and to manipulate Father, just like pagans try to control the false deities that they worship. In relating to Jesus, any merit-based approach on man's part is really just old-fashioned paganism, pure and simple. It's really sad, because the whole time, we're trying to figure out what to do to control Father. Meanwhile, he's teaching us his grace and love and showing us that he's all about grace, not merit. However, not everyone has a teachable heart and learns this about him. Nevertheless, everything he gives us and everything he does for us is free. It's *all* grace with no conditions or requirements whatso-ever."

"How do you mean that we try to 'manipulate' Father?"

"It's just like we mentioned earlier about prayer. Some people think that if they pray a certain way or get enough people to pray for a particular outcome or practice certain spiritual disciplines or fast long enough—or whatever—then God will *have* to grant them what they request. Imagine us puny humans—mere creations of the all-powerful, all-knowing, and infinite Creator—doing *anything* to try to twist God's arm to do what we want. It's ludicrous! That's not what prayer is for anyway. It was never intended to be a means to get whatever selfish thing we want from God."

Cindy chimed in after Walter. "There are people who search the Scriptures and 'discover secrets' to getting what they want out of Father—or so they think. And—*bless their hearts*—they probably mean well, but they just aren't getting to know Father for all their trying. They don't understand that what they're doing is far from relating to him in a grace-based way."

"Yeah, and some of those people," added Walter, "go on to write 'Christian self-help books' to teach others how to get what they want from Father, using their 'proven biblical techniques.'"

"They seem to sell a lot of books," I commented.

Walter raised an eyebrow. "Don't I know it!"

"But remember now, Honey Bunch," Cindy continued, "that *we* were in that same space years ago, trying to merit Father's love. Now, because we've been on both sides of that issue, we can pray for and encourage those people as Father leads us across their paths. We don't look down on them or pity them. After all, those believers are our brothers and sisters in Christ."

Walter nodded his head repeatedly. "You're right, Darlin'. You're right. So, Brother, we're just trying to help you to see through some of those deceptions as a ministry of encouragement to you and your family. We're not trying to speak self-righteously as if we were any better than anyone else. Father's grace means exactly that: it's *his* grace to grant as he chooses. While we may have learned and grasped some of these truths that many grapple with or somehow miss, there are others which we have yet to see. We don't claim or pretend to be omniscient, so there may well be areas in *our* understanding which are off center and need to be brought in alignment with the Scriptures. We remain open to the Spirit to guide us and to teach us as he wills."

I nodded in agreement.

"Sure, I understand, and I appreciate the insights. This not only helps me to see some pitfalls to avoid, but it also educates me a little better as to how to pray for those I meet who are affected by them."

"Then it's been a fruitful discussion," announced Walter. "We certainly don't want to load you up with all this information and engender any level of arrogance."

Elena had just finished cleaning up our plates and clearing off our small table. "I have a question," she said.

"Sure, Elena," replied Cindy. "What is it?"

"It's very exciting to know that Father doesn't use any shame or condemnation with us as we relate to him, but I'm not sure how fearing him fits into this exactly. You know how the Bible teaches us to have the fear of the Lord. Are we still supposed to fear him even in light of his great love and boundless grace for us? Or does the fear of the Lord just speak of reverence for him, like we have for our earthly fathers?"

"Oh my, Elena," said Cindy falling backward a few inches. "You ask a really deep question."

"Yet it's a very important question," interjected Walter, "with a significant and life-impacting answer."

"Then it's okay for me to ask?" she inquired meekly.

Cindy patted Elena's hand reassuringly. "It certainly is, Elena. And it's one of those topics that we all need to understand."

"Darlin', will you take this one, please?"

Cindy smiled at her husband. "You're so generous, Honey Bunch," she replied with a giggle. She drew her attention back to Elena. "This is a topic we studied pretty thoroughly in our first couple of years in Switzerland. We were ministering to some of the refugees pouring in from the surrounding countries, and I was helping a couple of missionary wives to disciple some of the ladies who were new believers. Proverbs 31:30 came up in a discussion we were having. That's the verse that defines or describes what a godly woman is. It reads: 'Charm is deceitful and beauty is fleeting, but a woman who fears the LORD will be praised.'

143

"The Old Testament phrase 'the fear of the LORD' struck a nerve with these new believers, who had had so much fear in their lives due to the various, terrorizing political regimes many of them had lived and suffered under. So, we did a word study and compared the different passages which use the 'fear' terminology. What we discovered is that it's a phrase associated with the Old Covenant identified with Moses. Y'know, it had the animal sacrifices, the temple, the law, and all that. As applied to the Israelites, it referred to those of Israel who had that covenant relationship with Father, being submitted to his will with a sense of reverence and awe. The original Hebrew word had several different shades of meaning, but as relating to these various contexts it generally referred to the kind of awe which draws people closer, not that which causes them to shrink back in fear. For what we are considering in answer your question, this phrase 'the fear of the LORD' and its similar expressions really only appear a couple of times in the New Testament. It's in Acts 9 and 2 Corinthians 5. It basically refers to those in Israel under the Old Covenant who have that covenant relationship with Father in which they are submitted to his will. It does indicate a sense of awe, but not in the sense of being afraid and hiding."

Then she turned again to Walter. "Honey Bunch, would you answer the rest of the question from a New Testament perspective?"

"Why, I'd be delighted, Darlin'," Walter answered. "With Christ as our ultimate high priest in the New Testament, we see that because of what he did for us in his death and resurrection, we believers no longer fear the punishment of an eternity without him in the lake of fire. In 1 John 4, the apostle refers to us as believers who have been perfected in love, since we reside in Father, and he resides in us. Verse eighteen states: 'There is no fear in love, but perfect love drives out fear, because fear has to do with punishment. The one who fears punishment has not been perfected in love.' In Christ we also have that relationship with him by which we are submitted to him in awe of who he is. But we have no fear of any kind of punishment because his love—perfect love—has driven out or banished such fear. Therefore, under the Old

144

Covenant, being related to him as a believer using the 'fear' terminology was the doorway to true wisdom, as Proverbs 9:10 teaches. Proverbs also teaches that women—godly women—who walk in that relationship with him shall be praised, like the verse my Darlin' quoted. Under the New Covenant in Christ, we believers have a sense of awe toward him, but without the fear of eternal punishment or any kind of condemnation, like we mentioned earlier from Romans 8:1."

Elena looked down at the table briefly, and then up at Cindy and Walter. "Oh. Well, is there a shorter answer to my question?"

Walter and Cindy grimaced from ear to ear. "Sorry, Elena," replied Cindy. "We made it sound a lot more complicated than it is. Here's the summarized answer: People who don't know Jesus would do well to fear him, but we who are in Christ don't truly *'fear'* him. Because we are overflowing with his love and grace, we love him back with a sense of awe for what he has done for us."

"Okay," she said with a bright, reassuring smile. "I've got it now."

There was still something in what they said which I wanted to verify for my own understanding. I voiced it to them as to a human soundboard.

"Jesus' love for us has taken away any fear of death or hell which we would have had, which is what the world lives with daily."

Walter nodded once. "You got it, Chief!"

Minutes later as we were walking toward one of the main mall exits, I reflected on our conversation throughout this whole lunch together. Then I realized something which seemed significant, so I decided that I would "test the waters" with Walter and Cindy concerning a thought.

"Walter, I think I just realized something."

"What's that, John?"

"Well, see how this sounds. Throughout our previous lives apart from Christ, we lived life and related to others and to him, if at all, from the perspective of a performance-based, shame-and-

145

fear dynamic. But now that we are in Christ and rightly related to him, we live life and relate to him and to others from a grace-based, gratitude-and-love dynamic—at least that's the ideal way we endeavor to live. Therefore, his grace and love working in our hearts yield gratitude, grace, and love as we relate to him and to others."

Walter's mouth fell open slightly.

"You know, Brother, that's a very precise and analytical way to express it."

"Thanks—I think. But you know, I'm a little curious about something. Even as I wallowed in my bitterness for those years, I was still a believer; I didn't forfeit my salvation or home in heaven due to Father's grace and Jesus' faithfulness, despite the fact that I wasn't being true to who I was in Christ. Even so, my attitude, words, and actions often made me *seem* like an unbeliever."

Walter put his hand on my shoulder. "Yet you had everything you needed as a believer to conquer the bitterness: Father's grace and love, Jesus' enabling and wisdom, the Holy Spirit's guidance and ministry, and the Holy Scriptures. You just weren't in fellowship with Father to be able to appropriate it all."

As we walked I stopped suddenly. "So then, that whole two-year ordeal was a total waste of time, spiritually speaking?"

Walter half shrugged. "If you're saying that all the stress, confusion, doubt, and disfellowship with Father was unnecessary, then I'd agree with you, but I wouldn't call it a waste of time. As a result of what you've been through and in the aftermath, you've learned some very crucial lessons and essential truths in this walk with Jesus. He's given you a perspective, understanding, and empathy for people in the trenches of hardheartedness which not all believers have. You've also grown in ways that perhaps you wouldn't have otherwise. Don't get me wrong, now. I don't mean to fan the flames of any potential introspective traps. I know it wasn't fun during those years. Just know that many if not most believers go their whole lives without gaining a good comprehension and grasp of the things Father has taught you as a result of that whole ordeal. And don't underestimate what he might do with your

146

experiences and what he's taught you. He may yet work something even more beautiful in your life for his glory. He delights to turn our worst messes into things which become precious and praiseworthy."

Being showered with Father's love and his grace upon grace results in tremendous freedom, I was learning. By then I was certain that I had been freed from the shackles of bitterness. The new grace-based perspective which Father had taught me was also casting out some of the residual paganism and shame which had dogged my days for so long. My relationship with Christ was becoming ever more liberating, refreshing, and relaxing. Now it was time for me to learn about some of the other freedoms I was blessed to receive in Christ and some of the intricacies concerning the development of bitterness in the human heart.

CHAPTER 8

"FOR FREEDOM CHRIST HAS SET US FREE"[1]

Perhaps it was due to my fresh new perspective on Father, his grace, and his love or perhaps due to whatever turmoil and ecclesiastical politics were going on behind the scenes, but for some reason the services at the local assembly we attended were becoming less appealing to me. The new leadership was steering us in a different direction from where we as a local body had been.

Originally our church had been known as a refuge, a place of healing. Over the years, many of the family members had referred to it as "a hospital for burned-out Christians." Our founding pastor had pastored other churches for a number of years; however, in the late seventies he decided to begin a new work. Other pastors in the area would ask him why he wanted to start a new church, since there were already so many. According to him in his own words, his reply was, "Because it's easier to give birth than to raise the dead." This comment didn't go over very well with local pastors who heard it, to say the least. Nevertheless, he began visiting neighborhoods and knocking on doors, reading the spiritual pulse of the community and evangelizing as he went. Many believers at that time, it seemed, had tired of the status quo of local congregations. Many assemblies often had very authoritative leadership with firm grips on the membership and expectations for everyone to "toe the line." The man who had started our congregation reached out to many of these individuals and began ministering to them as equals, applying God's grace. Apparently, he had also experienced some ill treatment at the hands of others in ministry and could easily empathize with those brothers and sisters in Christ. Therefore, he built a congregation on just such believers, forming genuine friendships with them and encouraging them with biblical teachings.

The edification and joy of the attendees inspired many of them to evangelize the lost. Members shared Jesus with their friends,

149

neighbors, and coworkers. There were people trusting Christ at work or in people's homes and others who trusted Christ after being brought to the preaching services. Excitement was in the air, because the fruit we saw was not the result of the evangelism programs typical of a lot of churches then. People were excited about Jesus in their own lives, and they were motivated by that joy and love to tell others about him.

We followed the path of other congregations by renting a facility, outgrowing it, then renting a larger one, and outgrowing that. Many of us members felt that we needed to have a more permanent location, so a building program was begun. Most of us gave toward this fund, sacrificing monies which had been set aside for vacations, new cars, home remodeling, etc. Even children were donating their allowances and savings originally intended for new bicycles and other expensive items. People kept saying, "We need a church building more than I need" whatever purchase they had originally intended. After a year or two of such sacrifices and giving freely, there was enough to begin building. The new, larger facilities kept the excitement going.

All this time, we as a local body had also been giving to different missionaries on the foreign field. We were interceding for them and doing what we could to encourage them. It was in this environment that I sensed a call to the mission field and joyfully accepted.

We experienced great unity, with our hearts being knit together in love. As different church family members had needs arise, others were quickly there to meet them. The membership practiced a lot of the "one another" passages in the New Testament by fulfilling a lot of practical needs. When someone was sick or hospitalized, others were there to provide meals, childcare, house chores, and companionship. When someone needed car repairs or home maintenance, it seemed that a few others were always there to network a solution and even help with the costs. When someone lost a job and had bills to pay, a collection would be taken up immediately to fill in the gap. The church staff provided counseling for other needs, and there were different groups ready to pray about any and all concerns. There was often a lot of events planned for the purpose of socializing and fellowshipping. Strong, long-lasting ties of friendship were forged. We cared dearly for one another, and the sincerity was evident in our actions. Looking back on those years with the founding pastor, we often referred to them as the "glory days" of our congregation.

Occasional problems did arise, of course; none of us claimed that we were a perfect local body of Christ. However, the challenges were approached with prayer, love, patience, biblical principles, and seeking the face of God. Grace and forgiveness covered a multitude of sins, and relationships were restored as we looked toward the future.

When I brought Elena home from Honduras, this fellowship welcomed her with open arms. In just one day, a number of church friends rallied together to provide everything we needed for our church wedding. Elena had brought with her a wedding dress made by a seamstress in her home town. Yet, thanks to the young couples our age who were my friends at church, she had also had her choice of three other wedding dresses and four bouquets from which to choose. These same friends coordinated everything from food and photography to the rehearsal dinner and bridal shower, albeit on a small budget. Elena was amazed at the outpouring of love she received, for none of them knew her and she couldn't even speak English then. Also, due to my whole secrecy about our engagement (in case her residence visa had not been approved after our civil wedding and I would have had to return to the States without her), everyone was both shocked and delighted to hear that I was returning with a bride. My church family knew me well, and they had a genuine love for people, so being a blessing to and befriending Elena was not an issue. After all, she has always been an easy person to love, and she won them over with her smile and her loving personality like she did me.

After the founding pastor retired, we as a local assembly experienced a transitional period. The young "interim" pastor who joined the staff next only stayed a couple of years or so. (My reference to him as the "interim" pastor is due to his unexpectedly brief stay.) As an outsider coming in, he had had a lot of new ideas, which were not always well-received. This change in leadership was to a more authoritative one, though on the surface it usually appeared cordial and friendly.

My most significant experience with him took place some months before we moved to Honduras. One day I approached him in his office for a request. Our Sunday School class wanted to ask for the use of the kitchen and fellowship hall for a Sunday school breakfast. He denied our request because we didn't have "a valid, ministry-based reason" for using the facilities during the Sunday school hour. I left his office that day puzzled and disappointed. Keeping up outward appearances and integrating slick programs for the whole family and every need seemed to be priorities under that administration.

When he left under disgraceful circumstances, the man he had hired to be the youth pastor then took his position as senior pastor. (This is the young man who counseled me to ball up and throw away a piece of paper to solve my bitterness.) He pursued a somewhat similar direction with the congregation as the "interim" pastor had, but after a while things became really odd. The authoritative nature of the lead pastoral staff continued. There appeared to be an attempt at tighter reigns on resources and people. Whatever the pastors said was to be accepted without question. There were also peculiar statements from the pulpit like, "If you walk through the sanctuary and pick up trash, that's a ministry." *So, now ministry includes sanitation duty?* I wondered. *I don't remember the word "janitors" in Ephesians 4:11-13. Why would a pastor say things like that?*

Once he presented his idea for us to build a gymnasium in order to reach neighborhood teens through a basketball program. There were a lot of talk and a lot of hype about the gym for months. Groundbreaking Sunday arrived in which different leaders (such as the pastors, the deacon board chairman, the Sunday school superintendent, and others) walked down the aisle toward the platform, each carrying a decorated shovel for the occasion. Each one was received with a round of applause. I refused to applaud, so I stuck out like a red thumb. I cringed in my seat, thinking, *'Are people really applauding decorated shovels? Is this what the gospel and the body of Christ are all about?'* The new philosophy, perspective, and approach were very frustrating and disheartening for me. Most of the other members didn't seem to have any issues with what was being said and done. I didn't want to be viewed as divisive or rebellious, so I didn't say anything.

Meanwhile, I had been enjoying the fellowship of a small circle of brothers and sisters outside the traditional church setting for several months. This was the band of brothers, along with their families, whom I had met at Stone Mountain. As time and opportunity allowed, we began visiting each other from time to time. Our friendships were blossoming. It seemed that these spontaneous, sporadic encounters which had led to great fellowship and conversations were more fruitful to me personally than any of the more formal, weekly meetings of which I had been a part for most of my life. Not being part of a regular routine, however, their occurrence was less frequent. Therefore, I found myself praying for and seeking more of these fellowship opportunities. Although we enjoyed visiting individual families as our hearts were knit together, there seemed to be a special dynamic in the mix of our more group-oriented gatherings with different depths of godly wisdom and biblical perspectives. If weeks passed and no one had scheduled anything, then I found myself making phone calls to arrange something. I realized that intentional meetings could also bear some of the same fruit. That was certainly the case for our next fellowship.

One summer Saturday afternoon, several of us met at a local park for a picnic. My family and I were joined by Tom, Sara, Steve, and Aby. Steve had known Tom and Sara since the late seventies through a mutual, local congregation where they were all active back then. He was the friend who introduced me to Tom's oldest son first and then to Tom and Sara themselves. This would be a great time of fellowship among old friends. I was delighted to be with them all, but since I'd had such a great friendship with

Steve for decades by then, and he and Aby lived over an hour away on the north side of Atlanta, I was especially glad to have him with us. The distance, responsibilities of family and work, and this American culture in general didn't make it easy for us to see each other often. I had learned that, just as in Central America, making time for relationships—both family and friends—is an essential priority.

For the picnic, each family brought a variety of items for making sandwiches and a few other picnic sides. Steve brought a game called Bocce, which consisted of wooden balls in a bag and was to be played outdoors on level ground. It was an unusual game which I had never even heard of before that day. We played three games as teams: boys versus girls. Little Nathaniel participated to some degree and also had a box of toys to play with as we prepared lunch.

As we ate together and enjoyed the mild breeze, fresh air, and sunshine, my heart was full of gratitude for so many blessings which Father had bestowed on me in recent months. By all out-ward appearances, no one would have noticed that anything had improved in my finances, job, health, or other circumstances. Yet things were different because I was different. Father had trans-formed my attitude and graced me with a fresh perspective after lifting me out of the mire of bitterness which had had me so beaten down. This had made all the difference in the world for me and my family.

I sat next to Elena at a park table at the pavilion which we had reserved for the afternoon. As I put my arm around her and smiled, I realized that I would not have been at this park in this moment enjoying the love and fellowship of great friends had it not been for Father's recent work in my heart. I whispered, *"Te amo, mi amor,"* to my wife and gave her a kiss.

Steve caught us and said, "You having a good day there, Brother?"

"Yes, I am."

"I think we all are," said Aby. "It's such a gorgeous day, and everything is so peaceful here."

154

"You're right, Aby," I replied. "And I just can't stop thanking Father for what he's done in me since March. If it weren't for him, I wouldn't be here enjoying this day with you all. I'd probably still be sulking at home, drifting farther and farther into bitterness. I just can't thank him enough. I'm so grateful that Tom invited us over for coffee that Monday night."

"But you didn't even have any coffee," said Tom playfully.

My smile grew wider. "You're right, but I got what I needed the most."

"It's encouraging to see the changes Father has made in your heart," he said, smiling. "Your blessing has become a blessing to us too."

"You know, for a while now I kept thinking that if only I had spoken to you sooner or brought Elena and Nathaniel over sooner or done *something* a certain way sooner, then it would have shortened the time of all that I put my family through."

"That's an easy game to play," Tom replied, nodding. "But as you've said yourself before, Father was orchestrating the events and sorting out the pieces. Matters of the heart take time and can't be rushed."

"Does that mean that there are no short cuts to spiritual healing?" inquired Steve.

"Maybe not in the way we think of short cuts. We can, however, turn to Jesus as soon as we realize that our hearts are not right. It may not provide an instant spiritual healing or solution— just like a physical injury takes time to heal—but it puts us on the right path. It's also one thing we can control: the choice we have to continue as we are or to seek Jesus for his grace to help in time of need. And Father is patient. He's used to waiting for the long-term goal. Just look how long he waited for the nation of Israel to turn around in the wilderness and in the Babylonian captivity. Even now, he still waits for the nation as a whole to turn to him. And it will happen one day in the future."

"Interesting," Steve said, pondering what he had just heard. "So many people struggle with bitterness, even believers in Jesus. Yet the details and reasons for one person's bitterness can be so

155

different from most other people's."

"Yeah," I admitted. "I can just hear some people saying, 'Your situation was easy because you just had some wrong thoughts about God. You didn't lose anyone through death or grow up an orphan or live with a debilitating disease or experience a divorce or lose your child, your house, your business, or everything you own, etc.' And, yeah, okay. So I *didn't* go through any of those things. My heart just aches for those who have had those devastating experiences and circumstances. I know quite a few people who have. I would never try to make light of anyone's suffering.

"But it doesn't change the fact that what I went through was still spiritually crippling bitterness. I'm still grateful for what Father has done to transform my heart. I know that I don't deserve the healing that he has worked in my hardened heart. I don't understand why he chose to do this in me when so many other people need this kind of breakthrough." Moisture clouded my eyes. "But I'm so thankful! I wish I could do something to help all those people and to encourage them to run to Christ and to allow him to heal them with his grace and love. He loves them so much, but I guess that they can't see that in the present due to their pain and hardships."

"You can still be an encouragement to others," said Tom in a placid voice. "Father delights in turning our sorrows into opportunities for ministry to others. And you're right, John; it was spiritually crippling. The details for each person's situation will be different, but the effects are about the same, though the intensity may also vary. What you and all those people have in common with bitterness is the distrust toward Father and the resulting distance you put between yourself and him. The wrong thoughts and unbiblical perspective that you had of him were byproducts of your own making from your experiences. Basically, you were in a difficult and disheartening situation where he didn't meet your expectations, so you felt like you couldn't trust him. At times we may not know him well enough from the Bible, walk with him closely in our daily lives, and surrender ourselves and our agendas to him and what he wants to do in our lives. When that's the case,

156

it becomes easy to form our expectations of him from what we see in the lives of others or from what we hear from the Christian community at large. Maybe not outwardly in your case but, in your heart, you began to grow cold toward Father and to distance yourself from him. To you he didn't seem to fulfill what you wanted him to do in your life, family, and ministry. During that whole time, your view of him changed a little here and there. You didn't realize that in your heart you were rewriting your whole theology about who you perceived Father to be to you. Perhaps you even used some Bible verses to justify those distrusting thoughts. Perhaps you slanted some scriptures to help yourself form this new theology, this different perspective about God.

"But Father's grace and love, poured out through Jesus and applied by the Holy Spirit, are always the cure. The details of how it all works out will be somewhat different for everyone. Notwithstanding, Jesus remains the fountainhead of God's grace and love and the treasure chest of all blessings, knowledge, and wisdom. If real hope, an effectual breakthrough of his grace and love, and genuine transformation are going to come at all, then they will only come from him. We can't simply conjure up or rationalize out our spiritual healing for ourselves. It's a work that only Jesus can do."

As Tom spoke, Steve chewed the last bite of his sandwich and displayed that look on his face, like the mental gears were turning. After he swallowed, he said, "Y'know, it sounds like the same kind of setup that Adam and Eve had in the garden. They had a limited knowledge and experience with Father. Then they were in the middle of the orchard where the snake was, who was selling a different view of God, one in which he was painted as untrustworthy. And this 'new theology,' so to speak, created a crossroads for them. The first man and woman each had to choose which view they wanted to believe: either that Father is trustworthy and loving with their best interests in mind or that he is untrustworthy and unloving, hiding what's best from them."

"I hadn't thought of it that way before, Babe," said Aby. "And now that you bring it up, I guess since the enemy was working through the serpent at that time, he probably moved him close to

157

the two trees. That way he would be in a prime location to talk them out of eating from the tree of life in case they were to head toward it."

"Well, what do you know?" Steve replied to Aby. "That could very well be the way it was. We're kinda speculating, since the text doesn't exactly give those details of locality and so on. But some of it can be inferred from the account, so it sounds plausible."

Sara began to put away some of the leftover food items as she said: "It sounds like the account of the temptation in Genesis 3 has more practical application to our lives than previously thought."

"Hmm," I pondered aloud. "I wonder how many situations and details in our daily lives are similar setups like that, where we are confronted with conflicting views of Father and have to choose which one to believe."

Tom pondered what we were saying, I'm sure of it. However, this was another moment where he allowed us the time and space to contemplate what we were discussing. A quick answer from anyone at that moment might have diverted us from what the Holy Spirit wanted each of us to take away from that part of the discussion.

After some time of silence, I said: "I'm also most thankful that Father led us to your house, Brother Tom, and used the situation to speak to my heart and even gave you the words to say. Words just can't express my gratitude."

"I understand. It all goes back to Father. You know that it would have been impossible for us to plan or anticipate what was going to happen that night. As always, Father remained sovereign through it all."

"Man," Steve interjected, "it must have been incredible! I can only pray that Father would use me in that way to encourage some-one else."

"It's no reflection on us, though," Tom admitted. "It's Father's handiwork among and through us. He usually does his best work in spite of us."

Then he turned to his wife. "Sara, would you share with them what you told me when we were discussing this topic just the other day?"

"Sure, if that would help." Sara cleared her throat. "We found out early in our ministry that we were no better or more spiritual than anyone else who loved Jesus." She grinned at us with raised eyebrows. "Big surprise, right? We just wanted to be a blessing to people who needed hope and encouragement. We told Father that we would be available for whatever he'd have us to do. That's basically what led us into missions—tribal work in particular. You see, as believers, we tend to believe that God won't use us. Maybe it's because we think that we're unworthy—as if it had anything to do with us." She stored the last couple of containers in a cooler that they had brought.

It sounded as if that's all she had to say, but I knew that I needed to hear more to understand fully what she meant.

"What do you mean, Sara, 'as if it had anything to do with us'?"

Sara turned her attention toward me. "This is something Father showed me many years ago. After we had worked ten or twelve years in the tribe, it suddenly dawned on me one day what was happening. The people were teaching each other, encouraging each other, praying with and for one another, and meeting each other's practical needs as things came up. They were being the body of Christ and letting Jesus flow through them, and it wasn't anything that we had done. We were simply there. We were just available. We went there to serve and to minister, true, but we were no super missionaries or special, spiritual people. We just spoke to the people when and what we thought Father wanted us to say to them, but it wasn't anything to do with us. Yet it's better that way, because then he receives the glory for it all, since it obviously wasn't anything we were capable of doing. We were basically just watching Jesus work among them."

"That," interjected Tom, "is God's grace in action: Jesus working in us and through us despite us since we really don't deserve anything anyway. All the glory for it belongs to him."

"Given that," began Steve, "could we say that preparing for mission work is basically preparing for what you know you need and then going to be available for whatever Father wants you to

159

say and to do?"

"That's basically it," Tom offered. "Missions is the ministry of letting Father express his heart of compassion, grace, and mercy through us to those in need. He does use us and work through our spiritual gifts as we function in the body. Functioning and using our particular gifts in the body of Christ is essential. That's why, wherever you are in the world, you needn't think that you're too unworthy for Father to work through you. Know that he *wants* to bless others through you. And abide in Christ, as he taught us in John 15. Be like a branch in the vine, depending on him and allowing him to flow and minister his grace and love through you. Be attentive to what he is showing you and where he is leading you by his Spirit so that he can make you a blessing to others. God's love for us, which indwells us and flows through us, reaches perfection in our love for others. It's like 1 John 4:12 says: 'If we love one another, God dwelleth in us, and his love is perfected in us.'*"

"Did you hear that, Aby?" Steve said excitedly, looking at her with his wide-eyed expression. "Father can perfect our love *wherever* we are in the world. Are you ready to pack your bags for Honduras?"

"Oh, I don't know," she said, flashing a quick, shy smile. "Let's talk to Father about that sometime."

Steve could have been kidding with her, but underlying his jest, he also may have meant what he said. Aby's family originated from Mexico, so she speaks Spanish, but she had never lived in Mexico other than visits for a few weeks at a time. Steve and I had both had a desire to return to Honduras on a more permanent basis. For the time being, however, it was just a wistful dream.

"Tom," I began, "what you talk about is so much easier to walk than what a lot of people preach about keeping rules to abstain from sin. I know that we've talked about legalism before, but I've always been curious as to how you learned all this freedom in Christ. I mean, I know that at least a couple of the local congregations you've been a part of in the past weren't all about celebrating our freedom in Jesus. It's the same with Steve and the church

160

environments in which he grew up. How did y'all either avoid or become free of the yoke of bondage of legalism?"

Tom took a sip of coffee from his trusty mug and looked around nonchalantly as he began to speak.

"For me, when Jesus got a hold of me in the military, I was hooked. Once I understood his great love for me, that's all it took. I knew I'd be his forever.

"Back in the early sixties, in the place where I was stationed there wasn't much in the way of a lot of ministries or outreaches to the military like there have been since. On weekends when most of the other guys were out on leave to pool halls, bars, and movie theaters, I pretty much stayed in the barracks and read my Bible. At that point, I didn't know much about how to read the Scriptures, and I didn't have any real resources to help me. However, I read as much of the Bible as I could, soaking in all that Father taught me. I just knew that he had to teach me, since I couldn't learn all this on my own.

"I was reading through the New Testament, and one day I read Paul's Epistle to the Galatians, which teaches about our freedom in Christ. When Paul wrote in Galatians 5:1, 'Stand fast therefore in the liberty wherewith Christ hath made us free, and be not entangled again with the yoke of bondage,'* I just believed it. So, I said, 'All right, Lord. You made me free, so I'm going to stand fast in that freedom and not be entangled with a yoke of bondage.' When Paul said later in verse thirteen, 'For brethren, ye have been called unto liberty; only use not liberty for an occasion to the flesh, but by love serve one another,'* then I just believed that too. I said to the Lord, 'I believe this one too, Lord. I'll not use my freedom as an opportunity to sin. Rather I'll serve others through love.' Then I read in verse sixteen where he said, 'Walk in the Spirit, and ye shall not fulfil the lust of the flesh.'* That's another one I believed. And I said, 'I'll take that one too, Lord.'"

Then he looked at us with a slightly more relaxed demeanor and a sudden impish grin, bordering on laughter.

"Now, I know this sounds like I was little Johnny Sunday School, just taking the Bible at face value and doing exactly what

161

it says. The truth is, I understood it and accepted it with my mind, but making it a part of my daily life took years. I had to be a student at Father's feet and let him teach me how to walk in the Spirit. And I failed many, many times. It used to make me so frustrated!

"Once in the heat of a battle with temptation, I just closed my eyes, and I told Father, 'Lord, I just can't do this anymore, so I'm just going to quit trying! If it's gonna happen, if I'm *really* gonna resist temptation, then *you'll* have to do it!' And to my surprise, the temptation just sort of lost its pull on me for that moment. And I opened my eyes, and I thought, '*Nothin's happened.*' And I looked around, and suddenly, I just didn't feel like giving in to temptation anymore. But that was just a first step for me. There were many more to follow.

"Now, I don't pretend to think that I've reached some spiritual plateau, because I haven't. But I know that as long as I'm surrendering to him—abiding in Christ, walking in the Spirit, letting him live his life through me, letting the word of Christ dwell in me richly (these phrases all mean the same thing, by the way)—then it's a battle against the flesh that I don't have to fight. Walking with him like this is something you don't perfect. You just look to him moment by moment to live it through you.

"And you know, I realize that in talking about this it's a lot of '*I* did this' and '*I* did that.' But that's not the way to understand it, because it's really about *Jesus* living in and through me, not about what *I'm* doing. And yet it's not passive. It's very active as I commune with him moment by moment.

"To answer your question, John, as long as Jesus is my life, then the laws, rules, and regulations just don't have any attraction to me or jurisdiction over me. There is no law against the fruit of the Spirit. That's a teaching from Galatians 3."

At first, I wasn't sure what to say. However, I did have a question.

"So, what did you do when those churches tried to impose their legalism on you?"

"I just didn't pay it any attention. I knew that Jesus had already said I was free from it all, because he himself freed me. Those rules that they set and tried to enforce and the intimidation and the pressure they placed on people to obey just didn't stick to me. Most of their rules had nothing to do with me because I was enjoying my walk with Jesus so much. I had no desire to do all those things that they were saying not to do anyway. If it ever came up in a discussion or a Sunday school class or something like that, I'd just say, 'Oh, I'm free from that anyway. Jesus would have to give me the desire to do that before it would have any sway over me.'"

My eyes grew large with amazement!

"And they accepted that answer?"

"No, not really. Some of them liked to control folks. They were confused by how I was neither breaking their rules nor heeding to them, giving them lip service. I didn't let those folks discourage or distract me from Christ."

"Amen, Brother!" interjected Steve with his characteristic, enthusiastic laughter.

I turned to Steve. "Okay, Flamen'. What's *your* story?"

"You basically know it already," he said nonchalantly. "I grew up in all the law culture, so I was exposed to it during an impressionable part of my life. I learned very early how to submit to it. I worked it so hard that shortly before I graduated from Bible college and soon afterward I got burned out on all the performance and demands."

"Was that about the time that you had scheduled every fifteen minutes of your day and endeavored to earn points to reward yourself with an hour of watching TV?"

"Good night, Brother!" he said chuckling. "You remember that?"

"How could I ever forget such a bizarre discipline system?" I replied with a grin.

Aby had a gawking, wide-eyed, incredulous look at Steve. "What was that, Babe?"

He giggled even more, and the rest of us joined in the fun.

"You should have seen his daily schedule, Aby," I offered good-naturedly. "He had it all written out in his Day-Timer, his daily planner. Everything was scheduled: meals, chores, daily devotions, exercise, work, study, sleep, and so on. And when he first showed me his schedule written out, he was so proud of his achievements! But there was a problem: he had every time slot allocated so that even when he fulfilled the whole regimen and earned an hour of watching TV, he didn't have time for it in his schedule!"

More laughter emitted from Steve, along with the rest of us.

"That's why I got so burned out," Steve replied, still laughing. "There was no time to enjoy anything."

"Steve, at least you learned that there's not much fun under law," said Tom, still smiling from our laughter. "You must have been highly motivated to give it up."

"Aw, man, that's so true," Steve admitted, finally reining in his laughter and composing himself. "But seriously, I really did burn out on all that stuff: the pressure to perform, the harsh expectations, the fatigue from so much church work and ministries day and night—the whole system of shame management."

"'Shame management'?" inquired Elena. "What is that?"

"Yeah, you know—the whole thing about rules and expectations that some congregations enforce on you to shame you when you don't meet their high standards. Instead of heralding Jesus' offer of grace and rest for weary souls, they work more toward a way to manage the shame as a motivator to get you to serve and to live godly. They don't want to remove the sense of shame completely, otherwise most people would feel so free that the leadership would fear that the members might lack the motivation to work the church programs and to keep the machinery going. Instead they just apply a little shame now and then as needed, managing it so that the different ministries keep going."

Tom said, "You mean saying things like, 'We're in need of workers for the nursery. Can't we have some volunteers to care for these precious little ones while their parents have the opportunity to hear the gospel in our services?'"

"Hey, that's pretty good, Brother Tom," Steve said in his levity voice. Then, changing to an announcer voice, he said: "We might recruit you as our ministry recruiter."

164

"To me," interjected Sara, "the legalism and shame management remind me of those talent show performers who used to spin plates on sticks long ago on TV." Her face lit up with a wide grin. "Sometimes they'd get ten or more plates spinning at the same time, just about head height." She began motioning with her hands. "And the audience is watching, and everyone is very impressed! The plates spin for a while, but then the person spinning them has to dash around and keep spinning them every few seconds to keep them from falling. After a couple of minutes, it becomes obvious that this guy can't keep these things going for very long. At some point they're going to fall. And sure enough, two or three start wobbling and slowing down simultaneously, then a few more follow suit. As the guy is running around in a panic, feverishly trying to get the wobbly plates spinning again, it catches up to him, and they all start to crash on the floor." Her laughter was contagious.

"I remember seeing those on TV in the seventies," I commented.

"Yeah, well that was entertainment back then," replied Sara, her laughter having mostly subsided, "watching some poor guy stress out trying to keep all those plates spinning."

Steve cleared his throat loudly. "I tried spinning plates for most of my life," he said with fake smugness in a character voice. "All it left me was *shattered* dreams."

"Oh, boy," said Tom. "We need to introduce you to Walter."

"Who's he?"

"He's a friend of ours, a good brother in Christ. His only downfall is his bad puns."

"Yeah," I agreed, "we'll have to introduce you two sometime, Flamen'. He's an encouraging brother. But let's get back to your story. What did you come to realize about the 'shame management' system?"

Steve sighed. "So much of that work and performance I did was all done in the flesh. I wasn't motivated by my love for Jesus; I felt pressured to perform, to measure up, to meet everyone's expectations of me. And because it wasn't done by the power of the Spirit and with the right motives, I suffered battle fatigue. Besides that, the fruit I bore wasn't fruit that remained like we read about in John 15. I think that because of all that, it burns out so many people. All the work and ministries are mostly done just to keep the machinery going and to keep the reputation of the church or the pastor in a glowing light. It's so that they can say, *'Look at us! We have ministries for the whole family! We have something for everyone! You're going to love our church! Come join us! Come grow with us!'* Never mind that the members are stressed to a frazzle trying to work all those programs and ministries to keep everything going. It may have started out as a desire to share Christ, to win the lost, and to advance the kingdom of God. But after a few years, you look back on it all, and you wonder whose kingdom you were really building."

"So then, the 'shame management' is just a tactic to get people to do what they want them to do?" I asked.

"That's about the gist of it. You know that the whole shame manipulation can't be from Father. We've already talked about how Jesus did all the work necessary to provide salvation as a free gift and that he wants us to rest from our works and to rest in him. Besides, Romans 8:1 teaches that Father doesn't employ things like condemnation, guilt, and shame in relationship with us. There's a *lot* of freedom in Christ. He motivates us by his grace and love for us, not by manipulating us with shame or fear."

"Right," I agreed. "So, the shame can only come from one of three sources: our own flesh, other people, or the enemy and his host."

"I think in this case it comes from people who probably mean well but don't realize what they're really doing to their brothers and sisters in Christ. They just think that they're teaching them to live holy, 'separated' lives."

"Yeah," I replied slowly. "Just think of what all that shame management to get people to perform is *really* teaching them about their walk and relationship with Christ."

There was silence as we each reflected on our own experiences with "shame management." Then a voice broke the silence.

166

"What people don't realize," Tom said, "is that they volunteer for the shame management by signing up as church members. It then becomes a dividing line of those who are 'in' and those who are 'out.' Membership brings with it a host of obligations, commitments, and loyalties. Then the pastoral staff can announce from the pulpit that they expect the members to agree with them on everything and to support everything they do without question. And those who dare to question pastoral decisions and the direction of the church are viewed as rebellious and divisive. But the church isn't an organization we join; it's a family we are born into through the new birth. The apostles didn't go around calling for people to join an institution they were starting. They preached Christ and him crucified, and they persuaded men and women of all ages and walks of life to *trust* the risen Savior so that they could have everlasting life through him. That's why formal membership isn't a biblical concept at all. It's a cultural device. It's just used to keep people in line. That's why we reject it."

Tom's comments really impacted me. I had known throughout my years of friendship with him that he was very passionate about the body of Christ. His stance on church membership made sense to me now, especially knowing his views on body life.

Tom realized that we were all gazing at him with new eyes, probably because most of us were hearing this perspective for the first time.

"I rattled on a bit too much," he said humbly. He smiled and motioned back to Steve. "Anyway, what were you two saying about what shame management teaches?"

Steve strained his eyes toward the distance and then remembered. "Just that it can adversely affect our walk with Christ. We can start to think that Jesus shames us like our brothers and sisters in Christ do just because we don't want to volunteer in the nursery or serve in the kitchen or help with the youth retreat or whatever."

This discussion about 'shame management' took me back to some of Walter's comments at the mall.

"And when we start feeling like Father is shaming us, it makes

167

it harder to approach his throne of grace confidently to receive mercy and grace when we need help, like Hebrews 4:15 tells us."

"You're right, Brother," concurred Steve. "When we treat each other like that, it only perpetuates that distancing and that sense of unworthiness before Father. It sounds more like something that the enemy does."

"Hmm," said Aby, pulling her long hair back and away from her face in the gentle breeze. "History is replete with examples of ecclesiastical leaders who have used peer pressure and social tactics to manipulate others to do what they wanted them to do. The same could happen in *our* gatherings as the body of Christ if we're not aware that it can happen so easily."

"You're right, Aby," I said. "And I agree with you too, Flamen'. We have to yield to what Jesus wants us to do, staying close to him so that he's the one directing us by his Spirit. We have to learn to say 'no' to anything he doesn't want us to spend our time, resources, and talents doing. Just because there are a lot of good activities and ministries which 'need' workers, it doesn't mean that we're called to every one of them."

"Yeah, well being a preacher's kid, I was made to feel like I was called to *all* of them. Eventually I got so burned out that I just cried out to Father. He directed me to Hebrews 4 and the genuine rest we can experience in Christ: rest from all the works, performance, and self-centered, merit-based approaches to the Christian life. I was so wiped out that I couldn't do any more. Eventually, I just had to drop out of all my ministry obligations and learn to say 'no.'"

"I bet that didn't go over well with the church family."

"Nah, they thought I was backsliden and rebellious," he replied nonchalantly. "But I had to go back to my first love. I had to look to Jesus and let him give me his rest. I started reading through the Gospels and Psalms again, just for the sheer delight of getting to know the Savior all over again. I especially read the Gospels over and over, trying to get a true image of Jesus' heart for people and how he related to them. Man, was it healing to my spirit! It was a soothing balm, and it really helped me recover from the ill effects that I had suffered under all the law and shame management that I had experienced."

"What did you say when people asked you why you weren't fulfilling those ministry obligations?" Elena inquired.

"I just told them the truth. I said that I was burned out and needed to rest. Then they would try to pressure me, saying things like, 'Well, Brother Steve, we really need you back in children's church, or the quartet, or this or that.' Or they'd say, 'It's just not the same without you.' Or, 'Our church really needs your talents and input.' One pastor even told me that if I didn't serve in the church, then I wasn't being a good steward of my spiritual gifts."

"Wow!" responded Aby. "That sounds like he was really pressuring you."

"He was, but I was just too exhausted. I had done so much for so long that I just couldn't do any more. I simply had to rest in Christ and let him restore my spirit."

Then an idea came to me. It was more of a question. Talking about the body of Christ in this light was helping me to view her from a fresh perspective.

"All of that pressure—and for what? Why does the church 'need' so many ministries?"

"Yeah, that's a question we should all ask," chimed in Steve, turning to Tom and Sara. "I was once part of a local body which boasted that they had forty-two different ministries. Can you imagine? And I was involved with eight of them."

"No wonder you were burned out," I observed.

"The apostles didn't need that many ministries in the New Testament," stated Sara. "You could make a biblical case that their only ministry was making disciples—according to Matthew 28:19 and 20. You might even argue that they didn't really plant churches, since Jesus said that *he* would build his church."

"The larger the local assembly," began Tom, "the more 'needs' are presented. Hence the more 'ministries' are believed to be required to meet everyone's 'needs' adequately. But if we view the body of Christ through the lens of a family, then things tend to work out a lot more simply. For example, as a family we all have the same Father and the same older Brother. As his spiritual children through the new birth, we each have his Spirit living in our hearts, who has placed us in the body and gifted us as he wills. We also have the Scriptures, so we already have all the resources we need for meeting one another's needs. The rest is more or less just loving people as Father loves them through us. According to Colossians 1:28 and 29, he will provide all the energy and strength we need for that. That's where Paul says about Christ, "Whom we preach, warning every man, and teaching every man with all wisdom; that we may present every man perfect in Christ Jesus: Whereunto I also labour, striving according to his working, which worketh in me mightily.'*'"

Here was the quote of another scripture passage which was somewhat familiar to me, though it was from an older translation. I thought to myself, *I have* got *to start bringing my Bible to these gatherings!*

"Hey, yeah," said Steve. "Ministry is making disciples with love as our motivation, and we minister empowered by Father's strength. He gave us the greatest commandment in John 13:34 and 35 when he said, 'I give you a new commandment—love one another. Just as I have loved you, you are also to love one another. Everyone will know by this that you are my disciples—if you have love for one another.'"

The greatest commandment? I had to process that one for a minute. My Bible college education and personal studies had always taught me something else.

"Hey, Flamen', I know that loving is the greatest commandment, but I thought that, more specifically, *loving God* is the greatest commandment. You know, like when Jesus was asked in Mark 12 what the greatest commandment was. 'Jesus answered, "The most important is: 'Listen, Israel, the Lord our God, the Lord is one. Love the Lord your God with all your heart, with all your soul, with all your mind, and with all your strength.' The second is: 'Love your neighbor as yourself.'"' So, isn't love for others the *second* greatest?"

"Love is simply the greatest period," Steve said calmly. "But at that time, Jesus was answering the question under the Old Covenant. That's why he quoted from Deuteronomy 6 and a verse from Leviticus. The whole Law of Moses was founded on those two principles of loving God and loving others. Therefore, even if we think of it from an Old Covenant perspective, love is still the greatest. But, as you already know, on the night before Jesus was crucified, he gave the Upper Room Discourse with a lot of teaching about the New Covenant and the soon-to-be-born church. You'll remember that this Covenant would be in force once Jesus resurrected just a few days later. He was about to show the disciples the greatest demonstration of love—his sacrifice for them and the whole world."

"Oh, yeah. You're right," I replied. "Since there would be a new dynamic of Jesus pouring out his love through us and toward others under the New Covenant, we would reciprocate that love toward him and be his vessel to shower it onto others too."

"That's it, Brother!"

"And that's a significant difference between the two," added Tom. "Under the Old Covenant, those commandments were really the stipulations Father set forth as Israel's side of their covenant relationship with him. They didn't have the Holy Spirit indwelling them then. However, under the New Covenant in Christ, Jesus' new commandment to love one another in John 13:34 was both a commandment and a promise. That's because we believers in the body of Christ now have the Holy Spirit to enable us to love one another—among other abilities. Now, you have to remember, Jesus' example was love unto sacrificial death. He really loved us to the end, unto death. He showed us how far true love will go, but he also gave us his Spirit to grace us with the ability to love—to that extent, if necessary."

"It's so sad," commented Aby, "that with the Holy Spirit in us and Jesus telling us to love one another that so many Christians have anything other than love for their brothers and sisters."

Tom nodded slowly. "That can be very telling in the life of an individual or a local body. But you're right. It is very sad and grievous to Father's heart. It would be to any parent whose

171

children didn't get along."

"It would do wonders for the cause of missions," said Sara, "for the people of the world to see those who make up the body of Christ demonstrating genuine love for each other. It makes it hard for people to believe we are his disciples if we all don't have his love for one another."

This juxtaposition brought a new realization to my mind. "I guess the legalists prefer to focus on the outward appearance rather than on the matters of the heart—like loving one another."

"Amen, Brother," said Steve. "It is bizarre how they get all upset about things like what believers wear, how they keep their hair, where they go, and some of the religious taboos *and* simultaneously practice and promote sins like manipulation, rejection, gossip, and outbursts of anger. It's just absurd!"

"Yeah. Hey, Flamen', what's that verse from 1 Samuel where God says he looks at the heart and not at the outward appearance?"

Steve was quick to answer. "That's from 1 Samuel 16, Brother. He said, 'God does not view things the way men do. People look on the outward appearance, but the LORD looks at the heart.' That's when Father sent Samuel to choose David as the next king. Remember? Samuel looked at Eliab's appearance and height and thought that God would choose him. Instead he chose David, a little shepherd boy. Father knew that David's heart was just the kind he wanted and the people needed in a king."

"If appearance is not that important, then why do legalists focus on it so much?" My question was really to anyone who would answer. As it turned out, Tom replied.

"It's a similar setup as when the Elders in the intervening years between the Old and New Testaments created and enforced new laws which went beyond the Torah under the Old Covenant. After the surviving Israelites returned from captivity in Babylon and Assyria to the Promised Land, they knew from the writings of the prophets that their captivity was a judgment for their many sins. It was because the nation as a whole had broken covenant with Father and followed idolatry.

172

"Therefore, after seventy years of captivity when the Israelites were released from bondage and allowed to return home, their leaders decided that in order to avoid any future captivities for generations to come they needed to add some 'hedge laws' to the Law of Moses. The 'hedge laws' were a body of laws which became known as 'the Traditions of the Elders.' They weren't actual laws from the Mosaic Law, but they were added to it as a sort of hedge or last defense to avoid breaking the actual God-given commandments. The traditional laws tended to be very strict and even far-fetched.

"For example, the Law of Moses said in Deuteronomy 14:21, 'Thou shalt not seethe a kid in his mother's milk,'* which meant boiling a young goat in its mother's milk. That was a pagan practice among idolaters in Canaan at the time. But the Elders decided to add a 'hedge law' which backed up a step even before that. It forbade the eating of goat cheese or milk and goat meat on the same day. The fear was the possibility of breaking the Mosaic Law because of the possibility that the milk in the cheese *just might* have come from the mother of the goat being eaten. They didn't want any 'boiling' going on with the two in anyone's stomach."

"Oh, my word!" Aby blurted out, amazed at the hurdles of reasoning required to fabricate such a 'law.'

"They reasoned that, if they could obey the 'hedge law' by not consuming goat dairy and goat meat on the same day, then they could rest assured that they wouldn't unintentionally break the Mosaic Law about boiling a goat in its mother's milk.

"There were many of those kinds of 'hedge laws' passed on to future generations. By the time of Jesus' incarnation in the early first century A.D., those traditions had gained a weight of authority in Israel equal to that of the Law itself. That's why there was such conflict between Jesus and the Pharisees. They were trying to defend the Traditions of the Elders on equal par with the Law of Moses. That's what all the commotion was about with their accusations that Jesus was 'breaking the Sabbath' by healing the sick or eating a handful of grain on the Sabbath, and so on. He was really just going against their man-made traditions, not the Old

173

Testament Law itself."

Steve commented: "It sounds like it was a system of rules based on fear—fear of another captivity."

"You're right, Steve, it was," Tom agreed. "Having had those captivities in their history and being willing to do anything not to repeat another, the Pharisees and Jewish leaders felt more than a little skittish about being subject to Roman rule. The Jews were still allowed to practice Judaism and to keep their nation, their land, their temple, the sacrifices, and the priesthood. However, they feared that one day it would all be taken away from them—which did happen decades later."

"Good night!" exclaimed Steve. "It sounds like 'perfect obedience'—or at least the outward appearance of it—was their goal. I guess that the contemporary legalists in the body of Christ today have a fear of displeasing Father and just want to obey as much as possible so as to please him—even though he's already pleased with us in Jesus because of what he did for us on the cross."

All this talk about legalism and obedience reminded me of an earlier conversation that I had had with Steve.

"Tom, a while back, Steve and I had a conversation about legalism and about how, when we first trusted Jesus, we were so excited and felt so loved that we delighted to do anything to please him, even submit to a bunch of man-made rules that we thought he wanted us to follow. How do we view that period in our lives now, since we didn't realize what we were doing at the time?"

"Father knew your hearts," Tom began simply. "He knew you were motivated by love to live for him and to please him, even though he was already pleased with you for Jesus' sake and because of his righteousness imparted to you. Remember: he looks at our hearts."

"So then, it was okay that we followed those rules?"

"I would say that your motives for following them were pure enough. From your perspective, you were expressing your love for Jesus—at least in the beginning like most believers. Some go for many years or even most of their lives caught up in the man-made rules. Eventually a number of them see through the smoke

174

and mirrors, tire of trying to please men, and begin to sense a dissatisfaction in it all. This is because it can easily be done in the flesh, and it's no substitute for intimacy with Christ. Whether they realize it or not, they experience a crisis of sorts in their legalistic walk. They see some inconsistencies, Phariseeism, pride, judgmental attitudes, and sometimes even some gross immoral sins in the whole system. Then they begin to wonder about and question things, either openly or secretly. Meanwhile Jesus has been there all along, ready to walk them out of it—if they so choose. But as far as you two are concerned, since then you've seen the errors of that whole system and are seeking Father to remove all vestiges of legalism. Therefore, as far as that goes, just as with other erroneous things in your past, don't sweat it."

I was grateful to hear that even this was resolved by Jesus' work. But Tom's mention of Jesus "being there all along" piqued my interest even further.

"You mean that Jesus just sort of waits to act until people choose to leave legalism?"

Tom's look was a bit pensive as he took a sip from his coffee mug. Then he answered.

"He did give us a free will to choose how we want to live. Some people start on the path of legalism and find that they really like it for whatever reason. And he does relate to each one of us as individuals, so he's known since before the dawn of Creation who would struggle with the system of rules and who would pursue it gladly. His grace is always there for us so that we can escape that system once we're ready. He's always there to teach us truth and to shower us with his grace upon grace, so it's an active waiting. And his love for us all never changes. He continues to relate to us like any compassionate parent who disagrees with their adult child's choices but keeps their relationship ongoing because of love. After all, whether we stay in a legalistic system or choose to leave it, we're still his kids. Yet he knows that we'll have more joy and satisfaction if we're not playing those games."

"That's it then," Steve announced in a definitive tone. "From now on, no more games. I choose *not* to be a part of the legalism any longer."

"That's great, Brother Steve," replied Tom. "I know that this is something you've been turning from most of the years that I've known you. I have, too. However, sometimes there's a little lingering legalistic residue that we have to let the Holy Spirit work out of our hearts, whether it's boasting, self-confidence, judgmental attitudes toward others, or independence from Jesus. Now, I'm not saying that I see any of those things in you," he added with a silly grin. "I'm really speaking about believers in general. This residue can take many different forms. While walking in this freedom in Christ can have its challenging moments from time to time, it's really fun because you get to see the Spirit working in your life, making you more like Jesus. So, don't get discouraged when he shines his light on an area in your life that needs his work. Be grateful that he's blessing you and lovingly taking the time to perfect in you the work that he began and that only he can do."

"You're right," conceded Steve contentedly. "I can't say that I've 'arrived' either. But I'm his, so it can be encouraging and exciting to see him continue to teach me and mature me in Christ."

As enlightening as this discussion was, I still had a burning question about obedience. "But if we truly love Jesus, we'll obey him, right? Isn't that what he said in John 14:15?"

"That's a common misinterpretation," Tom answered casually. "We've been made to believe that we prove our love for Jesus by obeying him, but that's not the intent of that verse.

"It's possible to go through the motions of obeying commandments while not being motivated by love. People do it every day. No, it's not that we obey *because* we love him or to *demonstrate* or to *prove* our love for him. It's that we love him because he first loved us and filled us with his love, and the *result* is that—in response to his love and grace and the Holy Spirit working in and through us—our lives reflect a walk of obedience to him. Do you see the difference there?"

"Sounds like a cart-and-horse thing," interjected Steve, pondering the statement aloud. "You're saying that if we allow his love to fill us and to characterize our hearts and lives, then the obedience will follow."

"See?" replied Tom with a smile. "You said it better than I did."

"Let me get this straight," I added. "Instead of taking that verse to mean, 'If you love Jesus, then you'll show it by obeying his commandments,' we should understand it to mean, 'If you're focusing on loving Jesus, then the byproduct will be acts of obedience evident in your walk with him."

"That's another great way to put it," encouraged Tom.

Aby's face lit up suddenly. "Well, then, if we just enjoy our relationship with Father, abiding in Jesus and allowing him to work in our hearts and lives, then we don't even have to worry if we're keeping the commandments. It will happen just as a result of us loving him and fellowshipping with him. Is that right?"

"You understand it better than I do, Aby," Tom replied, still smiling. "The Spirit within us will guide us and give us the desires of our hearts. He'll also let us know if we start to stray from the path of righteousness. Since we're accountable to Father and not to people, we can trust him to lead us into righteousness as we fellowship with him. As 1 John teaches, it's walking with Father *in* the light, not *according* to the light, the latter which would mean we'd never sin. That's not what that passage teaches."

"Wow!" she said coolly. "That really takes away all the pressure!"

Steve rejoiced in her understanding. "Doesn't it, Babe? And just think of how a lot of denominational leaders have used that verse as a tool to manipulate people to follow their rules and expectations."

"Making an effort to live a life of obedience in an attempt to fulfill that verse really *is* putting the cart before the horse."

"Hey, that's my babe!" Steve leaned over and gave her a kiss. Aby was all smiles.

I still had more questions for Tom.

"Okay, Brother Tom, I have another question. When people and churches make a list of rules to follow which are not even in the New Testament, it probably has little to do with love, right?" I asked slowly.

"It basically has to do with controlling the membership," he replied bluntly, "which brings us back to that unbiblical tradition of becoming a member."

"In which case, for a lot of folks, their Christian life or church life is about control and manipulation," I observed. "The laws really serve *their* purposes then."

"But, John, remember that law can't touch us believers, especially those of us who understand our freedom in Christ and are persuaded of his unshakable love for us. Paul says in Galatians that he's dead to the Law, just as we are in Christ Jesus. It's like punching a corpse. The force of impact is real, but it won't do any good because the corpse can't feel a thing."

Steve said, "Since we're yielding to Christ and letting him live and love through us, their laws have no effect on us. And concerning the *real* Law, Romans 10:4 says, 'For Christ is the end of the law, with the result that there is righteousness for everyone who believes.'"

"Amen, Brother Steve," Tom agreed. "We must remember that the Holy Spirit is a consummate gentleman. He won't force us or manipulate us to do anything against our wills. He will ask and try to persuade us, but he doesn't threaten us or twist our arms. He persuades with love, not force, guilt, or threats of any kind. In fact, 'persuade' is a key word in the New Testament. Do a word study sometime on 'persuade' and its other forms. You'll see that it is used very carefully. For example, Paul said that in his preaching of the gospel, he *persuaded* men. He presented the truth to them in a clear and understandable way. Then he respected them enough to allow them to choose freely whether or not to embrace it and to trust Christ. He communicated the very heart of God and his love to those who would listen. And each time, some chose to believe and others didn't. It's a ministry of persuasion, not coercion."

This perspective was so refreshing, like a cool breeze on a hot, arid day! Where had this kind of teaching been all my life? In all my years of Bible college, minister fellowships, and some of the other circles in which I had fellowshipped, I had never before heard these teachings. Granted that in those groups there was often some skirting around the issues to make it sound like we all believed in trusting Christ for our walk in him. However, it was mostly a token acknowledgment. There was hardly any real grace teaching about how to live this life in Jesus. What I did hear was a lot of teaching about duty, discipline, and responsibility. There was also a lot of talk about working and doing for God instead of yielding to him and letting him work in and through us. It was mostly a concentration on human effort, making most of the Christian life dependent on the believer. It was more man-centered than God-centered.

"This is all so freeing!" I exclaimed joyfully. "We have all this freedom in Christ. Is there anything that we *can't* do?"

My question was met with silence at first. I looked around to see if anyone would answer. Finally, Tom broke the silence.

"You are free in Christ to do *anything*. And yes, that even means that you are free to sin—even those terrible sins you hear about on the six o'clock news which other people commit. We still have Father's gift of free will. Likewise, his salvation is free, graciously given to us and secured for us for all eternity. However, if you're walking in Jesus—abiding in him, being filled with the Spirit, letting his word richly dwell in you—then he'll *give* you the desires of your heart. The old, sinful practices of your former life will not have much appeal to you as *he* becomes your life more and more. It's not that you'll want to run out and do a lot of wickedness. Rather you'll enjoy intimacy with Christ so much that you won't *want* to do those things. But again, it's not so much you doing anything. You're really just yielding to him and allowing *him* to do the work in and through you."

"But, when we talk about yielding to Jesus and letting him live through us, we're not talking about sinless perfection," stated Steve.

"Right, Steve. All our goodness and righteousness come from Jesus, not from our self-centered, fleshly efforts which we attempt apart from him. *He* produces the fruit of the Spirit in our lives, not we ourselves. *He* is the vine, and *we* are the branches. As I mentioned before, Galatians teaches that there is no law against the fruit which the Spirit bears in our lives. We won't live perfectly sinless lives, true, but the general character of our lives will be God-centered and Christ-honoring. And when we sin, we confess it, looking to him for his grace to cleanse us and to restore us to fellowship with him once again. After all, we are born again as new creations in Christ, the Second Adam.

"The problem comes when we let our sins fester without confessing them. It really doesn't make any sense *not* to go to Father with our sins. We're already forgiven eternally because of having trusted in Jesus and what he did for us. Therefore, the security of our salvation isn't the concern here. The kind of forgiveness we need spoken of in 1 John 1:9 is for *restored fellowship*. That much is clear in the context of the Apostle John's epistle. When we sin, what we need most is a fresh cleansing and restoration of fellowship with Father. He provides them when we confess our sins to him as that verse assures us. Our confession to him is us remembering and admitting how much we need Jesus every moment of every day. Our sins are evidences of those moments when we've tried to strike out on our own and to act independently of him. And Father doesn't use our prayer time as a chance to browbeat us, so to speak, with shame or guilt." He gave me a knowing look, with a sort of twinkle in his eye. "By now you're probably persuaded from the Scriptures that he doesn't do that to us. And he always welcomes us back, naturally. *He loves us!* We're his children, and he wants our fellowship with him to be restored even more than we do. So, you see why the enemy wants to discourage us from turning to Jesus when we sin. It's because he knows that we receive restoration and cleansing when we do. That's why he'll feed us negative thoughts about Father when we sin. It's all an attempt to build a barrier or wall between us and Father. He's not called the adversary and deceiver for nothing, you know."

"That was a big part of my bitterness for years," I admitted somberly. "I tried to confess my sins, but I looked at confession as shamefully admitting to failures that I couldn't conquer. To me it felt like a browbeating every time. I felt so guilty, and I don't know why, but I thought that *I* had to fix the problem myself before I could come to Father and ask for his help. That's why prayer wasn't fun anymore."

Elena's eyes were doleful. She gazed on me with compassion as I spoke, wrapping her arm around me. "Oh, Honey! You never told me that you were going through all that. Why didn't you say anything when you were having those struggles?"

"How was I supposed to talk about this?" I said, sighing. "*I* was the missionary, the husband, and the leader of the home. *I* wasn't allowed to have such struggles and problems with prayer and my relationship with Father—or at least that's what I believed. Besides, I was so cruel to you at the time, with all my anger, arguing, complaining, and bitter attitude. I knew that my prayer life was being hindered because of the way I treated you, but I just didn't know what to do about it. Everything seemed to close in around me." Just thinking about the way I had treated my wife made my eyes watery. "I'm so sorry for what I did to you, Elena, and I never want to mistreat you again. But I'm so imperfect that I fear I may do something like that to you again."

I suddenly held her tightly and buried my face on her shoulder. The tears flowed again, though not so harshly as before. Elena would never know how often I had wept in recent months, reflecting on the many vivid experiences I still carried of times when I had made her weep bitterly for hours on end due to my selfishness and hardheartedness. When I was alone at work or driving, I would remember those times, and tears would stream down my face. I was so blessed to have her in my life. Why did I ever abuse her so cruelly?

A little hand patted my head.

"What's wrong, Daddy?"

I looked up. It was Nathaniel. He had approached me, seeing us both looking sad, when we were now on the backside of sadness, dawning toward joy. I gazed at my little boy and pulled him in to include him in our embrace. "Nothing's wrong, Nathaniel. I love you so much, my precious son!"

181

"Don't cry, Daddy." His eyes examined me, as if trying to solve a puzzle. His expression made him seem wise beyond his years, yet I knew he couldn't discern tears of joy from tears of sorrow, which mine were initially.

"Okay, Son. I won't," I said, wiping away the tears. "I love you with all my heart, Nathaniel." I kissed his cheek and held him tightly.

"Our precious, little Nathaniel," Elena said, smiling and stroking his hair.

[1] Galatians 5:1a
*KJV

CHAPTER 9

LIVING LIKE THE OLD UNDER THE NEW

We finished cleaning up our area of the pavilion and had a moment for a restroom break for those of us who needed it. A few of us took a refill of soda, tea, or water. We returned to our seats at the picnic table, none of us ready to conclude our time together. It was still early afternoon. The sun shone brightly high above the trees, many of which shaded our area. A warm breeze blew gently, carrying a scent of honeysuckle, as the sounds of children playing in the distance fell softly on our ears. The weather and day were perfect.

Personally, I was so full of joy and thankfulness yet again that I sensed there was more encouragement to come from our time together. I love these people—my friends, my brothers and sisters in Christ. The fellowship we had experienced over the past few months was so exhilarating and inspiring. I hope for everyone to know this kind of encouragement.

"Tom," began Steve, "I really enjoy this freedom in Christ. Just knowing that I'm free to choose to live as I want really makes all the difference. But I also see the folly of sin, and it's not something I want to run into headlong."

"I'm glad to hear you say that," replied Tom. "Many completely misunderstand this freedom given us in Jesus. They think, 'We're forgiven and can do anything we please? Well that's just great! I have a list of sins right here that I've been hankering to commit!' But as we steep ourselves in the Scriptures and walk with Father, we realize that sin is *not* something desirable. That's the thing we *don't* want to do. But not because there's a list of man-made expectations for us to follow to feign some showy, man-made righteousness. Neither is it because we'll forfeit our salvation if we commit certain transgressions. In fact, our freedom in Christ means that we are free from sin's power, among other things. When we were spiritually dead in our old life, submitting to temptation was our default way of living because of our bondage to sin. Now in Christ, however, we have his power and victory over temptation and sin. Now we can choose righteousness over sin.

"But there's much more to it than that. Sin is folly. It's foolishness. It brings only death, loss, and destruction. Sin is shackles which we've been freed from. It simply makes no sense to pursue that same pattern and lifestyle. Paul said in Romans 6, 'How shall we, that are dead to sin, live any longer therein?'* So as believers in Christ, we're dead to it; we're separated from it and therefore don't have to surrender to temptation. It would be non-sense and foolishness to want to run back into sin. Spiritually speaking, we were raised in Christ to walk in newness of life. The apostle also said in Romans 6, 'Knowing this, that our old man is crucified with him, that the body of sin might be destroyed, that henceforth we should not serve sin.'* Therefore, sin is a mocker. It's slavery to the very thing that poisons us spiritually and distances us from Father, breaking our fellowship with him. It's much better to serve Father than to serve sin."

"I agree," Steve said firmly. "Romans 6 is one of the key scriptural passages for understanding the argument against sin. In fact, chapters six through eight are probably my favorite section in the Bible. They're so instructive and encouraging in our relation-ship with Jesus.

"I also like what Romans 6:11 says: 'So you too consider yourselves dead to sin, but alive to God in Christ Jesus.' This teaches us that spiritually speaking, we're dead to sin, all because of what Jesus did for us and worked in us. The next few verses talk about not letting sin have mastery over us. So, I see what you mean about sin being slavery."

"Could we also say," I asked, trying to process and to apply what I had learned from the previous conversation, "that *legalism* could likewise have mastery over us if we're not careful?"

"That's what I'd say," answered Steve. "It was for freedom that Christ set us free. And it's a freedom for many things, but he also freed us from the Law to be related to him and to enjoy knowing him as we walk with him moment by moment. That's what

Romans 7:4 teaches us. It says, 'So, my brothers and sisters, you also died to the law through the body of Christ, so that you could be joined to another, to the one who was raised from the dead, to bear fruit to God.'"

Tom nodded in agreement. "Yes, our freedom in Christ is a wonderful and magnificent blessing. And you know that we Americans are all about freedom. But in this case, we were freed from sin *and* the Law to be joined to the one who loves us infinitely beyond our comprehension. Hence, we are bought with a price to serve our beloved Lord. Also, we're like the younger son in the Luke 15 parable who returns to his father with nothing but trusts that his father will care for him and provide for him, even if it's as a hired servant. At least that's what he had thought."

"Those are examples that Steve and I have talked about before," I observed. "How cool that these teachings overlap!"

Steve started fidgeting like he was about to say something grand.

"I'll tell you what, brothers and sisters," he began, "I don't need some flaming legalist to hit me over the head with a Bible, telling me what I should and shouldn't do. I don't have to follow other people's rules and expectations, but I don't want to run into licentiousness either. I just want to bask in Father's grace and to enjoy walking with him, both in my relationships and in everything I do."

"Well, *'amen'* to that, Brother," Sara said decisively as she plopped down her cup.

"I have another question," I said with a smidgen of hesitation.

"Well now, Brother," Steve said in a baritone character voice. "Aren't you just full of questions today?"

"As always," I admitted. "Here's my question: What do we do to help legalists to recognize and to appreciate their freedom in Christ? I mean, how can we break their shackles or at least give them the keys, as it were?"

"That sounds like a job for the Holy Spirit," answered Steve. "I don't think that arguing with them and blasting them with Bible verses would help in any way. It would just cause them to be guarded and suspicious of you. Afterward they wouldn't want to discuss the topic any further with you. I know because I used to be entrenched in all that stuff."

Elena seemed surprised at this admission. "Steve, *you* were a legalist?"

He faked a blush, facetiously batting his eyes. "It's true—little ol' me!" Then he struck a pose like some kind of actor or body-builder, making his small waist seem even thinner. "I'm not a real Pharisee," he said in a serious-sounding announcer voice, flexing his arms as he showed first his left profile and then his right, "but I play one at church!"

This display was good for a few laughs, including Steve's own.

"Okay, Flamen'," I said, reining in the moment to get us back on topic. "So, I'd have to be diplomatic and *persuasive*. Well then, how did you really break free from it?"

"For me, I was broken and fatigued by all the works, performance, and rule-keeping. Like I said earlier, it just literally burned me out. I think Father allowed me to get to that point and then directed me to some key scriptures like Hebrews 4, Romans 6, 7, and 8, and Galatians. Yeah, especially the book of Galatians. I memorized several passages—like Galatians 2:20—that helped me to get Father's perspective. I believe that once I was at that point of desperation, then I was open in my spirit and ready to hear what Father wanted me to receive in those passages. It took a while for me to be convinced—I mean *persuaded*—that what Father was teaching me from those scriptures was not some excuse for disobedience to the things I didn't like about churchianity. That's when I *really* had to lean on the Lord, walking in his love, to guard me from swinging toward the opposite extreme of a life of blatant sin. For most of my life, my heart had been disposed to conform to the rules because I wanted to please Father. Once I learned that I had been deceived by the legalism most of my life, some serious indignation flamed up in me, and I didn't want it to be used to fuel a rebellious reaction, plunging me into worldly sins. However, I know that not all legalists will be like me and have that kind of burnout and rage followed by a deep longing for closeness with Jesus. Some of them will have their own struggles with bitterness, especially after they realize that they had been deceived by people when they thought that they were obeying Christ the whole time. Learning the truth can be a rude awakening and not so easy for everyone to accept."

"People who have this law problem in their lives," Tom began, "are not usually open to considering this understanding of our freedom in Christ as taught in the New Testament—not unless they are open to God's grace like Steve was after what he experienced. If you don't have the kind of caring friendship with them in which you have earned their trust, and if they don't understand that you care for them and have what's best for them in mind, then you will not have an audience with them on this subject. They will likely feel threatened or feel like they're being forced into believing and practicing something that they've always believed was wrong. Then you'll no longer be viewed as a friend but as an enemy. Just imagine how you would feel if someone tried to convince you to believe something contrary to what you've always accepted as true. Then you'll understand why they will resist this teaching.

"And if these truths are not presented carefully and according to the Spirit's leading and in his way and timing, some individuals will become embittered toward God. They'll blame him for the mistakes of men, once they realize how deceived they have been for so long. In such cases those folks have been known to run headlong into the sins of the world like Steve said, rebelling against anything resembling or even mentioning Jesus, church, or the Bible. I've seen it happen many a time."

"Oh. Okay," I replied soberly. "I don't want to cause *that* to happen. So, Father's grace would have to rescue those people who become embittered and blame him and rebel against him, right?"

"Exactly. His grace and love can heal anything and cover a multitude of sins. The rebellious may have to run the same cycle as the younger son in the parable we just mentioned. You all know the parable. He got a glimpse of 'freedom' out from under his father's authority and ran with it to a far country, squandering his inheritance. But when the hard times hit and he was humiliated by the consequences of his sinful lifestyle, then he came to his senses

187

and realized how foolish he was to leave his father. It can be a rough time for them during that rebellious stage, but the Holy Spirit will draw them with cords of kindness, seeking to rescue them from it and to turn them back to Father."

"Wow! It's a really fragile situation then." The serious reality of attempting to talk someone out of legalism didn't look like something in which I should be involved.

"Look, John," added Steve, "it's best to begin by bathing the whole situation and individual in prayer—lots of prayer. Just ask Father for his direction and see where he leads you. You'll never know how you can be instrumental as an encouragement in someone else's life like that. Just don't blurt out something offensive to them. And don't slap a book about grace or legalism into their hands either, unless you're absolutely sure in your heart and spirit that Father is leading you to do exactly that. That can easily be taken the wrong way as well."

"Hmm. It really is the Spirit's work then."

"It is, and you don't want to try to force anyone out of something by shattering his or her ideology. I've seen people do that— y'know, try to 'play Holy Spirit' in someone's life. Needless to say, it never ends well for either party involved."

"However," inserted Tom, "if Father impresses someone on your heart, it's usually for a good reason. And you can always pray for him or her if nothing else. Consequently, don't be afraid to love people and pray for them. Just be sure that Father is leading you before you say anything in this realm of correction. He'll let you know what to say or to do if it's his will."

Aby let out a sigh. "It's so sad that this freedom in Christ is misunderstood by so many. You would think that people would want to enjoy this freedom instead of submitting themselves to law all over again."

"They want to enjoy their walk with Christ," replied Tom, "but they're also aware that the enemy of our souls is very crafty. He has led many astray into error. Yet Father always remains sovereign. Remember 1 John 4:4: 'greater is he that is in you than he that is in the world.'* God often works behind the scenes and in people's hearts in ways that we couldn't imagine. Therefore, we often have to learn to be patient and to leave him space and opportunity to work.

"You can also look at it this way, Aby: If we didn't have such great freedom in Christ, then it wouldn't be so misunderstood. Then Paul wouldn't have had to keep explaining and defending our freedom in Christ through his letters. In this regard, it's interesting to note that his epistles frequently have an overall, sweeping theme of grace versus law or grace versus the flesh."

As Tom spoke, another scripture came to my mind.

"I just remembered a few verses in Colossians 2, which read, 'If you have died with Christ to the elemental spirits of the world, why do you submit to them as though you lived in the world? "Do not handle!" "Do not taste!" "Do not touch!" These are all destined to perish with use, founded as they are on human commands and teachings.'"

"Great passage, Bro!" exclaimed Steve. "Legalism really is a bunch of man-based teachings and rules. They often make sense as far as avoiding certain sins, and they may even *look* like God's laws. The enemy uses legalism to exploit people's hearts and good intentions of wanting to live for Jesus. We don't always realize that by obeying those rules in the energy of the flesh we're really just convincing ourselves that we can live a life that *looks* righteous apart from fellowship with Christ, even though it's just on the outside. All the while, we're 'obeying' in the flesh, independent from Jesus and intimacy with him. Nevertheless, dependence on the flesh for the appearance of obedience or outward conformity is no substitute for abiding in Christ."

"It's interesting yet sad," commented Sara, "how the enemy takes our good intentions and tries to use them against us in our relationship with Father."

"That is very telling," observed Tom, "because the deceiver tries to twist and to pervert our very understanding and view of Father. He knows that the Almighty is *the* infinite resource for us amid all the stresses and problems which we encounter in life. He also knows that he can't sever our relationship with Father.

However, if he can 'muddy the waters,' then he can frustrate our prayer life and walk, making us ineffective."

"Somehow," I said slowly, "that sounds familiar. Hmm."

I got that knowing look from the group.

"He really seems to delight in deceiving us," added Steve. "The enemy can get us to follow a bunch of rules and can make us think that we're depending on the Spirit when in reality we're depending on our own flesh. What a deception!"

"It appears," Tom began, "that most if not all the legalism I've encountered looks very similar to precepts lifted from the Law of Moses in the Old Testament. That makes it often look like those believers are still living in the days before Jesus' passion and resurrection. It practically always focuses on externals. They're things like dress codes, hair length and styles, whether and how much makeup women can wear, the kinds of places believers aren't allowed to go, certain activities which believers can't do, disciplines which they are required or expected to do, and so forth."

Suddenly, Tom had a raised eyebrow and a twinkle in his eye. "By the way, while we're on the subject, do you all know the five key differences between the two covenants or two testaments?"

"I must have missed that day in Bible college," replied Steve.

"You may find it helpful to understand the key distinctions, especially concerning this issue of grace versus legalism."

"Uh, okay," I said a bit frantically as I searched for a pen and paper in one of the bags we brought. "I'll probably need to write this down."

Tom smiled enthusiastically. "Don't worry, John. There are only five major differences, and I'm sure you'll be able to remember them."

I acquiesced in mid-search. "Well, okay." Not wanting to forget what I was about to hear, I still wished for a pen and paper during most of the time that he spoke.

"Okay. Now, this is not to insult your intelligence, because you probably already know ninety percent of what I'm going to tell you. Very little of this will be things you haven't heard or studied before. It's just that you may not have tied together some of these points from this perspective.

"First we'll start with the Old Covenant features. In the Old Testament, the Israelites had the Law, the temple, the priesthood, the sacrificial system, and the Sabbath. These really defined their covenantal relationship with God as a people. The relationship was initiated by God with Abraham, but it came into full force with all these features under Moses. It all took place in the land of Israel, which had been promised by God to Abraham and his descendants.

"The Law was given to Israel under Moses; hence it's referred to as the Law of Moses. It includes the famous Ten Commandments plus many more for a grand total of 613 total laws. The Law prescribes practically every aspect and detail of life and culture for Israel. In fact, it prescribes these other four features of the Old Covenant.

"In the wilderness under Moses' leadership, the tabernacle was the first meeting place or place of ritualistic worship. It was basically a tent with specific features and rooms surrounded by a fence. The priests served there, offering sacrifices and performing other rituals. Under Solomon, the tabernacle was replaced with the temple building, built of brick and mortar. That first temple was destroyed by the Babylonians, but a second temple was built over seventy years later under Nehemiah. That one was destroyed by the Roman general, Titus, in A.D. 70. In the second century A.D., the Romans built a temple to their god Jupiter on that same spot. After the Roman Empire fell, the Muslims built the Dome of the Rock on that same location in the seventh century A.D. Now, without the temple structure, the people of Israel today can't fully practice their rituals, particularly the priesthood and the animal sacrifices.

"In the Law, God ordained the priests to come from the tribe of Levi. There were many priests as well as other workers called Levites, but only one man at a time served as the high priest. The priests spoke to God on behalf of the people. (As a side note, the prophets spoke to the people with messages from God.) The high priests were the only ones privileged to go before the manifest presence of God in the holy of holies in the tabernacle or temple, but always with the blood of an animal sacrifice.

"The system of animal sacrifices was prescribed by the Law of Moses to be carried out by the priests—no one else. The most important sacrifice every year was offered on the Day of Atonement, and it was only presented by the high priest. It was a spotless lamb offered to make a covering of the sins of the nation once a year.

"Finally, there was the Sabbath, the seventh day of the week, which the Law prescribed as a holy day of rest for the nation. No work of any kind could be done on that day. It reminded the people of how Jehovah ceased from his work after the six days of Creation.

"In summary, we see that the five primary features of the Old Covenant are the Law, the temple, the priesthood, the sacrifices, and the Sabbath. Any questions so far?"

We were all quiet. What Tom said was very clear and understandable, but Steve just had to say something.

"No question, really," Steve said, breaking the silence, "but now I see why you said we already know most of this."

Tom chuckled. "These are pretty basic points. It's really the New Testament distinctions I'm working toward that are most significant.

"Under the New Covenant in Jesus Christ, we have five different features which somewhat correlate to and oppose the five features of the Old Covenant. Instead of the Law of Moses, we have the Holy Spirit living in our hearts, enabling us and giving us the grace necessary to live a life which honors Father. So rather than us trying to be good and to live righteously on our own, we have the Spirit to enable us with God's grace.

"Instead of the temple as a sacred place, now everywhere we go is holy, because we are aware of his presence with us everywhere. So not only does he accompany us through the Holy Spirit within us, but he is also already present everywhere. His omnipresence is comforting to us, because we know that, no matter where we go, we're always in the presence of our ever-loving Father. He's always available to help us with his grace, mercy, love, and all that he is.

"Instead of a formal, institutional priesthood, all of us who are part of the body of Christ are priests. We have direct and immediate access to the Father through Jesus. This is an important New Testament teaching referred to as the priesthood of the believer. There are no celebrities, superstars, big shots, or little shots in the church. We are all equal in Christ, and we all may pray to Father directly whenever we want. There is no human mediator between us and God. Jesus, who is both God and man, is our only mediator, and we each have direct access to him.

"Instead of dead animal sacrifices, we ourselves present our lives as living sacrifices unto Father, as explained in Romans 12:1. This is how we worship God—not through special music or 'worship' services, but by yielding our lives unto him. We die to self, submitting, yielding, and surrendering unto him and his will for our lives. He blesses us with his grace through the Spirit for us to be enabled to do this.

"Finally, instead of the Sabbath as a day of rest, in Christ we have the rest from our own works as taught in Hebrews 4, which Steve mentioned earlier. Father does want us to have physical rest, which the human body needs regularly. But this rest he speaks of is a rest from our own works—as if it were possible to earn salvation. So instead of us working hard to try to earn eternal life like the various cults attempt to do, we trust in the finished work of Christ—his substitutional death and resurrection—as the necessary work to provide for our salvation. We are sure of our salvation and don't have to do a thousand different kinds of works to secure it or to be pleasing to Father. Are there any questions now?"

Steve was processing something about all this, though I'm not sure what. Then he spoke.

"No, I guess not," he replied slowly. "I already knew all that too. I'm not sure that I've ever tied them all together like this, though. What concerns me is that a lot of Christians know all this and don't live like it's true."

"They live like we're under the Old Covenant," added Aby.

Tom nodded slowly. "In fact, the contemporary practice of

much of Christianity has its correlation to these five."

"And I can probably guess most or all of them," said Steve.

"Go for it, Flamen'," I said encouragingly.

"All right, let's see." He licked his lips, furrowed his brow, and gazed into the distance as he concentrated. "Instead of a temple, a lot of modern believers believe that the sanctuary of a church building is the holy of holies."

"Steve, you got one right off the bat," said Tom. "And what's the problem with that belief?"

"Well, it's just a building—brick and mortar. Some people think of it as 'the house of God', but that's an Old Testament reference to the temple or tabernacle. Buildings or rooms inside of buildings aren't 'holier' than other places simply because people pray, sing praises, read the Bible, and hear sermons in them."

"What does the New Testament teach regarding this?"

"In 1 Corinthians 6:19 it teaches that our bodies are temples of the Holy Spirit who indwells all believers in Jesus. And corporately, we as the body of Christ are also his temple, according to 1 Corinthians 3:16. Everything we do is in his presence, so we can rejoice in the fact that he is available to hear us and to minister to us at all times."

"That's very good! Can you name another substitute?"

"I think so. All right. Instead of a priesthood there are Christians who think that pastors, preachers, missionaries, and other ministers are exalted above everyone else in the body. And the problem with that is that it goes against the New Testament teaching of the priesthood of the believer in 1 Peter 2."

"You're talking about the clergy," I suggested.

"Yeah, that unbiblical terminology of clergy and laity. The New Testament teaches that there are no such divisions. We're all priests anyway, so we don't need a human mediator between us and Jesus."

"What is the New Testament teaching concerning this?" inquired Tom.

"John and I talked about that before, I know." Steve looked at me. "Remember Matthew 20, Brother, where Jesus said that the

194

disciples were not to lord over others the way the Gentiles did?"

"That's it! Matthew 20! Yeah, Jesus did say that." It was from our road trip conversation. "So why do so many believers practice lording their authority over others?"

"The only authority," Tom began, "which any of us has is the Bible itself. You don't have to have any special biblical education or training to stand on the authority of the Scriptures."

"But it sure helps," I said.

"Well, yes," Tom conceded, "an education in the Scriptures can be helpful and prepare us for many things. Nonetheless, it doesn't give us any greater authority or special favor with Father. It also doesn't make us superior to other believers who may not have the same knowledge."

"So, what do we do with passages like Ephesians 4:11 that have a list of the different types of ministers?"

"You'll notice in the context of that verse that it's speaking of Jesus giving gifts after his resurrection. Therefore, the apostles, prophets, evangelists, pastors, and teachers are 'gifts' to the body of Christ in order to promote the maturity of the whole body. This indicates that each of those ministries is a function, not an office. It's just like the lists of spiritual gifts found in Romans 12 and 1 Corinthians 12. In 1 Corinthians 12:12 it reads, 'For as the body is one, and hath many members and all the members of that one body, being many, are one body: so also is Christ.'* The analogy there is pretty simple. Paul compares believers to the parts of a human body, stating that all are equal, necessary, and worthy, yet with different functions."

"Hey, I'm somewhat familiar with that passage," Steve blurted out. "You're right, Tom. It *does* teach equality among the members, because somewhere in that twelfth chapter it says, 'those members that seem to be weaker are essential, and those members we consider less honorable we clothe with greater honor, and our unpresentable members are clothed with dignity.' Then it goes on to say, 'God has blended together the body, giving greater honor to the lesser member, so that there may be no division in the body, but the members may have mutual concern for one another.' So, you see? Father doesn't want any division in the body, whether that be clergy versus laity, these gifts versus those gifts, or what-ever."

Tom nodded and motioned with his hands. "You may also throw into that the different denominational divisions. They're man-made divisions just as much as 'clergy' and 'laity.'"

"Uh!" groaned Steve. "That's a tough one for most people. But I guess 'no division' means 'no division.'"

This was a lot to absorb and to process. I wasn't even sure that I was grasping everything being said. As I listened, however, I kept having more and more questions. There was no way that I could ask every question. I had to prioritize them and decide which ones were most essential to ask for my comprehension.

"Tom, I need us to back up for a second."

"Certainly. What's your question?"

"Okay, so you said that these different ministry gifts are not offices but functions according to spiritual gifts, right?"

"Yes, I believe I did." He turned to his wife. "Sara, can you rewind the tape, Dear, and see if that's what I said?"

"Oh," she half-moaned, "I'm not recording any of this. You'll just have to remember."

He smiled. "All right, Dear. If that's the way it has to be."

Sara gave him a half-serious look and then giggled at him.

He looked at us with a grin. "My wife assures me that that's what I said. That's good enough for me."

"Well," I continued, "I was thinking that I remembered some-where in one of the Pastoral Epistles that ministry was referred to as an office, like an official position. Maybe it was in 1 Timothy or Titus?"

"You're probably referring to 1 Timothy 3:1 which says, 'If a man desireth the office of a bishop, he desireth a good work.'*"

"Yes, that sounds like that's it."

"This may be hard to believe, but it's actually an error in translation."

"Oh, really?" *Did I hear that right?* I wondered.

"Sadly, yes. Many of the Bible translations phrase it as 'office

196

of a bishop' or 'office of an overseer.' The translators took one word which comes from a Greek root word for 'bishop.' It simply means *oversight*. Then they inserted a few other words to make it a phrase. In the Greek it reads like, 'If a man desires *oversight*, he desires a good work.' But that translation kind of sounds a little awkward to readers of English, so they try to smooth it out somewhat by adding the extra words to try to make it 'a better sounding translation.' However, they wind up leading people astray with the insertion of the word 'office.'

"You see, the body of Christ has always been a family, never an institution, business, company, or corporation. Just like a family, there are different functions and maturity levels, but not any offices or official titles. That should be easy for us to remember, since the New Testament uses familial terms when referring to God and the members of the body—words like 'Father,' 'Son,' 'brothers,' and 'sisters.'

"Besides, the general teaching about these different functions of ministry is that they are believers who are more mature to some degree and more experienced about living this life in Christ than are newer believers. That's why they are called 'elders,' a term which refers to an older, more mature person. The elders are to serve by encouraging and building up the body, not by lording over others with some 'special authority' they are believed to have because of their gifts or calling. It's a function of shepherding, not an office or position in an institution.

"I often explain the local body and shepherding like rolling a tire down the street. This was a pastime the kids my age and I did as we were growing up in the forties. Rolling a tire is easy, because it's round and has traction to roll well on the road. Plus, it's designed and manufactured to roll easily. In order to roll the tire, you just have to let the tire do what it was made to do: just let it keep rolling. The only time you have to touch the tire is if it starts to go off course, to slow down, or to get too close to bumping into something.

"In the body of Christ, Father has given spiritual gifts as he willed to the believers. As the body is being the body, they don't

197

need much to keep them going. They just need the freedom and opportunities to function as Father has equipped them. The function of an elder, overseer, or pastor is just to let the body do what it was born to do. It just has to function. So, the only time one of these ministers steps in and *'touches the tire,'* so to speak, is when the body is about to get sidetracked into doctrinal error, to become spiritually stagnate, or to allow open sin in their midst. If a course correction or encouragement is needed, then the ministers can step in and provide that. And by the way, leadership really must be shared among several. The shepherding and functioning of a local assembly is not to be a one-man show. The body is really all about functioning together and exalting Jesus, not about letting one or more personalities rule it."

This analogy was amazing! It was simple, yet profound. Though I heard it long ago, I carry it with me these many years later, and I know that I'll never forget it. It was the kind of simple truth which made me wonder why I never heard anything like this in Bible college. There I was given textbooks, charts, Venn diagrams, projected presentations, etc., about how to do ministry. Much of what I learned from the professors and through the courses was beneficial. Nevertheless, some of it did miss the mark or distract us students from a dependence on Jesus and the Spirit's guidance, though not intentionally. If only I had known before going to Honduras what I had learned from Father since returning, then things would have been a lot different. But I had to submit those thoughts to Jesus to avoid the introspective trap, as Bob called it. Therefore, I choose not to dwell on those thoughts.

"Good night!" exclaimed Steve. "Elders functioning in the body like rolling a tire! Too bad they didn't teach us that in Bible college, huh, Brother?"

I just had to grin and shake my head. "You're right, Flamen'. We'll just have to remember that analogy from now on."

"A lot of things," Tom continued, "dealing with church, ministry, and walking with Jesus can be understood better by looking at them from such simple perspectives. It just goes to show you that this life in Jesus wasn't meant to be so complicated."

198

"It's interesting," began Aby, "that we as human beings tend to complicate things too much."

"I agree," said Sara. "Working in the tribe all those years ago, we knew that we had to keep things simple. They were a people group who didn't even have their own language reduced to writing. This meant that they were not readers like those of us in the West who are used to receiving so much information in written form. Initially they had to learn everything audibly, which was fine, because most of them were audible learners anyway. So many of the typical teaching techniques used here wouldn't work over there. They learned the Bible stories quickly by listening to them and memorizing them by practicing them aloud. It took our team years of studying the tribal language before we could compose a complete alphabet, determine the grammar of the language, and begin translating the Scriptures into their language."

"True," agreed Tom. "But once they got it, *they got it*. After we taught them the stories from the Bible, they would even remind us later of doing certain things, because they remembered that that's the way Father directed people in the Bible to do it."

"So, your point is S.I.B.K.I.S.S.," inserted Steve. "*See It Big, Keep It Simple, Stupid.*"

I looked at him blankly. "Flamen', you could have just left off the last S for *Stupid*."

"Yeah, I know," he admitted smiling. Then he did one of his narrator voice characterizations. "But it's more fun with it than without it, Brother!"

Aby placed her hand on Steve's arm. "Yeah, we'll have to work on your definition of 'fun,' Babe." She giggled at him and gave him a kiss.

"Hey," I blurted out, "let's get back to the last three key features of contemporary churchianity."

"All right, Brother," Steve said, with a determined facial expression. "What do we have so far?"

"So far, you got the sanctuary for the indwelling Holy Spirit and the clergy for the priesthood of the believer."

"By the way," interrupted Tom, "excuse me for interrupting,

199

but it's important to know that I'm not saying that all pastors, teachers, elders, and missionaries in local assemblies treat their positions like a priesthood with the same clout and authority as what was under the Old Covenant. There are some who serve biblically and others who don't. Just because someone is called 'pastor' doesn't mean that they're doing ministry wrong. And those who are out of line with the Scriptures don't think of themselves as mediators between Jesus and Christians, hindering the functioning of its members. They generally believe they are being a blessing to the body and meeting needs."

"So," replied Steve, "we probably shouldn't blast them just for having those positions."

"Right. Always remember that anything like this that we discuss is not to be used against anyone else. That's not the spirit of love for our brothers and sisters that Father wants us to have. We're really discussing these issues to help you all to understand your freedom in Christ from the New Testament perspective."

"Got it. So just like for the legalists, we should pray and depend on the Holy Spirit to guide us before even thinking about approaching anyone about this."

"Exactamente," I said.

Steve opened his mouth to say something but decided against it. This was a rare achievement for him.

"Okay, Flamen'. What's next?"

"Uh, let's see." He had that serious, furrowed-brow expression again. "Oh, yeah—the sacrifices. So instead of yielding our lives as living sacrifices, some believers try to give money as their sacrifices."

"Money, huh?"

"Yeah, like tithes and offerings."

"Man, *there's* a big can of worms."

"All right, just let me—" he said as he stood, retrieving a pocket knife, "—I'll just get out my pocket can opener." He proceeded to retract the can opener on his Swiss Army pocket knife and opened an imaginary "can of worms." A few of us granted him a courtesy laugh.

"Babe, please," said Aby, sounding exasperated.

"Hold on there, Brother!" said Tom chuckling. "I think you've gone too far with this metaphor."

Steve raised an eyebrow, smiled at Tom, and then folded his knife and put it back into his pocket and sat down.

"Speaking of tithing," I proposed, "is that really a New Testament teaching or just for the Old Testament?"

"Tithing," explained Tom, "was really just a tax paid by the Israelites to support the priests and Levites. Tithing is mentioned a few times in the Gospels, but only as examples of what was practiced in Israel under the Old Covenant. The New Covenant wasn't ratified or in force until Jesus' resurrection, so he sometimes mentioned Old Covenant practices like tithing during his ministry."

"Did the early church not tithe?"

"There's no record of it in either the New Testament or early church history for the first few centuries. There was no priesthood or 'clergy,' so there was no need for it. When error started spreading among congregations in those early centuries, some elders rose up to declare themselves as having a title, like 'bishop' or 'overseer.' They professed these titles in order to declare that they were authorized to point out error, separating the chaff from the wheat. When these 'bishops' started lording it over the other believers for the sake of pointing out and combating doctrinal errors, they formed titles and positions for themselves, eventually including the tithe as a practice for the church. It was used to support them just as it was used for the priests and Levites under the Old Covenant."

"I did a study on New Testament giving once," Steve announced. "When the early church gave, it was for the poor in Jerusalem and for widows and orphans."

"Money was given just to those who were needy, huh?" I surmised.

"That's about the size of it," agreed Steve. "In other news, we all know that Paul worked as a tent maker to finance his ministry. That's how he paid for both his needs and his coworkers' needs."

"Yeah, I remember reading Paul's farewell message to the

Ephesian elders in Acts 20," I added. "He said that he didn't desire anyone's silver, gold, or clothes. He even told them that Jesus said, 'It is more blessed to give than to receive.'" I looked around at everyone and shrugged my shoulders. "It sounds like he was encouraging them not to accept money for their ministry."

Steve mentioned another relevant scripture. "That lines up with the instructions that Jesus gave when he sent out the Twelve to minister in Matthew 10. Remember how he told them not to charge for preaching the kingdom, casting out demons, healing the sick, or raising the dead? He said, 'Freely you received, freely give.'"

"But in that same context," I added, "he also told them not to take any money or extra sandals, tunics, or bags. He said, 'for the worker deserves his provisions,' inferring that Father would provide for those kinds of needs through the people who welcomed the kingdom. So, what can we deduce from those verses?"

"Hmm," Steve said pensively. "It would seem that that was a special instruction given to the Twelve as he was training them in the last days of the Old Covenant in anticipation of the New. So, it's likely not an instruction for us in the church today. However, it is an interesting example used by the disciples before they became apostles in the body of Christ which was born a year or so afterward."

"Maybe the most that could be said about it is that believers may help provide for the physical needs of traveling ministers, like missionaries, as long as it falls under the 'needs' category. If it becomes the 'so-much-that-I-don't-know-what-to-do-with-it' kind of supply, then that can be a real snare."

"In other words, no big checks surpassing the bare necessities."

Tom interjected at this point. "Brothers, you might want to do a little more studying and praying before coming up with a one-size-fits-all interpretation or application of that passage. I think for now we can safely say that tithing is not a New Testament concept and that any giving done by the early church was for the truly needy, like the widows, the orphans, and the poor. Just remember that while Paul didn't typically accept financial gifts from local assemblies, he did say that he accepted four separate love gifts from the Philippians to provide for his needs on a few occasions."

"Right," agreed Steve. "Consequently, in typical American fashion, churchianity believes in giving money instead of yielding their agendas to Father's will on a daily basis."

"Apparently so," I conceded.

"It's so easy to write a check," Steve said in his falsetto Keith Green voice. "It's so easy."

I chuckled at his impersonation, which I had anticipated him doing just a few seconds before. We know each other too well.

"As a footnote to this discussion about monetary giving," Tom mentioned, "it's important to state that when we as believers give, it is to be done cheerfully as freewill giving. There's none of this 'give the minimum ten percent because we are commanded to do so' jazz. The New Testament church is not exhorted to tithe anyway. We are to give cheerfully and when and how the Holy Spirit leads us, because he loves a cheerful giver. Remember that it's all about our hearts and our walk with Christ. Besides, if you think about it, Father doesn't really need our money. Instead he wants our hearts. As we walk closely to him and follow his leading, he wants us to follow him in all that he leads us to do."

"Good point," noted Steve. "Thanks, Brother Tom."

"You got two left, Flamen'," I reminded him.

"The Sabbath one is easy. Believers understand that salvation is by grace through faith in Jesus' work. Therefore, they're not trying to work to earn or to keep their salvation. But a lot of them do consider Sunday to be the Sabbath for Christians. Some of them have strict rules about what they can and can't do on Sundays."

"Don't those believers miss the whole point in Hebrews 4," I asked, "about no longer trusting in our works but resting and trusting completely in Jesus' finished work?"

"I'd say that at least somewhat they do. There's also the passage in Colossians 2, which says, 'Therefore do not let anyone judge you with respect to food or drink, or in the matter of a feast, new moon, or Sabbath days—these are only the shadow of the things

203

to come, but the reality is Christ!' Those Colossian believers were faced with some heretical teachings in their town with elements of Gnosticism and Judaism knocking at their door. They were being judged and pressured by some who observed holidays, monthly celebrations, and the weekly Sabbath as holier than other days. Ergo, there were some who were trying to thwart the believers' freedom in Christ."

"Observing the Sabbath and those other days," I mused aloud, "were only a part of the shadowy things under the Old Covenant. Besides, they all point to Jesus and the New Covenant, both of which are superior. So, could we say," I inquired of Tom, "that in Colossians Paul was really saying not to stress over others pressuring or judging them for not observing the Sabbath and other special days?"

Tom considered my question for a moment before answering. "Observing the Sabbath and other holidays ritualistically like the Israelites did under the Old Covenant was part of their relationship with Father. Now, for us as the body of Christ under the New Covenant, that is not a stipulation. We are free of those Old Covenant practices. The New Covenant is really the fulfillment of the Old Covenant. Like Paul taught in Colossians, the Old contains shadows; the New is the reality of the person of Jesus. That weekly Sabbath rest pointed to the spiritual rest we now enjoy in Jesus since his work of sacrifice, death, and resurrection provided for our salvation."

"Oh, okay." I blinked twice, and then said: "So, we don't have to worry about being judged for not keeping that?"

Tom chuckled suddenly. "Oh—yes, that's correct. I took the long way around, didn't I?"

"If he had asked me," Sara offered, "then I would have just said 'yes.'"

Laughter was heard around the table.

"Since we know Jesus," Steve began, "and he indwells our spirits through the Holy Spirit, there aren't too many outward features we practice besides baptism and the Lord's Supper. Those are the only two ordinances for believers."

"That makes sense," I replied.

At this point, Tom brought some balance to our discussion. "Concerning the Sabbath and some other peripheral observances that some carry over from the Old Covenant, we must bear in mind the teachings of Romans 14. That's where Paul says that we are not to judge the weaker brother who observes holy days and other Old Testament practices which are not necessarily good or bad."

"Oh, yeah," Steve uttered slowly, musing aloud. "Romans 14 and 1 Corinthians 8 are Paul's teachings about eating meat sacrificed to idols. Those passages include insights for considering questionable activities and the interaction of weak and mature believers on such topics."

"Speaking of covenants," I intentionally interrupted, "we only need one more key feature of the modern substitutions for the New Covenant. You got four so far, Flamen': church sanctuaries versus God's omnipresence/indwelling of the Holy Spirit, the professional clergy versus the priesthood of the believer, giving tithes and offerings versus living as sacrifices, and observing Sunday like a Sabbath versus resting in Jesus from our works."

"Only four?" He asked, a bit puzzled. "What did I miss?"

"You missed the most obvious one—the Law."

"It must have—" and at this point, he pulled the hair at the rear of his scalp, making it look like a toupee which had shifted "—slipped my mind." There was that laughter of his again. Everyone else who had not seen this trick of his before or who did not expect it, chuckled heartily. It was one of his staple tricks he pulled from time to time—pun intended.

"Except that in the New Covenant, we don't have the Law," I added.

"Right. We have the Spirit within us, enabling us to follow Jesus. Which also ties in with the fact that we don't need a temple or building. God is with us now. Hey, *Emmanuel*—God *with* us!"

"See how easy this is?" asked Tom. "It's all interrelated. Christ fulfilled the Law and indwells us through the Spirit, so he enables us to live a life that honors him. And because he's with us, we don't need special buildings or a human mediator; we commune with him directly. His Holy Spirit within us enables us to live our lives as sacrifices. Without a formal priesthood, there's no need to pay the tithe-tax to support them. Plus, we rest in Jesus's completed work, so we're free from ritualistic observances, such as keeping Sunday like a Sabbath."

"Well, isn't that tied up neatly with a bow," observed Steve in a silly, bass-sounding, character voice.

"But, Flamen', you forgot to guess the churchianity substitute for the indwelling Spirit instead of the Law," I reminded him.

"I did?" he replied, arching an eyebrow. "All right, let's see. The Law is Old Covenant; the indwelling Holy Spirit is New Covenant. So the substitute would resemble the Law."

He paused as he thought for a moment. He seemed to be having trouble with this one.

"Would you like a hint?" asked Tom.

"No thanks. I think I got it now." His facial expression reflected a resolution and confidence.

"And what is it?"

"It's all the principles people pull from the New Testament and try to live by—like a new set of Christian commandments."

Tom feigned a gasp. "Well, I'm impressed."

"You did it, Brother!" I exclaimed.

"My honey hero!" Aby said, giving him a big hug.

After the hug, Steve did a few silly bows. The rest of us joined in with applause. Nathaniel laughed loudly at our sudden noise. Any onlookers probably thought that we were having a birthday party.

"Those Christian principles can really trip us up," Tom said calmly, "especially since they are taken from the New Testament and sound so good. I mean, how could you argue against obeying those?"

"Oh, but you can," replied Sara with a serious look.

"Now, how is that, my dear wife?"

"We've already said that the Scriptures teach that Christ fulfilled the Law and freed us from it so that we're no longer bound by it. He didn't die on the cross, bearing all our sin and freeing us from the Law, just so that he could burden us with a *new* set of laws. Besides, in Galatians 3 and Romans 4, Paul teaches that there is no law to achieve righteousness before God."

"Would you listen to that?" Tom said with a widening smile. "I'll have you know, my brothers and sisters, that the voice you just heard was that of my wife—my precious, wise, and loving wife."

"Okay," Sara replied in a facetious, condescending tone, "what do you want?"

Tom's bright smile was skirting the edge of laughter. "Here I am being serious, and you think I'm scheming for something."

"After forty years, I just chalk it up to knowing you too well." She chuckled as did the rest of us.

"That's almost enough to hurt my feelings—if it weren't true." Tom's hearty laughter was priceless. It reminded me of our shared joy in Jesus.

The example of these two and their marriage relationship were beyond description. I have attempted to articulate how they cherished one another deeply, not necessarily through excessive public displays of affection, but from their mutual care, love, and respect. Those who didn't know them well may have been unsure how to interpret some of the zingers and give-and-take which they exchanged when others were around. Yet I had known them for enough years by that time to know that they shared a camaraderie and rapport which many married couples lack. They had a deep, abiding trust of each other and a sincere friendship, so that they really enjoyed their humorous exchanges.

I stood up to refill my cup with water.

"Do you need anything, Brother Tom?" I offered.

"He's all right," informed Sara, blinking. "He just needs his coffee is all."

Elena quickly found the thermos he had brought to the picnic and offered to pour him a cup. He accepted it gratefully.

I took a moment to reflect on so much teaching on our freedom in Christ which we had just experienced and in which we had participated. The thought was staggering and almost overwhelming. I felt as if someone had just lightened a load which I hadn't realized I was carrying. My heart seemed to expand a little more with gratitude and love for my Savior. I knew that I would spend the rest of my life seeking to know him and to love him better. How could anyone not want to reciprocate love to the one person who only knows to relate to us from a heart of perfect, overwhelming love? *Thank you, Jesus, for your great love and the gift of such freedom in you!*

"It's so amazing!" I exclaimed. "Father graced us with the gift of free will and his salvation. Along with Jesus, he also gave us all the blessings and freedoms which accompany this relationship with Christ."

"That's right, Brother!" Steve replied. "With Jesus, it's a package deal. Remember Romans 8:32? 'Indeed, he who did not spare his own Son, but gave him up for us all—how will he not also, along with him, freely give us all things?' This means that, when we received Jesus—the greatest gift—we also received all spiritual blessings along with him."

Aby annexed Steve's comment. "It's just like what Ephesians 1:3 teaches: 'Blessed is the God and Father of our Lord Jesus Christ, who has blessed us with every spiritual blessing in the heavenly realms in Christ. '"

"It's so awesome!" I remarked. "And I don't mean that in the overused way people wear out the word 'awesome' nowadays. I mean that it literally inspires awe—just realizing all that we have been given in Jesus. I can't imagine why anyone would want to substitute him with a set of rules or Christian principles. It just doesn't make sense to me."

Tom sipped his coffee and then replied. "People are different. They are raised spiritually in different circles and under the impact and influence of different personalities. Many believers are simply unaware of all that we have in Jesus. Oh sure, they've read Romans 8:32 and Ephesians 1:3 at some time or another, since they usually read the Bible regularly. But they are often swayed—or *persuaded* I should say perhaps—to follow impressive personalities who promote the 'cart' of what a righteous, moral life supposedly looks like before the 'horse' of intimacy with Jesus. When that's the case, it can result in enslavement to other's expectations, spiritual stagnation, and profound disappointment, among other things. Following someone else's prescription of this life in Jesus which is not New Testament will eventually lead to a hollow disappointment and a great sense of disillusionment concerning Father and our relationship with him. But the Holy Spirit can work with the resulting disillusions to draw people out of the legalism or whatever system they've submitted themselves to, albeit in all sincerity."

"Amen, Brother!" Steve blurted out enthusiastically. "I have seen some real bondage paraded around at Christian seminars and conventions. You should have seen some of the books, tapes, and presentations of teachings I've witnessed in some of those legalistic circles. Good night! It's ridiculous!"

"Do you still have any contact with any of those folks?" I inquired.

"I don't have so much direct contact nowadays since I don't exactly run in those circles any more. But once in a while when I'm out somewhere, I'll unexpectedly cross paths with someone I knew from those days. We usually do some catching up for a few minutes, and then they get around to inviting me to their church services or some important meeting or program that they're having. They might even discuss some of the 'good ol' days' with me, boasting of the law they're still under without realizing it."

"Flamen', what do you say to those people now when they try to pull you back into their systems?"

"I talk with them politely and cordially, even when they try to pressure me to get back into some of it. If they're persistent with it and take it too far, then sometimes I just have to say to them bluntly, 'No thanks, Brother, I don't care for all that anymore. It's all just man's attempts to limit my freedoms in Christ.'"

I stifled a giggle. "And that works?"

Steve relaxed his face as he was thinking of how to respond. "You might say that. They typically back off and end the conversation nicely and quickly, gossiping later about how rebellious and backslidden I've become." He gave us that knowing look. "Yeah,

I hear about that eventually. But on a couple of occasions, it has led to more secretive conversations later with requests for help to leave the system."

"Has it turned into a covert operation on occasion?"

"No, I wouldn't say it was all 'cloak and dagger'—like some kind of black ops thing. But, y'know, some people really want out of it. Yet the peer pressure and fear of repercussions of even talking about leaving is a real force in their lives. They just don't know how to leave without suffering the shame and wrath of their friends or even what they would wind up in afterward. All this freedom can be more than a little scary for some. Most of them view leaving what they've always known as somewhat of a free fall experience that they want to avoid at all costs. I guess those systems at least provide a sense of security, even if it is something that's not biblical or best for them."

"I'm just thankful for all the blessings and freedoms we have in Jesus," Elena said plainly.

"Amen, Sister," said Sara.

"All right, Brother," Steve said to me, "what are you looking forward to doing that you've wanted to do for so long, now that you understand your freedom in Christ?"

I sipped some water and let out a sigh.

"I just want my family and me to walk in this love Jesus has for us, thriving in it and enjoying it as much as possible. I know that technically I've always been a recipient of his great love, but I really want to enjoy his presence and to sense his great affection for me and everyone else."

"Aw, c'mon, Bro!" he said playfully, almost snapping. "You've *certainly* had some legalistic tendencies over the years. I know you must have *something* that you're itching to do, now that you've really broken free from that law mentality."

"Like what, Flamen'?"

"You remember how legalistic we were about music way back then?"

He just *had* to mention that!

"Well, yeah," I replied slowly and suspiciously, "but we're not anymore."

"All right. Now that you realize how free you are in Jesus, what kind of music would you like to hear?"

"I'm just curious," Aby interrupted. "What sort of legalism about music did you have?"

I looked away, not very eager to share this. "It's not really worth mentioning."

"What do you mean 'not really worth mentioning,' Brother?" Steve asked in a tone which was more than a little surprised. "This is better than my legalistic schedule to earn TV time. C'mon, Bro, you gotta tell 'em about it!"

"It's not something I'm happy about or proud of," I commented, hoping to slink away from the topic of conversation.

"No, no." Then he turned to face Aby with more excitement about the topic than I would have wanted him to have. "Aw, Babe, this is great! I'll tell you all about it."

Why don't we have a best friend signal for 'drop it'? I wondered quietly.

"Soon after high school, John attended this legalistic seminar in an arena in Atlanta filled with thousands of people. Everyone was given a red workbook for filling in blanks and taking notes on this 'legalistically perfect' law teacher and his teachings on basic life conflicts. He covered all kinds of topics like what not to wear, where not to go, what activities not to do, what music not to listen to—the works."

Steve seemed a little too animated in telling this story. He was enjoying this too much. He was even using exaggerated hand motions!

"John already had a head filled with all the backward masking controversy floating around churches at the time just before he attended the seminar. Then this guy gave a presentation on worldly music—not just secular music, but even Contemporary Christian Music. He said that it has certain nihilistic characteristics, a fleshly beat, and even 'satanic' lyrics. Just picture it, Babe: John's at this seminar eight hours a day for a week. At the end of the week he comes home—"

211

"—Flamen', they don't need to hear all the *boring* details," I offered, trying to dissuade him from continuing. Nevertheless, he persisted, not missing a beat.

"—prays about it, and then *burns* all his secular rock albums in the backyard!"

"Oh, my word!" exclaimed Aby.

"Really, John?" inquired Elena, somewhat surprised. "You never told me about that."

I looked down at the water cup I held in my hands. "Well, there's probably a reason for that."

Steve rocked back in laughter. Then he glanced at me to see my reaction. I can't remember what it was.

"So, from then on, he wouldn't listen to any secular music whatsoever. All he listened to was Christian music."

"Actually," I said, speaking up, "that legalistic teacher was promoting that we listen exclusively to the old hymns. But I didn't go *that* far."

"Yeah, Brother, but didn't you even question if it was okay for you to sing 'Happy Birthday' because it wasn't a specifically Christian song?"

"Aw, Flamen', you're making this up now!"

"I don't think I am," he continued enthusiastically. "I remember us having a discussion about it back then. Besides, you were really nervous whenever I or someone else would mention some secular song that you used to listen to. Remember?"

"It's hardly important now—"

"—You used to say, 'Don't stumble me, Brother.' Remember that?" Steve's laughter indicated that he was really enjoying this.

"Look, I was young and impressionable. I just wanted to please the Lord in every aspect of my life. That's all. I never thought I was perfect."

"But you did tell me that you struggled with all that rock music you'd listened to for years playing in your head at the worst moments—like when you prayed, read the Bible, or tried to listen to sermons or Bible study teachings."

"That's true. It kind of felt like psychological torture sometimes."

"Anyway," he continued, "the point is that he was really irritating people, looking unfavorably on people in Sunday school and church whenever they played a secular song in their car or talked about some rock or pop song. People began to avoid him and plan their social activities without him."

"They did?" I asked with surprise. "*That* explains a few things from back then."

"John and I used to listen to Christian artists like Keith Green, Michael Card, Steve Green, Don Francisco, and Steve Fry as we rode from place to place, singing in the car together like we were in a recording studio."

"Yeah," I mused, reflecting on those times with a smile. "Those were fun times. I also listened to Sandi Patti, Twila Paris, Kim Hill, and Amy Grant. But as guys, we didn't have the voices to sing along to female recording artists."

"We listened to other Christian artists and bands too. It wasn't secular music and it wasn't bad music. It just didn't meet the standards of legalism. Then later, when John went to Bible college, he found out that some of the students and professors there looked down on the Christian music we listened to."

"Yeah, that was weird and confusing at the time. There were different extremes. Some people would listen to secular music, just not openly. Others would listen only to music tapes of old-fashioned hymns sung by people who only performed at legalistic churches. Then one year Steve Green came to town for a concert, and rumor had it that his manager requested renting the facilities of the large, six-thousand-seat auditorium at the church which founded the Christian university."

"And they said 'no.' " Sara offered.

"They said 'no.' At that time, one of the girls in my missions classes boasted that she would *never* attend 'one of those concerts' because she had 'higher standards for music.'" I shook my head. "It was unreal!"

"But, do you see now," asked Tom, "that the standards they clung to became a system composed of man-made laws pressuring you and others to conform to their ideas of how to walk with Jesus?"

"I do now. But back then—especially when I attended that legalistic seminar a few months after trusting Jesus and before attending Bible college—I didn't have the kind of biblical thinking and teachings about our freedom in Christ that I have now."

"That's great to hear that you're free from all that now. I'm glad for you, John."

"So, we really are free to listen to any kind of music," I said, intoning it as a statement, but really hoping for an answer to it like a question.

"We're really free in Jesus," Tom replied, nodding slowly. "Now, I don't want to sound like I'm presenting any expectations or substituting New Testament principles for a vibrant relationship with Christ. However, the more you get to know Jesus better— walking with him and learning from the Scriptures—the more *he* teaches you what music is encouraging and uplifting and what music is not the better part of wisdom to spend your time with."

"Yeah, I was already thinking that Philippians 4:8 would be good advice to follow when it comes to choosing music."

"Oh," said Aby suddenly. "You mean the verse that says to think on things that are pure, good, virtuous, praiseworthy, and so on?"

"Yes, Aby, that's the verse."

Tom said: "Biblical wisdom does teach us that some things are not spiritually edifying to watch or listen to, especially if we want to avoid some form of bondage. Just let Jesus be the one to tell you what you may and may not listen to. Don't let others try to play the role of the Holy Spirit in your life, fostering their standards and expectations on you. As you walk with him daily, learning from him and following him, he'll teach you what is best."

"It's interesting," commented Steve, "that whether it's legalism or licentiousness, bondage is still bondage, no matter what form it takes."

"And we may not always recognize the many facets of such bondage or enslavement," Tom said as he stirred his coffee. "But if we open ourselves to Jesus and let him teach us, then he'll guide us around the pitfalls for everything in life, not just our music-listening habits and other forms of entertainment. Also, we don't have to stress out so much over music. For example, I'm sure that for you, John, you just want to hear something enjoyable that you don't have to analyze to the last degree to determine if it's okay for you to listen to."

"You're right," I admitted. "That's what I'd like to do: just relax and not worry about it." I took a long drought of water.

"Me too," agreed Tom. "That's why sometimes I just listen to country music."

Immediately, I did a spit take to avoid choking.

Steve guffawed, seeing the stream of water hit the gravel beside our table.

Aby and Sara chortled.

Elena winced and pulled Nathaniel a little closer.

"You mean," I said incredulously, recovering from a gasp, "you listen to Tim McGraw and Rascal Flatts?"

At this point, I need to make something perfectly clear. As I was growing up in the seventies and early eighties, my mom and stepdad loved country music. Therefore, I had the misfortune of being forced to hear it for most of my childhood. Whenever I had an opportunity to listen to "my music," it was always a rock station on the radio. To me these two genres, rock music and country music, were mutually exclusive. Since the seventies, music genres have changed and evolved, sometimes blurring the boundaries among various musical offerings available. But I have *never* been a fan of country music. My coworkers at that time usually listened to country music on the radio in the office, so *again* I was forced to hear it. Even though I don't like country music and don't follow it, because I had to hear it at work, I did have a context for knowing about who Tim McGraw and Rascal Flatts were. Therefore, I was both appalled and disappointed to think that Tom would listen to country music.

Tom heard my question and blinked a few times. "Who?"

"You know, from the Top Country Hits Radio Station?"

215

"I'm not familiar with those names," he replied simply.

"He doesn't listen to contemporary country music," offered Sara. "It's really the older stuff."

"You mean like Willie Nelson and George Jones?" These were country singers that my mom and stepdad enjoyed in the seventies.

Tom shook his head slowly.

"I'm afraid you've lost me again."

Now I was really confused. *He listens to country music, but he doesn't know about the old country music or the new country music?* I puzzled.

"You know," Sara continued, "to be fair, he probably shouldn't really call it country music. He just has a few CDs of instrumental music that our sons gave him for his birthday last year. Some are country-styled hymns and some are more like blue grass with a mix of some folk songs. But it's all instrumental without any singing. It's not something put on the market by any popular artists anyone's ever heard of, either old or new."

Tom was still grinning. "I just like to let it play in the background while I'm working or studying."

My heart started beating again. *Thank you, Jesus!*

"All right, Brother," Steve blurted out, "back to my question: What music are you all fired up and free to listen to now?"

I didn't have to contemplate his answer. There was one, artist in particular who came to mind. "Well, I don't know." *Should I say it? Dare I say it?*

"I was thinking about maybe..."

"Who, Brother?"

"Well, if I had to name one, . . . I'd say that . . . I'd kinda like to hear some of . . . 'Weird Al' Yankovik's music."

Almost everyone laughed. Tom didn't recognize that name either.

The fellowship ended on a humorous note. We packed our belongings, deposited any remaining trash, shared a final prayer together, said our farewells, and piled into our vehicles to head to our respective homes. These uplifting times with great friends in

216

Christ always left me with a sense of cleansing, refreshment, recharged joy, and renewed gratitude. Everything seemed right with the world.

This would change, of course. The next three months would bring both personal and national tragedy to my attention, showing me just how fragile circumstances can be. I was beginning to think that all my bitterness was far behind me. I couldn't have been more wrong.

*KJV

CHAPTER 10

OFFENSES AND UNFORGIVENESS

Jesus had changed my heart for the better, and it looked like he was making improvements in other areas of my life as well. For certain there were some significant changes on the horizon.

A couple of friends of mine from church who got jobs as computer networking technicians encouraged me to take some night classes to earn a one-year certificate in computer networking so that I could apply for a better-paying job. Since it seemed that I was out of the ministry as a career, I would need a career that earned more in order to provide better for my family, especially considering all the tax debt which still dogged my days. With a couple of college degrees already under my belt, I knew how to study and take tests. Computers were an interest of mine, so I was sure that I had the motivation and could find the time to earn the certificate. Therefore, I signed up for night school for the fall semester at a nearby college. I qualified for a grant which would pay for both the tuition and the textbooks. *Thank you, Jesus!*

Unlike me, Elena was blessed with time on her hands, and she used it to excel as a wife and mother. Instead of pursuing a career, she was a stay-at-home mom. I envied all the time available to her to spend with little Nathaniel. Nevertheless, I was so grateful to Father for this great blessing and to her for nurturing our son and having so much personal input into his life. Because of Elena having the time to spend with him, Nathaniel never had to attend a daycare. She also became a wonderfully talented cook! Elena learned cooking techniques and exchanged recipes with both friends and acquaintances. Nathaniel and I were blessed by her varied and original culinary creations. She even honed her crocheting skills and sold some of her designs and creations. Elena also kept the home looking immaculate. We didn't have a lot in the way of material possessions, but she did a terrific job keeping the house clean and running smoothly. Elena proved herself to be a Proverbs 31 woman, and Nathaniel and I were so blessed to have her as an integral part of our lives. *Thank you, Jesus!*

In all my busyness of work, school, and some left for family time, fatigue became a common condition of mine. I didn't have much time or energy to think too far into the future. Elena, however, did have her thoughts toward the future.

One afternoon I returned home from work to discover that she had answered an ad in the paper which read, "So you think you can't afford a house?" Not only had she contacted a mortgage lender and had started the ball rolling on getting us qualified for a loan, but she had also contacted a few realtors and settled on one who was very friendly and helpful in providing a list of affordable houses on our side of town. Elena was very excited as she told me all about it. The proposed monthly mortgage payment plus the escrow for home owner's insurance and property taxes was one hundred dollars more than the monthly rent on the duplex we called home. I didn't think it would be feasible; she believed it would happen. The realtor had scheduled an appointment with her for the very next day to take her and Nathaniel to see some of the houses in our price range. The next thing I knew, I was coming home from work and taking Elena and Nathaniel to houses they had already seen during the day and were excited about choosing.

It almost happened too quickly. We qualified for a first-time home buyer's loan and then set a date for the closing and the move. With the help of a couple of ladies from church who assisted us in cleaning the house we would move into, we were finally first-time home owners. That was a long, stressful, yet exciting day. As with every move during our marriage, we didn't sleep that first night until everything had been unpacked and set in its place. In just one year since our move back to the States, Father had provided us with a home to call our own. *Thank you, Jesus!*

Only a couple of months after we had returned to the States, the IRS letters began arriving in the mail. We were sending in the monthly payments as best as we could, but apparently it wasn't nearly enough on a $20,000 debt. The letters all included the threat to seize our property if we did not pay the debt in a timely manner. I had no real property in those months before we purchased the house, other than a used car. In our first few weeks back from the mission field, a good friend at church had helped me to find a 1991 Toyota Corolla which I purchased using the funds from the sale of our vehicle in Honduras. With so many threatening letters, I could only imagine that if the federal government could not be placated with seizing anything valuable, then their only other recourse would likely be to have me incarcerated. People we knew kept telling us, "That's nonsense! They don't want you in jail; they just want their money." Somehow, this was not a comfort to me. There had to be *some* kind of solution to all this tax debt.

A pastor friend of mine from one of the churches who supported us while we were on the foreign field gave me some hope. He convinced me to let his CPA look over our financial records and tax return. This pastor assured me that his accountant could help us. After all, he had over thirty years of experience doing tax returns and managing finances for ministers; he had an exact knowledge of specific tax laws which benefit missionaries. Therefore, we had a meeting. I submitted all my financial records to him for the years in question. After he combed through everything, the result two weeks later was that there was an inaccuracy in my filing. Instead of a $20,000 debt, it was more around $22,500. He was somewhat sheepish on the phone about informing me of the news. If there was a charge for his services, then I was unaware of it. Perhaps my pastor friend covered for it; I never knew one way or another. The extra debt was disheartening.

The situation only grew worse over some eight months. We received so many threatening letters. The multiple, lengthy phone calls I had to make during work hours only resulted in speaking to a different IRS phone representative each time. None of them had any viable solutions for me other than for me to pay the debt. All the tension and frustration this created made us feel that the only option left to us in order to achieve some semblance of peace of mind was to pay the IRS debt with credit cards. Therefore, that was what we did. Although with this move we may have leapt from the frying pan into the fire, at least the threatening IRS letters stopped. Having never had any real debt before this whole scenario, we were about to go on a different kind of adventure with the credit card companies. It became one of hidden fees, high interest rates, and a different kind of phone call placed about every six months to the credit card companies to negotiate more afford- able deals, smaller minimum payments, and lower interest rates. A year or two later we would learn that this may have been the wrong decision. Nevertheless, there didn't seem to be anyone with the necessary knowledge to know how to help us in these circum- stances. I was forced to traffic in a realm which was not my forte; because of that, I worried that I was making worse decisions for my family's future.

A couple of simple yet significant mistakes on my part shook things up for me at work. My manager, Ron, issued me a discipline letter which had to be signed by me to acknowledge that I had been made aware of my mistakes. Then it was placed in my employee file. It was all handled so coldly and callously as Ron had a differ- ent manager serve the letter to me. I felt so condemned before the eyes of men—men who didn't know me or appreciate me for who I was. They merely judged me based on my performance involv- ing these two mistakes. Receiving the discipline letter tore me up emotionally. I broke down crying at the manager's desk when he served me the letter. This discipline was the kind of thing that slackers and employees with sorry attitudes received, I knew, not hardworking employees who served the Lord with all their might in their work like I did. Ron also simultaneously moved me to a different area where I would have a desk in his building just a few cubicles away from his. There I would have very little interaction with my coworkers. At least my duties would take me to other buildings throughout most of the day so that I would only seldom ever cross paths with him. My manager continued to project a sense of disapproval and unpleasantness toward me, which now probably seemed justified to him. A few times I would catch my coworkers laughing at vulgar jokes e-mailed by Ron to everyone under him except me. That and a few other awkward moments gave me a sense of rejection as if I were an outcast. I worried that I would lose my job.

In early September of that year, just six weeks after we signed the mortgage and moved into our house, the events of 9/11 played out and were televised on all the media outlets. The detailed events devastated our nation with concerns for our security, our freedoms, and our future. On that day I was floating among several office buildings in the exercise of my duties. What I didn't have the opportunity to see live on television I heard from office workers in the hallways and elevators. It was very clear that the world had changed that day, and people were genuinely frightened. Somehow, we all managed to get through the workday.

After arriving home, I grieved along with the rest of the nation as the video clips of the day were repeated over and over on all the networks. Elena was frightened and worried, as were many people. She had not watched too much of the coverage throughout the day in order to prevent little Nathaniel from seeing or hearing what his three-year-old mind couldn't process or understand. As so many details of the events were reported, a deep sense of national mourning was expressed. Over the next several days, I wept many times and often unexpectedly. Things were changing in society. The world had been revealed to be a much darker place than we had been lulled into believing. Even after all these years since 9/11, I continue to grieve for the thousands of families who lost loved ones on that day. For so many unsatisfactorily answered questions, I long for the day when Father's justice over these matters and many others will prevail.

During Thanksgiving of that year, Nathaniel contracted something which at first we thought was an allergic reaction or symptoms of becoming overheated. After a couple of pediatric visits, we were told that his persistent fevers, mouth sores, and irritability were all symptoms of something called gingivostomatitis. We were so worried about him, especially since he had had almost no illness. We were not accustomed to seeing him ill, so as new parents, we were quite distressed. It was a sad week, and it was difficult to see him suffering and not understanding what was happening to his body. His recovery was slower than we had hoped, but we were so grateful once he was over it. *Thank you, Jesus!*

The problems during that part of that year were discouraging. Along with the mounting debt, the tight finances, some illness, and strained relationships at work, there were other issues which plagued me. There was a constant fatigue which I suffered from so much work, school, and family responsibilities. Other minor frustrations of life in American culture made me feel lost and out of place at times in my own hometown. In my heart I knew that these difficulties were no comparison to the devastating poverty, rampant malnutrition, crippling unemployment, persistent illnesses, and relentless homelessness of many people we knew and had met in Central America.

Our view of the world from America differed from what we had witnessed previously. While we lived in Honduras, we were informed of so many heartbreaking stories of suffering, loss, persecution, and other tragedies which are too painful to detail here. All those histories were of people we knew personally: friends, neighbors, acquaintances, and even some of Elena's extended family members and classmates. Yet this was only one tiny part of the world. From what I learned reported in the world news media and what I already knew about the suffering and tragedies I had seen and heard in Central America, I could well imagine what was going on in most of the rest of the world. This awareness of so many tragedies and hardships was literally overwhelming. Problems we viewed in the States as being "simple" with "easy solutions" had been unsolved in other nations for generations. With time they were only becoming worse. Instead of affluence and compassion, there were massive, wide-spread greed, selfishness, and political corruption devastating entire nations and people groups. While these same elements also existed in the United States, they were many times worse in other parts of the world, with little or no accountability whatsoever. Mankind's lesser traits were thwarting the humanitarian efforts of many who were trying to impact the world for good, and they resulted in the overwhelming majority of the world's sufferings.

I reflected on Father's gift of free will, and I was grieved over mankind's abuse of it. I could not begin to fathom how grieved Father's heart was over the insurmountable tragedies and suffering which humanity as a whole was fostering on the world's population. However, no longer living in a Third World nation, we found it easier to forget the world's problems from time to time. We were becoming complacent, and this bothered me greatly.

As a twenty-year-old, I had had my first exposure to the needs of the Third World on the very first day of my first trip to Honduras, and it had altered my perspective of the world. The poverty and suffering I witnessed first-hand during the trip had changed me forever, or so I had thought. By this time, we had been back from the foreign field for well over a year, and I worried that the urgency of so many needs of the world were fading from my immediacy and concern. We were becoming too Americanized, worrying about many of the petty problems of Western culture. While I continued to be grateful for Father's work of grace and love in my heart, my problems and frustrations were taking a toll on me.

My new attitude and outlook on life went from being fresh and exciting to comfortable and settled. As the months passed, my joy and gratitude plateaued, then gradually and steadily began to descend. Perhaps it was because of the demands of living in and rearing a family in this American culture, one which promoted selfishness, a fast-paced lifestyle, and having "more" over the importance of others and their needs. Perhaps it was because life became more pragmatic, with daily cause and effect situations being so predictable. Perhaps it was because the immediacy of a dependency on Christ no longer seemed as urgent or necessary. Perhaps it was for all these reasons and more, but the reality was that I didn't have the kind of walk which I had enjoyed with Father once his grace had broken through my bulwark of bitterness. The closeness I once had with him was fading, and that was also very disturbing and disheartening to me.

In the midst of all this, Elena awoke one Sunday morning feeling very sick. She was experiencing nausea and abdominal pain. It was enough to keep us home from church services that day, but not enough to warrant a clinic visit. At least that is what Elena said. She insisted that she merely needed some extra rest. The thought never occurred to me to leave her at home and to attend the morning service without her.

That mid-afternoon, I received a call from the new pastor. His tone was not friendly, and he wasn't concerned about Elena. In fact, he didn't seem to have noticed that we were not present that morning.

"I need you and Elena to meet me in my office this afternoon," he said flatly.

"For what?" I asked.

"I just need some clarity about something."

"Well, Elena has not been feeling well the whole day. She needs to rest. Can't we just talk on the phone?"

"No, this is important," he insisted. "I need both of you here in half an hour."

I was feeling stressed and a little irritated. *What does he want?* I thought.

"Can't we just meet some other day? Elena is sick today and needs to rest."

"No," he repeated. "Like I said, this is important. I need you both here as soon as possible."

"But we don't have anyone to watch Nathaniel for us."

"The nursery is open now for choir practice. He can stay there while we talk in my office."

There didn't seem to be any way out of this. I hung up the phone and told Elena that we would have to meet with the pastor. She had not eaten anything all day due to her nausea and was not well enough to go anywhere. Despite this, we dressed and came to the pastor's office.

When we arrived, it was almost an hour before the evening

service. The choir was rehearsing as usual. Under the circumstances, it was sort of an eerie feeling hearing them sing hymns and praises without an audience, especially since we were pressured to be in the pastor's office. His office was where I had met with the founding pastor countless times for prayer meetings, deacon board meetings, counseling, and even just for friendly, social visits. There were a lot of good memories for me associated with that room. But with the new pastor, it all seemed too different. There were new furniture and decorations, different books on the shelves, and different arrangements of everything.

The pastor had just stepped out of his office as we approached his secretary's desk. He shook my hand in a perfunctory way and said, "John, glad you could make it."

"I'm not even sure why we're here," I replied. "We should be home. Elena's hurting and needs to rest. What is this all about?"

He spoke matter-of-factly. "We'll discuss this in my office. I just need some clarity on a few things."

Before we turned toward his door, I saw a very familiar face. I was surprised to see Don, the Chairman of the Deacon Board, passing through the secretary's office from the coffee room. I had served with Don as a deacon for a few years before my family and I left for the mission field. Even before then, he and I had bonded and built a warm friendship since my salvation as a teenager. We had a long and cordial—even sometimes goofy—history together. Serving in the church together through all the ups and downs over the years, we understood each other well. We both knew how much we loved Jesus and cared for our church and its people. Although Don was a dozen or so years older than me, he was a great friend and somewhat of a mentor at times. I was simultaneously both happy and puzzled to see him there. He was just walking in with a mug of coffee, and he greeted us with his usual warm and friendly smile.

"Hey, John! How's it going?"

"Doing great, Don." We shook hands carefully, minding his coffee. "How about you?"

"Oh, doing just fine," he said, smiling as he raised his mug in one hand. "I got my coffee, so I'm fine."

Then he turned to Elena with the same big smile.

"Hey, Elena!"

"Hi, Don," she said, sensing some pain but trying not to make it so obvious. Nevertheless, the pain was evident on her face.

"Are you okay?" he asked with a concerned look.

"I'm not feeling well," she said, showing a weak smile."

"Bless your heart. I'm sorry to hear that."

The pastor stepped to the doorway of his office and asked the three of us to enter. We came in and took our seats on the plush furniture around the coffee table.

"I just wanted to start with a word of prayer," he informed us.

We bowed our heads and closed our eyes.

"Father, thank you for this time together," he prayed. "I ask you to give us clarity in the matters we are about to discuss. Help us and give us your wisdom. In Jesus' name, amen."

Something about this whole scene was giving me a feeling of dread. The pastor, who had counseled me nearly a year before to get rid of my bitterness by mentally throwing away my negative thoughts, still didn't know us very well at all. Although we had had dinner at his home with his family just a few days after Father broke through my bitterness, we had not spent any real time together nor grown any closer since then. What could have possibly happened to make him insist that we meet in his office today, even though Elena was not physically up to it? Why was Don present? I didn't mind at all him being there, but if it was something concerning him, then why didn't the pastor mention that Don would be meeting with us? It must have something to do with him being the Chairman of the Deacon Board. Whereas the pastor's whole demeanor was not at all friendly, Don's was just as friendly as always. Maybe he knew that nothing was wrong, and I was just looking for the "panic" button. Maybe he had no notion of what we were about to discuss.

"Now, tell me," the pastor began, leaning forward with his elbows resting on his knees, "what's going on?"

'What's going on'? I wondered silently. *You want to know about*

our problems, our struggles? Why would you call us into your office for something like this? But I had a feeling that this was not a question for concern regarding the current events and status of our daily lives.

Elena and I looked at each of them, trying to figure out what to say. Then we looked at each other. She was hurting pretty badly, and I could imagine that her pain had just doubled from what she just heard.

"I don't . . . I don't know," I heard myself say. "What do you mean?"

"I understand that there has been some talk going around, and I need to know what has been said." His tone of voice was even and a bit low; his eyes were stern and unblinking.

Talk about what? We don't know what has been said. What is he trying to get us to say?

"I don't know what it is you want me to say." My voice sounded weak, and I suddenly felt afraid of us being pulled into something very hurtful.

"Some things have been said, and I just want some clarity from both of you on what exactly was said." His voice had slightly more volume, and his eyes, intimidating, remained the same.

Don didn't show much of an expression one way or another this whole time. He seemed basically neutral. Maybe he didn't know what this was all about, the same as us.

"We don't know what you're talking about. Can't you just tell us what this is all about?"

He leaned forward ever so slightly.

"I'll give you one more chance," he said flatly, with his voice now sounding more serious and threatening. "Tell me what has been said. If you don't, then—"

"—Okay!" Elena blurted out suddenly. She obviously felt pressured to say something. She was trembling from being so nervous and experiencing so much pain. "We've been having a hard time with our finances," she said weakly, with a sad tone in her voice, "ever since we came back from Honduras."

"All right, Elena," he said. "And what have you been saying

229

about this?"

"Well, we've really been struggling with paying the bills, and I guess I may have mentioned it to someone at church." Her voice was starting to crack. Here I was sitting beside the love of my life, and it felt like a tyrant was forcing her to confess something she hadn't done. I wanted to sweep her into my arms and carry her away from this whole situation. For some unperceived reason, the idea of walking out the door never occurred to us. We felt like we were forbidden to leave and had to endure the whole encounter.

"Have you said something you shouldn't have?" Now his eyebrows were raised. "Have you said that the church wasn't helping your family?"

"Elena's not—" I started to say, but he interrupted me sharply.

"—I'm not talking to *you* right now. I'm talking to *her*."

She trembled and winced in pain. "I . . . I may have. *Oh!* I'm hurting so bad." She clutched her abdomen with both hands and starting rocking slowly.

I put my arm around her and began rubbing her back.

"It's okay, *mi amor*," I assured her. Then to the pastor, I said, "She's in a lot of pain. She's been sick all day and hasn't had anything to eat. I need to take her home."

"I want to make this very clear," he said, more sternly than before. "Gossip will *not* be tolerated in this church. When people start talking bad about the church and spreading rumors, we will confront it head on."

"Who said we were talking about the church?" I asked, somewhat irritated.

"That's not your concern. I just want to make it clear that gossip will *not* be tolerated. If it happens again, we'll confront it the same way."

"We don't have any reason to gossip about anything," I assured him with more strength in my voice. "We just came from Honduras where we were victims of gossip, so we know what it's like and how it feels."

I wasn't sure that what I had just said even registered with him because of what he said next.

"And another thing, John," he added, "on Wednesday nights, I don't want you going to the Teen Center anymore. I want you to come into the sanctuary for prayer meeting."

I couldn't believe it! He was ordering me like a little child! How could he take away the only encouraging thing I was getting out of these services? I had to protest in some way.

"But I've befriended one of the teens and have really made a lot of progress with him."

"You can spend time with him outside of church, but on Wednesdays, you're going to the sanctuary class."

I didn't know how to respond. I'd never had a pastor treat me like this or do any of these things to me. It all seemed so surreal, like I was being branded as a "bad Christian" or being put under church discipline. And being intimidated and pressured into confessing something we didn't say or do? And my poor Elena!— being treated like this after all that she's already suffered in her life, growing up in poverty and having been targeted by so much senseless gossip in her hometown over the years. Now she was going through the same kind of thing all over again, only this time it was in a foreign language and in a foreign land far from her mom to comfort her. It was even coming to her from our accuser—*a pastor, of all people!*—who knew all the while that she was sick and in pain! None of this made any sense. *Lord, why's he doing this to us?*

My mind was swimming in a daze of confusion, questions, and anger. I held Elena to try to comfort her. I didn't remember much about the last few minutes of the meeting; I just wanted it to be over so that we could leave and go home. Don was there, of course, but I don't remember him participating in the pastor's intimidation tactics. In fact, when I reflected on it later, I didn't remember any sort of reaction either positive or negative coming from him. He must have been quiet the whole time except for the last couple of minutes. I seemed to remember him saying something in a friendly tone, but I couldn't recall what it was. Did he see through this whole charade to realize what the pastor was doing to us? Maybe he viewed the whole scene differently.

231

As we left the pastor's office, the pastor said, "The evening service will start in a few minutes, so I'll see you then."

"But we need to go home," I protested. "Elena is sick, and she hasn't eaten anything all day."

"She can find something in the kitchen to eat."

This was a convenient solution that he offered, but after what we had just experienced, we were not about to have someone catch us raiding the church refrigerator just to be accused of "stealing food."

We separated. The pastor walked toward the sanctuary, Don walked down the hall with his now half-filled coffee mug, and Elena and I turned toward the dining hall. We passed through it and down the Sunday school wing and to the nursery to gather Nathaniel. Then we left immediately for home.

Our daze and confusion only compounded during the drive home. Elena had tears in her eyes, which was from both the excess pain and the shameful treatment she had just received. I still couldn't believe what had just happened to us—of all people! We didn't need this in our lives! How could the pastor not realize this?

My mind was busy and frantic, trying to wrap itself around what we had just experienced to make some sense of it all. I reflected on the three senior pastors we had had in the history of our church by that time.

Our founding pastor had served as a youth pastor, an associate pastor, and a senior pastor in a few previous congregations for a number of years before moving to Atlanta. At age thirty-eight, he began knocking on doors and meeting people of all walks of life, working hard to become acquainted with them and to get a sense of the spiritual pulse of the community. He longed to start a new church in our area that would minister the gospel to people who needed Jesus Christ. For many years he worked long and hard to build up the church and its membership from just two families to the twelve-hundred-member congregation and multi-building facilities on nine acres that it became. That's what it was when he retired. I knew him to be a kind, encouraging man of God with a

232

genuine love for people. He never would have ever done anything like the treatment we received to us or to anyone else. Over the years he had spent countless hours in his office, weeping on his face in prayer over erring members who had given into various temptations. Although the congregation had experienced its fair share of ups and downs like any other ministry, I had never known him to do anything even remotely like the intimidating manipulation we experienced.

The next minister, the aforementioned "interim" pastor who left abruptly and shamefully, was an out-of-state transplant. He had been a youth minister for only a few years when our pulpit committee found him. When he came to our church, it was already large and thriving, thanks to the tenacity, hard work, and faithfulness of the founding pastor. This "interim" pastor hadn't had to toil and to persevere to build up the congregation or anything else at the church. He merely needed to maintain what was already in place. While we were in Honduras, something detrimental to the congregation must have happened because people had left in droves. By the time we returned to Atlanta, there were only about half of the membership in attendance as before. At thirty-years-old by then, the "interim" pastor was about four years younger than me. The pulpit committee had touted his youth as an asset. However, it eventually seemed that he had been burdened with too much responsibility, expectations, and stewardship to lead such a large membership for his youth and lack of experience. The events which lead to his sudden and shameful departure just three months after our return to the States evidenced as much.

The next and current pastor at that time had been a friend and hiree of the "interim" pastor. He joined the church staff as the youth pastor, with about the same amount of experience. When the "interim" pastor left, a lot of people looked to him to step in and to become the senior pastor. It was only a matter of months before that happened. This pastor was two years younger than me. He likewise had youth and a lack of experience; he was also picking up the pieces of what remained in the wake of the "interim" pastor's effects on the congregation. He seemed to have an even tighter grip than the previous minister, taking the reins of leadership and somewhat plowing his way through to do things his way. Mistakes had been made by the previous pastor, and this new pastor would shore up any shortcomings in the way things had been managed to avoid any further situations. He evidenced very little *persuasion* in his speech.

By default, I had analyzed what I thought had occurred during our absence and why. I thought that the process would be cathartic and somewhat satisfying enough to soothe the wounds of what we had experienced that Sunday afternoon. I was wrong—again. Not running to Christ in all things as I had done for some months, I fell prey to the introspective trap as Bob called it. I was hurt and angry—again. Someone had used words and intimidation tactics to humiliate and to hurt my wife—*and I had done* nothing *to stop it!* Why didn't I just stand up when the whole conversation started and escort my wife out of that place? Better yet, why didn't I tell that pastor on the phone, "I'm not meeting with you until you tell me what this is all about." Then when he surely would have beat around the bush and would have tried some intimidating line on the phone, I could have said, "Don't worry about us anymore. We're never going back to that church." In my flesh, I seemed to have several good answers, solutions, and retorts in hindsight. Yet none of that was useful at all. It only served to intensify my hurt further.

Poor Elena was hurting physically and emotionally. I tried comforting her, but all she did was weep silently. Against my pleas and prayers, she went to bed that evening with nothing in her stomach. I could have wept for her and with her, but I was too angry and hurt myself.

There it was again—*anger*. It was a seething, loathsome, indignation, so much like what I had experienced previously. This ugly monster had ventured back into my life, and it was vying to take control. I agonized all over again about this reappearance. *Lord, I thought we had taken care of this!* I repeated prayerfully. I tried confessing this sin, running to Christ. *Okay, he hurt us, and it was wrong. But I shouldn't have all these negative emotions*

234

toward him. I'm sorry, Lord, and I was wrong to do it.

It didn't work this time.

I tried again, rewording my prayer a little differently.

It still wasn't working. I had no sense of comfort and cleansing. My prayer of confession was insincere. I didn't mean it from the heart; I just wanted all this anger and negative attitude to disappear.

Although I thought I was willing to release my anger and to surrender it to Jesus, I really wasn't. There was another emotion there, blocking what needed to be done in my heart. It was a desire for vengeance. In my heart, I felt that the new pastor should be punished somehow. I couldn't forgive because I wouldn't for- give—not without knowing that some punishment was adminis- tered, some justice was applied, and some recompense or ven- geance was made against that pastor. I knew the scripture which said that vengeance was the Lord's, and that he would repay. Right then, that was what my heart wanted most. That was why the un- righteous thoughts formed easily in my mind and tortured me so.

Any man calling himself a pastor should know better than to do that to another human being. The thought wasn't satisfying, and it didn't make me feel any better, but it spewed out nonetheless.

If he truly has the Holy Spirit indwelling him, then he'll be convicted for what he did and come to us to ask forgiveness and to make things right for restitution.

There was another one of those thoughts, those mental accusations. They kept coming, and I felt powerless to stop them. They continued throughout the evening, one after another. I didn't have a restful sleep that night because of them.

Since I could neither sleep nor pray, I searched some of the imprecatory psalms to try to justify my anger. Yet even as I read each one, I knew that my motives for doing so were not right. I was seeking to justify my complaints before God. What I didn't want to recognize was that this man was also a child of my Father—whether I liked it or not—and he would answer to God, not to me, for his own actions. The pastor had his own walk before the Lord, to whom alone he was accountable, just like I was accountable to Father alone for mine. There was no way that I

235

could know what Father was doing in the pastor's heart and on his side of this whole ordeal while he also sought to love the anger and bitterness out of my heart.

Those negative thoughts and accusations kept tossing around in my mind for most of the night. On the following day at work, they resumed torturing me. Try as I might to busy myself and lose my thoughts in my work duties, there was always a variety of those nagging thoughts which would come to mind. There seemed to be no end in sight for my anger—again.

Somehow, I needed relief from all this. I tried praying; it didn't help. I could collect my thoughts and make my petition known before the Lord, and I knew that Father was listening, but I couldn't bring myself to confess my sins with sincerity and without any feelings for revenge or insults. Whenever I tried to talk to Father about what that pastor had done to us, the Holy Spirit just reminded me of my heart condition. He gently brought to mind how I needed to release that man to him, yielding any ideas that I had concerning punishment or vengeance. There was a tangible soreness in my abdomen and muscles as I agonized over what to do. I *needed* to forgive; that much was obvious. But I didn't *want* to forgive, not without him suffering something equivalent to what he had put us through.

Overall, I was miserable. This was not what I had wanted to become, not again.

CHAPTER 11

DEALING WITH UNFORGIVENESS

Since my prayers were at a roadblock due to my own unyielded-ness, I needed help and counsel from someone with the wisdom and godliness to pull me out of this pit of despair. During a break at work, I called Tom at home.

"Hi, Tom," I said in a low voice. "It's me, John."

"Hi, John. How are you?"

"Not so great," I said wearily. I sighed, feeling the burden of having to share all the gory details of what had happened so that Tom would be knowledgeable enough about the situation to counsel me.

"Tom, I have a serious problem with unforgiveness, and I need to know what to do about it."

"All right," he acknowledged calmly. "Tell me about it. I'm listening."

I sighed again, feeling the stress and strain of all the emotional pain that I had experienced in the previous twenty-four hours. I wasn't sure if I could communicate all that I needed to say, but I knew that I had to try.

"Well, yesterday Elena was very sick. She didn't feel well and didn't eat all day because she was feeling nauseous and had some severe stomach pain. She's had this before, but this time it wasn't too serious. She said that she just needed some rest, so we stayed home from the morning service. In the afternoon the pastor called us and said that we needed to meet with him in his office so that he could get some clarity about some things. He wouldn't say what he wanted. He just kept using that phrase saying he needed 'clarity about some things.' I told him Elena was sick and was resting, but he insisted that we come to his office as soon as possible. So, we went, not knowing what he was going to say. He didn't tell me on the phone, and he wouldn't tell me when I asked him again upon arriving at his office. Plus, he had the Chairman of the Deacon

237

Board, who's been a good friend of mine for many years, to meet with us also. He hadn't told me that he would be in the meeting.

"And, Tom, it was so weird! He began by praying and asking God to 'give clarity on some issues.' Then he asked us, 'What's going on?'"

"You mean just like that: 'What's going on?'"

"Yes! We didn't know what he was asking or what he wanted us to say. After asking the question two more times, he said that we had one last chance to tell him what was going on. Then suddenly Elena told him that we've been struggling financially and that she may have said something to someone about us not receiving any help from the church. He pressured us into admitting something we didn't even do! He was using all these intimidation tactics. It felt like we were little children going to the principal's office! And Elena was hurting so much the whole time, and he acted like he didn't even care!"

"Bless her heart," he said sympathetically. "How is she now?"

"Well, she didn't sleep much. I called her earlier, and she said that she did have some oatmeal. My mom went over to watch Nathaniel so that Elena could rest. She took something for pain and said she was going to try to take a nap, so she's a little better.

"I just can't believe how this man treated us. He's supposed to be the pastor! *Our* pastor never did anything like this to us."

"Did he say anything else?"

"Yeah, he said that 'gossip would not be tolerated at this church.' He thinks we were gossiping! After all we suffered at the hands of the gossips in Honduras, yet he thinks we're bad-mouthing the church and spreading bad rumors. He really doesn't even know us! He's just listening to what others are saying about us. I just couldn't believe it!

"Then he said that I couldn't attend the teen meeting on Wednesday evenings, that I'd have to sit in *his* boring class in the sanctuary. The Praise Band's music has been a real encouragement to me ever since we came back from Honduras. But now he's ordered me not to go there—as if I were a child! So now if I go back to the Teen Center he'll say I was 'disobedient' and probably call me in for another meeting to scold me again.

"This guy's a couple of years younger than me, and he really doesn't even know us. He's only been there as senior pastor for less than a year since the previous one left, so he doesn't have any history with us or the church. He just has his position, his title.

"And I know I should forgive him—not just because it's the right thing to do, but also because I don't want all this junk in my heart again. But I just can't get past the way he treated us, especially with Elena being so sick and him not caring—just intimidating her into confessing something that someone gossiped about us. I know I could follow Matthew 18, and tell him how he offended us, but that guy's not going to apologize. He would just give us that intimidating look with his eyes and say, 'If we had it to do all over again, we would handle it the same way.'

My heart felt heavier than when I began the phone call; my voice felt rough as well.

"I'm just so tired of all this, Brother Tom. Father had already broken through my bitterness and soothed away all the pain and anger. I was doing so great! We had that closeness and peace again, and I was so grateful and tenderhearted." My voice was heard to crack as I articulated my heavy emotional state. "Then this pastor had to treat us so horribly like this for nothing! Now I feel stuck again with all this anger and unforgiveness. I can't pray like I was, because I know that things aren't right in my heart—all because of this pastor guy."

Tom had listened quietly, not even making an audible "mm-hmm" to let me know that he was actively listening. I didn't know if he had been taking notes or maybe he just laid down the receiver. After a long silence, and just as I was about to ask him if he was still there, he spoke in a very placid, measured voice.

"What he did—he was not acting as a friend but as an 'officer of the church.' He felt that he needed to exert and to maintain his authority and position. The whole scene was basically a power play on his part. And your friend—the Deacon Chairman—he was brought in as a witness in case you two became unruly. His presence there was for the pastor's protection, whether he realized it or not."

Tom didn't mince words or speak indirectly. He targeted exactly what I needed to hear in order to understand the situation. As I listened, I became teary-eyed with intense emotions. I had a mixture of sadness, anger, relief, and gratitude. The sadness and anger were from being hurt; the relief and gratitude were from hearing truth and sensibility in the midst of all my pain, confusion, and doubt.

"He may never apologize for fear of seeming to lose some of his 'pastoral authority.' You remember that we've talked about authority before and how the only authority any of us have is the same—biblical authority? Those who put stock in positions and titles believe that they have special authority that derives from those positions or titles, authority which they believe others in the body of Christ don't have. That's one way they justify 'lording it over' their brothers and sisters in Christ.

"What he did and his attitude at the beginning brought temptation, fear, confusion, and a stumbling block to you and Elena. Again, it's evidence of a power play. It seems he's making a real effort to maintain his hold over the congregation.

"And the whole situation was not handled scripturally at all. If it had been, then he would have approached you two in private first as Matthew 18:15 prescribes. Also, he was avoiding your question both on the phone and when you first arrived at his office. As you said, he would only say that he wanted to get some clarity about some things and to know what was going on. By avoiding answers to your questions, he wasn't speaking the truth in love. He shouldn't have infused the whole situation with fear and intimidation. He should have just spoken to you privately as friends and equals in the body of Christ, avoiding the whole come-to-my-office power play. He could have just seen you in the hall or vestibule or some other neutral area one day and sort of in passing said, 'Hey, John, I was just wondering about something. Someone said that you two had said so-and-so, and I just wanted to ask you about it.' I'm not saying that he should have discussed it when others were around, passing through the area at the same time. But by not meeting in his office—on his turf, so to speak—it would have avoided the whole intimidating feeling of 'going to the principal's office.' And it would have been with the two of you in private first without bringing an outside party to the meeting.

"Now, concerning you, the real problem is not the problem but how you deal with this whole situation. Your real problem is how you react to the pain of those who mistreat you and those you love, whether those who mistreat you are believers or unbelievers. When they do, you become angry, bitter, and unforgiving."

Everything Tom was saying was true. I knew that he loved me enough not to say these things about me to hurt me. Rather, he was piercing to the heart of my problem, showing me what the true problem was. Tom was probably the only individual in my life who could have spoken to me about myself like this at the time without triggering any negative reaction in me. He and I both knew that this situation with the pastor would not be the last time that someone tried to hurt me or my family. It was a blessing to hear what my core issue was so that I could be aware of it and look to Father to help me with it. I would need to find the healing and the solution for all this in Jesus so as to avoid this same kind of angry, bitter, confused, fearful reaction. Once he let me know this about myself, he then turned the conversation toward explaining the hope available to me in Christ throughout the situation.

"Remember how he had told you a while back that you should let go of your anger and bitterness and put it behind you?"

"The throw-away-the-negative-thoughts therapy." I almost cracked a smile at the reminder of that ridiculous suggestion. "Yes, I remember it."

"That's what the world says: 'Let go of your problems and put them behind you.' But Father doesn't say that. The Scriptures tell us to deal with the problem, not to ignore it or to try to will it away. The only way you can deal with this is to take it to Father and to look to him for solutions and healing. You probably know Philippians 4:6 and 7, right?"

"I do," I admitted a bit sheepishly. "This is one of those passages that I should have been practicing through all this."

241

"Great. What does he tell you in those verses?"

"He says, 'Do not be anxious about anything. Instead, in every situation, through prayer and petition with thanksgiving, tell your requests to God. And the peace of God that surpasses all understanding will guard your hearts and minds in Christ Jesus.'"

"That's what we do when we're anxious. We pray to Father and ask him to take away our anxiety and to heal our hearts. And it says we must tell him our requests 'with thanksgiving.' But it's hard to be thankful in situations like this. We can't make ourselves thankful, but Jesus can. Therefore, we yield ourselves to Christ in prayer, knowing that he alone can make us thankful. When you admit to him that you are not thankful but want to be, then the cleansing and his work begins. This is like the story of the little boy with the new shoes that his daddy gave him. You remember that illustration, right?"

The story and the images quickly came to mind. It also reminded me of the fellowship with the brothers we had atop Stone Mountain so many months ago where I first heard Tom recount this illustration. My stress level was still high, but it was beginning to soothe a bit. I closed my eyes and held my forehead in my hand.

"Yes, I do."

"That little boy knew that he couldn't fix the problem he had caused for himself, but he knew that his daddy could. That's why he ran to him, even though he was crying because he had disobeyed his father.

"You see, it's easy to coast along in our lives and to forget how much we really need to depend on Jesus for everything every second. We even depend on him to fill us with gratitude so that we can give thanks in all things as he tells us. Now, we can't be *happy* about bad things, but we can be *thankful* that God is with us, that he is sovereign, and that he loves us through all things. He gives us that hope and fills our hearts with gratitude. This reminds us of Romans 8:28."

"I know that one too," I said with a sigh. "It reads, 'And we know that all things work together for good for those who love God, who are called according to his purpose.'"

242

"That's a great scripture to remember. It's an encouraging scripture to remember. From it we know that because of our love for God—our relationship with him and our calling according to his purpose—he is working in our hearts and lives. When we look to him for help, yielding to him so that he can do his work in and through us, then he *does* work all things together for good. We may not believe that it's for our good from our limited perspective, but it's for the ultimate good. That is, it *is* for our good, but not for some of the selfish things and purposes which we think are our good. It is to conform us more to the image of his Son, Jesus Christ.

"There's another important aspect to this. When we come to Christ in prayer, admitting that we're not grateful but want to be, we can come to him presenting our sins to lay at his feet. This means that we confess or admit the wrong that we have done for our part. Jesus does want us to grieve over our sins just as he is grieved. Like we are told in James 4, he says, 'Be afflicted, and mourn, and weep: let your laughter be turned to mourning, and your joy to heaviness. Humble yourselves in the sight of the Lord, and he shall lift you up.'* Therefore, he wants us to grieve or to mourn over our sins and what they have done to us and our relationship with him, but he doesn't want us to beat ourselves up over it. This kind of prayer of confession in which we humble ourselves before him is not to put us down as if we were worthless. It's to put us in the right condition to allow him to work in our hearts. Remember that we're still his children. Just like you don't want your child to despair over some wrong he's committed, Father doesn't want you—his child—to despair over what you've done wrong either.

"He knows that we, his children, will not walk perfectly, but he is pleased when we come to him to deal with our sins."

He's pleased when I bring my sins to him? I thought silently. It was another scenario in which we always go to him with everything. I should have realized this by now.

"Oh," I said weakly. "I must have forgotten that. I *still* need to run to Christ in all things."

243

"We all forget the importance of this sooner or later," Tom assured me. "But he loves us anyway. He's working through our failures and pain, and his purpose behind it is for our good, like Romans 8:28 says, to conform us to the image of his Son, like Romans 8:29 says. So, you see, our good throughout all this is to make us more like Jesus. Therefore, when we come to him in repentance, confessing our sins, he rejoices greatly! It's joy just like Jesus taught in the parables from Luke 15 about the shepherd and the lost sheep, the woman and the lost coin, and the father and the lost son. We sometimes get sidetracked or disoriented amid all the sins and hurts. But once we realize that Father has loved us through it all and that he waits patiently for us to turn to him and then we *do* run to him with our muddy shoes, he rejoices so much. He's just like the father from the parable running to his wayward son and showering him with love and gifts."

Once again, the parable of the gracious father communicated the truth of Father's heart to me. *I* was that wayward son, returning in humility to admit my wrongs and failures. Just like that son in the story, I didn't necessarily expect to be cleansed, forgiven, and blessed with his grace. I just wanted to return to some semblance of living rather than merely surviving spiritually and to find a way out of all this turmoil and doubt churning in my heart—again.

"So . . . he really does rejoice when we come to him with our sins?" I asked in a low voice.

"He really does, John. He rejoices, knowing that in that moment he can begin to cleanse us and grace us with what we need to heal our hurts. He also gets to do his work of making us more like Christ, which is the very purpose for him allowing trials into our lives. Think about when little Nathaniel comes to you with something he needs help with. Don't you delight to express your love to him by providing him with what he needs?"

Several images flashed in my mind: times when I tied Nathaniel's little shoes, helped him with a toy that was broken, comforted and bandaged him when he had scraped his knee, and even when he had done wrong and come to me in tears. He was my precious, little son whom I loved more than anything in the world. In some of those moments which saddened him, I would feel sadness along with him, but I would always comfort him and shower him with love and affection. I wanted him to know that he could always come to me and share any problem with me. I realized then that Father was teaching me to come to him always as a child of his.

"I do, Brother Tom," I said, with fresh tears forming in my eyes. "It's easier to understand this as a parent."

"You're right, John. I learned many lessons with my three boys over the years. In fact, I'm still learning about Father's relationship with me through my relationship with them, even though they're all adults and fathers themselves now." He chuckled slightly, and I could picture his winning grin. "God is the best parent, and even as we relate to our children and sometimes stumble along the way, if we're open to his teaching, we can learn a lot from our children about his love and care for us as his children."

"Wow! His love for me is so great, even when I sin!"

"Of course he loves you when you sin! He doesn't like the sin, because that's what's hurting you and your relationship with him. His anger is really aimed at the sin, but of course he loves you! You're his precious child! He gave his Son to rescue you from the clutches of sin and death. And he only knows how to relate to us out of a heart full of love, even when discipline is necessary. From our finite, imperfect perspective, we don't always understand it that clearly, but it's true nonetheless.

"And because he loves us, he will continue working in us to make us like Jesus. Paul was sure of this in Philippians 1:6, where he said, 'Being confident of this very thing, that he which hath begun a good work in you will perform it unto the day of Jesus Christ.'* That word 'perform' is the old King James English way of saying 'complete' or 'perfect.' He'll keep working on us to finish the job of making us like Jesus, even if it takes until the day of his visible return to finish the job. And in verse thirteen of the next chapter, Paul says, 'it is God which worketh in you both to will and to do of his good pleasure.'* So, he really delights to take our sins

245

and failures—all the junk in our lives—and turn them into opportunities when he can do the important work in our hearts. We just have to let him do it. Remember that he won't force his way on us; he lets us choose to let him work. And as an extra blessing, we learn to trust him throughout the process."

"That's very encouraging!" I said, wiping away tears.

"Now, getting back to the gratitude: You can be thankful, not for the hurt this pastor caused, but for the fact that Father used it to bring this problem to your attention so that you would have to run to Christ for him to deal with this. It is in this sense that you can 'rejoice in the Lord always'* like Philippians 4:4 tells us."

"Tom, this is all wonderful," I began, feeling somewhat relieved, "but what if he never apologizes?"

"Whether he apologizes or not, you must forgive him from the heart graciously, just as Father forgives us and remains in relationship with us despite our continual sins against him. We can do this because of what Ephesians 4:32 tells us. Do you know that verse, John?"

"I do," I replied, sighing on the inside. "It says, 'be kind to one another, compassionate, forgiving one another, just as God in Christ also forgave you.'"

"We see the same teaching in Colossians 3:13, which likewise tells us to forgive others because we are forgiven. In fact, this forgiveness we received in Christ is our motivation for forgiving others who sin against us. In Christ we are enabled to forgive others with his grace because of the grace we received when we were forgiven. This means that you're not forgiving without Jesus' enablement. That's why we can forgive one another, because we do so 'in Christ,' just as the Father forgave us in his Son."

"You're right, Tom." Again, I sighed. "I know that I'm supposed to forgive him. It's just so hard to do right now."

"That's further proof of why we need to run to him and to depend on him every second for everything. We can only forgive others because we do so in Jesus, that is, with his grace enabling us. This forgiveness is you giving up your right to be avenged or to see him punished. And just know that the forgiveness is more for your sake than for his. It's so that you won't have this unforgiveness and resentment pent up in your heart, getting in the way of your relationship with Jesus and everything else like it did before. Besides that, Jesus delights to pour out his grace through us to forgive others, except that we must choose to let him. Obeying is always more fun knowing that it pleases him. We have his grace to enable us and pleasing him to motivate us. I'd say that's a pretty good deal, wouldn't you?"

"Well, I guess so. Knowing that forgiving others is pleasing to him *does* make it something that I want to do. But I can't help thinking that throughout this whole thing, forgiving will be the hardest part."

"It always is," he agreed flatly, "but remember to keep running to Jesus. Depend on him to give you his heart of grace and love to forgive. Talk to him about it—what you feel, the anger, the frustration. Keep seeking him and letting him know how you're feeling and how you're doing with this. As you do, he'll enable you with his grace to be grateful, to grieve over your part of the wrong, and eventually to turn from the unforgiveness and to release the pastor from the heart. After Jesus does the work in you and you have the peace of Christ concerning this matter, then you can approach him humbly, submitting to one another as brothers, like Ephesians 5:21 tells us. Jesus will have healed you with his grace so that you can be gracious to him and forgive him. You'll find that you'll have pity for him and his sin, not anger or resentment."

"Really? That's going to happen in me?" I couldn't imagine pitying someone who hurt Elena and me like that pastor did.

"It's what happens when we understand by Father's grace his perspective on sin and on those who commit it. But again, it's a work that only he can do through the Holy Spirit. If you allow him to work in you, to love and to forgive others through you, then you'll be surprised at how your heart starts to resemble Jesus'. You'll have more of Father's perspective and understanding; you'll start to have his *agape* kind of love for people. The most important thing is to run to Christ whenever you have negative thoughts about the man. And when you do forgive him, forgive graciously with no strings, no stipulations. Forgive as if the whole thing had never happened."

As I listened to Tom's counsel, though I still felt burdened, my spirit lifted somewhat.

"Thanks, Tom. You've been so encouraging! I don't know how to thank you for all this."

"We're all brothers in Christ," he stated happily. "I'm sure you would do the same to help me if I needed it."

I laughed halfheartedly, wiping away a tear. "I don't think you'll ever have this problem."

"You never know. We all need Jesus all the time. And he's always with us to shower us with his grace for the difficult times in life like this."

I thanked him again and hung up the phone.

His words were very enlightening and enabling. I was somewhat relieved, yet I also felt as if I had butterflies in my stomach. This was going to be extremely hard for me to do. Nevertheless, according to the Scriptures, it would be Jesus doing it in and through me. At that point, I still couldn't imagine having Father's heart of love, forgiveness, and especially pity for a minister who should know better than to treat other believers the way he treated us. Then again, I was learning that Father can do astounding things, even in the likes of someone like me.

This conversation with Tom played repeatedly in my mind for the rest of the day. I also kept reviewing Romans 8:32: "Indeed, he who did not spare his own Son, but gave him up for us all—how will he not also, along with him, freely give us all things?" It seemed to me that "all things" included not only spiritual blessings but also Father's grace to enable me to love and to forgive when it was most difficult. *He* would do the forgiving; I only had to die to self and to let him do his work in and through me. Although this would be arduous for me, it would not be impossible with Father.

I had seen before on television instances where some family members of murder victims repeated, "I forgive you," when they faced the convicted culprits who ended the lives of their loved

248

ones. They must have allowed Father to grace them with forgiveness and to let it overflow to those murderers. My case didn't even compare with those, concerning the tragedy and the depth of difficulty. Regarding my unforgiveness, no one had been killed; we were simply hurt unexpectedly by someone whom we never imagined would hurt us like this.

The days and weeks passed. I had the Scriptures and Tom's counsel in my mind and heart for spiritual nourishment and edification. However, whenever I saw the pastor in the worship services or even anticipated seeing him, my heart would pound, and the butterflies and nerves would work overtime. I knew that it meant that I had not yet forgiven him. Whenever he was on the platform, and especially while he was preaching, I found myself looking away from him. His eyes seemed to pierce through me, and at times he seemed to be preaching directly to me. *How could he do anything ministry-related after what he did to us, and that without even apologizing?* I thought over and over.

One Wednesday evening, I couldn't take it anymore. During the sermon I decided to sit in with Elena while she volunteered keeping the nursery.

"What are you doing here?" she asked, surprised to see me step through the door.

"I just thought I'd sit here with you," I offered.

Her facial expression revealed her thoughts. "You've been acting weird lately. What's wrong?"

"Nothing. I just want to be with you." I knew what was wrong, but I didn't want to discuss it.

Amazingly, Elena had long since forgiven the pastor. Thanks to Tom, I knew how she had done it, but I couldn't bring myself to release the man. She had been hurt by him more than I had been, yet I was the one still wrestling with unforgiveness. My love for her made me ache because of the way she had been abused. But if she had forgiven him and put all the abuse in the past, then why couldn't I? These thoughts swirled around in my mind as I attempted to read 1 Corinthians 15 in the nursery, taking observa-

249

tional notes on the passage. The speaker overhead transmitted the pastor's voice as his sermon was being piped into the nursery. It was impossible for me to focus on what I was reading.

Occasionally someone would stop by the nursery and chat briefly with Elena. Everyone who saw me sitting there either raised an eyebrow or asked why I was there. "I'm keeping Elena company," was my reply. Some of them probably figured out that something was wrong, but they never commented.

The following month, there was a birthday party for a child from church who was Nathaniel's age. Nathaniel and the other three- and four-year-olds were invited to the celebration at a local kids' pizzeria and playhouse. We accompanied Nathaniel there. My heart stopped momentarily when I saw the pastor enter the door with his wife and his young daughter. I should not have been surprised to see them there, since his daughter was four-years-old, and she had obviously been invited. I tried to stay aloof, remaining close to Elena and Nathaniel. Nevertheless, after twenty minutes or more, the pastor found his way around to me and casually approached me.

"Hi, John. How have you been?"

"Fine," I heard myself saying, avoiding eye contact. *You obviously know how I've been doing,* I thought silently. *It's been two months since that day in your office, and this is the first time you've spoken to me.*

"I just wanted to say hello and check on you to see how you're doing."

Nervous tingles and anxiety permeated my body. Suddenly I felt as if the room were extremely warm. I wanted to be anywhere but there at that moment. *How can I get out of this corner politely?* I wondered.

"Excuse me," I offered weakly. Then I slowly made my way through the crowd and went to the men's room, feigning the appearance that a restroom break was my excuse for leaving.

After the party, Elena asked me what had happened and why I walked away. She said that another father, whom I passed in the crowd, walked up to the pastor as soon as I stepped away.

"Brr!" he uttered, shuddering, as if shaking off a sudden chill. "What was that all about?" he asked the pastor.

"I have no idea," the pastor replied flatly, following me with his eyes.

"You embarrassed me," Elena said plainly in the car as we drove home. "Why can't you just forgive him?"

"I don't know," I said trembling. "I'm just so hurt because of what he did to you."

"Yes, but I'm fine. Everything's okay with me." Then she posed a question that pierced my heart. "Is it really worth all this?"

Elena was right. I needed to forgive, and it *wasn't* worth all this that I was going through. I prayed daily and throughout each day, running to Christ and talking to him about me and this situation just as Tom counseled me to do. My heart condition showed no noticeable change.

There was no real progress with me in the forgiveness process. I must have thought that, after conversing with Tom that day, I would hang up the phone and the unforgiveness, resentment, anger, and bitterness would just melt away like it had before. But this seemed different to me. It probably wasn't different to Father, but to me it was in many ways worse than what I had experienced during those two years of my previous bitterness. This time it wasn't just some wrong thoughts and warped perspective I had about Father which needed correcting with truth, love, and grace. This time it was mistreatment from a pastor—someone I expected to be an encouragement to me instead of a stumbling-block. Therefore, it was something personal from one individual against my wife and me. I knew what I needed to do, and I couldn't do it. I just wanted all this to end.

Elena still showed no signs of unforgiveness. Once from a distance, I even saw the pastor speak with her in the hall after the Sunday evening service. He spoke with her about a solo she was planning to sing in one of the up-coming services and then about the nursery schedule, asking if she could substitute for someone a

251

week later. Elena accepted, seeming to have no problem at all conversing with him as if that day in his office had never occurred. She was modeling what it looked like to forgive someone graciously, with no requirements and no lingering resentment. *Why can't I be like her, Father?*

One day Steve called me at home. He was being factitious as usual until he quickly noticed that I seemed to be in a bad mood. I would have to admit to him what my problem was. He wouldn't judge me, I knew, but admitting it would seem to make me feel worse. Then again, maybe he could help me in some way.

"I'm still dealing with this unforgiveness," I admitted loathingly. "I wish I could just turn it off, but I can't. I know what to do, but I'm having the hardest time doing it."

"Man, that's tough, Brother," he said with sincere empathy. "We all struggle with that sometimes."

"What makes me look worse is that Elena got over it so quickly. She forgave him the next day and hasn't held a grudge since. I don't understand how she does it!"

"She's a loving person."

My scowl was not visible over the phone. "Thanks a lot, Flamen'."

"No, I don't mean it that way. I'm not saying that she is and you're not. I just mean that she naturally has a love for people. You know how she is with people, especially with children and senior citizens."

"Yeah, I know," I admitted sheepishly. "She's closer to Jesus than I am."

"It's not a competition, Brother," he replied plainly. "Don't let your thoughts lead you into a downward spiral."

"I know," I sighed. "It's the introspective trap. That's what these friends of Tom's call it."

"'*Introspective trap.*' Hmm. That's about right. It can become a snare for you if you let it. When we meditate on negative thoughts about ourselves, we tend to believe them."

"I just want this to be over," I stated with frustration. "I've had

252

this before—for two years! I don't need to go through this again. I learned my lesson last year, and I just want the bitterness to end."

"Are you still talking to Father about this and your heart and how you want to be thankful and to forgive—like Tom suggested?"

"Yes, I am, throughout each day. But there's still this roadblock, and I still can't look the pastor in the eye, not even from a distance."

"Have you focused on Father's love?"

"Yeah, Flamen', I have. I've thought about that night at Tom and Sara's house with Nathaniel, going over the scriptures Tom told me and remembering my son running into my arms. It gets me all teary-eyed, but I still have this nagging thought that *I've got to forgive that man.* And I just can't! Father's love for me is great—I know that. He takes me back, just like the parable of the gracious father, but he keeps reminding me that I need to forgive."

"Hey, that sounds like progress there!" he voiced with excitement.

"What do you mean, 'progress'?" The suggestion was irritating, especially since it didn't feel like I was doing anything but regressing.

"Brother, if this had happened before Father's grace broke through to you last year, then you wouldn't have *dreamed* that he would take you back. Remember? You thought Father was frowning at you with his arms crossed, sort of like a military drill instructor."

"That's true," I replied softly. "I guess that counts for something."

"Aw, c'mon, Bro! It counts for a lot more than just 'something'! You realize now that you can go to him with your problems and that he'll listen and that he won't frown and turn away from you. You know now that he rejoices to welcome you with open arms—all because of his grace and love. It's just like in some of the psalms where the writer starts out moaning and complaining about his problems. After he's cast his burden on the Lord, by the last few verses of the psalm he's rejoicing in Father and his

253

forgiveness."

"Yeah, you're right. I could read some of those psalms. That would probably help."

"They'll help you to see your problems from a biblical perspective. Besides that, you'll get some additional insights to help you find the grace to forgive."

"'*Find* the grace'?"

"Yeah, y'know, to forgive."

The phrase suddenly seemed peculiar to me. "So, I have all the grace I need in Jesus . . . I just need to *find* it?"

"It's mostly an expression. I don't know that 'finding' it is the issue. But he does shower us with grace upon grace according to John 1."

"Okay." I was trying to dissect this whole process and to figure it out so that I could do what was necessary. "So, I have the *means* available in Jesus; I just need to *choose* to forgive."

"Yeah, basically. Good night, Brother! You really are analytical!"

"I'm just trying to figure this out."

"You may not want to hear this, but while analyzing it *could* help you to understand it a little, it may not provide the big breakthrough to forgiving him that you're looking for." His voice sounded serious yet compassionate. "Brother, learning to forgive is not some one-size-fits-all program that you learn. Don't expect this to be 'How to Forgive Others in Five Easy Steps' or 'The Three Keys to Dealing with Unforgiveness.' You probably just need to run to Jesus, pour out your heart to him about this whole ordeal, and allow him to let his grace heal you. He usually works through our problems like this in relationship with him instead of us learning some formula or short-cuts for doing what only he can do in us and through us."

Another audible sigh proceeded from me. "You're right, Flamen'. I'm just so tired of the way I feel and the way I'm reacting to this. How about if we just talk about what I've learned so far?" I asked, still determined.

"If that's what you really want, then I suppose it won't hurt."

254

"Okay, thanks. Where do I start?"

"I'd say to start with what you know about Father and his great love."

"Yeah, that's perfect," I said resolutely.

At the time, this exercise seemed encouraging, but it may have simply been too pedantic to penetrate into the heart of the matter. Reflecting on what Steve had just said, I was convinced that the road to forgiveness is not a series of the same "how-tos" for everyone. I had already learned that Jesus works with us individually in the details of our lives for our spiritual growth. We continued with the conversation, however, since I felt that I simply had to do something to help me to understand what was going on in my heart.

"I know that he loves me more than I can imagine," I began, "and that he only knows how to relate to me out of a heart full of perfect love."

"Right. He loves you even when other people don't."

"I also know that the Creator who sacrificed his Son for me to rescue me from sin, death, and the lake of fire has unwavering, perfect love for me." It was a blunt truth that I had known for some time, yet it didn't seem to impact me much at that moment.

"That's great, Brother. Also know that your circumstances and other people's words and actions toward you don't indicate that his love for you has changed."

"Father *knows* me better than anyone else does," I reminded myself aloud, "and he *loves* me more than anyone else does. He knows what's best for me too."

"With that being true, what does it matter if other people don't love you or even hate you or mistreat you? Jesus' love for you is enough."

"Enough?"

"Yeah! His love is enough for you to endure hardships and abuse of all kinds. It doesn't mean that he's responsible for it. It's just imperfect people acting selfishly. Y'know—people abusing Father's gift of free will."

"You're right," I accepted calmly. "So much suffering and

injustice is carried out and 'justified' in Jesus' name. Men every-where and throughout the ages have blamed God for their sins, saying that he led them to commit the most horrendous atrocities, yet it simply isn't true."

"Despite what others say, do, or think about you or against you, Father's love for you doesn't change. He's still giggly excited with love for you. After all, you're his child, and he gave his Son to save you."

Another truth needed to be vocalized. "He is grieved when we hurt each other," I remembered, "just like any parent is grieved when his or her beloved children hurt each other."

"Father loves that pastor as much as he loves you, Bro. His love for either of you doesn't change. Father doesn't love him any less or you any more just because of what he did. He loves you both infinitely. In fact, he loves you both so much that doubtless he's working in that pastor's heart just as he is working in yours, probably just in different ways. We can't see what he may be working in his heart. You just never know."

"That's true. So, I can't hate him or wish evil on him."

"Aw, no way!" I could imagine Steve's wincing, furrowed-brow look, though I couldn't see it. "But it's also important to understand something else about the people who hurt you."

"What's that?" *This may be where he lowers the boom and gives me the truth that's extremely difficult to bear*, I thought hesitantly.

"Now, what I'm about to say may not be true for this pastor. I don't even know him, so I'm not swayed one way or another. But I've had a lot of people hurt me, my family, and others as a fleshly tactic to get their way, to hide something, or whatever."

"Okay, I guess I'm ready to hear it." I tried to brace myself emotionally.

"All right, here it is: When someone tries to hurt you, understand that their comments and actions were *meant* to hurt you. In fact, that's why they did what they did. It was an attempt to hurt you, maybe even to break your heart."

This seemed too obvious.

"Well *duh*, Flamen'! Of course, they're trying to hurt me! What else would they be trying to do?"

"Hang on, Brother. Just hear me out for a second. When someone hurts you analytical guys—"

"—Wait a minute. 'You analytical guys'? Aren't you basically analytical and introspective also?"

"Maybe to a point."

"Or to a fault."

"Here's *my* point: What you're hearing from them—the criticisms, insults, complaints, all that negative talk against you—has nothing to do with the truth about you. If it did, Father would have delivered it in a more *persuasive* way, not through someone who's behaving in a mean way and who doesn't have your best interests in mind."

"Well, that sounds different." I was expecting some crushing blow to my ego or perhaps something to shake the foundations of my understanding. Reflecting on it now, I don't know why I thought that way.

"Y'see, a lot of people treat us the way they do because they think we have a big button labeled 'hurt me' that gets pushed when they say or do certain things. As sickening and as sad as it is, some people delight in hurting others. It boosts their egos in their own view or does something for them on some level."

"That does sound sad, sickening, and ludicrous," I acknowledged. "I can't imagine delighting in hurting others."

"It happens—a lot more than we may know. Oftentimes, if you could peel away the layers and look behind their actions, words, and attitudes to see what motivates such malice, you'd find some bitterness of a different kind."

"Really? There are different kinds of bitterness?"

"I don't really mean it like that, Bro. Maybe there are. I guess what I'm trying to say is that a lot of people don't realize that they're bitter. Did Tom ever talk to you about the basis of all anger?"

"Yeah, he did. He said that, in reality, it's *all* aimed at God, whether we know it or not."

"I tend to agree with that."

257

"I do too. I mean, it broke my heart to hear it the first time. He told me just before Father's grace and love broke through my bitterness and anger that night at Tom and Sara's house. But I really believe that when that truth hit home with me, it was one of the steps of Father's work in my heart. It helped me to understand the graveness of my spiritual condition."

"Think about the people of the world: their choices, their actions, and the multitudes of heart-wrenching tragedies that mankind has fostered on one another. When you look at society at large and contemplate some of the things that people do, it becomes clear that there are tons of bitterness and anger in this world."

"That really makes sense."

Since being showered with Father's grace the year before, I seemed to have acquired a sensitivity to noticing anger and bitterness in others around me besides just myself. Far from being a reaction of condemnation, it was always a scary acknowledge-ment, since I humbly realized that that had been me just a short while ago. Now I had the perspective to pray for those in the grip of bitterness. Furthermore, I knew that if Father had not broken through the shroud of bitterness I wore for those years, then I would have continued in the same spiritual mess.

"Steve, this world needs Jesus and his grace and love like never before."

"Don't we though? Now *that's* the heart of a missionary!"

"Yeah, well, I wish I could go back to Honduras."

"Me too, Brother. I was delighted and content working there more than in any other segment of my life so far. I just wish I had met Aby before I went. Going to the mission field as a single man wasn't the best of ideas."

"Flamen', now that we know these truths about bitterness in society," I stated, "what do we do with them?"

"Seems like we need to pursue Father—or rather, to be aware of and enjoy his pursuit of us—and to look to him for guidance. He could lead us back to Honduras one day. But whether he does or not, we can always share his grace with those we cross paths

258

with—just not in the fleshly, programmed, man-centered, performance-based ways we were used to using in our earlier years."

"Amen to that, Flamen'. So many of those church programs and outreaches seemed so plastic and fake. All those formal visitations, bus ministries, and evangelistic ministries—I'm not sure how much good they did."

"I don't know," he contemplated aloud. "I wouldn't discount them all. A lot of people came to know Jesus through those programs in the seventies and eighties—even today. And sure, not everyone who shared Jesus had the purest of motives or complete dependence on the Holy Spirit. But in Philippians, even Paul rejoiced that Christ was preached regardless of the motive. Father can use practically anything and still fulfill his will and receive the glory."

"I know you're right, Steve. I just don't think that I could stomach much of what passes for evangelism in a lot of Christian circles these days."

"Yeah, I can relate to that. But we can always share Christ with others out of our relationship with him. As we build relationships with others and sort of win their trust and earn a hearing with them, they'll be more inclined to hear what we have to say about him if we speak the truth in love."

Then I released a sigh. "Which brings me back to dealing with this unforgiveness I have. I'm not really going to be effective in *anything* for Father if this isn't resolved."

"All right," he agreed. "We can table that discussion for another time. Let's get back to talking about people hurting us.

"As the world is, people get angry for a lot of reasons," he continued analytically, "whether it be disappointments in life, missed opportunities they had their hearts set on, unexpected tragedies, or other things. But in the end, they usually aim their anger at someone else and, in their heart of hearts, that someone is mostly God."

"Yeah, I know. I've met people who claim to be atheists due to losing one or both of their parents in their childhood. I mean, not

259

to make light of their pain, but they blame *Father* for it. Even if it's sometimes evident that their loved ones passed away due to their own lifestyle choices or from unanticipated accidents, I just don't believe that Father goes around snuffing out people's lives like that. A lot of people think that he ends people's lives just because he feels like it or 'they deserve it.'"

"That's a valid point," Steve remarked. "From a lot of people's perspectives, Father is blamed for probably most of the deaths that occur. Like Tom said, we blame Father because, in his omniscience, he knew that these tragedies were going to happen, and he could have prevented them—like the events of 9/11 for example."

"Oh, I know!" The reminder of what happened on that catastrophic day was emotionally and spiritually painful. "Man, that was a most awful and tragic day! To think that people could conspire to perpetrate such a series of events—it's just unbelievable to think that people would agree to plot and to scheme something like that! It was such an abuse of Father's gift of freewill."

"You're telling me! And think of the families of all those victims. They've been more than devastated by the losses of their loved ones. We may never know how much bitterness and how many atheists resulted from that one day."

"Man, I haven't even thought of that!" I exclaimed. "I remember that there was an increase in church attendance immediately following 9/11. However, it died down after a few weeks."

"People were looking for answers then; not all of them found the answers they were looking for. What they really needed was believers to be there for them to demonstrate Father's love, grace, and compassion."

"That's a constant need that we *all* have despite any residual bitterness. But, getting back to our topic," I said, backing up, "about people getting angry for many different reasons: If their anger isn't resolved, if they either openly or secretly blame Father, then bitterness quickly sets in."

"Exactly, and a symptom of their bitterness is to lash out at those around them."

"That's exactly what *I* was doing," I admitted. "Steve, I was awful to people! I hurt Elena so many times, making her weep profusely. And I just can't shake those memories of her crying—all for my fault."

"Don't beat yourself up over it, John," he said firmly. "I'm sure you've apologized to her and she's forgiven you."

"That's true, but I still live with those memories. Steve, I even lashed out at strangers in Honduras and then to strangers here in the States." This was easier to talk about over the phone than face to face.

"Again, you've confessed and repented, all as a result of Father's grace working in your heart. What you learned from those experiences can be vital in helping others who don't even realize the depth of their anger and bitterness or that they blame Father for things in their lives. It can also help your perspective to understand some of what people are going through when they hurt you for whatever selfish reasons they have."

"Yeah, Flamen'," I agreed. "I know you're right."

"It can even serve as a building block towards forgiving others for their wrongs against you."

"What do you mean?"

"Look, Bro. I don't want this to sound like I'm tootin' my own horn, but when I realize that people are just lashing out of their own anger and perhaps even bitterness, then I know that their actions and words against me are not really personal."

"It seems pretty personal most of the time."

"And that's probably their intention. Just think: What would do the most damage from their perspective: personal insults detailing your faults and shortcomings or generalizations expressing dislike and hatred?"

"Oh, okay. I see what you mean now."

"I believe that Father's grace has diffused a lot of the hurt aimed at me before it even started by making me aware of this from his perspective."

"You mean that when someone hurts you, you just say, 'Well, that's just the bitterness talking'?"

"No, I'm not saying that." He probably had that furrowed-brow look again. "I don't make excuses for people's behavior. What I mean is that when people hurt me, instead of letting their comments sink in and do any real damage, I just think, 'Wait a minute. They only said or did that to try to hurt me. They're just venting some anger, and I happen to be in their path.' *That* means that their opinions—or supposed opinions—are not based on truth. Therefore, I don't have to hide in a corner in a fetal position, worrying that what they said about me is true, because it's not true. When Father wants to reveal something to me about my heart that needs work, he is much gentler and caring. Remember, he wants to make me more like Jesus, and he knows that using the voice and words of the enemy through another human being to lambaste me is not an effective way to accomplish that."

"But what if some of it sounds true?"

"Even if it sounds true, even if it has a sliver of validity as to some needed character improvement on my part, it's still not Father communicating something with me. It's still some ploy of the enemy filtered through a human being, and Father doesn't partner with the deceiver for our sanctification. Y'know, when we let him, the enemy can gain a lot of ground if we play the recordings of those comments over and over in our minds."

"Yeah, but it's easy to let those thoughts run wild, Flamen'."

"That's why we need to renew our minds by meditating on the Scriptures, not negative thoughts we hear from the world, the enemy, and our flesh. Meditating on Father's thoughts for us and about us can repel and drown out all those negative thoughts. Otherwise, replaying those negative memories and thoughts will lead you to despair. You definitely don't want that."

"No, I don't. That sounds like bitterness to the nth degree. So, how do I apply all this to my unforgiveness with this pastor?"

"All right, let's consider this. You said that his control of the whole deal was a power play, right?"

"That's the term that Tom used, and it seems to fit."

"All right, so here's this guy who has a title, and he has to try to live up to it. He believes the gossip without checking with you two first in a nonconfrontational way to see if what he heard was valid."

"You're right so far."

"He uses a few intimidation tactics like calling and insisting that you come in, avoiding your direct questions about what he wants or is doing—"

"—Bringing in a witness to validate his side if the confrontation ever gets out, making us feel like it's a 'trip to the principal's office,' being rude to me and mean to my wife while she was sick. The list goes on and on."

"I get the picture. He sounds like a real piece of work. Anyway, all that stuff he did was directed at you two. However, it was probably just his struggling and floundering with trying to control the congregation. That doesn't excuse what he did, obviously. It just gives us a clue as to what could have been his motive. Therefore, if it only takes a couple of side comments from people to get him all geared up into manipulation mode, then what does that really say about him?"

My mind went blank. I tried to think of something to say as a reply, but I couldn't think of a fitting answer.

"I—I'm not sure what it says about him."

"All right. Think about security," Steve suggested. "What would a *secure* person in Christ have done?"

"Oh, you mean to say that he's insecure."

"Eh, his actions and words would lead one to that conclusion, so it's quite possible that he is. What would a *secure* person in Christ have done?"

"Well, Tom said that he should have talked to us on the side after a service in a nonthreatening way to say, 'Hey, I just wanted to check with you about something. Somebody said that you all had commented about such-and-such. Is that true or is there something you need help with? '"

"Yeah, Brother, that sounds *much* better. A secure person in Christ could have viewed it as *an opportunity to meet a need* or to reason with you calmly if you had said something inappropriate. That would have been more of a familial- or relation-oriented way to handle it for the good of the body, rather than the iron-fisted method of law, conformity, and punishment."

263

"I agree with you, Flamen', but I don't really see how this is helping me."

"All right. Here's where we bring it home. The fact that he used a fleshly tactic rather than a relational, grace-based application lets us know that he has his own spiritual issues to deal with."

"Exactly! I couldn't agree with you more."

"Hang on, Brother. We're not going the condemnation route. We're trying to see things from Father's perspective. After all, Father sees *both* of you as his children having this unresolved conflict. It has hurt you and stirred up some bitterness. So, as you can imagine, Father is concerned about you. Obviously, he wants you to release the guy and to forgive him. But, what has this ordeal done for him?"

Again, I was drawing a blank. "I just can't see it for now," came my frustrated reply. "What *has* it done for him?"

"Well, it's given him an opportunity to show his true colors. The fact that he resorts to the flesh instead of depending on the Spirit to lead him in addressing this issue shows his insecurity. Hence, with all Father's love for the pastor as a child of his, and nearly two millennia ago having already taken care of this bag of sins he committed against you, how would Father view the pastor from his heart of love and compassion?"

It was then that I understood what Tom had said to me. I was both surprised and amazed at the conclusion that I drew.

"He would think . . . 'How sad that my child is doing all this instead of depending on me.' He would *pity* him, Flamen'!"

"Uh-huh. You got it, Brother!" The glee in his voice over this breakthrough was undeniable. "He would *pity* him! He would feel sorry for him. You see, just like we talked about with Tom at the park that day, sin *is* slavery. Sure, it's an offense against God's holiness, and it hurts other people too, but it's also slavery. You see? This poor guy doesn't recognize all the resources that he has in Christ. Therefore, he resorts to these fleshly, manipulation tactics. How sad is that?"

The clouds were breaking in my mind and spirit. Like long shadows shrinking with the approaching light, my frustration and indignation were beginning to diminish.

"Man, you're right, Flamen'! I never thought of it like this before."

"See? When people hurt others, the fleshly tactics they use reveal what enslaves them. Believers—who have that intimacy with Christ and the wisdom, insight, and perspective which he provides in the Bible—can see that amid all the sinful cries for help. When the fleshly folks act out, lashing out at other individuals, they're really just wallowing in their own pain and sin for all to see. It's almost like they're wearing a T-shirt that reads, 'Insecurity is my spiritual hang-up,' or 'Bitterness toward God is my *real* problem.'" He enunciated these T-shirt messages in his silly, baritone, narrator voice.

I repressed a smirk. "Aw, Flamen', now you're just being goofy!"

"How'd ya guess?" he inquired in the same, voice-over tone. "C'mon, Brother! After all you've been through, you *gotta* see the humor in this!"

Finally, I cracked a smile, which Steve couldn't see on the other line. Then I sighed again.

"This stuff has hurt me so much, Steve. That guy had no clue what he did to me."

"You're right. He probably just had tunnel vision, thinking that he was 'protecting the flock.' Maybe he's just heard too much gossip and reached the breaking point that day. You'll probably never know his side of the ordeal. People with positions and titles rarely feel the need to explain their actions. That doesn't really matter, though. We forgive because Colossians 3:13 tells us to be 'bearing with one another and forgiving one another, if someone happens to have a complaint against anyone else. Just as the Lord has forgiven you, so you also forgive others.'"

"Did you get that from Tom?" I asked suspiciously.

"No, I got it from Paul. It's in his letter to the Colossians."

"Cute, Marie. Real cute," I replied with a roll of my eyes. "That's a verse that Tom mentioned to me. He told me that this one and Ephesians 4:32 teach us to forgive others because in Christ

265

we have been forgiven by Father."

"Yeah, that's a great verse too."

"He said that we can only forgive people in Christ because he gives us the motivation and grace to enable us to forgive."

"Tom's right, of course. Now that you know that you have Father's grace in Christ to forgive that pastor and in Christ you can love him concerning his needs and pity him for what he did in his fleshly weakness, it sounds like you've seen you're way clear to forgive him. Am I right?"

A whirlwind of thoughts swirled through my mind. This was quite a leap from having all the pent-up bitterness I had harbored to having the grace to forgive and the pity and sadness over the pastor's methods for 'overseeing' the congregation. It seemed like something was missing.

"Wait a minute," I thought aloud. "I need to review what we just concluded to see how we got here."

"Fair enough, Brother," agreed Steve plainly. "Let's go over your perspective first. For now, you're dealing with unforgiveness. What have you been doing for *your* part?"

I took a deep breath. "Well, I've been talking to Father constantly, asking him to help me to forgive the pastor and to be thankful to Jesus. I've let him know that I realize it's wrong not to forgive, and that I really want to forgive, but that it's just not something that I can do apart from him doing it through me."

"That's great! You haven't been playing some game with Father or yourself, trying to ignore your feelings and sweep it all under the rug without dealing with it as a heart matter. And you've kept running to Christ, convinced that Father deeply loves you as his child and that this whole situation is no indication that his love has changed in the least."

"Right. Although I haven't consistently run to Christ, at least I can rest assured that Father's love for me has always been steady and strong. He loves me despite my sin of unforgiveness."

"Now, that's the kind of progress I'm talking about!" exclaimed Steve with joy. "You're on the right track, Brother. Then for *his* part, there's this game that the pastor has been playing."

266

"Yeah, there's that," I agreed with a heavy heart. This was the extremely difficult part.

"He wronged you and Elena in several different ways. But you realize that what he did was intended to produce pain in you, which means that it wasn't personal. It just indicates that he was resorting to a fleshly means to do what he thought he was supposed to do. Or maybe he was just being overbearing and trying to control the congregation. Or maybe he had had it up to *here* with hearing so much gossip, and he decided to make examples of you. We really don't know what his motivation was. Anyway, how did we say Father views him from his perspective?"

"Well, in the end, we're both his children, and he's grieved that the hurt has happened." My analytical tendencies seemed to shine through, helping me to see things clearly by God's grace.

"Exactly! He really is grieved over the pain and suffering we cause one another, first because he loves us all. Second, he's grieved that after all he did through Jesus to break sin's hold on us and to give us his Spirit so that we have all the resources of grace available to us in Christ, we still use sinful means to relate to and to try to manipulate one another. Here we are as believers acting like people who don't know him, who haven't been released from the shackles of sin, and who haven't been sealed with his Holy Spirit who resides in us and enables us by his grace to live better. *That's* why it's so sad and grievous."

"And," I added, "that's why we can pity those who sin against us and hurt us so much, whether they're believers or not. We can especially pity them if they're the last person you'd expect to hurt you, like someone who claims to be a minister for Jesus. *Man*, I can't believe this has happened to us!"

There was a pause on the other end of the line. Then Steve said, "Brother, with Jesus' love and grace to sustain us, we can endure the sins of others against us. Truthfully, we can thrive, secure in Christ, despite *any* circumstances."

This was a truth that I was still learning.

"So . . . I should be able to release the man and to forgive him, holding no desire for punishment or retribution."

267

"Sin is probably doing enough of that in his own life, if that's the way he's trying to 'minister' to people. Remember how we talked about sin carrying its own punishment? It brings us consequences that we seldom see beforehand. Knowing this about sin is motivation enough for us not to want to pursue it. There's no need for us to promote a fear of Father since we can't sin without him seeing it and knowing about it. As true as it is, that kind of thought tends to drive us further from him when we sin. Instead, we should view his continual presence with us as an encouragement; it means that his help and hope are constantly available to us. That's why we can be thankful and rejoice!"

"Yeah, I agree with that, Flamen'," I replied with a sigh. "It's hard to turn to Father for cleansing when I think that he just condemns me for what I've done. And you're right about sin being so damaging. This unforgiving spirit has hurt me on a lot of levels. But I think there's something else that bothers me," I said with some hesitancy. "Flamen', shouldn't I tell somebody what this pastor's done to us so that he can be stopped and won't do the same or worse to others?"

"That's a great question, Brother," he replied placidly. "What do you think?"

Something unseen and intangible seemed to impede the suggestion, frustrating my attempts to consider a course of action.

"I just don't know, Flamen'. It seems like I should go to the Deacon Board or to someone. But I wouldn't know how to approach the topic without it becoming a full-blown, drama ordeal."

"What has Father led you to do?"

"Well, that's the thing. I haven't gotten any peace in my spirit or leading about doing *anything* like telling *anyone*. I've shared this with you and Tom because y'all don't even know this guy, and you're two brothers I can trust to counsel me and to pray with me about this. Besides, I'm really seeking godly counsel for my problem with the bitterness resulting from this, not as some juicy bit of gossip to affect this pastor's life and ministry."

"Then it sounds like you've just answered your own question."

"I did?" I replied with surprise and confusion.

"Yeah, Brother. I hear you saying that you're seeking Father about what to do and not doing anything unless and until he directs you. That's what you should do, I'd say."

"What about scriptures like Matthew 18, which says to approach him privately and, if he doesn't listen, to take another person with me? Or what about 1 Timothy 5:19 which says only to accept an accusation against an elder by the word of two or three witnesses? Elena and Don and I make three witnesses."

"You *could* invoke those," Steve answered slowly, "following the steps. But knowing the way this pastor operates, wouldn't he have the upper hand and figure out a way to make *you* look bad and to get you booted out as sinful and rebellious? That would be a worse situation to recover from, and it would compound your problem of forgiving him."

"So, because of his sin, those Bible verses are thwarted?" I asked a little impatiently.

"Brother, I wouldn't say that at all! Those Scriptures *do* give you recourse, but I don't think it means that you *have* to follow them like some spiritual commandments, regardless of what Father is dealing with you individually in *your* circumstances. Remember that we're not living the Christian life by a set of New Testament principles. That would be replacing the Holy Spirit with a set of 'Christian Laws' that you *must* follow no matter *what* individual work he's doing in your life. It's not that you're discounting the Bible. It's just not setting it up like Old Covenant Law in New Testament clothes. You see what I mean?"

"Hmm. Well, I guess I do," I said calmly, seeing his point. "We *did* discuss this with Tom quite a bit at the park last year."

"Besides, if you *did* go that route of calling him out, wouldn't there be a small amount of satisfaction on your part, as if you had gotten some form of revenge?"

"Yeah," I admitted, "that was a nagging thought on the back burner of my mind."

"That's probably why Father isn't leading you to follow those Bible verses; he knows your heart all too well."

"That he does," I said plainly.

"I'm sure he'll take care of it his way and in his timing. Remember what Galatians 6:7 says? 'Do not be deceived. God will not be made a fool. For a person will reap what he sows.' Meanwhile, I say, just concern yourself with *you*—that is, with your heart and your reactions."

"So, I can pity him, forgive him by Father's grace, be thankful, and rejoice."

"You're on your way, Bro! So then, what does having Father's pity for him *really* motivate you to do?"

There was only one answer to this question. "It motivates me to—*to pray for him!*" The realization was sudden and unexpected. "*That's* it. His spiritual need calls for prayer."

"There probably aren't too many people who see this weakness in his life and could pray for him and this specific need right now, are there?"

"Wow, I guess not. Wait a minute, Flamen'." Something connected with me just then. "Are you going to tell me now that Father *let* this happen so that he could work his grace in me to the point where I *could* pray for this specific need in this pastor's life?"

"No, Brother, I don't think I have to suggest that." Another character voice followed. "*You just did that yourself!*"

"Way to flame, Flamen'!"

"Anytime, Brother. That's what brothers are for!"

"Man, this has been some phone call!"

"Yeah, it has. But I gotta split now, Bro. I'm building a chicken coop for my mom, and I have to run by the hardware store to get some more materials."

"Chicken coop?!"

"It's to raise chickens for fresh eggs. Fresh eggs are the best, Brother!"

"That's life in the country for you."

"Amen!"

"I don't envy her for having chickens. Fresh eggs *are* the best, but I can't take those roosters crowing at all hours of the night like they did in Honduras."

"We'll see. Gotta go, Bro."

"Thanks, Steve. You're a great friend and a wonderful brother in Jesus."

"Thank you, Brother. So are you. You'd do the same for me if I were in a mess, right?"

It was the same thing that Tom had told me when I thanked him for his counsel and encouragement. Here was another friendship based on grace instead of merit and indebtedness.

"You bet, Flamen'," said I with a grin.

When my call with Steve ended, I felt much more relieved. Ending it talking about chickens was a welcome diversion to all the heavy, serious talk about these spiritual, heart-heavy matters. It also re-established the rapport in our friendship so that I didn't feel like some needy, erring brother whose problem was so grave that he couldn't relate to the everyday of life. The humor points were likewise refreshing.

Practically all the clouds but one were dissipating under the light of Father's grace and love. One stubborn cloud remained, however. It seemed that I had forgiven the pastor in theory, due to the dose of Father's grace evident as a result of my conversations with Tom and Steve. *Genuine forgiveness*, however, would only be evident if I could see the man and have the heart and compasssion of Christ for him. I would have to face the pastor soon. The Wednesday night prayer meeting was the very next evening.

All day that Wednesday, a lot of emotions and thoughts raced in my heart and mind; the flurry only increased as the afternoon waned and evening descended. I felt tingly with anxiety, wondering how I would feel when I saw the pastor. Would I have a heart of forgiveness? Would I return to my now routine and almost complacent mood of anger and bitterness? Or would I play some deceptive game with myself, 'going through the motions of forgiveness' while deceiving myself into thinking that I had really forgiven when it hadn't been sincere? These last two possibilities worried me greatly. Either option would be the continuation of my second bout with bitterness, which meant that it would be that much harder to conquer afterwards.

271

Just before the Wednesday night prayer meeting began, I escorted Elena to the nursery where she volunteered. The heightened emotion I sensed made my palms perspire. *It's only a matter of minutes before I see him*, I thought. *Father, please help me to be grateful and forgiving. As unworthy as I am of your grace, I need you to do your work in me, please.* I took my leave of Elena and entered the vestibule just after the service began. Someone was leading the attendees in a hymn. My hands trembled slightly. I bowed my head at the door to collect my thoughts and to pray.

Time passed slowly. I couldn't quite bring myself to entering the service just yet, so I detoured to the men's room to splash cold water on my face. A myriad of thoughts cascaded in my mind.

The real problem is not the problem, but how you deal with this whole situation.

. . . It's easy to coast along in our lives and to forget how much we really need to depend on Jesus for everything every second.

. . . "Do not be anxious about anything. Instead, in every situation, through prayer and petition with thanksgiving, tell your requests to God. And the peace of God that surpasses all understanding will guard your hearts and minds in Christ Jesus."

. . . "Always giving thanks for all things in the name of our Lord Jesus Christ to God, even the Father." . . . We can't make ourselves thankful, but Jesus can. Therefore, we yield ourselves to Christ in prayer, knowing that he alone can make us thankful. . . . You can be thankful, not for the hurt he caused, but for the fact that Father used it to bring this problem to your attention so that you would have to turn to Christ for him to deal with this. It is in this sense that you can "rejoice in the Lord always"* like Philippians 4:4 tells us.

. . . We can't be happy *about bad things, but we can be* thankful *that God is with us, that he is sovereign, and that he loves us through all things. He gives us that hope and fills our hearts with gratitude.*

. . . "And we know that all things work together for good for those who love God, who are called according to his purpose."

Our good throughout all this is to make us more like Jesus. There-fore, when we come to him in repentance, confessing our sins, he rejoices greatly!

. . . Father can use almost anything and still fulfill his will and receive the glory.

. . . He doesn't like the sin, because that's what's hurting you and your relationship with him. His anger is really aimed at the sin, but of course he loves you! You're his precious child! He gave his Son to rescue you from the clutches of sin and death. And he only knows how to relate to us out of a heart full of love, even when discipline is necessary.

. . . He really delights to take our sins and failures—all the junk in our lives—and turn them into opportunities when he can do the important work in our hearts. We just have to let him do it.

. . . Other people's words and actions toward you don't indicate that his love for you has changed.

. . . By realizing that people are lashing out of their own anger and perhaps even bitterness, then I know that their actions and words against me are not necessarily personal. . . . They only said or did that to try to hurt me. They're just venting some anger, and I happen to be in their path.

. . . Whether he apologizes or not, you must forgive him from the heart graciously, just as Father forgives us and remains in relationship with us despite our continual sins against him. We can do this because of what Ephesians 4:32 tells us. ". . . be kind to one another, compassionate, forgiving one another, just as God in Christ also forgave you."

. . . This forgiveness we received in Christ is our motivation for forgiving others who sin against us. In Christ we are enabled to forgive others with his grace because of the grace we received when we were forgiven. This means that you're not forgiving with-out Jesus' enablement. That's why we can forgive one another because we do so "in Christ," just as the Father forgave us in his Son.

. . . That's further proof of why we need to run to him and to depend on him every second for everything. We can only forgive

others because we do so in Jesus, that is, with his grace enabling us. This forgiveness is you giving up your right to be avenged or to see him punished. And just know that the forgiveness is more for your sake than for his. It's so that you won't have this unforgiveness and resentment pent up in your heart, getting in the way of your relationship with Jesus and everything else, like it did before. Besides that, Jesus delights to pour out his grace through us to forgive others, except that we must choose to let him. Obeying is always more fun knowing that it pleases him. We have his grace to enable us and pleasing him to motivate us. I'd say that's a pretty good deal, wouldn't you?

. . . Remember to keep running to Jesus. Depend on him to give you his heart of grace and love to forgive.

. . . And when you do forgive him, forgive graciously with no strings, no stipulations. Forgive as if the whole thing had never happened.

. . . Jesus will have healed you with his grace so that you can be gracious to him and forgive him. You'll find that you'll have pity for him and his sin, not anger or resentment. . . . It's what happens when we understand by Father's grace his perspective on sin and on those who commit it. . . . It's a work that only he can do through the Holy Spirit. If you allow him to work in you, to love and to forgive others through you, then you'll be surprised at how your heart starts to resemble Jesus'. You'll have more of Father's perspective and understanding; you'll start to have his agape *kind of love for people.*

. . . With all Father's love for the pastor as a child of his, and nearly two millennia ago having already taken care of this bag of sins he committed against you, how would he view the pastor from his heart of love and compassion? . . . He would think, "How sad that my child is doing all this instead of depending on me." . . . He would pity *him! He would feel sorry for him. . . . Sin is slavery. Sure, it's an offense against God's holiness, and it hurts other people too, but it's also slavery. This poor guy doesn't recognize the resources he has in Christ, so he resorts to these fleshly, manipulation tactics. How sad is that?*

. . . Father's grieved that after all he did through Jesus to break sin's hold on us and to give us his Spirit so that we have all the resources of grace available to us in Christ, we still use sinful means to relate to and to try to manipulate one another. Here we are as believers acting like people who don't know him, who haven't been released from the shackles of sin, and who don't have the means to live better through the Holy Spirit. . . . That's why we can pity those who sin against us and hurt us so much, whether they're believers or not. We can especially pity them if they're the last person you'd expect to hurt you.

. . . With Jesus' love and grace to sustain us, we can endure the sins of others against us. Truthfully, we can thrive, secure in Christ, despite any circumstances. . . . I should be able to release the man and to forgive him, holding no desire for punishment or retribution.

. . . I hear you saying that you're seeking Father about what to do and not doing anything unless and until he directs you.

. . . After Jesus does the work in you, and you have the peace of Christ concerning this matter, then you can approach him humbly, submitting to one another as brothers.

The next thing I knew, I was sitting on a pew in the vestibule outside the closed doors of the sanctuary. Through the large glass windows and main doors, I could see that it was already night. The lighting in the vestibule and the soft voices of a few people walking the hallways brought me back to where I was. Time had passed more quickly than I imagined. *How did I get here without remembering? How long have I been here like this?* My face and hands were no longer wet or cold from the water that I splashed over me from the men's room sink. I felt a peace settle on me for no discernible reason. As I concentrated on Jesus' love for me, my heart was filling with joy and gratitude.

Yes, Father, I do forgive him. Finally! Thank you, Jesus!

My head suddenly felt lighter. I had not realized how much heavier than usual it had felt, as if I had something almost like sinus pressure.

As I listened to the overhead speaker, I heard the pastor closing the service in prayer.

I waited, patiently yet eagerly. I knew what I must do.

There was a final "amen." Then the sanctuary doors swung wide open. Two other sets of doors down either hallway swung open next. People began to exit and to go in various directions. I made my way through the sparse crowd leaving the sanctuary. Only a few dared to look at me. They were used to seeing me with a suppressed frown for over a couple of months now, so they probably expected nothing new. But this time, things with me were much better. Jesus had showered me with his grace upon grace to forgive!

I walked quickly toward the front where the pastor stood behind a simple podium used for Wednesday evenings, placed on the floor below the platform, level with the congregation. I stopped short, waiting and giving space and privacy to two members to finish their conversation with the pastor. He stood there looking at them and talking, nodding his head as appropriate. His eyes looked about the same, but not so menacing. His facial expression looked caring toward those with whom he conversed. He was wearing a tweed suit. I didn't remember having seen it before.

The couple said farewell and turned to leave.

I approached the pastor slowly. He looked at me with uncertainty in his expression. Then the waterworks began.

"I'm so sorry!" I exclaimed, tears pouring from my eyes. I embraced him and buried my face into his tweed jacket. He let me stand there crying. He put an arm on my back. All I could do was weep and say, "I'm so sorry!" repeatedly, wetting his jacket with my tears. The pastor was silent for almost a minute. Then he said quietly, "Amen. I forgive you, John."

There may have been others watching, but I didn't care. I was sensing such a relief and cleansing as I continued sobbing and hugging him. The thought occurred to me that he probably misunderstood what was happening at that moment. He probably thought that I was apologizing for "being such a gossip," with my tears of repentance proving that he had been right all along, but that didn't bother me either. I was letting Jesus flow through me and showing repentance for my unforgiving spirit and forgiveness for what this brother had done to my wife and me. Later I thought, humorously, that he had the right to misunderstand all he wanted, just like Walter had said. For the moment, I knew that I was doing exactly what Jesus wanted me to do and what he wanted to do through me.

When I finally came up for air and my sobbing had mostly run dry, I looked at the pastor. "I'm really sorry," I repeated one last time.

"I'm glad to hear it, John," he replied with a smile. "I'm glad to see that the Lord has done a work in your heart."

"So am I." I blinked and smiled, wiping away a few more tears.

"That's all right," he said, beginning to smile.

I didn't want this moment to pass without doing one more thing that I needed.

"Would you please come with me," I asked humbly, "so that we can tell Elena that everything's okay between us now?" This was most important to me at that moment. She had seen the repressed bitterness I had gone through for months. I knew that she would not believe the news from me if she were not to see me with him.

"I surely will," he answered, "just let me return this mic to the sound room."

He unhooked a corded microphone from his tie and belt; then he took it to the sound room on his way out the back of the sanctuary and into the vestibule. I followed him like a little, lost puppy.

We then passed through the vestibule, into the dining hall, and down the Sunday school wing hallway toward the nursery at the far end. This took some time because every few seconds someone would stop the pastor to converse with him about something. Most of them would notice me beside him and change their facial expressions. The rumor mill must have been working overtime in recent months because everyone looked surprised to see me by his side. Also, my countenance, red and puffy from all the weeping I

277

had just done, must have made me look like quite a mess, further fueling whatever interpretation people were getting from seeing me like this. My quiet, personal rebellion of late had kept me distant from the pastor. Therefore, most of those who saw us together probably didn't know what to think of this new development.

By the time we passed through the throng of people and reached the nursery, Elena was down to one toddler awaiting her parents in the nursery. Nathaniel was there too on the floor by her side, working in a coloring book. My wife was standing at the half door as we arrived. She looked the most pleasantly surprised of all to see me walking with the pastor as if we were long-lost friends. "Hey, Buddy!" she said cheerfully, greeting me with a big smile at the sight of me with the pastor. "How are you?"

I responded with a hug and a quick kiss.

"I'm doing great!" I replied, beaming at her and then at the pastor. I opened the door to pick up Nathaniel in my arms. "I just wanted you to know that everything's okay between us now."

The pastor grinned as if he were in on the whole thing. "It looks like things are back to normal," he said to her.

"Oh, that's wonderful!" exclaimed Elena with a sparkle in her eyes that matched her smile.

"Jesus has done a work in my heart," I explained. "So by his grace, I've been renewed."

"Well I must say," the pastor commented with an extended grin, "this is an answer to a lot of prayers. I know a lot of people who'll be so glad to know you've had a change of heart."

I took a deep breath and let out a relieved, heartfelt sigh. "I'm sorry it took me so long. I guess it just took me a while to work through some things."

"God sure is good, isn't he?" asked the pastor.

Elena and I both nodded in agreement.

"Now if you'll excuse me, I have a few rounds to make before leaving. John, Elena—I'll see you both Sunday."

We exchanged farewells, and the pastor took his leave.

On the way home, Elena had some questions about how all this happened. I explained a condensed version of what Father had been doing in my heart for over two months as well as some of my conversations with Tom and Steve.

"Did he really ask your forgiveness?" she inquired.

"No, but I knew he wouldn't. And that's okay."

"But, what did you say to him tonight?"

"I just cried on his jacket and kept repeating, 'I'm so sorry,' over and over. I didn't know what else to say."

"*You* apologized to *him*? But how does that make everything okay if he didn't apologize for what he did to us?"

"Oh, no," I replied reassuringly. "Don't look at it that way at all. Father gave me the grace to forgive him, so I don't have any bitterness. I'm free from an unforgiving spirit because of Jesus working his grace in me!"

"But isn't he supposed to apologize and make things right with you?"

Gratitude was flooding my soul and making my spirit soar.

"Well, he may not think that he has to do that. But that's okay with me. Jesus has forgiven me of a lot more and a lot worse, so I can put it all behind me and forgive him from the heart—with no strings attached."

"What strings?"

I stifled a giggle. "It just means that I forgive him unconditionally. That is, it's Jesus who's enabled me to forgive him by pouring his grace through me. I just happen to be the vessel or conduit. I have the blessing of watching him work through me. And I'm so thankful that he hasn't given up on me."

Elena still looked a little puzzled, but she couldn't question that I was obviously back to my grateful self. In the end, that's what really mattered.

I couldn't control someone else's actions to meet my expectations no matter what I did. For my part, I had done what Jesus wanted me to do. If the offender didn't make proper restitution, then he would be accountable to Jesus for that and not to me. As far as I was concerned, Father's grace and love were enough for me to forgive unconditionally. Finally, I could move on with my life and my walk with Jesus. This meant far more to me than anything the pastor could have done for his part.

Learning to forgive, or rather yielding to Christ to allow his grace to forgive through me, was a greater ordeal than it needed to have been. Nevertheless, it was a wonderful experience to see Father at work in my heart.

There was far more to learn on this whole adventure: things involving people, love, and the places where they all mix.

*KJV

CHAPTER 12

A SIMPLE SHARING AMONG FRIENDS

By his grace and love, Jesus had broken through my bitterness and changed my heart again. Admittedly, I was troubled that I had had another period of bitterness. After my previous experience, I never would have imagined that bitterness would ever again be a problem for me. By then, however, it was evidently too presumptuous of me to expect that any temptation would be victorious over me only once. God's grace and love were more than sufficient. The weak link in this equation, of course, was me. Although during this second round I had understood that Father's heart was toward me and that my attitude was not directly aimed at him, the observation that Tom had made about all anger being toward God either directly or indirectly had made a lasting impact on me. It wasn't something specifically taught in the Bible as fact, as far as I could find; however, in the words of one of my former doctrines professors, it had "the ring of truth to it."

The biblical topic of anger, unsurprisingly, became of great interest to me. As a result, I searched the Scriptures to learn as much about it as possible, especially its place and effect on my walk with Jesus. Tom's comment became a little more refined in the light of my search in the Scriptures. Eventually I realized that his statement about all anger being aimed at God was not intended to be as absolute as it initially sounded. After all, biblically speaking all anger fell into one of two categories: human or selfish anger used for one's own selfish, fleshly interests, and righteous indignation expressed for selfless, godly concerns. The previous was obviously sinful by definition; the later reflected or paralleled the same anger that Father had toward sin and unrighteousness.

On the one hand, I could be selfishly angry because of some perceived injustice that I suffered or some unfulfilled expectation. On the other hand, I could be righteously indignant over sinful concerns which likewise angered God. Examples of the later which came to mind were things like injustices and transgressions committed against the innocent, the poor, the needy, and the downtrodden. Interestingly enough, I discovered that I could have a general sense of anger toward large, distant injustices. For example, I could have righteous indignation due to those corrupt governments which profited by allowing many of their governed citizens to subsist in poverty or whom they otherwise exploited to their advantage. I could also be angry about the near genocide of over six million Jews in the Holocaust in Europe during the 1930s and 1940s or about the tragic events of 9/11. Although this kind of anger against such atrocities were constant, they were not often very active or even made much of an impact on my daily life or that of anyone else. It was always much easier to justify any course of reaction in which I lashed out for the sake of personal, selfish anger. Indeed, James 1:20 proclaims: "For human anger does not accomplish God's righteousness." This selfish, human indignation was that to which I finally understood Tom to be referring. Therefore, I could agree that all *selfish, sinful* anger was aimed either directly or indirectly toward Father.

Yet all anger, even righteous indignation, was to have its temporal limitations. It is taught in Ephesians 4:26, "Be angry and do not sin; do not let the sun go down on the cause of your anger." To me, this passage showed that not all anger necessarily led to sin and that even godly anger only persisted for a number of hours, rather than days without end. I understood this resulting limit to be reflective of one's trust in Father as the ultimate Judge and Righter of all wrongs, whether or not he acted according to our expectations or on our timetables.

It was also interesting to note the Bible's teachings about the limited uses of anger. The Scriptures teach, I learned, that anger should be a last resort rather than the first line of defense or attack. Before announcing in James 1:20 that selfish anger does not produce God's righteousness, verse nineteen of that same passage states: "Understand this, my dear brothers and sisters! Let every person be quick to listen, slow to speak, slow to anger." My observations of society had convinced me that practically all visible human anger was of this fleshly, sinful sort which was used as a first resort. *Oh, Father, how we need you so desperately to fill our hearts and lives, to become our all in all! Rescue us from this selfish anger!*

Since I had succumbed to the throes of bitterness for two different time periods in my life, being transparent with Father became a conscious priority with me. The Scriptures were also a motivation for humility, for it states plainly in James 4:6 that "God opposes the proud, but gives grace to the humble." Father had already proven his love to me in so many ways that I hoped never again to question his affection for me. His love and grace, I knew, were constantly available to me through my relationship with Jesus Christ. However, pride, spiritual coldness, and selfish anger were realistic temptations for me, and I did not want to miss any of his grace toward me because of submitting to them. Yet I was also aware of the dangers of setting any legalistic rules for myself in an attempt to achieve any form of godliness apart from my relationship with Christ. As Greg and Walter had reminded me nearly a year previously, Christ had saved and transformed me so as to live his life through me. It was not my responsibility to arm myself with a list of Christian principles to attempt to fulfill apart from Jesus and his enablement. Abiding in Christ as taught in John 15:1-8 was to be the norm for this life in Christ, this walk with Jesus. This walk was definitely not about performance, I had understood finally; it was about yielding to the one who loved me most and letting him live through me.

Therefore, I would need to continue renewing my mind with the Scriptures, as Romans 12:2 teach. Also, I would run to Christ as often as possible, turning to him as my *only* resort, depending on him totally, and looking to him to guide me in all things. I didn't expect to accomplish any of this perfectly; I had been made all too aware of my limitations. However, by Father's grace and not by my imperfect efforts, I endeavored to do this, leaning on him and his grace and trusting the Spirit to inform me when I was off track.

In the final analysis, Jesus is my everything, and I have been blessed with everything through him. The words of Romans 8:32 sounded regularly in my heart: "Indeed, he who did not spare his own Son, but gave him up for us all—how will he not also, along with him, freely give us all things?" This truth was worded as a rhetorical question, I noted, with the expected answer to the effect that, of course we are freely graced with all spiritual blessings. This was evidenced by his great sacrifice of his unique Son for us. Why would he bless us with the greatest gift, the Lord Jesus Christ, and then deny us any of the other gifts deemed lesser in comparison to his Son?

As the weeks and months passed, I enjoyed my walk with Jesus so much more. As had begun a year before, the gratitude, joy, and love I had for Christ grew steadily. My life was no longer an attempt to avoid sins and to keep faithfully a list of spiritual disciplines, as if Father were some pagan deity to appease with my performance. No, he is a real friend and presence in my daily life. He is my Father, Savior, Lord, and a host of other realities to me. As he sought me in the individual moments of each day, I practiced communing with him and delighted to follow him and to learn from him. He teaches me to trust him, and he wins my trust a little each day. My awe, wonder, and adoration for him likewise grow exponentially.

My relationships at home, work, church, and elsewhere sometimes reflected marked improvement and other times did not. I came to realize that the reality of walking with Jesus in a fallen Creation didn't make every moment in life heaven on earth, but it did make difficult situations more bearable and enjoyable. Whereas before in my years of bitterness, some relationships, situations, and tangible objects all seemed to oppose me at nearly every turn, this new outlook based on Father's grace and love had given me clarity of perception regarding many of these. By meditating on the Scriptures, I was renewing my mind, which yielded positive effects on my perspective. Various options and opportunities to problematic scenarios and challenging relationships became available to me as I allowed Christ again to be the Guide in my life. This resulted in my previous pessimism seeming unrealistic and absurd. I was still confronted with problems in my daily life, but I began to view them as opportunities to seek Father and to trust him to work as he willed. Learning to trust him was not so scary anymore, and I realized that it was far better than trusting myself or anyone else.

My hope expanded as did my understanding of his role in my life, especially as I witnessed the evidences of him working behind the scenes in various situations. A couple of thorny situations in my personal relationships cropped up through no intention of mine. They greatly stressed me for weeks and then months. I was tempted and even pressured to confront the individuals in an attempt to fix each situation. The "conflict resolution" steps I had learned from the law man's red workbook and seminar so many years before had made it seem predictable how I could resolve any personal relationship as I wanted—which, as the red notebook assured me, was "God's will" after all. However, there was a sense in my spirit that I should be patient, though I knew not why. Some very agonizing moments led me to the edges of frustration and hopelessness. Then, without any indication, both individuals approached me at separate times and apologized on their own, demonstrating regret for how they had treated me and thoroughly apologizing so as to restore and to renew those relationships. My heart was touched and refreshed. *Father, you did this, you alone. Thank you for nudging me to wait for you. You know how I can easily ruin things when I try to force my own will upon them. Thank you, Jesus!*

A certain observation made by Tom to me on the phone that day rang true: Father gave me his heart of love and compassion for people, so that I began to view from his perspective the individuals whom I encountered daily. No longer did I consider people to be problems, annoyances, irritations, or timewasters. Father showed me that everyone was a child whom he had created and cherishes. Some were believers, having been born again as spiritual sons and daughters through their faith in Christ. Most were not believers nor were they fully cognizant of the loving Father who had given his all in pursuit of them and an everlasting relationship with them.

285

Whether the individuals with whom I crossed paths knew Jesus or not, I saw the gracious father and his two sons from Jesus' parable concerning them practically every time. Various ones, like the younger son early in the narrative, were pursuing their own interests using the gifts with which he had blessed them. They had little if any recognition of Father and his incredible love for them. Others were like the younger son later in the parable after he had come to his senses and returned home. They were relishing in Father's love, walking with him, and depending on him. Still others, like the older son in the parable, served and toiled begrudgingly under what they misunderstood as the heavy hand of a taskmaster. Their lives demonstrated certain marks of "obedience" to Father, but their misinformation and ill-conceived perceptions of him resulted in a life with very little joy and understanding of what their Father was really like. Many others did not fall neatly into any of these three categories but were some mixture therein.

Regardless of how they could be viewed, each person was one for whom Christ died in Father's relentless pursuit of them. Father loved them all and was intimately familiar with every facet and detail of their lives: their origins and backgrounds, their joys and sorrows, their strengths and shortcomings, their interests and peeves. He loved them all, though he didn't agree with their every motive, thought, word, choice, and deed. The Christian circles I had been a part of years previously didn't always have these distinctions in focus, and by this time I wondered why. Father showed me that I could love people for who they are—beloved children of his at some stage in the parable—without either agreeing with or demonstrating disgust for their choices, habits, or lifestyles. My heart would sometimes grieve over the things people did and the self-inflicted sufferings they endured. However, I knew that the love engendered in my heart for them was but a sample of Father's incomparable love for them. While serving as a missionary in Central America, I had imagined that I understood his love for all people; now I was learning a better comprehension of his affection for people of all walks of life. *Thank you, Jesus, for changing my heart!*

◊   ◊   ◊   ◊   ◊

My perception of things at church had also transformed. The genuine growth of my love for people likewise included those of my own local congregation. Time spent with individuals in conversation and fellowship drew my heart closer to them. However, schedules, programs, ministry commitments, and time restraints in general interrupted and constrained these moments. We attended services in which we had to sit quietly and attentively as one or more individuals on the platform exercised their spiritual gifts. Nevertheless, once we were dismissed from these formal meetings, we fulfilled our preconceived plans to share a meal as a group to enjoy times of fellowship.

Our group fellowships always seemed to revolve around food. Although our times together weren't typically a Bible study format, we grew close and became well-acquainted with one another through our conversations, interactions, and leisure activities in which we participated. Some afternoons or evenings we would agree to meet at a designated restaurant and stay late, enjoying each other's company. At other times, a married couple would volunteer their house as the meeting point after different ones of us had purchased meals from a variety of fast-food restaurants. One Sunday afternoon, after we had agreed to dine at a local dive, I glanced over the menu and casually commented, "If we each put in a few dollars, then we could buy some groceries and have an impromptu cookout with burgers, sandwiches, and sides which would taste better and cost less than if we ordered from here." To my amazement, the idea enthused the others. "Hey, yeah! Let's do that!" were the excited responses. We quickly exited, ditching the menus on the restaurant tables, and in less than half an hour we were all preparing an enjoyable meal together in one family's backyard. At times we would order pizza and watch a movie together or play Charades or some other party game. Sometimes we would have a potluck and watch a sports game together. While sports were never an interest of mine and occasionally the movie was lackluster, the important thing was to spend time together and

287

to share in the fellowship and the love of Christ. Unsurprisingly, children were welcomed and encouraged to participate, since we were mostly young couples with small children. Nathaniel benefited from the godly influence of older "siblings" and "aunts" and "uncles" with whom he bonded through these fellowships.

The relationships that we forged with both long-time acquaintances and newcomers to the group, were spiritually edifying. Occasionally someone would feel comfortable enough to share their problems and needs, and various ones would offer encouragement and even lead in prayer for him or her. Sometimes someone would pull out a guitar or sit at the piano in the living room, if one was present, and share a song or two of praise or encouragement. These moments would sometimes lead to more praises, prayers, or even testimonies of Father's grace and provision. The larger the group, the more splinter conversations and prayer groups would form. Nothing much was ever planned or programmed, other than the details of where, what, and how we would have our meal together. There was no charismatic leader directing us or doing most of the ministering; we simply and genuinely enjoyed each other's company and leaned on Jesus to show us how we were to spend the balance of our time together. None of us could wait to reunite again after the next scheduled service. These opportunities allowed us to grow close and to practice some of the *one-anothering* exhortations in the New Testament. It reminded some of us of our local body's "glory days" with the founding pastor as described previously.

These fellowship times I began referring to as "having church in spite of church." This was born out of my observation that we were all more comfortable, participatory, pleased, and interactive like a body of believers during these fellowship times at someone's home as opposed to a straight-laced, programmed service. The first time I used this phrase, it was well-received with a round of laughter. It seemed to communicate and resonate with those in our group, especially since the services were becoming less effective, more perfunctory, more out of touch with where the membership was, and, frankly, more boring. It especially became woefully obvious on those evenings when we would sit together during the service as a group, having predetermined our post-service fellowship plans. We waited with great anticipation on the edge of our seats during those final minutes for the last hymn, the last announcement, the last prayer, and the final "amen" which would signal the start of our evening adventure together.

For us, building and encouraging relationships became a crucial reason for meeting at the local church facilities, although the pastoral staff may have felt otherwise. Perhaps they viewed the preaching, teaching, and other formal ministry expressions as essential and what we were doing beyond the services as non-essential, if they even knew of our fellowships at all. The attempts made by the ministerial staff to fabricate new ways and formats through which to present the gospel from various scriptural passages resulted in mostly ho-hum presentations. The congregation was practically composed of all believers, and in some ways, these preaching appeals were making the listeners inoculated to the immediacy and power of the gospel of Jesus Christ. Surely this was not the intended effect. Our quaint fellowships apart from the formal functions, we found, were much more invigorating, personal, and edifying.

With so much time being devoted to the relationships shared through "having church in spite of church," it had dawned on me that there was little time to meet with Tom and his circle of friends who had encouraged me so much throughout the previous year. For the longest time, it had been my desire for Steve and Aby to meet these brothers whom I met on Stone Mountain as well as their families. However, some were also busy with a multitude of family needs and ministry commitments. After a few months I wondered if we would ever gather together again for fellowship and encouragement.

Then the perfect opportunity was presented for us to meet. It was Easter Sunday, 2002. There would be a large group of us including all us brothers who had met on Stone Mountain, our wives and children, and Steve and Aby too. Oddly enough, this day was free for us all to meet due to each of us cutting back almost entirely on our formal ministry commitments to allow for more relational, spontaneous, family-centric opportunities like this.

Even more oddly, however, was the location for our Easter celebration. One might think that to commemorate the single, most significant event in the life of the body of Christ, we would have chosen a huge, citywide gathering of Christians in down-town Atlanta, perhaps some historic locale, or even a picturesque lakeside or mountain top spot for a solemn sunrise service. None of those possibilities were even considered.

Steve's voice on the phone was ecstatic when he told me about it.

"We're all meeting at Six Flags, Brother!"

"What?! Flamen', you're kidding me! Right?" I retorted, all the while thinking, *He really means this, doesn't he, Father?*

"Man, it'll be awesome! We can meet at the picnic area, have a picnic lunch with the Lord's Supper, fellowship for a bit, and then go ride the roller coasters!"

"You do realize, Flamen', that you're suggesting we take communion on Easter Sunday at an amusement park, right?"

"John, you won't believe how few people will be there on that day. There'll be no crowds! We can ride everything with almost no waiting in line! How cool is that?"

"Look," I replied, trying to be the voice of reason, "you're just a big kid at heart. That's great and all; it makes you a very entertaining brother. But—seriously—Easter Sunday communion *at Six Flags*? What did Aby say about all this?"

"She said she wants to sit at the front of the Water Log ride this time."

No, Father! I winced silently. *Not Aby too!*

"Wait a minute, Flamen'! You talked Aby into this whole thing?!"

"Brother, *she* made the suggestion," he replied calmly.

"Oh. Well, okay," I said quietly. "But I don't think that Tom and Sara will go for this. They're not our age, you know."

"Tom said it would be fine. In fact, he just called me a few minutes ago and said that he's already spoken with the other guys, and they're all looking forward to it. You *will* be there, right, Brother?"

My mind was racing a mile a minute. I had to say something.

"Yeah but, Flamen', I can't afford those tickets for the three of us."

"Now, Brother, would I invite you, Elena, and Nathaniel to Six Flags without planning everything through first?"

"Well, I don't know. But, on *Easter . . . ?* "

"Aby and I have some free tickets and parking passes through our membership in the investors association, enough for Aby and me *and* for the three of you."

Suddenly my face felt flush.

"Oh. Wow. Thanks, Brother. I had no idea." This was becoming more of a possibility than I would have thought.

"The other guys are taken care of too. Walter and Greg have already bought family passes which include some free tickets for friends, and Bob received tickets from work." He paused briefly, adding a tone of uncertainty to his voice. "Or maybe it's Greg and *Bob* who have the family passes. I don't know. I may have their names mixed up. But the point is that with all of us together, we have enough free tickets and even parking passes for Tom and Sara and you all to be there without it costing you any money. You just need to bring some food to share at the picnic like before and the gas to drive there. So, what do you say, Brother?"

A day at Six Flags would be fun, especially with it being free, I thought, somewhat toying with the idea. *But, on Easter?*

"It sounds like crazy fun, Flamen', but are you sure we can do this on Easter Sunday?"

"Yeah, I'm sure." Judging by his tone of voice, his furrowed-brow wince must have kicked in at that point. "Why not? It's the best day for us all to meet. We can fellowship and have a blast all at the same time."

"Well, I'd like to, but—"

"—But what, you don't think it's right? Like there's some Pharisees from your congregation who will look down their noses at you judgmentally for going to Six Flags on Easter Sunday?"

"Flamen', you gotta admit: It *is* forging new territory for me."

"Yeah, but—*good night!*—we've already *burned* those legalistic bridges! You know God's omnipresent, so he's already everywhere simultaneously. He's always with us, he's at Six Flags right now, and he'll meet us there when we get there."

"Well," I said, thinking aloud, "I have been trying to purge any residual bits of legalism in my relationship with Father."

"This will help you to do that, Brother."

Thus, I agreed. As it turned out, it was a great time of fellowship and edification which I would not have wanted to miss.

When I told Elena about it, her reaction was similar to mine. In fact, while driving to the park that morning, we were still talking about how strange it would be to have the Lord's Supper at Six Flags on Easter Sunday. It felt especially strange for us to dress so casually in T-shirts, jeans, and sneakers on Easter morning instead of our Sunday-best attire. Little Nathaniel was excited about the outing too. We sang along to a Veggie Tales CD on the way to Six Flags Over Georgia, just a few minutes west of Atlanta.

The air was crisp with a gentle breeze that morning. The sun shone fairly brightly, though there was a haze of clouds burning off, a remnant of the early morning mist. A chill still hung in the air on this final day of March, and though Spring had sprung, the temperature in the fifties along with the wind made it a little too cold for me. Elena felt that the air was very comfortable. Having lived in Honduras most of her life, she did not enjoy warm weather. Being cold-natured, however, I would have preferred a temperature in the seventies. That is why I wore a light jacket.

As we entered the park, we were amazed at the lack of vehicles and crowds. Six Flags was an amusement park which I had visited several times over the decades, so I was used to seeing the parking lot packed. Driving to the back of the parking lot toward the picnic area, we saw that it was only about one-fifth full of vehicles, and there were only a negligible number of cars added throughout the day. Near the picnic area, very close to the woods and picnic tables, were the familiar-looking vehicles of our friends, most of whom had arrived before us. I backed the car into a space with the car trunk facing the trees. Steve was already visibly enjoying himself in his surroundings, decked out as he was in a ball cap, T-shirt, shorts, and sandals. Aby, content at his side, was similarly dressed, with her face beaming and her long, dark hair being occasionally tussled in the slight breeze. The other families in our group were similarly dressed in jeans or shorts and T-shirts. They were setting out the items each of them had brought for the picnic. The children of these families were playing and exploring in several spots around our chosen picnic area, skipping, jumping, and looking like they were enjoying an adventuresome field trip. Only Tom and Sara were missing, but their vehicle was soon seen crossing the parking lot just after Elena got Nathaniel out of his car seat and I heaved out a cooler and picnic basket from the trunk of the Toyota. Feeling a chilly breeze, I decided to continue wearing my light jacket.

"Hey, Brother, ya made it!" Steve walked toward me, and we did our routine how-ya-doin' greeting with the loud, deep voice characterizations and back slaps. A few of the younger children giggled at our goofy greeting.

"We just couldn't miss it, Flamen'. But not because it's Six Flags and not just because it's Easter either."

"Now who's using the 'E' word?" came a familiar voice. It was Walter, who walked up behind me and gave me a friendly hug. "Good to see you, Brother! Boy, it's been a while, hasn't it?"

"Something like that," I replied, smiling and returning the hug. "It's so good to see you, Walter!"

The other wives greeted Elena enthusiastically, with their high-pitched greetings, smiles, and hugs. Although we had only visited occasionally with these brothers and sisters over the past year, Elena was faithful to keep in contact with them by phone and e-mail. She had been sharing her life with these ladies as they bonded through crochet patterns, recipes, homeschooling, and prayer concerns. Elena had continuously encouraged me to call and to keep in contact with my friends. However, the night classes, work responsibilities, and time spent with Nathaniel left me little opportunity to do so apart from planned visits.

"I'll never understand this culture," she had remarked frequently. "It's so hard to see friends without making an appointment. Friends don't make appointments with friends! Who ever heard of that?" I always agreed with her, bearing the same sentiment.

In Honduras, it is the norm to walk to a friend's or neighbor's house unannounced and spend hours just socializing, even as the family busies themselves with household chores and other responsibilities. Such freedom expressed in that culture is the kind for which I long here in the States, although I know that in this society most people frown upon such spontaneous visits. "Houses here aren't built as closely together as houses there," I would explain repeatedly. "And here everyone drives to go places; there everyone walks everywhere." When I voiced these explanations, even I thought that they sounded like excuses. Then she would add, "And there, people are more important than things; here things are more important than people." Reluctantly I would agree, yearning to see it reversed here in the States. Sometimes I would add to that list: "In the U.S. we're too independent and too concerned about our own interests, schedules, and agendas more than those of others, like we are in Honduras." While both cultures have their own pros and cons, I often desired to return to my "second home" in Honduras, where relationships meant more to people than anything else. However, in some pockets of American society, relationships *do* take priority with those who share Father's heart and perspective. Elena and I have endeavored to practice this aspect of Latin American culture in our relationships by making people more important than possessions and schedules. We have found that it is possible to live by one's heart in the United States, valuing people over personal interests and agendas, despite the natural progression and drift of the culture at large.

We heard that Steve and Aby had gotten acquainted with Bob and Linda, Greg and Kathy, and Walter and Cindy just before we arrived.

"Flamen', how did you recognize them if y'all hadn't met

before?"

"Oh, Steve's *really* easy to spot from a mile away," offered Walter, slowly shaking his head with his facetious, wide-eyed expression. "From all the things I've heard about him, he's just too hard to miss."

"Well, thank you, Brother!" Steve said, with his standard baritone voice characterization and a chuckle.

Without a sense of time restraints of any kind, we all exchanged warm, individual greetings with one another and socialized for a few minutes while working together to set up the items brought by Tom and Sara to accompany the picnic spread. We talked joyfully for the longest time, simply enjoying each other's company and our mutual bond in Jesus. For a few seconds, I gazed around at the friends before me, feeling so very blessed. Both adults and children were relaxed and joyfully sharing in the fellowship of one another as caring friends. We were more than friends; we were family in Jesus because of him.

It was a touching scene, and I was so thankful to be a part of it. I realized that what brought us together was not sports, hunting, entertainment, games, politics, or any number of other interests which people typically rally around to find commonality. As I listened to snippets of each conversation, I realized from the comments that it was evident that our common bond was Jesus. He is our life, our sustenance, and our reason for everything. My heart basked joyfully in the glow of the love and fellowship of these brothers and sisters in Christ. It seemed like a preview of the joy and communion we would share together in heaven one day. *Father, this must be the kind of thing that delights you: seeing your children sharing, caring, and fellowshipping with one another. Each one is looking out for the interests of the others without any selfishness or disagreements, only harmony, unity, grace, and love founded on our common bond with Jesus. Thank you, Lord!*

The moms called their children to join us once it looked like all the food and preparations were in place. We had gathered around two of the stone picnic tables which were closest together so that we could enjoy fellowship in proximity. As we formed a wide circle around the tables under the tall trees, the conversations began to quiet down. Each child stood with his or her parents. Once all the attention was on Tom, he began to speak.

"What we share in our Lord Jesus is a special bond," he said in a gentle voice. "It is because of him that we can celebrate him, his work of redemption on our behalf, and the great love and grace he poured out for us. As we enjoy the freedoms and blessings we have in Christ, we celebrate him, not just today but every day. May every one of you know that Father's love for you is mighty and far beyond what we can fathom. He has proven it to us in a multitude of ways, the greatest of which are the sacrifice of himself and his resurrection for us. Thank you for being here with us, for being a part of this fellowship, and for the testimony and example that each one of you is to Sara and me. God bless you all."

Then he turned to Greg. "Greg, will you lead us in prayer, please?"

Greg began to lead us in a brief prayer of thanksgiving. I quickly glanced at Walter just out of curiosity. Then I realized why I was looking, and I thought better of it. When we opened our eyes, I saw Bob reach for a paper plate with some freshly-baked, unleavened bread on it. He passed it around, and each one of us broke off a piece of the bread. Next, Greg took a pitcher of grape juice, and he and Walter poured some into the disposable cups which were on the table before us. Then they helped to pass the cups around to everyone.

Turning to Steve, Greg said, "Steve, would you share a scripture with us?"

Steve nodded. "We're told in 2 Corinthians 5:21 that 'God made the one who did not know sin to be sin for us, so that in him we would become the righteousness of God.' Our Lord Jesus' body was broken as he bore our sins so that we may be spiritually alive, free, restored in relationship with Father, and righteous in his sight. Thank you, Jesus, for your sacrifice and love." Then we all ate a piece of the bread.

Next, Walter raised his cup, and said, "This is the blood of the New Covenant in Christ. It was poured out for our forgiveness.

'To the one who loves us and has set us free from our sins at the cost of his own blood and has appointed us as a kingdom, as priests serving his God and Father—to him be the glory and the power forever and ever! Amen.'[1]" We all echoed his "amen." Then we drank in unison, standing silently and pensively.

My heart was so full, and my spirit was soaring. *Thank you, Jesus, for all you have carried me through and for where you have brought me!* Again, I felt misty-eyed. I simply could not adequately express my love and gratitude for all that he had done for me. For so long I had had no tears; my heart had been so hardened during those years. Now the tears flowed easily, even when I least expected it. *Thank you, Jesus, for tears and for a heart softened by your grace and love.*

The trees swayed gently in the wind. A few distant voices drifted in from other picnic areas farther away. The soft silence was broken as some hugs were exchanged, and a few quiet expressions of "I love you, Brother," "I love you, Sister," and "Thank you, Jesus," were heard. We gradually formed lines around the tables to fill our plates.

[1]Revelation 1:5, 6

CHAPTER 13

LOVING JESUS BY LOVING PEOPLE

Most of the adults sat at one table, and the children sat at the next. Linda and Kathy sat at the end of the children's table closest to the adult table since we outnumbered the children present. I helped Nathaniel with his plate and sat him next to Walter and Cindy's sons, Timmy and Joey. After cutting his food into bite-sized pieces and filling his sippy cup, I gave my son a quick hug and sat down beside Elena.

For a few moments, the conversation was light, mostly about the fair though chilly weather and the delicious food provided for our lunch. I looked around the table at these precious people for whom I was so thankful that Father had brought into our lives. Each one was a blessing I had missed for some months. Though we had visited separately with them as families and tried to keep in contact with one another, there was an inexplicable charm and rapport evidenced whenever we were all together like this. It was especially exciting to have this opportunity to include Steve and Aby in the fellowship. They have likewise been blessings in my life; they would easily complement the rest of the group.

Walter's words about us enjoying this one day in Father's kingdom stayed with me. It led me to do a little daydreaming about what it will be like having delightful fellowship together with Jesus in eternity.

"Whatcha thinkin' 'bout there, Brother?"

Steve's question brought me back to the present. My smile grew slowly as I replied.

"Oh, I'm just imagining what it will be like when Jesus takes us home."

"Amen, Brother! That will be a glorious day!" Then he began to sing, "'What a day that will be, when my Jesus I shall see.'¹" After a few lines, he succumbed to his own joyful laughter.

"You're right, Flamen," I agreed. "It *will* be a glorious day. Finally, to see and to embrace the one who demonstrated his great love for me through his sacrifice and resurrection, and who loved me and walked with me through all those moments in my life! I just can't imagine anything being better. But you know, when I was growing up as a kid, there were a lot of preachers pushing a message of fear about Jesus' return. They talked about the rapture of the church and about some not being ready and being left behind. It was a lot of scary talk, especially for me as a kid back then."

"I can relate to that, Brother," he replied, nodding his head. "I was in literally thousands of church services growing up as a preacher's kid, and so many of the appeals at the invitation time were based on the fear of being left behind." He looked around the crowded table and asked, "How many of you all heard preaching about the rapture and Jesus' return as something fearful when you were growing up?"

His question was met with nods, verbal replies to the fact, or raised hands from almost everyone. I noticed that Tom was perhaps the only one who didn't respond. Part of his story, I knew was that he didn't hear the gospel of Jesus Christ until he was an adult in the military. Although by that time I had not heard his whole testimony, I had hoped to hear it soon.

Greg wiped his mouth with a napkin and said, "I've met quite a number of *believers* who are afraid of Jesus' return to take us home. They don't like talking about it because they've feared it most of their lives. Even now as adults, it frightens them just to talk about it."

"Wow!" I replied. "How is that even possible?"

"They've heard it used as a threat their whole lives, so they associate it with only negative feelings. Plus, they listen to a lot of the fearful hype that goes around in certain circles, and sometimes even in the media, making it sound like the end of the world."

"I would think that *all* believers in Christ would rejoice over it, since it means that we're going home. What do you say to those believers?"

"I use a simple analogy," said Greg, wiping his hands with a napkin. "I put it to them like this: Imagine that you have a relative whom you've known and loved your whole life. He's someone close to you, like an older brother or favorite uncle, who spent a lot of time with you constantly as you were growing up. The two of you had such a special, kindred bond; your hearts were knit together. Maybe your siblings or parents were even a little envious.

"Then one day, he has to leave on a long trip—maybe even to another part of the world. But he keeps in contact with you through postcards. In the postcards, he keeps saying that he'll be back one day, maybe when you least suspect it. In his last note you received, he tells you that he'll be out of contact with you for a while, but that you're not to lose hope; he'll return just as he told you he would.

"The years pass, and you do some growing up. You often think about your favorite relative with a certain fondness, and you miss him greatly. Your heart just longs to see him so much, but you don't know where he is or when he'll return. When other family members mention him, they all agree that he's coming back some day, just as he said that he would. You get busy with your life, family, and work. Then one day when you're busy at home or at work or somewhere else, out of the blue, he just walks through the door! He calls your name and opens his arms wide for a big hug."

At this point, Greg clasped his hands together. "Then I ask them: Would you be excited to see him and run to give him a hug, or would you be filled with fear and dread that he had returned?"

"That sounds amazing!" I said almost gasping.

"Yeah, who wouldn't be delighted?" remarked Aby.

"Some believers tend to forget," Greg continued, "that Jesus—the Creator of the universe, our Lord and Savior who rescued us from sin, death, and hell—loves us with a passion beyond description. For us, his return to take us home *will* be a joyful event. It'll be what we've waited for our entire lives! How in the world could we as believers in him ever fear that moment? I know why, of course, since I explained that just now. However, there are people out there dishing out a message of fear, trying to frighten people into the kingdom with their scary preaching and talk about doomsday."

"Yeah," said Walter sarcastically, cocking his head, "because *that* seems to work so well."

"The sad part," said Bob, "is that when people respond to those kinds of invitations, it really fuels those preachers' fires, making them think that they're doing Father's work by 'scaring people into trusting Jesus.' They don't realize that not only is that contrary to the gospel of grace, but it doesn't result in as many 'decisions' as they think it does. A lot of those people are reacting to their fears and not exercising divine faith in Jesus, becoming truly born again and beginning a genuine relationship with him."

"Good night, have I seen plenty of those cases!" exclaimed Steve, putting his sandwich down. "Those preachers choose fear over love as a motivator."

"Maybe," I suggested, "they forgot that Romans 10:4 teaches us that God's kindness leads us to repentance."

"I don't see how someone can claim to know Jesus and not re-member that. His kindness expresses his love."

"We participated in a discussion about this when we first started as missionaries in Eastern Europe," Cindy began. "Because of the fearful political situation that had ravaged that part of Europe for generations, we weren't about to import those American ministry tactics into our gospel presentations."

"It wasn't just because of that," added Walter, "but also because we learned before we even left for the mission field that the love of Jesus for sinners was motivation enough. Even though he talked about hell more than anyone else in the Scriptures, Christ never used the fear of hell or even missing his return to motivate people to believe in him or for any other reason."

"'There is no fear in love,'" I began, "'but perfect love drives out fear, because fear has to do with punishment. The one who fears punishment has not been perfected in love.' I've learned that well enough from 1 John 4:18 since I've been back in the States. Thanks, Walter."

"It's all Jesus, Brother," he replied. "I've learned a lot, but I still have a long way to go."

"Amen, Honey Bunch," chided Cindy. She jabbed his ribs, and

he jabbed back at her.

"Jesus speaks the truth in love," said Steve, "*persuading* us to believe in him. But those who choose not to believe are still free to reject him. It's profoundly sad, though. So many people have heard the gospel—or what they're told is the gospel—in a presentation mixed with the fear of going to hell and 'hatred for sinners.' Those so-called 'church leaders' who give that kind of appeal should know that the love of Jesus is more powerful, lasts longer, and is more effective than fear."

"It makes you wonder," said Kathy, "what it would be like if people were only drawn to Jesus by cords of his love, with no mixture or mention of hell or the fear of it. What would that really look like?"

"The love of Jesus is what drew *me* to him," commented Tom casually.

I was surprised to hear a response to Kathy's rhetorical question. Some may have felt a longing in their hearts when Tom spoke. I know that I certainly did.

"Tom," said Greg, "I don't think most of us here have ever heard your testimony of how you met Jesus. Would you share that with us please?"

"Okay, but I'll warn you that it's not a flashy, fancy story. It's when I was stationed in Greenville for a few months after graduating from boot camp. Someone on the street invited me to a church service one Sunday evening. I didn't have anything better to do, so I went. I heard the man in the pulpit talk about Jesus for a while. Then he invited us to come forward if we wanted a lifelong friend in Jesus. I went forward, filled out a card, and shook the man's hand."

"That was it?" Aby asked incredulously.

"No, that wasn't it," he replied with an impish grin. "I really didn't learn anything about trusting Jesus then."

"They didn't make you recite 'the sinner's prayer'?" asked Steve.

"Oh, no, it was nothing like that. They just wanted to mark my decision on a card. I didn't trust Jesus until a couple of weeks later when I was reading the Gospel of John. I read about John the

Baptist, and I was really impressed by him. He seemed to me like he'd be the greatest man in the whole Bible. Then I read his comment about Jesus in John 1:29 where he said, 'Behold the Lamb of God, which taketh away the sin of the world!'* When I read that, I realized that *Jesus* took away my sin, that *he* was the one who saved, *not* John the Baptist. I was captured by his love—hook, line, and sinker. All I wanted to do was read the Bible and pray and get to know him more, the Lord who loved me so much that he gave his life to free me from sin and death."

"Amen!" said Bob with delight in his eyes.

"That's so cool!" said Steve with a chuckle. "You mean you didn't hear any of that talk about hell or fear or God supposedly 'hating' sinners?"

"Not a bit of it," Tom replied, shaking his head slowly. "We didn't have much in the way of church services on base back in the sixties, so I just stayed in the Scriptures for most of my free time on base. I learned so much about Jesus: who he is and his love. It wasn't until a year or so later after I met Sara that we started getting involved in a local body that I heard *that* kind of preaching."

"What did you do when you heard that type of preaching?" inquired Aby.

"I didn't know anything about questioning or challenging the leadership; therefore, I didn't say anything about it. I just knew that they were wrong because Jesus didn't teach me that from the Bible. He taught me that he *loves sinners* and gave his life to *free them* from sin, not that he hates them because they sin. I knew that he didn't send people to hell. They do that to themselves if they reject him, not trusting in his love."

"You could see it that way, Tom," interjected Bob, "because you knew that those preachers and church leaders didn't have any authority that you didn't have, which was the Scriptures themselves."

"That's true," he answered. "Those with the positions or titles of 'leaders' claim that they have authority from God to lead us. They say that if we oppose them, then we oppose God. Whether this is actually verbalized or not, pretty soon we see how true it is.

304

Then one day we finally realize the real truth, which is that their 'authority' is only *assumed* authority, not *granted* authority. You see, God did not grant them an authority above their brethren in some special act or calling. In fact, if you look hard enough, you'll find that they actually get their authority from those they lead. This means that *the people* allow them that authority by submitting to them and following them. Then eventually you suddenly realize to your amazement that they share the same authority *you* have, which is biblical authority. That's one of the reasons why Jesus made us all equal with the same authority in the body of Christ, so that no one would 'lord it over' anyone else in the body. Even the apostle Paul didn't lord any authority over anyone."

"Maybe people back then were just more compliant," Steve suggested. "After all, the Roman Empire was a force to be reckoned with. Slavery in the empire was widespread, and the few uprisings they had were usually squelched quickly by Roman troops."

"While I know that historically that was the way the Roman Empire and their citizens and conquered peoples were, I'm not so sure about that being the reason," Tom answered. "But picture who Paul really was. He was a Hebrew of the Hebrews, a Pharisee of the Pharisees, a man who practically had the whole Torah if not most of the Old Testament memorized. He's a man recognized even by secular scholars as being one of the brightest intellectuals of the ancient world. He was also called to be an apostle through a supernatural encounter with the risen Lord Jesus Christ on the road to Damascus. The Holy Spirit used him to pen over a dozen epistles inspired by God and which incorporate a significant portion of the New Testament teaching. Paul was a missionary who evangelized many cities and planted numerous churches throughout the Roman Empire. He was a minister of the gospel who literally suffered persecution and more than once almost died for his faith and love for his Lord Jesus. Imagine such a man sharing Christ with a lost world of pagans, watching them come to know Jesus, seeing them repent of their idolatry, spiritism, and debauchery. Imagine him discipling these new believers for months or several years in each city.

"Then the Lord leads him to other lands, and later he hears that some are in sin and are not following Christ. Does he wield his 'apostolic authority' to command them to repent and to obey the truth? No, he doesn't. You won't find that anywhere in the New Testament. What he does is he implores them as a father tenderly speaks to his beloved children. He beseeches them as brethren, as equals in the body of Christ. He *persuades* them—there's that word again—reasoning with them from the Scriptures. He doesn't say, for example, 'I'm the apostle, and you'll do as I say. You'll stop committing fornication immediately!' No. What he does is he *persuades* them in 1 Corinthians 6, saying, 'know ye not that he which is joined to a harlot is one body? for two, saith he, shall be one flesh.'* He also says in that same chapter, 'What? know ye not that your body is the temple of the Holy Ghost which is in you, which ye have of God, and ye are not your own? For ye are bought with a price: therefore glorify God in your body, and in your spirit, which are God's.'* He always *persuades* them to obey the truth, choosing to do it apart from fear, intimidation, or other such manipulative tactics. He respects their free will, presenting them the truth, but ultimately leaving the choice in their hands. He doesn't 'lord over them' any imagined special authority. Oh—well, there I go." He suddenly displayed a shy smile. "I've done too much talking again."

Tom's humble admission was inspiring, though unnecessary. His words were so penetrating that I had to let them adjust my understanding. I ruminated on them mentally as I chewed on my sandwich physically.

"No, Brother Tom," said Steve. "We enjoy hearing you speak your heart."

"Yes, it's very edifying," I added.

Others expressed the same sentiment.

"Well, all right," said Tom feigning a begrudging reaction. "I must let you know one thing regarding what I just said. I hope that you're all careful with this information." He added a little chuckle. "It's not my intent to incite rebellion in your local congregations.

306

If you don't like the way your local body handles authority, and you've spoken to the leaders about it calmly—but only after a season of serious prayer and following the Spirit's leading—then you're always free to go somewhere else."

"I think we all agree," replied Walter, "that causing a scene and displaying a rebellious spirit full of anger wouldn't be the *Holy* Spirit leading us in that case. It might be the spirit of self or of vengeance or of chaos, but that's not *Father's* Spirit leading that way."

A consensus was conveyed in the nods and facial expressions around the table.

"I find it amazing," began Aby, "that you learned about Jesus in a context of nothing but his love from the Bible. I know that I wish that I had learned about Jesus that way without having to have learned it years after coming to him in faith. I'd like to hear more about that."

"Certainly," replied Tom. "You know, I have been known to be very long-winded," he confided with more laughter. Then he continued.

"Jesus' love is powerful. It attracts us to him, drawing us with those cords of love. He hates sin because of what it does to us. It enslaves us, draws us away from him, and hurts us—the objects of his affection. Perfect Love has no desire that sin continue to hurt us and others through our sinful lifestyles. That's why his grace and love change us. As finite beings, we can become confused easily, thinking that Father hates the sinner—especially if that's what we're used to hearing. The power of Jesus' love is what breaks the chains of sin. He wants to let his love flow through us as his vessels to shower others with his love."

"There are certainly a lot of folks out there," said Bob, "who need to see the love of Jesus." He released a sigh before continuing. "If we as the body of Christ did a better job of demonstrating and communicating his love to the lost, then people would flock to Jesus. Abiding in him—that is, yielding to him and letting him flow through us—is intended to be a lot easier than we make it out to be, just like everything else in this walk with Jesus.

307

Nevertheless, as it is today in the church at large, too many of us harp on other people's sins and don't love them like he does. We're more worried about being offended by their sins or about trying to protect God's holiness—as if it were in danger of being tarnished or as if we were capable of protecting it. Instead, we need to see them as hurting people who need Jesus to love them and to mend their broken hearts and lives. It's sometimes too easy for us to forget that, as we love people, we're loving Jesus also."

"Amen to that, Brother Bob," said Greg. "If we don't see people as Jesus does, then it'll be much more difficult if not impossible to let Jesus love them through us."

This made me think of something I wanted to discuss with these brothers and sisters, but I didn't know how they would take it. With a small amount of trepidation and a large dose of curiosity, I decided to breach the topic. First, I glanced around at some of the faces.

"Now, I don't know how this is going to come across," I began, only glancing briefly at a few, "but I'm wondering what y'all will think about this. It may make me sound really weird or way out in left field, but I think that Father has taught me to be more patient toward people and their sins."

"How so?" asked Steve.

"Well, before, when I was a real Pharisee-type person, I was kind of offended being around cussing and alcoholic drinking. It used to make me very uncomfortable. When I'd go to the grocery store, I'd stay far away from the beer and wine aisle as if it were the plague or something. Even now I don't walk through it if I can go around some other way. Having been raised in a home with an abusive, alcoholic stepdad, I don't have anything positive associated with alcohol. I've also seen what it can do to people, so I've never had any desire for it, not even to taste it." I looked down at my now empty plate, realizing what I was about to admit. "I used to judge people when I saw them drinking beer or some other alcohol." Then I looked up, seeing that all attention was on me. "But now when I see people in restaurants or other places with some kind of alcoholic drink in their hands, I don't think badly of them because of Father's work of grace and love in my heart. Jesus has given me his perspective to see beyond any sins so that I can see the person whom he loves. That makes it easier to love them too."

"That's a great thing!" exclaimed Walter. "That's spiritual maturity, if you ask me."

"Thanks, Walter," I replied, slightly abashed. "But I don't bring this up to brag. This is just something I've noticed in the last year, and I was wondering if I'm being too lenient or if it's how I should be."

"When you read about Jesus in the Gospels," began Greg, "you see that Jesus was known as 'a friend of sinners' and that people were attracted to him by his love for and acceptance of them. The self-righteous, religious crowd—the Pharisees, the Sadducees, and the like—*they* were the ones who had so much condemnation for people. Therefore, being less judgmental and condemning of people, like the self-righteous, and more accepting and loving of people, like Jesus, is what Father wants for his children."

"Whew!" I said with relief. "That's good to hear!"

"Being like Jesus," added Bob, "doesn't mean that we always applaud everyone's behavior—every deed, every word, and every thought. Jesus loves all people so much that he wants to rescue them from whatever bondage to sin they may have. You see, Jesus' love wants what is *best* for people and their spiritual well-being, and that means doing what's necessary to free them from their sinfulness. It also means changing their lives for the better, making their lives revolve around him instead of around sin and be characteristic of him instead of characteristic of sin. Christ has already made our freedom possible through his sacrifice and resurrection. Now through the gospel, he invites people individually to trust him and make their release from bondage a reality in their lives."

"Those who condemn people," said Greg, "often forget that their condemnation and self-righteous attitude are just as sinful as the sins that they are judging in others."

"Amen, Brother Greg," Bob responded with a nod. "When we remember that we all start out coming to Jesus as unworthy sinners, it's easier to keep that humble perspective and not to judge others. Father's grace and mercy are free to all who trust Christ, despite their sinful past or present."

"Love for others," Walter said, "is what the Holy Spirit produces in us. 'The fruit of the Spirit', according to Galatians 5:22 and 23, 'is love, joy, peace, patience, kindness, goodness, faithfulness, gentleness, and self-control. Against such things there is no law.' You won't find judgment and condemnation on that list. Those are more in character with the works of the flesh listed a few verses before that."

Bob continued. "Showing love, patience, kindness, and the like toward people can only happen when we allow the Spirit to yield his fruit in our hearts. Therefore, we don't have to be offended when people sin around us."

"That's what I believe," I answered. "It's the same way I feel toward people who cuss around me. Sometimes at work or out in a store or somewhere else I'll meet someone whom I've never met before. Then they start using all their foul language as if that's expected and acceptable everywhere. It used to upset me pretty bad, because here's someone who hasn't had any interaction with me to know if that's even something that I care to hear, yet they use the vulgar language. Sometimes they use the worst words in the English language in the very first sentence they say to me. I'm still not a fan of it; nevertheless, Jesus has shown me to look beyond that to the person who needs him and for whom he died."

"Love really *does* cover a multitude of sins," commented Sara nonchalantly.

"Oh, that vulgar talk really gets to me!" admitted Aby, twitching suddenly as if startled by an insect bite. "Such filthiness—when I hear it, it makes me feel so unclean that I just want to run away from it. I wasn't raised around that kind of language, and I can't get used to hearing it."

"I understand that, Aby," I assured her. "Believe me, I do. But I just know that, despite the horrible words that some people use, they are still loved by Jesus just as much as he loves all of us. I'm not happy to hear all the cussing and foul language—not at all. Yet

I still want Jesus to love people through me. I don't want to be unforgiving toward people just because they swear. I want them to know that they are accepted regardless of the words they use, their habits, their lifestyles, or whatever."

"It's where the compassion of Christ overrules any offense," explained Bob. "It's another benefit we receive from the grace of God working in our hearts. We grow to where we're not so easily offended by what others say or do. The closer you know Jesus and the more intimately you walk with him, you'll see that you're hardly offended by anything that people say or do. His love and grace let you see past all that."

"In reality," added Tom, "we *choose* to be offended. Some things we let slide, others we don't. But ultimately, we decide what we will take offense to and what we won't."

"Now, *that's* an eye-opener!" I exclaimed. "Tom, I've never heard anyone say that before now."

"If each one of you thinks it through," he continued, "then you'll realize that the things which have offended you in the past were really predetermined. That is, they've been decided by either your sensitivity to certain things or your strong opinions about them or perhaps even by the way you were raised to be offended by specific things. It's almost like having an unwritten list with you at all times of things which can quickly change your attitude and sour your mood."

"And," added Bob, "there are people out there who notice what offends you. They actively work it to your detriment and their advantage."

The facial expressions of both men seemed to reflect that they agreed and had gained firsthand experience in this field. Their wives' expressions concurred as well.

"When interacting with people," explained Tom, "it helps not to be offended by anything they say or do. It makes life a lot less stressful for you, and it allows you the freedom to be a blessing to people in need."

All these comments were reassuring. Then I remembered that I probably needed to clarify one of my points.

"Oh, and just to be clear about what I said earlier, I didn't mean that drinking a beer or a glass of wine once in a while is wrong. I know some believers who do that. They're free to do it, so if they can handle it, then it must be okay for them. It's just not something that I myself have ever had the desire to do. I've gone my whole life without alcohol thus far, so I don't ever plan to start drinking in the future. I know that drunkenness is what the Bible teaches against, not any consumption whatsoever."

"In that case," Walter began, slapping the table, "I'll break out the wine coolers I brought with me!"

"Oh, stop it!" said Cindy, swatting at his arm. "We don't drink either. Honey Bunch, even when you're funny, you're not funny."

"Now, come on, Darlin'," he half whined with his same, old song. "You can't blame me for trying."

"Hey, Walter," Steve said, obviously enjoying the moment, "if it makes you feel better, I almost believed you there for a second."

Walter suddenly sat up a little straighter. In an instant, his expression changed from wounded to uplifted.

"It *does* make me feel better!" Then, leaning to Cindy on his right, he said with fake sheepishness, "Darlin', I'm going with what Steve said so that I'll feel better."

"You would," she said with a playful and harmless smirk. Then she propped her elbow on his shoulder. "Let's get back to our discussion. What's a good scripture about Jesus loving through us?"

"'We love because he loved us first,'" I volunteered. "That's 1 John 4:19."

"Hey, good job, Brother!" remarked Steve, flashing an encouraging smile and using a silly voice. "It sounds like you have 1 John 4 memorized."

"No, not really. However, I have been reading and studying that passage quite a bit recently. It teaches a lot about Father's love for us and how we love him and one another because we have his love in our hearts. Love is an essential, defining attribute of a believer."

"That's right, Bro. Jesus did say in John 13:35, 'Everyone will know by this that you are my disciples—if you have love for one another.'"

"In the preceding verse," Greg added, "he also gave *the extent* to which we are to love. He said, 'Just as I have loved you, you also are to love one another.' Since he loved us to the point of death by sacrificing himself for us, we are to have that same kind of love for each other. Therefore, we are to have a sacrificial love for one another that even extends to death—if that were ever necessary."

"Love is hard to fake," Kathy observed. "Sometimes people try to imitate it, going through the motions of what they've seen of it in others. But if it isn't genuine, then it becomes pretty obvious."

"I've heard it said," added Cindy, "that you can give without loving, but you can't love without giving."

"God is the Father of all love," said Bob. "He is its originator and its source. Biblically speaking, any 'love' not empowered by his enablement isn't genuine love."

"Oh, wow!" I blurted out. "That just connected with me. Now I know why I've had this love for people in the last year!"

"Why's that, Brother?" asked Steve.

"It's because Father has showered me with his grace." Then I reflected on what I had just said. "Or . . . well, maybe it's more accurate and biblical to say that I've *yielded* to him to be more open to his showering of grace, since he never ceases to give us his grace upon grace. Throughout my life as a believer, I've had a few moments when Jesus gave me a strong love for people in certain situations. But since his grace and love broke through to me a year ago, I've had this undeniable sense of love for people, even strangers. I don't quite know how to explain it."

"Father flows his love through us," suggested Steve, "letting us view people from his perspective of compassion—just like Tom said."

"Oh, yeah. Brother Tom *did* say that I would love people with Father's *agape* love once I saw them from Father's perspective. But I didn't know that he had told *you* that, Flamen'."

Walter reached across the table and patted my shoulder. "He's probably said that to just about *all* of us at one time or another."

313

Then he chuckled a little as did several others.

I glanced at Tom. His countenance displayed that knowing grin.

"It's not original with Tom," added Sara. "It's from the Bible. It's even taught in the verse you just quoted, 1 John 4:19."

"Hey, you're right, Sara. Wow! I'm kind of amazed that now I really enjoy people, not just those who are 'pleasing' to me or who 'fall well to me,' as we say in Spanish. I was so judgmental before, looking down at people's appearances, their clothes, their personal hygiene, and their actions—like if they smoke, drank, cussed, or had tattoos. I was a real Pharisee. But Jesus has freed me from that whole mindset, that whole attitude. I really enjoy people's company now, regardless of all that stuff. And I don't see them as bothersome or a waste of time."

"That's encouraging," said Tom. "He's making you more like Jesus in that respect. You now see people with the same compassion and heart as Father does. He sees them as people with needs, people who need him."

Suddenly, my face felt a little flush.

"Is it okay to agree with that, or will I look like I'm boasting?"

"Not to worry," Tom said cordially. "It's all a work that Father is doing in you."

"I really do enjoy people, getting to know them, their personalities, their hopes and dreams. We all have so many needs in common. Sometimes people don't know how to express their needs, and they do things that before would really get to me. But I think that all the grace, love, and freedom that Jesus has given me have opened a door, allowing me to see the needy hearts of people with whom I cross paths."

"It's a blessing to see Father work in your heart, isn't it?" asked Bob. "Knowing that he's still in the business of meeting needs that we didn't even know we had and conforming us more to the image of his Son is both a blessing and an encouragement."

"It really is, Brother Bob. I'm thankful and humbled. I know that I don't deserve all this, but I'm ever so grateful for these changes that he's brought about in me."

"He really has changed," volunteered Elena. "The John he is now doesn't compare to the John he was before. He's so compassionate and caring now. It's like I have a new husband!"

Laughter was heard around the table.

"He's a better brother for it," commented Steve with a grin and the same silly voice.

"Thanks," I replied, a little embarrassed from all the attention. "I know it's not anything that *I've* done. The good in me is all Father's doing. He deserves all the praise. I'm nothing without him."

"That's the way we all feel about his work in us," added Greg. "We owe all to Jesus. He's the one who's made us what we are today."

"I'm so thankful that he's teaching me so much now. In fact, I've learned so much about his grace and love that sometimes it's almost overwhelming, but in a good sense."

"Why don't you share some of that with us, Brother?" asked Steve, sipping from his cup.

"Okay. Well, let's see," I said, mentally reviewing some recent lessons. "One thing I've learned is through these fellowship groups with the couples from our Sunday school class. We usually meet after the services at someone's house. I call it 'having church in spite of church' because we have better fellowship and more opportunities to be the body to one another than we do sitting passively in a service for an hour while other people exercise their spiritual gifts."

"Wait a minute!" exclaimed Walter with mock surprise on his face. "*You* noticed that too?"

"Well," I replied with a grin, "it doesn't take much spiritual perception to notice that. I mean, there's not that much interaction when you have to look at the backs of each other's heads the whole time.

"But I've learned through these fellowship opportunities that Father truly loves the body of Christ. Of course, I've known that for the longest time. What I really mean is that he has shown me some of his heart toward the body. It's like, when you spend time

315

with people and really get to know them, you see their sorrows and joys, their passions and concerns. The more time I spent with these individuals, seeing beyond whatever image or persona some of them might portray, the more Father drew my heart to love them with his kind of love. It's the same for people who don't know Christ. Father loves them and longs for them to be in a relationship with him through Jesus."

"Now, *that*," said Walter, indicating me with his cup, "is the heart of a missionary."

"This reminds me," began Greg, "of 2 Corinthians 5:14. 'For the love of Christ controls us, since we have concluded this, that Christ died for all; therefore all died.' In the context of the passage, Paul is talking about the gospel being the message of reconciliation. I'll spare you the technical details, but the way the Greek grammar expresses the phrase 'the love of Christ,' it seems to refer both to Christ's love for us and our love reciprocated back to him. It's because of that relationship we have with Jesus and the love we share in both directions that we come to understand his heart for people."

"His love is a great motivator for so many things," interjected Cindy. "When you think about it, Jesus' love motivates us to resist temptation, to forgive others, to love the unlovely, to share him with others—even to love him back with our lives."

"Jesus is the Great Motivator," added Steve, "and I'd rather have him motivate me and give me purpose and meaning in life than anything else."

"I have a picture in my mind of love," I said, reflecting in the moment. "It's back when we first moved to Honduras, just before my bitterness began.

"Our container with all our possessions and personal effects had just arrived at the capital, and we had an appointment to meet with the customs officers to have our container checked into the country. We were staying at Elena's parents' house. Elena and I had to wake up at 4:00 AM and ride a bus over five hours to the capital to make our appointment the next morning. That night I had the hardest time sleeping because of all the crowing roosters and

316

barking dogs. Whoever started this idea that roosters only crow at dawn never spent a night in Central America, I can tell you that for sure."

This was worth a few chortles and an "Amen, Brother," from Steve.

"I think I finally fell asleep that night around 2:00 from sheer exhaustion. Nathaniel, who was almost seven months old at the time, stayed in the same room with us in a small bed beside ours. Around 3:00, he woke me up. I think he was thirsty or was awakened by a noise or something; I can't remember now. I was so exhausted and irritated, because I had only been asleep for about an hour, and I knew that I would have to wake up an hour later for that five-hour bus ride, so I wasn't a happy camper. I grudgingly turned on a little lamp and gave him some water and picked him up to rock him back to sleep. When little Nathaniel first saw me in the light of the small lamp, he sat up in his bed, looked straight at me, and gave me the biggest smile. Then he reached out to me and hugged me."

My eyes began to grow moist. "I have that image in my mind, that snapshot of my little son: so happy just to see me and to be with me. He didn't know that I had had almost no sleep and would have to wake up an hour later. But just the love and joy expressed on his face was such an encouragement to me."

I looked up at Steve and Walter. "I've carried that moment with me and treasured it ever since as a moment of pure love. During my years of bitterness, I often reflected on that moment and longed to have that kind of love for and joy with Father."

"Honey," Elena said, putting her arm around me, "you never told me about that."

"I let you sleep through that night because I knew you were tired. Besides, it turned into a precious father-son moment."

"Aww! That's so sweet!" She kissed my cheek. I stroked her long, shiny, dark hair and looked into her deep brown eyes.

"Good night, Brother!" said Steve. "It sounds like Father's been teaching you *tons* of things through your son. I wish I had one."

Steve's eyes were playful, yet serious. I knew that he longed to be a dad and to have his own children; yet I didn't know how to respond to him. Then Tom rescued the moment with his wisdom.

"As Father's children, we can always look to him to teach us in different ways. Whether it's through our children, our siblings, our parents, our friends or whomever, Father is always teaching us through our relationships. And you know what? He does a pretty good job with what we give him."

"I'm just so thankful to be his child," said Bob humbly, "and I want to be open to learn from him as much as possible."

"So am I," I concurred. Others around the table expressed their agreement also.

"Getting back to what we said about loving people," I said, "another thing I've noticed is that so many people are quick to write off others just because they don't like something about them."

"Give us an example, Brother," Steve said.

"Okay. Sometimes I'll meet someone for a brief moment when I'm out somewhere. I don't know any better, so I just enjoy the person's company and the conversation as usual. Then when he or she leaves, someone who wasn't even part of the conversation will make a judgmental comment like, 'Can you believe what she's wearing?' or 'Man, that guy's effeminate! You know what that means,' or 'He's a real freak. Why do you even talk to him?' or 'She acts so haughty, it's disgusting,' or whatever opinion they express to discount them. It's just so crazy! People just judge others from a brief impression without even trying to get to know them! Why can't they just try to accept other people different from themselves for a moment and find something that they like about them?"

"Now, Brother," Steve replied in his baritone characterization voice, looking down at an angle with his eyebrows arched, "do you *really* need an answer to that question?"

I released a huff of exasperation.

"Okay, I already *know* the reason. But it just gets so disappointing. It's almost like they're trying to spoil my enjoyment. Then sometimes the first person might return a few minutes later, and the second one, who was judging the first, puts on a front like they

318

had no ill thoughts toward them at all. How fake and hypocritical that is!'"

"Brother, you know when they share those judgmental opinions, it really speaks volumes about themselves and not about those they're criticizing."

"It sure does! It reveals how they talk about *everyone*—including me when I'm not around! It's not a happy scenario."

"Because you know that already," Steve continued, "*you* can rise above it by loving everyone the same—even the judgmental folks. Remember: that used to be *you* not so long ago."

"I know, Flamen'. It *was* me. And they *do* need Jesus' love like everyone else. That's why I'm so amazed at how Jesus has affected this heart change in me."

"Speaking of 'loving everyone the same,'" began Tom, clearing his throat, "when it comes to loving and accepting others, there's a particular sin that a lot of believers commit that they don't even realize they're doing."

"What's that?" I asked.

"The Bible refers to it as 'respect of persons.' It's also referred to as showing partiality or favoritism. It's valuing one person over another in our behavior or how we treat others. I'm guilty of this sin as much as anyone, though I don't want to be. I'll admire some people for whatever selfish reasons I have for considering them more significant to me than others are. Other people I consider less significant to me for various reasons, so that I count on them less. I do this in my mind, and then it plays out in the way I treat people."

He halfway shrugged and threw his hands up.

"I know that it's unwise and ugly not to see everyone as Father does. I also recognize that it's a serious problem, both in my life and in the church at large. In many pockets of the body of Christ, they tout it as if it were a virtue."

"How so, Brother Tom?" inquired Steve.

"If you listen long enough, you'll usually hear church members brag about their pastor and all the great qualities he has as superior to others. 'Oh, our pastor is a great, godly man! He preaches straight from the Bible.' On and on they go. The same people brag about their local congregation in a similar vein, extolling their great programs, facilities, practices, and characteristics. They—including us too—can get caught up in the trap of treating some folks in the body like 'Christian celebrities' or 'Christian royalty' at the expense of disrespecting, rejecting, or slighting others whom Father loves just as much. Very few of us realize that we are practicing and promoting the very sin spoken against in James 2:1-9. Does anyone know that passage?"

I had been waiting for this moment since I left home, because *this time I brought my Bible!*

"I got it!" I said, springing into action. I whipped out the Bible that I had concealed in the inner lining of my jacket. There were a few giggles as I flipped through the pages to James chapter two. I began reading in verse one.

"'My brothers and sisters, do not show prejudice if you possess faith in our glorious Lord Jesus Christ.'" I stopped and looked up at Tom.

"*'Prejudice,'*" he repeated pensively. Then he nodded. "That's a good translation for it. The old King James Version calls it 're-spect of persons' there. Read through verse four please, John."

"'For if someone comes into your assembly wearing a gold ring and fine clothing, and a poor person enters in filthy clothes, do you pay attention to the one who is finely dressed and say, "You sit here in a good place," and to the poor person, "You stand over there," or "Sit on the floor"? If so, have you not made distinctions among yourselves and become judges with evil motives?'"

"See?" Tom asked. "It's a heart issue, because it has to do with our motives and our judging people. In this example, it worked itself out by following a cultural practice in that day of assigning seats of favor or disfavor in a meeting. In the context of the passage there, James was pointing out a particular, preferential treatment of the rich over the poor. And we may read those verses and think, 'Oh, I'd never do that!' But this is just one practical example. We do much the same thing—practicing 'prejudice' or 'respect of persons' when we treat some more favorably than others. Another cultural example is written about in Galatians 2:11-13. That's where Peter stopped eating with the believers from among the Gentiles and ate only with believers from among the Jews to try to impress the Judaizers who were visiting the local body. He was hypocritically snubbing those Gentile believers just to look good to the group visiting from Jerusalem. As you know, Paul confronted him publicly for that. Still another example is explained in 1 Corinthians 1:10-12, where the Corinthian believers were taking sides and following their favorite apostle or elder. This evil of 'respect of persons'—this type of 'prejudice' or favoritism—causes divisions in the body.

"John, drop down to verses eight and nine, please."

"'But if you fulfill the royal law as expressed in this scripture, *"You shall love your neighbor as yourself,"* you are doing well. But if you show prejudice, you are committing sin and are convicted by the law as violators.'"

"Thank you. When we love everyone as equally as we love ourselves, beginning with the way we consider them and carrying over into our behavior toward or treatment of them, then we allow Jesus to be Jesus through us, sidestepping the whole issue of 'respect of persons.'"

Steve shook his head and then motioned with his hand.

"Okay, Tom, question: Does Father really treat all people equally? If so, how can he give the same significance to everyone, and how can he expect us to do the same?"

"Those are good questions," Tom conceded. "Let's think about this: What makes *all* people equally valuable?"

There was silence at the adults' table. The children had already finished their meal and were getting a bit antsy and noisy. Just then, the *whooshing* sound of a roller coaster, the rapid *clickity-clack* noise associated with the wheels on the tracks, and a few excited screams were heard emanating from the rear of the park. The children reacted to the sounds, verbally expressing their joy and amazement.

Meanwhile, the facial expressions of Bob, Greg, and Walter revealed that they already knew this answer. They were probably giving the rest of us time to think through the question to give a response. It made me wonder how many theological discussions this group had had together over the years and which issues concerning which they had reached conclusions.

Steve looked like he was thinking. I was trying to process through to an answer. However, the only thing I could come up with was that it had to have something to do with Jesus. Then I thought of an answer, but before I could speak, Aby casually replied.

"It must have to do with what Jesus did on the cross."

Tom nodded happily toward Aby.

"That was excellent, Aby," he said in an encouraging tone. "You're exactly right. What Jesus did for us all on the cross to provide salvation and his resurrection from the dead on the third day—that is what makes us valuable. Therefore, it's not what *we* do, accomplish, achieve, or work. It's not who we are, which family we are born into, what social or financial status we have reached, or even what we own. What Jesus did for us on our behalf and in our place gives us *all* equal value and worth as human beings. This is something the world simply doesn't comprehend.

"Therefore, our own worth is based on Father's grace through the work of Jesus Christ. Once again, it's all Jesus, and it's all by his grace. That's why we can treat everyone equally as Father does—by his grace, his enabling—since we know that Jesus' work of salvation was for all, whether everyone receives it or not."

These thoughts were new to me—at least the connections and applications were new. The principle truths were ones I had known and believed for years.

As the gears were turning in my mind, Steve asked another question.

"So, Tom, how does this work out practically for us? What does a walk devoid of this sin of 'prejudice' or 'respect of persons' look like?"

"You may think of it as equal respect for all persons instead of more respect toward some and less respect toward others because, in a nutshell, it translates into that. For example, when you have an opportunity to be a blessing to or to fellowship with two or more people, do you reject the one who's 'less significant' to your life and always gravitate toward the 'more significant,' so to speak? I'm not saying that it's a sin to spend time with your friends instead of with strangers. Remember that I'm not trying to put you back under the law of New Testament principles. What I'm saying is, be open to let Father guide you toward whomever he will. Re-cognize that 'respect of persons' is one of those secret sins that we all do, and we all need to lean on Jesus to draw us away from that propensity. You'll find that you'll be quite pleasantly surprised where he'll take you and how he'll bless you.

"Here's another application: Do you credit one person with a speaking-type spiritual gift over another? Do you honor one who ministers over another? Do you call 'inferior' the gift that God has given to some? You see, this 'respect of persons' sin is as rampant as gossip, envy, self-importance, and some of the other sins permitted or even encouraged in the body of Christ at large. We don't always realize its seriousness and the consequences we bear."

"I just thought of something that might help," said Greg. "May I, Tom?"

"Certainly, Greg. Go right ahead."

"Think about the small, humble people Father used in the Bible to accomplish great things: farmers, shepherds, widows, fishermen, tax collectors, people in poverty. The Book of Judges is full of people like this: the weak, humble, and uneducated through whom Father delivered Israel from their human enemies, the Philistines, who surrounded and thwarted them. If he had used the biggest and the best, then it would have been harder to see that the God of Israel was working their deliverance and not some hero for people to admire. In 1 Corinthians 1:26-31, Paul talks about how Father chose those considered weak and foolish by the world's standards to shame the strong and the wise."

"Samson," I suggested, "was an exception though, right?"

"He was the strongest, but his strength was by God's grace and linked to his divinely directed sanctification of his uncut hair. I would guess that he probably looked like a man of average build.

Therefore, when he performed all those feats—like striking down a thousand Philistines with a donkey's jawbone—the Israelites knew that his power was not in his muscles or in the jawbone he used as a weapon. Samson's power—his might, his strength—was divine in origin, from the Spirit of the LORD. His vanity and ignorance were evidences of his human frailty."

The children started walking around the table toward us. They were a little rambunctious and obviously ready to go to the park, especially with all the sounds of the park rides luring them.

"Well," commented Bob, "we'd better get these youngun's on some rides."

The children cheered and began dancing around the tables.

We all began picking up the remains of our trash and putting away the leftover food. It was a neatly coordinated effort. With all of us working together, the area was cleaned, the garbage was thrown away, and any leftovers were sealed in containers and placed in the coolers in our vehicles in less than five minutes. Everyone worked happily and expressed gratitude for such a beautiful day and an edifying discussion.

I pondered where we were on such a grand day and smiled. My somewhat rhetorical question was to no one in particular; it mostly expressed my incredulity.

"Man, can you believe we're celebrating the Lord's Supper and Easter at Six Flags?"

"There you go with the 'E' word again," sighed Walter playfully.

He didn't seem offended, but I wasn't sure what he was accomplishing with the comment. I had learned over a year's time that Walter usually had a point with his comments like this. Cindy overheard what he had said and gave him a nudge.

"Go on, Honey Bunch. Tell him what you mean so he can solve the mystery."

"You got it, Darlin'! We *definitely* want the mystery to be solved, otherwise we might have to call Scooby and the gang."

"Scooby-Doo!" howled Steve.

On second thought, it may have been wiser *not* to introduce these two.

Walter nodded at Steve's impersonation while rubbing his palms together. Maybe it was a pun reference to Palm Sunday from the previous week. I could never really tell with him.

"Yeah, well that word 'Easter' has some uncertain origins. Now, it's not *necessarily* of pagan origin. It could be of German and Hebrew etymology simply referring to the Passover, which is fine. However, contemporary use of the word doesn't really communicate to the world that we're celebrating Jesus' resurrection, his Second Coming, and our consequent, future resurrection. I just prefer to refer to it as Resurrection Sunday."

"Hey," I responded lightly, "that does have a nice ring to it."

"Yeah," agreed Steve, "and it even points out the essential truth we're celebrating." Then his voice was imbued with a characterization. "That way people won't think of it as a celebration of spring, bunnies, ducklings, and *egg hunts*."

"Right!" exclaimed Walter sarcastically, adding, "As if we needed a holiday to celebrate all that."

"Why don't we just call it Resurrection Sunday from now on, Flamen'?" I suggested.

"Hey, John," interjected Walter, cocking his head like a terrier reacting to a high-pitched noise, "why do you keep calling him *Flamen'*?"

Steve slighted a suspicious yet humorous glare at me with a sneaky grin. I almost stifled a smirk—almost.

"It's just a nickname," I answered.

"There must be some interesting story behind it."

"Yeah, there is." I glanced back and forth between Walter and Steve a couple of times. Then to Steve, I pitched the question: "Do you wanna handle this one, Flamen'?"

Steve backed away slowly, changing to another characterization voice—his classical baritone narrator. "Yes, I believe I will. But let's *table* that discussion for the Mind Bender, the Ninja, or the Scream Machine."

"Or the Water Log ride," said Aby, approaching him from behind and squeezing his shoulders.

Timmy, Joey, and Lynette followed Cindy and Walter. Elena held Nathaniel by the hand as she walked near us toward the car.

"Hey, John," she called out to me, "remember, I may not ride too many things."

"But we're here *for free*," I protested, "and the lines are almost nonexistent!"

"It's okay, Elena," Aby said reassuringly. "If you don't like roller coasters they also have easier rides like the Carousel, the Bumper Cars, the Antique Cars, and Monster Plantation."

"'Monster Plantation'! What a joke!" quipped Walter. "That's the ride where couples float on little boats through a house full of cartoon-styled animatronics and smooch in the dark." At this point he wrapped his arms around Cindy and made a loud smooching sound near her ear.

"Ow! Stop it!" she half-scolded and half-teased.

"I'm not saying we won't ride it, Darlin'. I'm just seeing the humor in things."

"As you always do," she replied with a smile and a friendly roll of her eyes toward Elena and Aby.

We took a few last-minute items, such as caps, sunglasses, sun screen, and a collapsible stroller for Nathaniel. Then we secured our cars and walked toward the rear entrance gate. The children were elated as they skipped and talked. Excitement was in the air for us all. Steve was like a big kid, being just as excited as the children. We all bonded a little closer throughout the day.

The whole day was hilariously fun and memorable. Returning home in the evening, we were exhausted yet content. This walk with Jesus was becoming ever so much more enjoyable than it ever had been in my legalistic or bitter years. My heart was filled with gladness, joy, love, peace, and gratitude. I was learning to walk with Christ joyfully, and I basked in Father's love without any fear, guilt, or pressure to perform.

Soon, however, I would be confronted with the heart of the gospel message and wonder if what I was hearing was cult-like/heretical in nature or biblically sound doctrine. If it were the former, then I would be devastatingly heartbroken and forced to disassociate myself from these brothers and sisters. If it were the latter, then I would have to re-examine the gospel all over again.

[1] "What a Day That Will Be," Jim Hill. © Copyright 1955, Renewed 1983. Ben Speer Music/SESAC (admin. by ClearBox Rights). All Rights Reserved. Used by Permission.

CHAPTER 14

THE SHAME GAME

We brothers and sisters in the fellowship group couldn't always meet as the entire set of families like we did at Six Flags, but for as many of us as could meet, we did so as often as possible.

Fellowship with these believers in Christ always held a sense of expectancy, with none of us knowing how the Holy Spirit would lead us in our times together. Whenever we met together, there were moments of sincere prayer, uplifting praise, godly counsel, and edifying discussion, none of which we could have anticipated or planned beforehand. As I communed with Father throughout the day leading up to these socials, I would sometimes ask that he lead us in our fellowship time together and that all we would say and do together would be for Christ's glory and for our mutual edification. Then I would simply trust him to bless us as he always did. I prayed this way individually, not wanting to open the meetings with this prayer, as if it were invoking some spiritual ritual to "guarantee a blessing." We all seemed to understand the fallacy and trap in forging a dependency on that kind of thing. None of us wanted to turn what we shared together in Christ into some ritual or product of the flesh.

Concerning any sort of "preparations," they only concerned the meal. Each family would prepare a dish to contribute to the meal, and most of us began bringing our Bibles. Although we studied the Scriptures, our time together was never a formal Bible study like what I was accustomed to doing for so many years. Therefore, no one person served as the sole speaker or teacher. We neither had a predetermined guide or outline to follow nor a booklet for filling in blanks and taking notes. We each contributed to the discussion as the Lord lead us individually. There was simply no way to foresee how our time together would proceed.

The awareness of Father's presence and work among and through us during these times together was humbling, because

329

there was no way to predict how Father would lead us and through whom the Holy Spirit would present various teachings, although we all sensed that we were vessels for his ministry to one another. Sometimes the rightly spoken word of just a sentence or two at the right time from the least likely of saints in a meeting rang in my ears for months or even years afterward. Truly, those were moments when God was teaching me or others present specific things. Elena and I never sensed that people left disappointed that they didn't hear from Father. Quite the contrary, we left feeling encouraged and loved by him and one another; we shared a sense of awe that he would bless us in such a simple way. I remember sharing meals with these believers in our fellowship times, having that expectancy of wondering where the evening's conversation would take us, what we would learn, who among us would share and encourage the rest of us, or who would have his or her understanding grow concerning something he or she may have wrestled with for years. In such a family-style meeting of fellow believers in Christ, Father would bless us in ways we could not anticipate. Elena and I were always so encouraged and refreshed in these fellowships. Eventually I saw some parallels of our participation in our gatherings with 1 Corinthians 14:26-33. This too was uplifting to me.

Even the mealtime conversations at the table were precious! We had no cliques; we simply talked, laughed, and loved like we were all old friends, having known each other all our lives. All the children got along well, talking and playing despite their differences in age. Most in this group did have quite a few years of history together, apart from my own friendship of many years with Tom, Sara, and Steve. However, since the beginning, Elena, Nathaniel, and I had always been accepted as equals and integral parts of the group. The same was true for Steve and Aby. Banter, prayers, songs, and various other elements of intimate fellowship were shared among us. Whenever we ate together, I would sit with different ones each time, not picking any favorites, but longing to get to know everyone as much as possible. At times someone would share a concern or a question with the group at the table. A simple comment might begin as, "Did you ever wonder why . . . ?"

330

or perhaps as, "I was reading in Psalms this week, and I had a question about . . . ." A conversation would often grow and develop from such simple beginnings and would occasionally take most of our time together to bring to any sort of resolution or conclusion. It was a true family fellowship for which only Jesus received all the glory because none of it apart from the meal had been planned or steered by anyone of us. Of course, we were also grateful to him for providing the food.

As we fellowshipped together, we grew closer. As we each matured in our own walks with Jesus, not unfailingly but by his grace and enablement, his life flowed through us individually and into the group as a whole. The results of seeking him as individuals and together were amazing and much like what I had read about in the New Testament. Our hearts were being knit together in the love of Christ for him and for one another. We were experiencing fellowship in the Spirit, being of the same mind, having the same love, and being united in spirit and purpose. I was awestruck that I could ever be a part of such a group, especially given my history of hardheartedness and spiritual coldness. God's grace is truly unmerited and transformative!

As Elena and I discussed afterward what had taken place during each of our fellowships, we realized that, as a family of believers, we all shared a bond that was not based on doctrinal agreement or consenuality, although both were in great supply. There were no selfish motives or hidden agendas among our group, from what we could observe. We each viewed one another as more important than ourselves. There were no programs to maintain, schedules to follow, systems to manage, or expectations to fulfill. Our ties to one another were based simply and solely on Christ and our relationship with him. Everything else in our lives together flowed from that.

Much of this Elena and I had already been practicing weekly for a number of months by then with the couples from our Sunday school class in our "church in spite of church" fellowships. However, there were some marked differences. Those fellowships were scheduled almost like appointments for taking place after most of the services. After several months, many of the participants began to exhibit certain noticeable expectations. Furthermore, on occasion one or two couples might talk about others unfavorably or demonstrate some selfish tendencies. To my dismay, the tone or ambiance of the group seemed to allow for that and even encourage it in some ways. As a group we also began to seek a few agendas, which sometimes excluded others. My little joke about these times being "church in spite of church" was probably to the group's detriment, for I started to notice that many began to cling to what they could glean from the time we shared together. It was as if some of them expected their spiritual needs to be met through this format, much like the expectations typically had for a formal worship service. Some made comments about preferring these social gatherings to anything they garnered in their individual walks with Jesus. This issue became especially troubling to me at least, because it signaled that they were looking to receive spiritual life and sustenance from the group instead of contributing to it from their own relationships with Christ. To me, it seemed backwards. Contributing to the group as an overflow of what we received in our personal walks, instead of depending on the fellowship of others to get our needs met, was the more biblical model and Spirit-led practice.

These symptoms of illness in the body were quite apparent, yet I was perplexed as to how to approach the situation. It was never my purpose to seize the reigns and to try to steer the group toward what I envisioned for us together. I desired that we corporately have much more freedom from those kinds of agendas; therefore, I made an effort to resist doing that. This spiritual climate in the group became a matter of frequent prayer for me, but I didn't receive any clear guidance as to what to do to address the situation practically. The contrasts between this church group and the other fellowship became undeniable, yet only Elena and I perceived them, being the only family common to both.

Walter and Steve really connected that day at Six Flags. These two jokesters seemed to share a kindred spirit of sorts as they bounced their comments off one another. With their complementary brands of humor and their hunger for Jesus, their personalities authentically resonated with one another. Their wives also enjoyed each other's company, probably due in part to being so used to the zingers, puns, and one-liners of their husbands. During our adventure at Six Flags, there were times when we would split up for about an hour, since we formed such a large group. The ones my family and I tended to flock with at the park were Steve, Aby, Walter, Cindy, and their children, Timmy, Joey, and Lynette. With these brothers and sisters in Christ, we experienced a joy and freedom that are practically indescribable. It was very relaxing and edifying to spend time with fellow believers who shared a freeing walk of grace with Jesus, a desire to know our Lord more in all pursuits, and a great, healthy sense of humor.

Our time together was a continuation of the fellowship and discussion we had shared just before the amusement park adventures. That whole day had been like a celebration of Christ and who we are in him. As a real bonus, Steve and Aby had the opportunity to play "aunt" and "uncle" to the four children, who also enjoyed the attention from this caring couple. The food, fun, and fellowship in the context of our families made the day that much more exceptional. Somewhat unbelievably, we enjoyed all this on Resurrection Sunday, which seemed like the most fitting day for the activities we shared. It had been a day of celebration, fellowship, joy, and gratitude.

Although Steve and Aby lived on the north side of Atlanta, a fair distance away from the rest of us south of the city, our three families found excuses for meeting socially whenever possible. Because we wanted to spend time together, we all found it easy to arrange our schedules to do so. Opportunities were planned for about every other weekend. About a month or so after Resurrection Sunday that year, our three families met one Saturday afternoon for a special lunch at Walter and Cindy's house.

It was to be a cookout/potluck, or so I thought. Walter would provide the meat and man the grill on his back deck. The rest of

us would bring the side dishes. With this group of language aficio-
nados, there was, of course, the anticipated debate as to what to
call the event. Steve, the northern transplant, and Aby, the Texan
of Mexican descent, were used to calling this kind of event a "barbecue." Those of us from Georgia were calling it a "cookout,"
since we would *cook out*side on the grill, and not all the meat
would be *barbecued*. This brought the use or nonuse of sauces into
the debate. It was a fun discussion in which I only participated just
to goad Steve a little and to see if he would go the distance. I also
wouldn't have minded to have seen him lose this nomenclative
debate. Personally, I didn't care what it was called as long as we
could all enjoy the time while sharing a meal together.

As sort of a compromise, I suggested that we call it a "grill out,"
seeing that the *grill* was employed and the cooking was being done
*out*side on the deck. Steve thought that we should call it a "meat-
grilling," but with the recent addition of both corn on the cob and
buns to the grill, the whole idea of calling it a "barbecue" or "*meat*-
grilling" seemed illogical. He then countered with the suggestion
of "grilling with meat *et al*," at which point the wives stepped in
and said that we were all being "ridiculous." Specifically, this was
Cindy's word choice. She conveniently ended the debate by saying, "Let's just call it 'lunch', and let's eat!" Even though Walter
started in with his "now, Darlin's" and Steve proceeded to "good
night" the whole ordeal, it was all done in playful fun. The children seemed to enjoy it near the end as well, spurring us on with a
few suggestions and giggles along the way. Needless to say, it was
entertaining while it lasted.

The mealtime was exciting and enjoyable outside on the deck.
There was a variety of food and plenty of it for the ten of us. This
day in particular held much camaraderie and banter. We ate,
talked, and laughed, enjoying each other's company. The children
were cheerful with us adults and each other, delighting in the warm
sunshine and the shade trees stretching over much of the backyard.

As we ate, my heart was grateful for the food and the company.
Having visited the homes of many impoverished families in
Central America, I reflected on the abundance we had in the United

334

States in stark contrast to the abundant poverty, starvation, and malnutrition in most of the world. These kinds of thoughts usually milled around in my mind whenever I saw large spreads of food like this. To me, it was very humbling and somewhat melancholy to see so much food easily available before me, yet beyond the reach of those who needed it most in the world. Mealtimes with large groups like this always affected me the same way. I knew that I would never completely forget the images of so many in need, nor would I desire to do so. Those of us present had seen poverty on varying scales in the foreign field, be it in Central America or Eastern Europe. Even Aby, who had seldom traveled beyond the borders of our country, had encountered some deep poverty, starvation, and malnutrition in both rural and urban locales in other States in the families of her former students. Therefore, we were all grateful for the provision of food and humbled by the blessings before us. All leftovers, we knew, would be donated to needy neighbors or otherwise consumed later and not wasted or thrown away.

We were also thankful for this fellowship and bond which we shared in Jesus Christ, being all too aware that many other believers were likewise hungry for this gift of mutual oneness and fellowship in him. Our gatherings seemed so simple yet rich in fellowship and encouragement. Had I known that such was possible, I would have sought to meet with such a group of brothers and sisters in Christ long before then. As I contemplated our other fellowship of "church in spite of church," I longed for those believers to have the same understanding and communion of relating to one another biblically like this fellowship. Then there would be an ambiance of grace among us as we met and shared our lives in Christ together. Instead, there was too much vying to drain the group dynamic for selfish gains. It was a problem I contemplated often when we met with these other believers.

As the meal was ending, the children were excused to play in the backyard, within earshot and view of us adults on the deck. Some of us took a break from the splinter conversations taking place around the table. Walter rubbed his belly contentedly.

"Thank you, Jesus, for such wonderful food!" he exhaled aloud, resting his arm on Cindy's shoulders. "I was tempted to overeat, but this time I resisted."

"Well, Honey Bunch," remarked Cindy amusingly, "if you're tempted to clean up, then that's a temptation that you're welcome to plunge into head first."

"Now, Darlin', you know the boys and I always clean up after meals," he pretended to whine. "I'm just giving them the afternoon off for them to spend time with Nathaniel. I'll still do my part and theirs."

Seated at his side, she reached out and caressed his cheek.

"You're right, Honey Bunch! What would I do without you?"

Walter's eyes darted from one side to the next, then rested again on Cindy.

"You'd clean up by yourself?"

Cindy flashed a quick grimace, and then handed him a napkin.

"Why am I not surprised by your retort?"

His grin was classic. *"Masz szczęście, że mnie masz, kochanie,"* he replied in a foreign language.

"Hm, czyżby? Właściwie to o co ci chodzi?" she answered with a playful smirk.

None of us knew what Cindy and Walter were saying! We presumed it was from some European country where they had served as missionaries, but I didn't recognize it as any language to which I had been exposed.

Walter half-shrugged. *"Przepraszam, ja tylko tak próbuję żartować."*

Cindy gazed at him with a smile. *"Dobrze już dobrze, bardzo cię kocham!"* Then she gave him a kiss.

"Wiem, po prostu nie możesz inaczej."

Steve just *had* to outdo them both, so he blurted out in Spanish: *"Si ustedes van a hablar así, entonces nosotros vamos a platicar en otro idioma también. ¿Verdad, mi bella?"*

"Ándale pues, mi amor," replied Aby with a perky grin.

"Ni saben lo que empezaron," I added, joining in the fun. *"Éste será un día muy largo para ellos."*

336

With that, Walter stood and held up his hands. "Okay, Brothers! We give up! Y'all win!" To a round of laughter, he picked up some plates and took them inside as he tried to whistle the moment away.

Steve and I, still grinning, arose from our seats and began to help Walter clear the table and refrigerate the leftovers. The ladies remained at the table for a moment, still giggling and conversing in English about the silliness which just transpired. It didn't require much convincing from us husbands to get them to relax as we assured them that we would do everything involved in the cleanup.

Steve started singing in a silly voice some song which I imagined was his own invention. Within a few minutes we had cleared everything from the table, sanitized the cooking and eating areas, and filled the dishwasher with dirty dishes and the refrigerator with sealed evidences of our meal. As we worked, I reflected on our conversation with Walter and Cindy at the mall the previous year and remembered something said then that connected with a conversation I had had with Steve during our errand/road trip the previous year.

"Hey, Flamen', you remember how we talked about Jesus removing shame, right?"

He paused for a second, looking up.

"Oh, yeah," he replied casually. "In the truck that day we got the appliances for my mom."

"That was it. Well, I just remembered that last year at the mall Walter, Cindy, Elena, and I had a conversation which included a little discussion about shame and what Jesus did to remove it from people's lives in the New Testament. He agrees that at the cross Jesus freed us from both our sin *and* our shame. Therefore, we don't have any sense of shame from Father. The only sources of shame for us now are the world, the flesh, and the enemy."

"You got it, Chief!" Walter answered in agreement. "As we let Jesus teach us and conform us to his image as we walk with him, he'll mean so much more to us; then, as we allow him to shower us with his grace and love, the shame from those three sources will gradually have little to no effect on us. In fact, whenever we *do*

337

sense any shame in relation to him, it's a red flag that we're not fully walking in or trusting in his love for us at that moment."

"Good night!" said Steve slowly and contemplatively. "That really makes sense, Brother." He folded his arms and positioned his back against the kitchen island. "We know that Father loves us beyond our wildest dreams and that his heart is toward us, rejoicing in us as his children through the new birth. That's always true no matter what we feel. But if we don't let his love fill us and meet our need to be loved, impacting us moment by moment, then we'll wind up letting certain people, our flesh, and the enemy and his forces load us up with shame. That'll *really* have a spiritually negative impact on us."

"Okay," I said, pausing to absorb and to process as much as I could, "but what are the signs or symptoms of shame in our lives? It can't just be a general sense of feeling bad about ourselves. That would be too vague and difficult to identify as being the result of shame itself. Besides, we may not always recognize shame when we're acting out of the flesh instead of abiding in Christ, filled and drenched with his love and grace, right?"

"'Drenched!'" exclaimed Walter. "What a picturesque word choice, John! Have you ever thought about becoming a writer?"

"Maybe we can talk about that later," I answered. "For the moment, I'd really like to learn about eliminating shame. What symptoms evidence the presence of shame in our lives?"

"The evidences are many, and they are all varying forms of transgression or sin." While speaking, he piled our used cleaning rags in a corner basket for the laundry room. "But first it's important to understand that part of shame's *modus operandi* is hiding or distracting. That is, it's shifting the focus off us, since we feel so bad, and onto someone or something else. It's what psychologists call a defense mechanism." Walter turned to face us, squaring his feet with his shoulders as he explained. "Shame seeks to be covered—like Adam and Eve sewing fig leaves—and the defense mechanism of hiding or distracting is employed to force some sort of covering. When we feel ashamed, our flesh likes to pump us up, trying to make us feel good. So certain sins, like gossip and

338

bullying, 'exalt' us by putting others down and making them look worse by comparison. They serve as covering-type sins."

"Man! That really opens up a few things!" exclaimed Steve. "That means that when shame is doing a number on us, then we, acting out of our flesh, try to promote ourselves and try to make ourselves look good in an attempt to cover ourselves or to hide the shame."

"You got it, Chief!" agreed Walter. "If we work off our own weak, fleshly resources instead of running to Christ to let him deal with the shame we're feeling, then we walk in the flesh, trying to avoid, to repel, to cover, or to numb the feelings of shame. That's why it makes our flesh feel somewhat better when we put others down through gossip, insults, comparisons, or the like. It's a sinful dynamic that we may pursue, even as believers, it's sad to say."

"In the same vein," I suggested, "you could also add to that list sins like judging or condemning others, shifting blame, and lying and making excuses to avoid responsibility."

Walter nodded approvingly. "You're right, John. Those also fit shame's bill."

"Boasting and a competitive attitude," added Steve, "are also used to make us feel good and to make others look bad. I don't mean to say that all competition is fleshly, but if the motive is to promote oneself at the expense of others, then it's not a healthy competition."

"Okay, Flamen'," I said, turning to him. "What determines a healthy competition?"

"Well, y'know, if you're competing in a sport or some kind of game, you can compete to make it fun for all and to bring out the best in each other. That's not a bad thing, I don't think. But if you're competing to exalt yourself and to squash your opponents, trying to make them feel bad, then that has traces of ungodliness running all through it."

"Agreed, but what if you're competing because you just want to win?"

"Wanting to do your best and wanting to win aren't necessarily bad." He touched an index finger to his lip as he pondered this.

339

"But if the win is an opportunity to boast or to flaunt some arrogance, then it's pretty obvious that someone's motives aren't the purest."

"And if you're hurling abusive threats and insults at your opponents, stating how horrible they are and how you're going to destroy them off the face of the earth?"

I got the furrowed-brow look for that one.

"Aw, no! That has 'flesh' written all over it!"

"Just kiddin', Flamen'."

In a flash, the furrowed-brow wince relaxed and was replaced by a contented grin.

"That's all right, Brother. I knew that you had to be."

"I tell you," added Walter, "religious competition can be just as fleshly as anything else. And it's tricky, because most people don't view it as wrong or selfish. When churches or church leaders say things like, 'We have the biggest *this* or the best *that*, or the most *whatever*,' they may not think of it as boasting, but it is. At its core it's all shame-based behavior."

"Hmm!" groaned Steve. "I've been a part of some religious structures like that. For some local congregations, it seems that's all they ever do. They justify it by saying that they're trying to draw in more people to share the gospel with them."

Walter half-shrugged. "Justifying wrong behavior is making excuses, which is still a shame-based behavior."

To me, this made a connection with Genesis chapter three.

"So, back when Adam and Eve first sinned, obviously they hid from God because of their shame."

"Exactly," concurred Walter. "Father knew that they had sinned. That's why he sought them out, even though they only wanted to hide from him because they felt ashamed. It's important to note that the sin which distanced them from Father also produced the shame which made them fear him and feel unworthy of him."

"That's very insightful!" I said, almost gasping. "Not only did their sin result in spiritual death, depravity, and broken fellowship with him, but it also shrouded them with shame and guilt so that they only wanted to hide from the one who loved them the most."

"You're catching on, Brother," Walter observed, noticing the realization coming over me. "Thereby we see the core problem with shame: it makes us feel unworthy of Father. It makes us cower and flee from *him*—the source of all life, freedom, healing, and hope. That was Adam and Eve's reaction when God approached them after their first sin. Yet he was *the only one* capable of restoring and rescuing them from their tragic spiritual condition. Nevertheless, their shame made them fear him and shrink back from him. That's why Jesus dealt with both our sin problem *and* our shame problem."

"That's what kept tripping me up during my years of bitterness," I said aloud with a tremor in my voice. "With every transgression, I felt myself spiraling further and further away from fellowship with Father because of the compounded shame which weighed me down."

"That's a common problem for a lot of believers, John," remarked Walter soberly. "We've *all* experienced that before— even repeatedly. Shame is such a part of the complete package of sin that, when Jesus solved our sin problem at the cross, he broke the power of shame in our lives as well. It's just like any addiction or other sin with a stronghold in our hearts and lives. Because of the cross and the resurrection, shame no longer has any power over us any more than any addiction or other sin does. That's why, as believers, we're no longer slaves to sin or shame. This may not always be our experience, but the finished work of Christ makes it true. Therefore, we must always run to Christ, trusting in what he did to free us and allowing him to make that freedom our continual reality."

"That sounds like what Hebrews 12:2 tells us," offered Steve, "where it says that Jesus, 'For the joy set out for him, endured the cross, disregarding its shame.'"

"You got it, Brother! As Christ took on our sin, he also felt that same shame and separation that Adam and Eve experienced in the garden and which we ourselves also experience as a consequence of sin. He felt that sense of shame and that sense of lostness just

341

as we've experienced. However, like I said, the shame we sense between us and Father *and* its power were destroyed through Jesus on the cross."

Walter casually threw his hands upward. "I don't understand it fully, Brothers, but when Jesus suffered and died on the cross, he resolved the shame of the fall. Now as believers, we no longer have any reason to fear Father or to shrink back from him. Our shame between us and Father has been removed because Jesus offered a better sacrifice than those under the Old Covenant. He did the spiritual work, dealing with the 'consciousness of sin,' or our shame, as Hebrews 9 and 10 teach. *That's* why we can approach his throne of grace with confidence, because it's not about what we feel—our 'consciousness of sin,' our shame—it's about what Jesus did to resolve the entirety of our sin problem. You both know that the animal sacrifices under the Old Covenant couldn't do that. In Hebrews 9:9 it states that those 'gifts and sacrifices were offered that could not perfect the conscience of the worshiper.' *Jesus* did that; only he could 'perfect the conscience' by removing our shame. He broke the power of all our sin and shame through the sacrifice of himself. In verse fourteen it reads, 'how much more will the blood of Christ, who through the eternal Spirit offered himself without blemish to God, purify our consciences from dead works to worship the living God.' He doesn't want shame to hinder us from turning to him so that he can cleanse us and restore us to fellowship with him. Restoring our fellowship with Father just doesn't happen when we feel ashamed and guilty. When we're hurt, broken, devastated, bitter—no matter what we're going through—because of Jesus, our Great High Priest, we can go to him with our sin. Remember what Hebrews 4:15 and 16 tell us?"

That was one of the 'run to Christ' passages on my list. I was about to quote it, but Steve beat me to it.

"I sure do, Brother. 'For we do not have a high priest incapable of sympathizing with our weaknesses, but one who has been tempted in every way just as we are, yet without sin. Therefore let us confidently approach the throne of grace to receive mercy and find grace whenever we need help.'"

Walter nodded approvingly. "Steve, that's it! Jesus experienced all that sense of shame and feeling lost before Father on our behalf and in our place at the cross. When we trusted him for salvation, it became effective in our lives, whether we feel like it did or not. Obviously, it's a lot easier if we trust in his love and work of grace for us and in us, but it's still true nonetheless. Whatever shameful past we may have had, that's no longer who we are. Our sin, shame, and brokenness no longer define us. *Father's love and grace* define who we are. *Being in Christ Jesus* defines who we are. *Christ* is now our identity, not our sins. As a result, being believers in him, we don't have to hide in shame, whether it's because of past sins or present sins. We turn to Father confidently, being honest with him about what we've done, yielding our sin and brokenness to him without any shame. Then he blesses us, showering us with his grace upon grace, and restores our fellowship with him once again."

"That's why," added Steve, "we can walk in the reality of Father's love, with joy minus any shame, since he removed it all and doesn't relate to us using shame."

"Don't forget about Hebrews 10:22 either," I mentioned. "It encourages us by saying, 'let us draw near with a sincere heart in the assurance that faith brings, because we have had our hearts sprinkled clean from an evil conscience and our bodies washed in pure water.'"

"That cleansing from an evil conscience," replied Walter, "or from a sense of shame, is why we can talk to Jesus honestly about our sins and brokenness. Hiding our sins or pretending that they're not so bad isn't the kind of surrendering to him on our part that allows him to do the genuine cleansing work in us that needs to be done."

"Okay," I said with the dawn of another realization, connecting what had just been said with the garden in Eden. "That's why, in Genesis 3, *God* approached Adam and Eve after they sinned. He wanted to give them the opportunity to confess it and to turn to him for healing. That's why he asked them about their sense of shame.

'Who told you that you were naked? Did you eat from the tree that I commanded you not to eat from?'"

"And by asking those questions," Steve said, "it was less confrontational. I mean, yeah, it was obviously *somewhat* confrontational, but the purpose was not to condemn them. It was really just Father's way of giving them an opportunity to confess their sin and to ask for his forgiveness. It was their moment to depend on him to solve their sin problem, not to keep relying on the fig-leaf underwear, which was their own fleshly work or attempt at a solution."

Walter expanded on this idea of God asking questions. "Asking questions encourages the listener to think. It's something that Father did throughout the Bible. He sent Old Testament prophets to kings and to other individuals to ask them questions. Jesus asked a lot of questions of people to get them to stir their thinking about what he was teaching at the moment. I really think we miss that perspective of Father's purpose for those questions in Genesis 3 if we read them as if they were spoken in an angry tone. After all, Father wasn't breaking off all contact with Adam and Eve any more than Jesus was with the Pharisees and Jewish religious leaders when they sinned. Father had to approach them to provide a solution to their problem, because their newfound shame only made them want to stay away from him."

"Yeah, but instead of confessing their sin and asking for forgiveness," I observed, "they just shifted the blame and made excuses."

"Hence, even with the first sin in the garden," Walter deduced, "we see that shame-based behaviors are the result of sin."

"You got that right," interjected Steve. "Adam blamed Eve, Eve blamed the snake, and the snake didn't have a leg to stand on!"

I half-winced at that one. "Flamen', you know that's an old joke, don't you?"

"You can't beat the classics!" he intoned with a grin and his baritone character voice.

"Well, that's debatable. Especially since your jokes and one-liners have a short half-life."

Walter motioned with his arms, preparing to present his next point. "Okay, now, Brothers. Let's keep it friendly," he said, humorously. He continued.

"We see that the fall of mankind in the garden really demonstrated how shame works. However, Jesus broke the power of shame as well as sin itself. Now the power of sin is broken in our lives, and we have full, continuous access to him, unhindered by shame."

"It's really interesting," Steve mused aloud, "that whenever we're not trusting in the truth of what Jesus did for us and walking in Father's love, it's *then* that we fall back to our old fleshly ways of sinful behaviors. After all that Jesus did for us, we *still* act out in these sinful, shame-based ways which we use to try to cover, to divert, or to numb that sense of shame. Hmm! That's really sad, but it also explains a lot."

"It really does, doesn't it?" Walter asked with a solemn look. "All of what we've mentioned so far of these shame-based behaviors or sins are outward expressions. However, shame can even be expressed inwardly as well. For example, self-pity, self-condemnation, and even certain forms of depression are shame-based behaviors."

"But not *all* forms of depression, right?" I asked.

"Right," he agreed, "not *all* forms. Some forms are the results of chemical imbalances, diet, or even genetic factors, from what I understand. There are really many factors that contribute to the onset of depression, and I'm not trying to diagnose or to blame anyone here. No, I'm talking about the kind of self-induced depression which results from self-pity and self-hatred. It's a passive-aggressive behavior turned inwardly. So even though self typically tries to avoid or to cover the bad feelings produced by shame, some people's flesh condemns them, which just increases their feelings of shame. And by 'shame' I don't mean the godly sadness which works repentance, as 2 Corinthians 7:9 and 10 describe."

"Wait a minute, Walter," I said, holding up my hand. "That brings up another question. Doesn't sin just naturally carry with it its own sense of shame? Just because we're believers in Jesus and

345

have been forgiven and freed from the power of sin and shame, that doesn't mean that we shouldn't feel ashamed even now when we sin, does it?"

"That would be the wrong path to take in understanding this," Walter replied thoughtfully. "Obviously, sin produces shame. And yes, we can experience shame from our sins even as born-again, forgiven believers in Jesus. Shame is simply a natural consequence of any sin. What we're really saying is that God doesn't heap shame upon us or wield it against us *in his relationship* with us. The Holy Spirit convicts us, of course, but that ministry of his is not one of shame and condemnation. It's one of pointing out to us that we have transgressed by going our own way instead of yielding to Christ and following him. Therefore, we'll still feel shame in the moment, but that's a consequence of our sin, as is our flesh condemning and shaming us in the moment—or for however long we go without confessing it to Father and making things right. Remember that he wants to restore us to fellowship with him *even more* than we ourselves do. Therefore, even in that moment of us sinning, he desires that we run to Christ and let him clean us up, just like in Tom's analogy about the boy who muddied his shoes."

"Oh," I replied contentedly. "Well, that clears it up for me. Thanks, Walter."

"Nevertheless, through his crucifixion, Jesus resolved the whole sin-problem package for us—including the problem of shame. As believers in him, shame doesn't stand between us and God. I've probably repeated this enough now for it to sink in," he added with a grin and a twinkle in his eye. "That's why we can run to him and not be afraid whenever we sin."

"Yeah, I think I got *that* point now," Steve replied, matching his facial expression. "Besides that, even as forgiven saints, we *still* don't want to live in sin. Being forgiven doesn't mean that we just want to sin as much as possible, even though we have the freedom to do so. Hey, Brother," he said, addressing me, "remember our discussion about Romans 6 with Tom and Sara at the park last summer?"

"I remember it quite well," I replied enthusiastically.

"We talked about sin being slavery and said that it carries its own punishment. It's deceptive, because temptation entices us to submit to it; and once we do, the shame and condemnation begin. From this discussion, we now see that shame simply doesn't originate from Father. The Holy Spirit convicts us out of love, calling us back to Father to cleanse us and to restore our fellowship with him."

"It's also important to recognize," said Walter, "that as unbelievers in the past, we were depraved and spiritually dead. We were sinners because of being related to Adam, as Romans 5 teaches. As we're told in Romans 5:19, 'through the disobedience of the one man many were made sinners.' So, there's no need to prove to people who don't trust Jesus how lost they are by their sinful lifestyle. That's something that the Spirit does his way."

"Yeah," agreed Steve. "I've always wondered why that was such a popular method of sharing Jesus with the lost."

"Flamen'," I said mildly, "those who do that are just trying to make people realize that they are sinners and how much they need Jesus."

"But it's so misleading," Steve replied. "Asking people things like, 'Have you ever lied or stolen anything? Even once? Then that's against one of the Ten Commandments. So, you've broken one of the Ten Commandments at least once. And James 2:10 says, "the one who obeys the whole law but fails in one point has become guilty of all of it." That means that you are a sinner.' While it's true, that whole reasoning gets people sidetracked into thinking that it's some game of how many sins or which sins they commit that makes them sinners and worthy of hell. However, according to the Scriptures, individual acts of sin don't condemn us; it's the sin nature that we're born with, that we all inherited as descendants of Adam, which makes us unworthy of heaven."

"It can be misleading," agreed Walter, "though I don't think that the believers who share Jesus using that type of logic think of it in those terms. Our condemnation as the human race definitely comes as a consequence of that first sin in the garden in Eden. Whether people who are not in Christ 'look' or 'feel like' they're sinners really has no bearing on their condemnation and need for Christ. The first sin of Adam in the garden in Eden made him and all his future generations' sinners."

"That would be a much more accurate way of presenting mankind's universal spiritual problem."

"You're right, Flamen'," I concurred. "We'll just have to make that clear when we tell people about Jesus." I then turned to Walter. "Did you have anything more to add about sinning and the sense of shame?"

"Just one more thing," answered Walter. "Getting back to the sense of shame produced by specific sins: Back before Christ became our life, as sinners ourselves, we didn't think much about our sin. We didn't have the Spirit's ministry of conviction. Even so, we may have still felt ashamed for certain sins we committed then. Like I said, shame is simply part of the sin package. Lost people who sin long enough can grow numb to sin's effects of shame. In 1 Timothy 4:2, Paul mentions 'the hypocrisy of liars whose consciences are seared.' Some sinners become so desensitized by their sins, having their hearts cauterized or seared. They've lived such a long lifestyle of sin that they no longer distinguish between right and wrong. The context of that verse is identifying false teachers as pawns of the enemy, but that kind of numbing or deadening of the conscience can also happen to others who live a continuous lifestyle of sin, regardless of what the sin is."

"Hmm!" groaned Steve. "That is profoundly tragic! If those folks had understood what was going to happen to them, they probably would have avoided their life of sin altogether."

"Hence the deceptive nature of sin," Walter stated with a bit of a sorrowful expression.

"Good night!" Steve exclaimed. "This 'shame game' can get pretty ugly!"

"You're right, Brother Steve. It deceives and thwarts many. It's also used by people against others. Different personalities and temperaments can wield it in different ways. It's really up to each individual what kind of fig leaves he or she prefers to wear. All this is bad, obviously. None of it has either godly motives or is led by the Holy Spirit. And Father is grieved over the hurt and distance it produces in the ones he loves."

At that moment, the sliding glass door leading to the deck opened, and our wives entered the dining room. They were talking and giggling about something that they had just been discussing.

"Hi, Honey Bunch," said Cindy, giving Walter a kiss. "What are you boys doing?"

"We finished cleaning up a few minutes ago, and we just started a discussion about shame."

"Ooh, that's a great topic!" she replied enthusiastically. "And thanks so much for cleaning up. So, are these the introductory remarks leading up to the meaning of the cross?"

Walter slowly and casually bobbed his head. "It sort of looks that way, Darlin', but you may have just spoiled it for them."

The meaning of the cross? I wondered silently. *I already know what the cross means. What could they possibly mean?*

"What you talkin' 'bout, Willis—I mean, Walter?" said Steve in a predictable voice characterization.

Walter now had Elena and Aby's attention as well. They were intrigued, to say the least.

"Well, Brothers, you know that Jesus bore our sin and broke its power on the cross. In resolving the whole package of our spiritual problem including sin, he also resolved our problem with shame."

"Right," agreed Steve. "That's what we just explored in this *shameful* discussion."

"You also know that Jesus removed shame from people as he ministered to them and loved them individually throughout the Gospels."

"Sure," I replied. "We've talked before about that as well." *Father, where is he heading with this?* I prayed, feeling a bit uncomfortable.

"Great," he said contentedly. "Understanding shame as it relates to the cross is one of those essential truths for the believer— at least in my opinion it is. Getting to the meaning behind the cross of Jesus takes some preliminary steps or building blocks in our understanding. In fact," he looked at us a bit sheepishly and

349

awkwardly, "ya'll might need to sit down for this."

CHAPTER 15

THE MEANING OF THE CROSS

We passed from the kitchen into the dining room and sat around the large table. We could still see the children playing outside through the sliding glass door.

Cindy spoke cheerfully to Walter. "Honey Bunch, why don't you share with us briefly what y'all have already covered so that we'll all be on the same page."

"That's fair enough, Darlin'," replied Walter. He glanced around at each of the ladies as he spoke. "We were talking about the essence and expressions or manifestations of shame in people's lives. Shame is basically the bad feeling we have for ourselves, that 'consciousness of sin' we usually sense when we do something wrong or when others make us feel worthless, unloved, or unimportant. When we as human beings feel ashamed, we typically try to hide or cover ourselves. We might also try to deflect attention and shame from ourselves and onto other people. Shame can be used as our motivation to try to make ourselves look good while making others look bad or shameful."

Walter then directed his attention to Steve and me. "Hey, Brothers, help me out here. What were some of those sinful behaviors we listed?"

Steve grabbed a nearby pen and a sheet of paper to jot them down quickly as he named them aloud.

"There's gossiping, bullying, lying, making excuses to avoid responsibility, shifting blame, judging and condemning others, insulting others or saying things to make them feel bad, boasting, and competing in a mean-spirited way. Then there are the more internal expressions, which are having self-pity, condemning oneself, and choosing to be depressed."

"Yeah, and it's better to say it that way," I added, "so that it doesn't sound like we're deeming that all depression is sinful. Some of it is because of brain chemistry, hormone level changes,

351

diet, genetics, specific medical conditions, grief, stress, or other external causes not related with shame."

"Right, John," agreed Walter. "I've known some people who've struggled with depression, and it wasn't at all a spiritual issue involving shame. The sense of shame motivates different people to express it in different, negative ways of what they are feeling. It sort of depends on their personalities, backgrounds, experiences, and history of choices. Whenever we walk in the flesh, we all try to deal with shame in some way in an attempt to jettison the bad feelings and to restore or to fabricate good feelings. Some people express it outwardly in forms like gossiping, bullying, insulting, and others we listed. Other folks turn it inwardly, making themselves feel worse with self-pity, self-condemnation, and self-depression."

"Oh, that's kinda interesting," commented Aby slowly, "in a creepy sort of way, I guess. It's profoundly sad when you really think about it."

"What about insecurity?" I asked cautiously. "Is that a product of dealing with shame?"

Walter and Steve looked at each other, contemplating the idea silently for a moment. Then Walter spoke.

"Seeing that insecurity is basically a lack of confidence or a lack of assurance, both of which are provided for us in Christ . . . it would seem to be related to a sense of shame. Feelings of inferiority are just that—feelings. As believers, we are more than adequate, more than conquerors in Christ."

Steve nodded slowly in agreement. "Yeah, I'd say so too, Brother. If we're walking in the security and assurance that Jesus provides, then we're not following any imagined shame or the shame that the world, the flesh, or the enemy try to impose upon us. We shouldn't have a sense of insecurity or inferiority."

"That's what I thought," I replied reluctantly. "Insecurity is one that I've been known to have from time to time. And the baggage that accompanies it usually entails things like low self-esteem and a sense of inferiority to others."

Steve gave me the furrowed-brow wince.

"But why would that be an issue for you if you're running to Christ moment by moment and being who he made you to be?"

"That's just it, Flamen'," I said with exasperation. "Those moments when I *do* have those symptoms is when I'm *not* running to Christ."

"Then it should be easy to fix" he quipped. "Just run to him all the time and depend on him for your security and confidence."

I shook my head wearily. "Flamen', it's just not that easy to do all the time. Besides, remember that Tom said that this life in Christ is not so much what *we* do but what *Jesus* does through us when we yield to him?"

"Yeah, I remember," he conceded calmly. "I guess it's not like turning on a switch, then."

"If I may, Brothers," interjected Walter, "there's something that may help with this. As we've discussed before, Jesus is our source for everything: righteousness, wisdom, faith, peace, joy, love, gratitude, confidence, security, and so on. We know that he wants to live his life through us even more than we desire it. Perhaps we make this walk more difficult than it was meant to be. If we share with him our thoughts on this—our insecurities, worries, fears, or whatever we may be going through at the time—as we go through our day and encounter different moments and situations, then we *are* running to him and yielding to him, giving him our willingness and asking him to be Jesus in and through us."

"It's the prayerful attitude of confession like Bob and Tom talked about before, right?" I asked.

Walter motioned with his hands. "That's what I'd say. I mean—don't get me wrong—this life in him is not about finding the 'secret formula' or 'perfect balance' to living 'the victorious Christian life,' as many of us heard growing up. Father relates to us all individually as his children, so we can go to him with anything. His Spirit will guide us and teach us as he wills. Just like our children don't always grasp everything we teach them the first time out of the gate, neither do we. So don't feel disappointed if you seek Father time after time and don't see much happening. We're imperfect human beings, after all. We must also remember that Father has his reasons for not granting every request we present to him."

"I agree with you there, Brother," replied Steve. "Sometimes he's teaching us something deeper or more important, and sometimes he's at work behind the scenes, orchestrating events and guiding or shaping hearts. At other times, we must be patient, waiting for him to mature us in certain areas or for circumstances to line up or to play out as he desires. From our limited perspective, we won't always understand what he's doing."

"And like we've said before," Walter continued, "he's not worried that he'll be misunderstood. Misunderstanding him is something we do easily without even trying. Therefore, part of trusting him is letting him choose to do as he wishes in our lives when and how he wants to do things."

"Good night!" exclaimed Steve. "Looking over this list of shame-based behaviors, I think we could probably link almost every kind of sin either directly or indirectly to shame by one of these on the list."

"Wow, you're right, Flamen'," I said, glancing at what he had just jotted down on paper. "And this is just a short list of some obvious sins stemming from shame. It must be that a lot of sins are fundamentally fleshly expressions of our sense of shame."

"That tells us a couple of things," added Walter. "It shows us why it was so important to the enemy that he get Adam and Eve to disobey so as to experience shame. It also helps us to understand why dealing with shame at the cross was so important to Father."

Several of us nodded in recognition.

This was turning out to be a profound and significant discussion! Shame was not anything I had ever really heard taught much in sermons, college courses, or Bible studies—at least not in this light. Whenever I had heard the word "shame" in those settings, it was usually in a statement such as, "what a *shame* it is that we aren't living for Jesus like we should" or "how *ashamed* certain individuals should be" for their behavior. Thus, it was mostly examples of Christians being a source of shame and imposing it on others, not a biblical understanding of how Jesus had dealt with it and freed us from it.

"Y'know," interjected Cindy, "this list that y'all have compiled is pretty impressive. But this whole discussion is not intended to teach y'all how to go around recognizing shame in people and judging them for the way they behave as a result of it."

"You're right, Darlin'," agreed Walter. "It's really just meant to help us to recognize those moments in our own lives when we're dealing with shame and may not even realize it. These are some insights that have helped us in our own walks with Christ, because at some time or another, we all struggle with shame. It's important to note that, even though we're believers, this can be a recurring issue if we're not continuously trusting in Father's love for us."

"Honey Bunch, why don't we talk now about the solution for shame."

"You know me well, Darlin'," he said with a grin. "That's where I'm heading now.

"As we've mentioned before, Jesus dealt with our sin and shame on the cross. I'm sure you sisters are familiar with Hebrews 12:2. These brothers and I discussed it a few moments ago. It reads, 'keeping our eyes fixed on Jesus, the pioneer and perfecter of our faith. For the joy set out for him he endured the cross, disregarding its shame, and has taken his seat at the right hand of the throne of God.' Christ didn't let shame—that sense of separation from Father which Adam and Eve experienced in Genesis 3 and which we've all experienced—or the agonies of crucifixion deter him from his mission. He endured until the very end, knowing that his work on the cross would please his Father and provide a rescue for the world from sin and the lake of fire. After his resurrection, he would rejoice to see many turn to him to be forgiven, born anew, and freed from the enslavement of sin."

A few "*amens,*" "*thank you, Jesus,*" and similar expressions were heard around the table. Walter and Cindy beamed upon hearing our responses.

"As you already know," he continued, "being God the Son incarnate, Jesus was incapable of dying, even from the excruciating pains of crucifixion. He was human—apart from any sin or sin nature—and as God he was also divine. Nevertheless, the

355

tortures he endured at the hands of the Romans simply couldn't have killed him. He said in John 10:17-18, 'This is why the Father loves me—because I lay down my life, so that I may take it back again. No one takes it away from me, but I lay it down of my own free will. I have the authority to lay it down, and I have the authority to take it back again. This commandment I received from my Father.'"

Steve's mind was working; I could see that much on his face.

"The Old Testament does teach that the soul that sins will die. That's somewhere in Ezekiel."

"You're right, Steve, it does. Since Jesus was without sin, he had to *submit* himself to death, *surrendering* his life in order to die. That's evident from his last words on the cross. Just before he died, he said, 'It is completed!' Then to Father, he prayed, 'Father, into your hands I commit my spirit!' He chose to finish the work necessary for dealing with everything related to sin, including shame, to provide for our salvation. Then he succumbed or relented to death. The Gospels say that he 'gave up his spirit,' and 'breathed his last.' It makes the case that he yielded his life to death, because he couldn't have died otherwise. And we all know why he died, right?"

"Right," I answered. "He was our sacrifice for sin."

"That he was," agreed Walter, nodding his head. "But he wasn't offered up like the pagan sacrifices where a merciless, false deity 'required' blood and death from an innocent party. Remember when we talked about how my darlin' and I used to relate to Father like a couple of pagans would?"

"Boy, do I ever! That conversation has really stayed with me. I don't want my walk with Jesus to have any bitterness, legalism, shame, *or* paganism."

"For a lot of us, when we first hear the gospel, it's easy for us to misunderstand it as if Father were one of those false gods requiring human sacrifice."

'Misunderstand'? I wondered quietly. *Is he implying that we don't understand the gospel? Where is this going?*

"Wait a minute, Brother!" interjected Steve in a serious tone and with his furrowed-brow look. "What exactly are you saying about the death of Jesus?"

Walter blinked a couple of times, glanced at Cindy, and then smiled slightly at us.

"See if this sounds familiar: God is so holy that he can't look on sin. In fact, his holiness requires a just punishment for our sins. As sinners, we could never pay for our sins ourselves. Therefore, God sent his Son to bear all our sin—the sin of the whole world. He was made guilty for our sins and received the punishment that we deserved. Therefore, Christ suffered God's wrath as the perfect sacrifice for sin. On the cross, Jesus bore so much sin—the sin of all humanity—that God couldn't look at him, so he turned his back on his own Son. Jesus was forsaken by his Father during those hours on the cross. Because Jesus suffered God's wrath in our place, God's holiness and justice were satisfied. Now we can have Jesus' righteousness imparted to us the moment we trust in him as the sacrifice for our sins." He paused for a second, probably look-ing for some sense of recognition on our faces. "This is sometimes called the appeasement-based view of the cross."

"Brother," said Steve firmly, his furrowed-brow still in place, "are you saying that's not what *you* believe?"

"Not exactly. Parts of it are true, and parts of it are not exactly in line with the scriptural view of the gospel."

"Which parts do you believe are wrong?" I inquired, feeling a sense of dread with what he might answer. Emotionally I was stunned, and I noticed that my heart was pounding at an accele-rated rate. *Father, what is it that he believes? Don't tell me that Walter doesn't believe the true gospel!*

"Let me explain it to y'all this way. Father is holy, and in his holiness, he can't look on sin *with approval*. He is bigger than sin, and he's not so offended by it that he turns his back on us. As sinners, we were spiritually dead and enslaved to sin. There was only one way to cure us of the sin problem, to break sin's hold over us. That was for God the Son to bear the sin of the world and to endure God's wrath against sin so that we could be liberated from the power and penalty of sin. Second Corinthians 5:19 states that, 'in Christ God was reconciling the world to himself, not counting people's trespasses against them, and he has given us the message of reconciliation.' Therefore, instead of *forsaking* Jesus in that moment, *Father was right there with him at the cross,* reconciling the world to himself! He poured out his wrath on Jesus, true, but it was in order to deal with sin once and for all. That was the cure we needed in order to break the spiritual shackles of sin in us and to release us from bondage to it. So, you see, it's not that Father was so angry about our sin that he simply *had* to take it out on someone and that Jesus stepped in to take the beating for us. It was all according to their divine plan for our salvation.

"The Holy Spirit also had a role to play in Christ's crucifixion. As I mentioned earlier, in Hebrews 9:14 the Bible says that Jesus 'through the eternal Spirit offered himself without blemish to God.' Our Lord exemplified the way to live this life in him by depending on the Spirit; that's how he lived and ministered in his incarnation, doing everything through the Spirit, even when he offered up himself on the cross. Therefore, the Father, the Son, and the Holy Spirit were all three working *together* at the cross for our salvation. As God's wrath was poured out upon Jesus, he offered himself through the Spirit to the Father. All this was necessary to condemn sin and to affect the cure we needed to be finally freed from sin."

Steve had a faraway look as he listened and contemplated Walter's words. I listened intently, but with trepidation, easing up a little toward the end of the explanation.

"You mean," Steve said aloud, "it was more *curative* and not so much *punitive*."

Walter nodded happily. "You got it, Brother! It was more curative because the main goal of his wrath was to heal us of sin and to release us from its dominion over us, not to hurt us. You see, sin is such a serious problem that God's wrath had to resolve it through Christ and his work. By the way, his wrath is *also* an expression of his love. It's because Father loves us that he brought the totality of himself against that which destroys the ones he loves. His wrath isn't aimed at us; it's aimed at sin. Just like the Bible says in Romans 1: 'For the wrath of God is revealed from heaven against all ungodliness and unrighteousness of people who suppress the truth by their unrighteousness.' Truly his wrath is against sin, although people put themselves in harm's way by their godless life-styles and choices. In the Old Testament, there were people who gave themselves over to sin with such a passion that their bent was rebellion against God's grace and mercy. They made it clear that they wanted no part of God in their lives, and their sin became their life. Therefore, they were eventually consumed by God's wrath. Examples of this in the Old Testament are Sodom and Gomorrah, Jericho, Achan, and Nadab and Abihu to name just a few."

"That's very heartbreaking, but also very true," replied Steve quietly. "Throughout the Scriptures, we read that Father's wrath does consume sin—one way or another. It has a cleansing effect on the Creation."

"Okay, Walter," I interjected, "how about giving us some scripture verses to back up this viewpoint about Jesus and his work on the cross?"

"I'm glad you said that, John. You brought your Bible, right?"

"It's in the family room," I replied. "Let me get it."

I darted into the next room and returned quickly with my Bible in hand, relieved to have the opportunity to look at what the Scriptures teach about what Walter was saying. *Father, please guide us in this discussion and teach us what you want us to learn. If I'm wrong in what I believe, then please reveal it to me and show me your truth too.*

Cindy had just passed a Bible to her husband. "I'll be right back," she said before slipping away to another part of the house.

Walter took a deep breath and smiled. "As you probably know, most of the Old Testament imagery of the future Messiah's sacrifice and death used terms of punishment. In fact, let's look at Isaiah 53 as a great example of this."

Cindy returned with two more Bibles and passed them to Elena and Aby.

We all opened the Bibles and turned to Isaiah 53 as did Walter. Steve read along with me in my Bible as we read the following scriptures.

359

"Here are just a few examples of the 'punishment' or 'punitive' vocabulary. In verses three, four, and five it speaks of the future Messiah, Jesus, saying: 'The chastisement of our peace fell upon him. But he lifted up our illnesses, he carried our pain; even though we thought he was being punished, attacked by God, and afflicted for something he had done. He was wounded because of our rebellious deeds, crushed because of our sins.'

"See how the passage uses words like 'chastisement,' 'pain,' 'punished,' 'attacked,' 'afflicted,' 'wounded,' and 'crushed'? These words evoke images of punishment, which make the cross *look* like appeasement. From the Old Testament perspective, a lot of things are viewed through the glasses of extremes such as rewards and punishments, blessings and curses, righteousness and sin, life and death, and so on. That's why there are a lot of opposites and contrasts. It's a characteristic of the Old Covenant which God made with Israel. So, yeah, there's some of that 'punishment' aspect at the cross, but that's just the view of the cross from our human perspective. From God's perspective, there's a lot more going on there. Under the Old Covenant or the Old Testament age before the cross, shame permeates a lot of the outlook on everything. There's some talk about shame in Genesis, and the Psalms refer to shame as a motivation for and a consequence of certain behaviors.

"Coming to the New Testament, we see that Christ is referred to as the power of God. In 1 Corinthians 1:18 we're told, 'For the message about the cross is foolishness to those who are perishing, but to us who are being saved it is the power of God.' And in verse twenty-four it reiterates this, where it says, 'But to those who are called, both Jews and Greeks, Christ is the power of God and the wisdom of God.' Jesus and his work on the cross are the power of God."

"It's so amazing!" Aby commented. "Just to think of all that he did for us in providing for our salvation—Jesus really *is* the power of God, without a doubt."

"Yes, Aby, he absolutely is. I know that y'all are familiar with the teachings of the Book of Hebrews and what it says about Christ's role as our high priest. Let's look at Hebrews 9:26-28."

We then turned to the Book of Hebrews in the New Testament.

"Starting in the middle of verse twenty-six, it speaks of Jesus as our high priest. Aby, will you read those verses for us please?"

"I will," she replied. "It reads, 'But now he has appeared once for all at the consummation of the ages to put away sin by his sacrifice. And just as people are appointed to die once, and then to face judgment, so also, after Christ was offered once to bear the sins of many, to those who eagerly await him he will appear a second time, not to bear sin but to bring salvation.'"

"Thanks, Aby," said Walter. "By his own suffering and death on the cross, Jesus 'put away' or did away with sin as he 'bore the sins of many,' that is, the sins of the whole world. What he did for us on the cross provided for our forgiveness; however, his sacrifice and death accomplished so much more beyond the forgiveness of sins.

"In order to do the necessary work of Father's wrath consuming and dealing with sin so that it would no longer have a hold over us, that is, so that it would no longer reign over us and keep us enslaved, the Lord Jesus *became the embodiment of sin* as Father's wrath was poured out on him. However, it wasn't that Jesus had to be punished for us just because God's holiness and justice had to be satisfied like in a court of law. I know that a lot of people use that imagery when they talk about what happened at the cross in order for our salvation to become a reality. Yet Father is infinitely *compassionate*, and you just won't find much com-passion in a courtroom. It's a cold, stuffy, and legal setting. It's a place of opposing sides with mediators and a judge to decide who will win and who will lose. Father's heart simply isn't like that. He has a heart full of compassion, love, affection, grace, and mercy for all humanity. His work of salvation through Christ at the cross was all about reconciliation. You could really say that God lost the most, since it cost him dearly so that he could rescue us from sin, free us from its tyranny, and reconcile us in our relationship with him."

"Who would ever imagine," interjected Steve, "that the offended party, God, would give his all to reconcile sinners back to himself? It's just unfathomable!" It was then that I noticed that his furrowed-brow was relaxed.

"Amen, Brother!" replied Walter. "I'm tellin' you, it really is. Father delights to do the unfathomable. Speaking of which, let's look at the first few verses of Romans 8, which tell us that sin was condemned in the flesh through Jesus. John, would you read verses one through four please?"

"Sure. It's a great passage." After we turned to the chapter, I began to read. "'There is therefore now no condemnation for those who are in Christ Jesus. For the law of the life-giving Spirit in Christ Jesus has set you free from the law of sin and death. For God achieved what the law could not do because it was weakened through the flesh. By sending his own Son in the likeness of sinful flesh and concerning sin, he condemned sin in the flesh, so that the righteous requirement of the law may be fulfilled in us, who do not walk according to the flesh but according to the Spirit.' That's really powerful!"

"The Law of the Old Testament," commented Steve, "basical-ly just identified what sin was. That's all it was capable of doing. It couldn't lift a letter to help us."

"'Letter'?" I asked incredulously. "You just had to say that, didn't you, Flamen'?"

With a gleam in his eye, he replied: "It seemed to fit, Bro. But the point is that, since our flesh was no match for the Law, Jesus came in the flesh so that Father could condemn sin in the flesh *through him*—that is, through his fleshly body."

"That's right, Steve," agreed Walter as he turned a few pages in his Bible. "Father's wrath was poured out on Jesus—who at that moment became the embodiment of sin—in order to condemn sin and to deal with it completely. It wasn't an act of appeasement like pagan sacrifices are. It was substitutional on our behalf and in our place because we ourselves never could have endured God's wrath. Nevertheless, since Jesus was God the Son, he couldn't die. He suffered through the whole agony of wrath, and when it was finished he said, 'It is completed!' Then he willingly gave up his life for us.

"And remember what Paul says in Romans 6 about us being dead to sin? Here it is: 'Are we to remain in sin so that grace may increase? Absolutely not! How can we who died to sin still live in it?' Then in verse four he says, 'that just as Christ was raised from the dead through the glory of the Father, so we too may live a new life.'"

"Hmm, no argument with you there," said Steve, showing a pensive look. "We definitely have new spiritual life in Jesus since our salvation—hence the expression 'born again.' I remember that later in Romans 6, he says—where is it?" Steve scanned Romans 6 in my Bible to find the verse he wanted to reference. "Here it is in verse six and following: 'We know that our old man was crucified with him so that the body of sin would no longer dominate us, so that we would no longer be enslaved to sin. (For someone who has died has been freed from sin.) Now if we died with Christ, we believe that we will also live with him.'"

"You got it, Bro!" said Walter encouragingly. "Look at verse seventeen, where he says, 'But thanks be to God that though you were slaves to sin, you obeyed from the heart that pattern of teaching you were entrusted to, and having been freed from sin, you became enslaved to righteousness.' The whole passage uses terms to show our liberation from sin: 'died to sin,' 'no longer dominate us,' 'no longer be enslaved to sin,' and 'freed from sin.' Paul made it a point to say that Jesus' work on the cross and his resurrection really and truly made us free from sin. Therefore, it wasn't an appeasement transaction like the pagans attempt to do for their false deities. It was a curative work necessary to condemn sin and to break its hold over us. This obedience of the original recipients of this letter referred to here was obedience to the gospel by trusting Jesus for salvation. The same is true of us and everyone else who trusts Christ: we are freed from sin and made slaves to righteousness."

"I already knew," replied Steve soberly, "about this passage teaching that we were freed from sin, but I guess I still thought his substitutional sacrifice meant that he suffered our punishment because Father was so angry about our sin. I thought that at the

363

cross Father turned his back on Christ, not being able to look at his own Son and forsaking him while he bore the sin of the world. But I'm kinda seein' it differently, now that I see how these different passages reflect the same idea."

"That's good to hear, Steve."

Aby squinted slightly as if thinking about something as she was turning pages in the Bible that Cindy loaned her. "There's something about this that reminds me of Colossians 2. Let's see. It begins around verse thirteen, where it says, 'And even though you were dead in your transgressions and in the uncircumcision of your flesh, he nevertheless made you alive with him, having forgiven all your transgressions. He has destroyed what was against us, a certificate of indebtedness expressed in decrees opposed to us. He has taken it away by nailing it to the cross. Disarming the rulers and authorities, he has made a public disgrace of them, triumphing over them by the cross.'" She looked up from reading. "We were spiritually dead because of the sin nature we inherited from Adam and Eve, but then, at the moment we trusted Christ, he made us spiritually alive through Jesus' work on the cross."

"That's another great point, Aby," responded Walter. "Jesus freed us from sin, shame, *and* the Law, and he quickened our spirits, making us spiritually alive with his eternal life. The individual laws or 'decrees' as Paul calls them here—all 613 of them—resulted in our 'certificate of indebtedness.' Jesus' resurrection, however, proved that what he did was effectual and accepted by the Father. You can't have the cross without the empty tomb. That's why Romans 7, and a few other passages, affirm that through Christ we were freed from the Law. Elena, would you please read Romans 7:4-6 for us?"

"Yes, I will, Walter." After flipping through a few pages, she said, "Here it is. 'So, my brothers and sisters, you also died to the law through the body of Christ, so that you could be joined to another, to the one who was raised from the dead, to bear fruit to God. For when we were in the flesh, the sinful desires, aroused by the law, were active in the members of our body to bear fruit for death. But now we have been released from the law, because we have died to what controlled us, so that we may serve in the new life of the Spirit and not under the old written code.'" She looked up, glancing at Walter and me. "That does say clearly that we 'died to the law through the body of Christ,' and that 'we have been released from the law.'"

"Released from the Law and joined to Jesus," interjected Steve in a sing-song way. "That's how we love to be!"

"And remember what I said earlier about all this being about reconciling relationships?" asked Walter. "We read about that in 2 Corinthians 5."

"I'll read that one," Steve volunteered.

"That doesn't surprise me," replied Walter with a grin.

After turning in the Bible to 2 Corinthians 5, Steve began. "All right, I'll start in verse fourteen. 'For the love of Christ controls us, since we have concluded this, that Christ died for all; therefore all have died. And he died for all so that those who live should no longer live for themselves but for him who died for them and was raised. So then from now on we acknowledge no one from an outward human point of view. Even though we have known Christ from such a human point of view, now we do not know him in that way any longer. So then, if anyone is in Christ, he is a new creation; what is old has passed away—look, what is new has come! And all these things are from God who reconciled us to himself through Christ, and who has given us the ministry of reconciliation. In other words, in Christ God was reconciling the world to himself, not counting people's trespasses against them, and he has given us the message of reconciliation. Therefore we are ambassadors for Christ, as though God were making His plea through us. We plead with you on Christ's behalf, "Be reconciled to God!" God made the one who did not know sin to be sin for us, so that in him we would become the righteousness of God.'" Then he looked up at us. "That last verse, verse twenty-one there, is one of my favorites."

"It's the one you shared with us at Six Flags during the Lord's Supper."

"And it really says a lot. It's such a beautiful conclusion to that passage, too."

"Amen, Brother! So here it says that Jesus became sin—as much the embodiment or personification of sin as was possible. Lining up these verses with these other passages like Romans 8, we see that it was so that he could endure Father's wrath and do the spiritual work necessary to 'condemn sin in the flesh.' See how Father is more concerned about reconciliation—restoring the relationship with those he loves—than he is about merely resolving a conflict like in a court of law? As y'all know, the main thrust of mission work *is* this 'ministry of reconciliation.'"

"And, hey, what about Romans 5:8-11?" Steve suggested. "Let's look at that one." He turned back some pages and read the verses. "This touches on several of these points: 'But God demonstrates his own love for us, in that while we were still sinners, Christ died for us. Much more then, because we have now been declared righteous by his blood, we will be saved through him from God's wrath. For if while we were enemies we were reconciled to God through the death of his Son, how much more, since we have been reconciled, will we be saved by his life? Not only this, but we also rejoice in God through our Lord Jesus Christ, through whom we have now received this reconciliation.'" Steve's voice was full of excitement as he said aloud, "Here it teaches that we are spared from Father's wrath because Jesus endured it for us!"

"That's exactly it, Brother Steve," said Walter, nodding. "So, if you notice, we've really talked about six elements involved at the cross: the Father, the Son, the Holy Spirit, the sin of the world, shame, and the wrath of God. The Father was reconciling the world of sinners unto himself as the Son bore the sin of all humanity, offering himself through the Spirit to the Father. According to the Scriptures, Jesus became sin for us. Father poured out his wrath on Jesus, but not as a punishment. It wasn't, as is some-times implied, so that he could 'exhaust his rage' over our sin and satisfy the requirements of his holiness and justice and finally 'cool his temper' to be able to love us. That kind of imagery doesn't describe Father at all. Christ's work on the cross was really the necessary cure to condemn sin in the flesh so that sin's power could be broken in our lives and we could be free from it. It's his love and grace in action." Walter paused briefly and said the next sentence very slowly. "And it's unbelievably humbling to think that Jesus, the Darling of heaven and of all Creation, did all that . . . for us."

Silence hung in the air for a moment. Walter's words were profound. While I was truly in awe of such love expressed by both Father and Son for a world who turned their backs on an infinitely loving God, I was also in a theological quandary.

This whole discussion gave me a whirlwind of emotions and thoughts. On the one hand, it easily renewed my gratitude again for all that Jesus had done for my family and me and for what he had meant to us. (It didn't make sense at all, of course, apart from his infinite love, for which I was most thankful even though I still didn't fathom it completely. But I suppose that if I were to understand it perfectly then it would seem somehow less than what it truly is—miraculous and divine.) On the other hand, while for most of my life I had read, studied, and pondered these same Bible verses we were considering—some of which I had even memorized—Walter's view interpreted them differently than I had repeatedly been told to understand them.

It's not that what Walter was saying was far off from what I had always been taught. In fact, some of it was *exactly* the way I had understood most of the details regarding the redemption provided through Jesus' passion. The main difference was calling it "curative" and not "punitive" or "grace-based" and not "appeasement-based." That last term sounded somewhat offensive, as if I were being accused of misunderstanding the gospel or viewing the cross like a pagan would. No one had ever referred to my understanding of the gospel as "appeasement-based." I don't know that I had ever considered Jesus' sacrifice as "appeasing an angry God." Admittedly, I could accept the fact that some of the religious circles in which I had found myself in previous years leaned more toward legalism than grace. But were they *all* wrong about this "appeasement-based" view as Walter called it? Was I going to change my view of Christ's sacrifice from "payment for my sins" to "cure for my sin" in just one afternoon of conversation? After all, this was really just Walter telling us all this. How did I even know that Tom, Bob, and Greg agreed with this theological view? What if Walter were secretly a heretic, and he had craftily invited us all to his home under this pretense of a cookout—or whatever it was—in order to "persuade" us to adopt his heretical view? Well, I didn't want to be convinced so easily. I would have to do my own study on this to be sure that I clearly understood what the Scriptures teach about Jesus' work. Nevertheless, I had to admit that his comments about shame seemed to be on target, both from a biblical view and from what I had experienced in the world. For the moment I was troubled and perplexed as well as uneasily undecided.

Suddenly I looked up from my thoughts and noticed Cindy closing the sliding glass door to the deck. She smiled and mouthed the words, "They are fine," pointing back to the children outside. I looked out back just in time to see Nathaniel laughing at something silly that Timmy just did. My son was having a blast, and he was safe.

Walter stated it very plainly: "Brothers and sisters, I assure you that if you don't understand the biblical meaning of the cross and the work that Jesus did there concerning sin and shame, then you'll be very much manipulated by different sources in the world. Because Jesus dealt with our sin, death, shame, and the Law through his death and resurrection, we are completely liberated from all four. However, not understanding this point about shame will leave us vulnerable to shame-manipulation and legalism from both secular and religious systems."

"I've seen how people enforce legalism on others," I began, "but what do you mean that shame-manipulation comes from both secular and religious systems?"

"I mean simply that pretty much any group of human beings in which you're involved is very capable of and will have a bent toward fostering a sense of shame upon you. This is true for the work place, a community or social group of some kind, and even a local congregation or group of believers. It's especially true if they don't share a grace-based relationship with Father and walk in the truth that Jesus took care of both our sin and shame at the cross. There are people out there who work shame like a charm to control and manipulate others into conforming to their group expectations."

"Good night!" said Steve. "That really explains a lot of what was happening in some of the circles that *I've* previously been a part of."

"We've *all* been there and done that, Steve," admitted Walter. "I thank Jesus for walking us out of those situations, which he has used since then in our lives in various ways for his glory. Admittedly, the 'shame game' can be hard to catch at first, especially if that's most of your life experiences. But once you pick up on it, you start to see it in other settings and relationships as well."

"Walter, if this shame management started with the fall of man in Genesis 3," Steve observed, "then it's obviously been a mainstay throughout the world and throughout history."

"I'd have to agree with you. People who work the shame on others usually have learned it early in life from their parents. For example, without even realizing what they're doing, parents can pass on and promote the myth of Santa Claus as a shame management tactic for desirable behavior in their children. They say things like, 'You'd better be good, now, or Santa won't bring you what you want.' Or even, 'Ooh! What if Santa sees you doing what you just did? It won't be a happy Christmas for you!' Some children grow up thinking of God in the same way, that he's just there to catch us doing wrong so that he can punish us or withhold blessings from us. Then there are many schools and sports competitions which reward conformity to their systems of rules and shame those who don't conform to their expectations."

"Let me guess," Steve said, adopting a different voice characterization. "'Look at what a great job Susie did on her paper! A gold star for her! Oh, but little Bobby didn't do so well. No gold star for him. Maybe he'll do better next time.'" Then he spoke in his baritone announcer voice. *"It's The Shame Game by Flesh-O-Matic!"*

Walter grinned and shook his head. "You really enjoy doing those voices, don't you, Brother?"

Steve shrugged playfully with a beaming smile. "They help me get through the day."

"Wait. Let's back up a second," I interjected. "Walter, you're saying that because of our inherited human depravity, we're born with this sense of shame and that many parents, schools, and other institutions and groups manipulate it as a tool against people for coercing conformity and behavior."

"You got it, Brother."

"Because we're born with it, and most of us were also raised this way, even unintentionally, our flesh has been trained to use it. We have a knack for wielding it on others and propagating the whole shame-manipulation from generation to generation."

"You're right again!"

I looked at Elena and squeezed her hand. Then I glanced out the glass door to Nathaniel in the backyard, who was playing with Walter and Cindy's children. Looking back at Elena, I said, "I know I've said this before, but I don't want to treat my family like that anymore."

"You don't have to, especially now that Father has broken through to you and you're aware of the problem and are seeking to relate to him based on grace instead of shame-based performance."

"Brother," began Steve, looking at me, "if Father's grace and love can get through to me, then a major byproduct of having a transformed heart is reflecting his grace and love in all my relationships."

"Exactly!" said Walter. "That's a main reason for Father reconciling us unto himself. He wants us to live out the grace we receive from him and to relate to others in grace-based, reconciled relationships. Imagine how refreshing it will be for those around you and for those who cross paths with you to be treated with grace and love instead of manipulated through shame."

"It all sounds so wonderful!" I exclaimed.

"Oh, it is," concurred Cindy. "In the countries where we

370

worked in Europe, we saw many people impacted in positive ways. Through the orphanages, refugee camps, and summer camps we've been a part of, we've come in contact with hundreds of people who've lost so much that they literally had nothing else to lose. So many of them had survived such crushing, political circumstances in the upheaval of their families and lives. To be manipulated by some of the governmental and international, humanitarian, relief organizations after such devastating losses left most of them just feeling numb, empty, and used for other people's advantages. They felt so used and abused for whatever gain these groups could somehow benefit by 'helping' them in such degrading and demeaning ways. We would meet these people, accompanied by friends and fellow believers from our mission, and just love them back to some sense of normalcy."

"My darlin's right. For a lot of these folks, it would take months or years of just letting Jesus love on them through us before they would experience their own breakthrough of Father's love and grace. As they experienced his love month in and month out, year in and year out, they came to realize that we had no selfish agenda and no hidden motive for ministering to them. We just loved them like Jesus would. Only then would the walls in their hearts gradually start to tumble down. They saw that we didn't leverage any shame or use any other manipulative tactics to get them to perform certain ways and that we didn't receive any benefit as a result. These are some of the things that they noticed and told us themselves after some time. Eventually we would see hearts transformed and lives changed and a community or body of believers taking shape. This transformation, this new life, is the hope of the resurrection."

"The resurrection!" I exclaimed. "Walter, how does Jesus' resurrection fit into this whole picture of 'the curative view of the cross' as you call it?" Here I was asking questions for which I already knew the answers, but I wanted to hear the curative-based view's perspective on the resurrection of Jesus.

Walter rubbed his hand from his forehead, down his cheek, and to his jaw and chin. Then he shook his head slowly with a simple smile.

"Whew! That's *another* awesome part of the whole picture! The very second that Jesus submitted to death on the cross, God won the victory over sin, death, and shame. His glorious resurrection on the third day was the undeniable evidence that our Lord Jesus Christ had conquered and rendered powerless sin, the grave, and shame. He also fulfilled the Law, making it have no relationship to all of us who trust in him. Jesus' resurrection was the final proof that his work on the cross succeeded and that he resurrected as the Victor, the Son-of-God-in-power!"

"Amen, Brother!" Steve almost shouted.

"Thank you, Lord Jesus!" Cindy said with laughter in her voice.

"Jesus, Jesus, Jesus!" Aby exclaimed, raising her hand into the air.

"Yes, Lord!" Elena said, closing her eyes blissfully.

"Thank you, Jesus!" I heard myself saying.

Walter nodded, with joy apparent on his face and in his voice. "And just as all three members of the Trinity were active at the cross, so they were active in the resurrection. Jesus rose again as the firstborn of the resurrected—which will include us one day! He pioneered the way for a new body of believers: the saints, the sons and daughters of the living God!"

Steve scooped up a pepper grinder from the table to use as a pretend microphone and, rising to his feet, burst into a chorus of "He Holds the Keys" by Steve Green. He belted out the notes in a range that crescendoed ever higher than his typical baritone voice was used to singing, reaching them with an exaggerated, dramatic effort. It was a joyful though silly moment full of celebration.

Steve's loud singing attracted the attention of the children outside. They rushed to the sliding glass door and peered inside, cupping their hands around their eyes to see through the glass despite the reflected sunlight. Once they saw that Steve was singing into a pepper grinder with us cheering him on, their curiosity deflated. They slowly turned back to whatever game they were playing.

"What love!" Abby exclaimed. "What love for us all!"

"Yes, glory!" said Walter. "What an undeniable demonstration of God's love for us! It's because of the cross and the empty tomb that we can live as his children, truly loved. We don't have to live under any oppression from an angry deity who must be appeased. We are truly loved, and we can walk every day of our lives confident in his love for us."

While I wanted to ask about walking in Father's love, the phrase "undeniable demonstration of God's love for us" struck me first, so I decided to ask about it.

"Walter, I agree that Jesus' resurrection is undeniable. Recently I've encountered a couple of people who are following online some big atheist with a PhD who's touring the country to discount the claims of Christ—especially his resurrection. From the few things I've read about him on the Internet, he seems pretty smug in his reasons for denying Jesus' resurrection. What are some good, historical proofs for the resurrection of Christ to give to these friends of mine who seem to have been lured into this guy's orbit?"

"That's a great question," Walter replied. "People of the world won't look to the Bible for answers, but there are some historical evidences which can't be explained any other way apart from the resurrection of Jesus Christ. After all, every cause has its effect, and the resurrection of Christ resulted in several undeniable effects or results."

"I'd say that the most obvious," suggested Steve, "is what resulted due to the lack of a corpse. The disciples, who later became apostles, wouldn't have gotten far if there had been a corpse. It would have struck down the whole idea of a resurrection."

"That's right," agreed Aby. "There wasn't even any record of an attempt from any opponents to disprove his resurrection by presenting a substitute corpse. Both the Jewish religious leaders and the Roman officials each had their own reasons for wanting to silence any talk about Jesus rising from the dead. The lack of a body to disprove the resurrection of Jesus is a historical fact. If there had been a body to disprove Jesus' resurrection, then Christianity would have died quickly and never would have spread around the world."

Steve put his arm around her shoulders and grinned. "That's

my wife, ladies and gentlemen—the great history teacher!"

Aby revealed a shy smile. "Aww! Thanks, Babe!"

Steve gave her a quick kiss.

"Yep," replied Walter, "those boys went from being a small, ragtag band of peasants who had scattered and were scared out of their wits on the night Jesus was arrested to being a bold and fiery group of men. They proclaimed wherever they went that Jesus really *did* rise from the dead. They wanted everyone to know him and to trust him for eternal life. It was a message that they carried with them to the end of their days, some of them even suffering tortures and martyrdom without ever denying Christ's resurrection."

"This transformation of the disciples," added Steve, "from fearful men hiding from the authorities to bold witnesses proclaiming Jesus' resurrection publicly, happened in the space of just a few days. Anyone who looks at the historical facts and understands cause-and-effect relationships would think, 'Hmm! Those boys must have really seen Jesus alive after seeing him crucified. There must really be something to their insistence that he rose again.'"

"You got it, Bro!" said Walter. "And those tired, disproven theories that they went to the wrong tomb or that perhaps Jesus didn't really die but just 'swooned' and revived in the dark, dank tomb, having the strength and ability both to roll away the stone *and* to overpower the Roman guards—none of that holds any water."

"Yeah, really," I agreed. "Obviously Joseph of Arimathea knew which tomb he loaned them for Jesus' burial, and those who prepared Jesus' body knew which tomb they placed it in. What good would it have done to have gone to the wrong tomb and to have lied about a resurrection when their opponents would only have had to extract the body from the correct tomb to derail their claims—if such had happened?"

"Brother," asserted Steve, "I think that as far as the world is concerned, the Journal of the American Medical Association concurred that Jesus really did die. They detailed it in an article they published back in the eighties. Their interpretation of the

374

historical evidence for Jesus' suffering and crucifixion from a modern medical standpoint concluded that there is no doubt that he died before being taken down from the cross."

"Wow!" I exclaimed. "I didn't know about that article! You'd think that that would be enough to quiet any disputes about his death and that the post-resurrection appearances would verify his resurrection. I don't understand why some people believe such falsehoods to the contrary, especially when they don't make any sense."

"Some people," offered Cindy, "just refuse to believe in Jesus because of their past hurts and disappointed expectations. It's sad, really: all that love and grace for them demonstrated publicly before the whole world, yet they prefer to believe a lie instead of the truth."

"That brings us to another observable proof," Walter interjected. "The proof of millions of believers in Jesus for the last almost two thousand years and continuing still today."

"Yeah, Brother," said Steve. "If it were all a lie, then the gospel wouldn't have *possibly* been carried by the apostles throughout the Roman Empire and later by others to the ends of the earth. And they couldn't have suffered persecution and even martyrdom for something they knew to be false. People who plot conspiracies don't all go to their graves sticking to their stories like the disciples did. Besides, conspiracies are challenging enough for two or three people to maintain. These were the eleven disciples plus Mary Magdalene. And according to what Paul wrote in 1 Corinthians 15:6, over five hundred believers saw the resurrected Christ at one time."

I tacked onto Steve's comment. "With two thousand years of growth in the faith and so many new followers believing in his name each year, if it *were* all a hoax, surely it would have come to light long before now by his opponents. That first generation of individuals who wanted to stop it before it grew any further would have had the prime opportunity way back then to do so."

"We also have the New Testament," Walter said, raising his Bible. "Think of how the apostles wrote the Gospels, the epistles, and the other documents—all of which were copied, distributed, preserved, and translated into hundreds of languages over the millennia. There are whole languages and people groups who have had missionaries, like Tom and Sara, learn those languages and reduce them to writing for the sole purpose of translating the New Testament and Old Testament scriptures into them. Just think of the hundreds of tribal languages which have the Bible as the only book published in those languages—along with maybe a lexicon and grammar or two for the purpose of those indigenous people groups to learn how to read and to write their own language. No other book in existence has ever had *that* kind of publishing record. And it just couldn't have happened and have been accepted as true by so many people if it were all founded on a lie. Any fact to the contrary would have surfaced long ago and would have averted such popularity and fame. As it is, a number of historians in those first centuries, both secular and Christian, referred to Jesus Christ as a historical person. Most atheists and agnostics don't agree with this, obviously, but then again, there have been a number of them who have examined the evidence for Jesus' resurrection with the result that they became persuaded and trusted Christ. These include Simon Greenleaf, C.S. Lewis, John Warwick Montgomery, and Lee Strobel."

"What about Sunday?" asked Elena. "The Jews had kept Saturday as their Sabbath for thousands of years. Those Jews who trusted Jesus as their Messiah—would they have changed their special day from Saturday to Sunday for the resurrection of Jesus on Sunday if it hadn't really happened?"

"Excellent point, Elena," said Walter encouragingly. "It would have taken a miracle—like Jesus' resurrection—to get those early believers from among the Jews to break with their age-old tradition and to celebrate on a different day besides the Sabbath. And here we are—the church of Jesus Christ—nearly two thousand years later. You know, with all our flaws, disagreements, and other problems, we still commemorate Sunday as the day of the week when Jesus rose from the dead."

"'At a girl, Elena!" said Steve. "That's one of those obvious proofs that just stares you right in the face so much that you tend to overlook it."

"That's *my* wife, ladies and gentlemen!" I exclaimed, quickly putting my arm around her and giving her a kiss. "Sharp and insightful beyond her years!"

Elena smiled with a slight blush in her cheeks. "Aww! Thank you, Honey!"

"Copycat!" called Steve playfully.

"And—wow!" exclaimed Cindy. "Speaking of those early Jewish believers with their traditions, wouldn't it also take a resurrection kind of miracle for those Jews to associate and to meet together with believers from among the Gentiles? They were former pagans, y'know, and in joining the body of Christ, those former Jews and former Gentiles had to get along with each other."

"And that's *my*—" Walter began, reaching his arm around Cindy.

"—Oh, stop it!" she chided softly, swatting playfully at his arm. "And don't try to kiss me, either. You've had your quota for today." She eyed Elena and Aby with a sly grin.

Walter feigned a whiny look on his face. "Now, Darlin', you know I don't have a quota on kisses."

Cindy rocked softly in her seat, displaying an impish sneer as she glanced around at us all. She seemed to be playing a coy game with her husband.

In an attempt to rescue the moment for Walter, I annexed Cindy's point with another comment.

"Getting back to the Jews, they had to compromise quite a few traditions, such as their dietary laws, so that they could associate with their fellow believers from among the Gentiles. Conversely, the Gentiles also compromised in some areas of their customs as well, as seen in the letter from the Council of Jerusalem in Acts 15."

I wasn't sure if anyone had even heard what I had just said, since they were all glancing around the room silently to see what would transpire between Walter and Cindy. The charged air made the moment feel like high school all over again. Then suddenly, Cindy

377

popped up and broke the silence.

"Oh, Honey Bunch!" exclaimed Cindy, snapping out of her game face. "Tell them about *He Loves Me!*"

"I'm glad you said that. Thank you, Darlin'!" Then turning back to us, he said: "My brothers and sisters, I know that a lot of this discussion we've had about the meaning of the cross of Jesus is probably a little different from what you've usually heard—all this talk about shame and wrath and Jesus not being a sacrifice in quite the same way as you've usually been told that he was. It might even make us sound like we're mixed up in some kind of heresy."

He and Cindy chuckled at that. I smiled nervously, but I couldn't quite bring myself to laugh.

"However," he continued without missing a beat, "most of what we've gone over in this discussion is some of what we've read in a book entitled *He Loves Me!* by an author named Wayne Jacobsen. It's a wonderful book which talks about the love of God. He explains in greater detail all about shame, sin, wrath, the appeasement-based view, and the curative view of the cross. I'll even let you borrow my copy if you'd like to read it."

The glass door slid open, and in came the children, fanning themselves and commenting about the heat. They were ready to cool off and to enjoy some playtime inside for a change. I was glad to see that Nathaniel was having so much fun. He really enjoyed spending time with Timmy, Joey, and Lynette.

During a more opportune moment, I expressed interest in borrowing the book. Walter handed it to me and also shared with me some other scripture references for further study. I jotted down the references: John 10:11, 14, 15, 17, 18; Romans 5:8-11, 18, 19; 1 Corinthians 1:30; Galatians 2:20, 21; 3:11-14; 6:14, 15; Ephesians 2:1-7, 13-16; and Hebrews 9:15; 10:10-14, 22.

"It's just too much to absorb in one sitting," he explained amicably. "This isn't really the kind of interpretation that anyone can be expected to adopt in an hour. It takes a while to examine it on all sides. And the truth is," he said with a raised eyebrow, "that I might not think so highly of you if you embraced it that quickly."

378

He chortled as he looked me in the eye. "But as with everything, run to Christ. Talk to him about this as you read and study the Scriptures and see what he teaches you."

The rest of the afternoon and evening at Walter and Cindy's house was less doctrinal and more frivolous since we played a few party games. After having had such a deep and challenging discussion, I was thankful for the levity. I was more than a little worried that this interpretation of the cross might be heretical or at least borderline heretical.

On the drive home that evening, I asked Elena about what she understood from the discussion. I couldn't help but notice that she was mostly quiet during that whole time.

"You didn't say much during the discussion about Jesus' sacrifice," I said softly.

"Yes, but I was listening," she replied.

"Did you understand everything that Walter was saying?"

"Of course, I did. I know English."

"No," I chuckled. "I mean, did the theology and the way he explained those Bible verses make sense to you?"

She stared ahead as we drove. "Well, it was a lot to consider. But it seemed to be what the Bible teaches, so I thought it was pretty good."

What an easy faith you have, my sweetie. I wish that I didn't have such struggles over so many things that I hear. Sometimes I can't even enjoy a simple song without wincing over some glaring unbiblical teaching or inference in the lyrics. Father, is that a good thing or a bad thing?

"Do you believe that what Walter was saying is true?"

"About what?"

"That what Jesus did on the cross was to cure our sin problem and not that he was punished in our place."

"Well, he sort of was punished in our place."

"Not according to Walter."

"Yeah, remember what he showed us in Isaiah 53? That passage uses the word 'punished.' And remember that he said that

Jesus endured God's wrath because we couldn't have survived it. So, he did what we couldn't have done. And the Law wasn't able to help us either. Steve said that it couldn't 'lift a letter' to help us." She rolled her eyes at me with that last statement. Then she giggled.

"Yeah, that Flamen's a hoot." It seemed like Elena was content to end the conversation, but I simply had to pursue this further.

"Did they teach the gospel like that at the mission, or did they say that Jesus was punished for our sins?"

"They usually said that he was punished for our sins."

"Doesn't that seem like a big difference from what Walter taught us?"

"Yeah, I guess it does a little," she said slowly. "But Walter showed us in the Bible that it's what the New Testament teaches, right?"

I was feeling more than a little flustered. Apparently, she had no struggle over accepting this teaching.

"I guess it does," I finally said weakly. "I still need to study the Scriptures to see if this is really true."

"Didn't Walter give you a book?"

"Yes, he did."

"Then, why don't you read that? It will probably help you."

The next day, Sunday afternoon, I called Tom's house. There was no answer. Later I learned that Tom and Sara were on a ministry training retreat for a whole week.

They just never ceased to amaze me. Even as retired missionaries, when others would choose to play it safe in their later years, this couple continued to travel locally and far and wide, spending what little they had in traveling expenses and whatever other expenses were required, to pour their lives into as many as they could. There were always summer camps, children's Bible clubs, evangelism outreaches, native Malaysian fellowships in Atlanta, discipleship meetings, fellowship meetings, or other ministry training opportunities for them to participate in, despite Tom's poor health condition. My gratitude for them as individuals and as a couple increased continuously. They were an exponential blessing to so many, and probably very few of us even knew how to appreciate them. *Thank you, Jesus, for this brother and this sister in our lives!*

Steve was available by phone, so I called him next.

"Flamen', I need your honest opinion," I said to him in a serious tone. "Do you think that what Walter was teaching us was biblical or heretical?"

"Aw, no! Not heretical!" he exclaimed. From my end of the phone call, I pictured his furrowed-brow wince. "Definitely not heretical. It's New Testament, Brother. It's what we've longed for the gospel to mean without even realizing it."

"Okay, explain it to me."

"Brother, it just all ties together! Father *can* look on sin. He's powerful enough that it doesn't sway him or tarnish his holiness at all. I don't mean that he *wants* to look on sin, just that he's not so offended by it that he can't get his hands dirty to fix it. He can look on sin; he just doesn't *approve* of sin. That's what Habakkuk 1:13 means when it says that he's so holy that he can't look on sin."

"Yeah, you're right," I agreed quietly. "Walter did explain that, didn't he?"

"Yeah, he did. And remember different times in the Bible when God approached those in sin? As soon as Adam and Eve sinned, he came to them to offer them his grace. He didn't come to scold them. He wasn't even angry with them. He was mostly just grieved, knowing that they had chosen to die spiritually and to break fellowship with him. By asking them some questions, Father gave them the opportunity to confess, to repent, and to look to him to reconcile them back to himself. But, because they felt ashamed, they only hid in fear, making excuses and shifting the blame. Adam even blamed Father, saying 'The woman whom you gave me, she gave me some fruit and I ate it.' I mean—good night! Imagine having the audacity to blame God for your own sin! What's even more tragic is that, being omnipresent, God was there with Adam and Eve while they were surrendering to temptation.

Plus, being omniscient, God knew long before then that man would take Father's gift of free will and abuse it to trust in his own understanding, instead of trusting in Father's loving character. Their choice to submit to the temptation was based on their decision to trust in themselves and their own understanding. Yet all along, God had a plan to redeem mankind. Thus, while he was grieved about their choice, I believe that he was also positive or optimistic in spite of their transgressions. That's because he knew that he had a plan to resolve the whole sin tragedy. The Trinity knew that their plan would center around the Son enduring Father's wrath poured out upon him—all so that we could become liberated from the bondage of sin. Man, that is some powerful love! His love provided us the means to redeem us by his love and grace and even graced us with the freedom and will to choose!"

"It really is awesome, Flamen'! What are some other examples that come to mind?"

"There's the account about Cain. When he sinned by killing his brother, Father approached him immediately. There are really *tons* of examples throughout the Old Testament where Father sent prophets to confront kings, other individuals, and even whole cities—like Jonah in Nineveh—when they were in sin. Plus, look at Jesus in the New Testament. He confronted the Pharisees, Sadducees, and experts in the Law on many occasions, even though they were lying through their teeth to him and accusing him of being illegitimate, demon-possessed, and a sinner. Despite it all, he loved them enough to communicate with them on their level. He wanted their hearts to look to him, even though most of them simply wouldn't in their arrogance. He didn't shy away from the religious crowd because of their many sins.

"And there are others too. Jesus drew close to many people in sin, offering them love, grace and forgiveness. He did this with the woman caught in adultery in John 8, the demoniac boy's father when he was struggling with unbelief in Mark 9, Peter in John 20 after he denied Christ three times, and Mary of Bethany in John 11 when she was struggling with doubt after her brother Lazarus died. Most people may not think that doubt and unbelief are much in the way of sins, like they're not as bad as murder or adultery or others that seem like 'big ticket' transgressions. Obviously, all sins are equally terrible and offensive to a holy God, which we already know. We could probably even argue that all or most sins are committed as a result of doubting or disbelieving Father and then choosing to go our own way instead of his. But in a sense, unbelief and doubt are really serious spiritual problems, because they are proofs that we distrust Father and the Scriptures. Imagine yourself telling Nathaniel how you love him and care for him, and then one day he looks back at you and says, 'I just don't believe that, and I don't trust you.' Brother, what would that do to your heart?"

"It would crush me, Flamen', that's for sure."

"We say that we have faith in Christ and that we put our trust in him, but then we live like he's untrustworthy. Imagine how hurtful *that* is to his heart."

"Wow! I see what you mean."

"You see? He wasn't so offended by our sin that he couldn't get close enough to us to take on human flesh and to bear our sin in his body—in Jesus' body, that is—so that he could 'condemn sin in the flesh.' Brother, I know I must have read that verse in Romans 8 at least a hundred times, but it just never really sank in what was meant by that phrase. There's probably a lot of other believers who've glossed over the phrase and not really thought about what it means and what its implications are for us and our freedom from sin."

"Yeah," I replied. "I know that I've glossed over it all this time too. It really seems like a key phrase at the heart of Walter's argument."

"'Argument'?" Steve seemed startled at my use of the word. "Brother, this is much more than just an 'argument' for a theological position. It's a window into the love of God."

"Well, I guess you're right."

"You bet I'm right! Just consider it this way: If the appeasement-based view were true—"

"—Do you *really* have to use that term?"

"Just hear me out, Bro. If that view were true, then what would

383

it say about Father?"

"What do you mean, 'what would it say' about him? I don't get your point."

"Okay, let me put it this way to make my point: If Father were so boiling angry about our sin that he had to take it out on someone just so that he could stand to look at us and to love us, and since Jesus is the only Being in all Creation who's even qualified to be punished in our place for us, then what would that say about Father that he would have had to send his own Son to the cross and to let him suffer cruelly for us, even turning his back on him because 'he couldn't bear to look on all that sin'?"

I listened closely to Steve's long, drawn out question, trying to understand the implication clearly in my mind. "Uh . . . well . . ."

"Think of it like this analogy," he added, interrupting my thoughts. "If I were to commit some great offense against you, and you got so angry that the only way you and I could be friends again is if you beat the living daylights out of your own son, what kind of father would that make you?"

That did it. I understood it then. My son was too close to my heart for me to miss the point. Just the thought of something like this was beyond tragic for me.

"Flamen', you know that I wouldn't—! I just couldn't *ever*—!*"

"And do you imagine that I would want to have anything to do with a 'friend' who would treat his own son that way? What would you do to *me* then? Maybe one day you'd decide that I needed the same kind of treatment to appease your anger for some other transgression, especially if you were to treat your own son that way."

"What . . .? I mean, how . . .? Flamen' I don't even know how to form the question!"

"It would demonstrate, not the heart of a loving father, but the heart of a sadist—someone whose only solution for his own uncontrollable temper would be to inflict pain on others. Could it be that in our heart of hearts *that* is what bothers us about the way we've always heard the gospel preached? The way a lot of gospel presentations are worded, there's often the unspoken implication that Father was in such a rage of fury due to our sin that he just *had*

384

to quench his wrath on someone. Maybe we've unconsciously viewed him for so long as an angry God rather than a loving God because of that misperception."

My face suddenly felt pale and drained of strength. The thought of this being a real fear broke loose like a dam bursting from a towering, menacing wave of water.

"I guess so, Flamen'. I . . . I just don't know what to say."

"The appeasement-based view makes Father look like a sadist, a psycho. The curative view makes both Father and Son together to be heroes, working out a rescue and reconciliation for us in regard to sin, death, shame, and the Law. The Trinity knew that we were too weak to overcome the sin problem without their intervention. Therefore, they worked together at the cross to bring about the cure that breaks sin's bondage in our lives, freeing us from the power of sin and giving us the way of escape from God's wrath against sin. Because Jesus endured all that wrath, we won't have to endure God's wrath at the end of the age."

"Really? *That's* the reason?"

"Yeah, John! Think about what the New Testament teaches. For example, in Romans 1:18, Paul wrote, 'For the wrath of God is revealed from heaven against all ungodliness and unrighteousness of people who suppress the truth by their unrighteousness.' This demonstrates that Father's wrath *has* to destroy sin. Wrath has to consume sin and to cleanse the whole Creation of it. Since Jesus let sin be consumed in his body, we can trust in what he did *for* us as a humanity so that he can deal with the sin *within* each of us as individuals. If people don't trust him and accept his work on their behalf, then they'll spend eternity in the lake of fire. Nevertheless, as believers in Christ, we miss out on all that, thanks to Jesus. And at the end of the age, during the Tribulation period, God's wrath will ultimately cleanse all Creation from sin. But we won't have to go through any of that! In 1 Thessalonians 1:10, Paul wrote to those saints in Thessalonica that they were waiting 'for his Son from heaven, whom he raised from the dead, Jesus our deliverer from the coming wrath.' Then in 5:9 he says, 'For God did not destine us for wrath but for gaining salvation through our Lord

Jesus Christ.' Don't tell me that you didn't know this already."

"No, of course I knew it. I did an inductive study of First and Second Thessalonians about twelve years ago. I guess with the distraction of my bitterness since then, I had forgotten about those verses. Thanks for reminding me about them, Brother!"

"Sure thing, Bro! Here's one last scripture about wrath. Romans 5:9 reads, 'Much more then, because we have now been declared righteous by his blood, we will be saved through him from God's wrath.' You see? It's a done deal for those of us who trust Christ."

"Praise Jesus for that!" Then my excitement was tempered by a stark reality. "But, Steve, there are *billions* who *still* don't trust him or even know about him!"

"That's a fact which spurs us all on to tell others, whether we're career missionaries or not."

It was a sobering fact, one which communicated the urgency of the need for others to know Jesus. Nevertheless, another thing about the cross concerned me.

"Flamen', not to transition from the needs of the world to something else, but I still have one thought just gnawing away at me."

"What's that?"

"Why did Jesus say what he did on the cross if he didn't lose fellowship with his Father during those hours? Why did he say, 'My God, my God, why have you forsaken me?'"

"Hey, that's an excellent question!"

"Do you know the answer then?"

"I think I may have *ferreted* it out. You know that Matthew and Mark recorded Jesus' actual words in the Hebrew as *'Eli, Eli, lema sabachthani,'* which was a quote from Psalm 22:1."

"That I do know. The Jews near the cross didn't recognize it, since by then that generation mostly just spoke Aramaic and usually only heard Hebrew at the synagogue when the rabbis read from the Torah or something like that was happening."

"And that's why they misunderstood him and thought he was calling for Elijah."

"Right, that's what they *thought*. So, why did he quote from

386

Psalm 22:1?"

"There are a couple of reasons," he replied. "For starters, he was saying that, through his crucifixion, he was fulfilling that psalm as a prophecy. You remember that Psalm 22 has some vivid details which are described just like an actual crucifixion and that it was written centuries before crucifixion was even invented by the Persians. Sometime later, the Romans used and further developed that execution method. And as a psalm of David, it has some messianic ties to it. That's why, instead of translating the verse into Aramaic for those Jews to understand, he quoted the words in the original Hebrew to say that he was fulfilling that prophetic psalm, not simply communicating that his Father had forsaken him."

"Okay. That seems to work. What's the other reason?"

"All right. You know how Hebrews 4:15 says, 'For we do not have a high priest who cannot sympathize with our weaknesses, but one who has been tempted in all things as we are, yet without sin.'"

"I do."

"When Jesus was bearing the sin of the world and experiencing God's wrath being poured out on him, he felt that sense of loss, abandonment, and shame that we often feel in times of agony and despair as a consequence of our sin. Even though Father was still there with him as always, his *feeling* or *perception* was that of despair. Therefore, as our high priest, he knows what it's like to feel lost, abandoned, and despairing. He can *empathize* with us."

This took my appreciation to another level.

"Wow, Flamen'! That really hits home for me! He truly does understand all the heartbreaking stuff we go through—the fear, the doubt, and the anxiety."

"Uh-huh!" he remarked jubilantly.

"His words in Hebrew from the cross communicate that! What a Savior!"

Then he began to sing, "'O what a Savior! O hallelujah!'¹ Jesus breaks the power of sin—condemning it in his own body—frees us from sin, shame, the Law, and the grave. He quickens our spirits with his resurrection life, rescues us from wrath, seals us with his Holy Spirit, prepares a home for us in heaven with him, and far and above all the other blessings he showers on us, he empathizes with us when we are broken and confused and feel lost and abandoned."

"It's all so amazing, Steve! It just sounds too good to be true!"

"So, you're with us then?"

I blinked quickly a few times, trying to follow. "With whom for what?"

"With us on the curative perspective of the cross."

I wasn't sure that I wanted to commit to it then. I still wanted to study more in the Scriptures.

"Don't rush me, Flamen'. I still want to look over some scripture verses."

"Aw, c'mon, Bro! Can't you see that it's not heresy and it's not a cult?"

"Well, I still want to look at it some more. Besides that, I want to read this book, *He Loves Me!* by Wayne Jacobsen."

"Hey, that's right! Walter says that that book goes into more detail on this. I'll have to read it too."

"Yeah, you do that, Flamen'. We'll both read it, and afterward we'll regroup on the subject. We'll discuss any questions or concerns that we might have."

"That sounds like a plan."

Both Steve and I read the book. It was the most encouraging and heartwarming book about the love of God which I had ever read—apart from the Bible, obviously. It *did* help me to understand the curative view of the cross much better than before. Eventually, I humbly and gratefully accepted this view as the New Testament teaching on the meaning of the cross.

Walter's words rang in my ears for years: Jesus is the Darling of heaven and of all Creation! He's so worthy of all praise, honor, and glory! I could not fathom the most precious one of all that is, who is so worthy of more than all that is, gazing lovingly on us, his rebellious people, and choosing to endure God's wrath on the cross. He willingly suffered such agonies and heartbreak, all so that he could redeem us back to himself, breaking the power of sin in our lives, quickening our spirits, and providing us with his eternal life.

Thank you, Jesus, for what you did for us through your suffering, death, and resurrection!

---

[1] "What a Savior," Marvin P. Dalton, © Copyright 1948. Stamps Quartet Music, in "Guiding Hand." Renewal 1976 by Stamps Quartet Music/BMI (admin. By ClearBox Rights). All rights reserved. Used by permission.

CHAPTER 16

WALKING WITH JESUS

Setting aside the appeasement-based view of the cross, I came to understand that what Jesus did for us via Roman crucifixion was much more than to suffer Father's wrath as an innocent victim in place of us, a world of guilty sinners. It was an effectual antidote to break the power and bondage of sin in our lives so as to allow his resurrection to regenerate us as new creations in Christ. Through the Lord Jesus' dual work at the cross and the empty tomb, God reconciled us unto himself. He quickened our spirits to be spiritually born anew; showered us with his righteousness, grace, mercy, and all other spiritual blessings in Christ; sealed us with the Spirit as his personal pledge of our heavenly abode to come; and adopted us into the family of God through the new birth as his very own sons and daughters. As believers, we have been graced with the everlasting life of Christ, which includes both a present grace-based relationship with Father through Jesus as well as a future, eternal home with him. We have been sealed with the Holy Spirit, who ministers to us in a myriad of capacities on this journey. The effectual work of salvation wrought for us by Jesus provided so much more than all this, clearly, both as present realities and future blessings.

The appeasement-based view of Christ's work on the cross seems more pagan-like in nature. That perspective does make Father in the whole Passion play appear to be as if he were an ill-tempered deity with an uncontrollable need to make someone pay for the sins of the world. Some view him in exactly this way. It seemed like a ploy of the enemy to foster this concept on the world as a twisted, sadistic misinterpretation of Christ's work of salvation. As I reflected on the multitude of times that I had shared the gospel with people throughout the years, both in the States and in Central America, I would cringe as I remembered the image of Father that I had unwittingly portrayed to so many people. It's no

391

wonder that masses of people struggled to share a closeness with Father as the Lover of their souls. They had distanced themselves from him emotionally because, as they had been told countless times through appeasement-based gospel presentations, he was misunderstood to be like an ill-tempered dad who, needing to take out his anger on someone during a rage, mercilessly beats the first family member who walks through the door. No one would want to get close to *that* kind of god, I knew.

Appeasement also seems to be the explanation for the way a number of believers in Jesus approach their relationship with Father. Some try to please him by tithing, praying, reading the Bible, witnessing to the lost, attending worship services, and doing other good works. These good works are likewise deeds that some cults promote "to earn" or "to bring about" their own salvation. At other times, believers try to cover or to hide themselves by sinning against others, as our discussion about shame revealed that day at Walter and Cindy's house.

My search through the Scriptures revealed that there was definitely some of the punishment terminology which related to what Jesus did for us. I couldn't deny the Old Testament teaching that the one guilty of sin had to be punished and that Jesus accepted that guilt and the consequences of it on our behalf to make our forgiveness effectual, nor did I want to deny this truth. However, I also saw the other scripture passages showing the perspective of Christ's work of enduring God's wrath as a curative, liberating, and life-giving operation. The most significant of the passages were those we discussed at Walter and Cindy's house.

In my reading of *He Loves Me!* by Wayne Jacobsen, I read an interesting analogy of his on pages 121 and 122 comparing the curative view to a medical scenario. Jacobsen explained it as an antidote for a terminal disease—like chemotherapy for cancer—which was too deadly for the patient to survive. In this analogy, a parent could accept the sick child's blood as well as the antidote, suffering the pain and side effects of the disease and probably dying. However, the parent's body would produce antigens that could be reintroduced back into the child and cure him or her of

392

the disease. Not being trained in the medical field, I was uncertain how accurate this analogy was concerning oncology and chemo-therapy. As with most analogies, it most likely broke down here and there, but for the purposes of communicating what Christ did for us as our substitute, it connected with my understanding.

Another thing that I accepted in relation to the appeasement-based view of the cross was to acknowledge that probably most of the believers who espoused it did so unaware of its implications and potential harm. Much like those who followed legalism, its adherents were convinced in their hearts that appeasement was the only biblical way to understand the cross of Jesus, having never heard any other perspective. Since spiritual warfare is a reality biblically speaking, I understood that people are not enemies, but that the true enemy himself and his hosts are very real indeed, though unseen by human eyes. My brothers and sisters in the body of Christ who followed the appeasement understanding of the work of Christ did not require criticism or condemnation, least of all from me. From a perspective of a grace-based relationship with Father, I recognized that they needed prayer, encouragement, grace, mercy, love, friendship, and time. Whatever adjustments needed to be made in their understanding would not be made by me confronting them. I would merely step back and allow the Holy Spirit to do as he pleased, not forcing my own agenda on others.

Another point in relating to those who followed the appease-ment view was all too real. The fact did not escape me that until just recently, I had been one of their number for most of my life. Therefore, I understood very well how people could follow it unquestioningly. In fact, Father had taught me so many biblical perspectives, issues, and teachings (which were new to me back then) since his grace and love had broken through my bitterness that I was beginning to wonder if I should question and reexamine most if not all of what I had previously believed. This did not mean that I began to doubt biblical orthodoxy. Rather, it was my resolve to be open to the Holy Spirit's guidance and correction for every-thing that I believed. This included my understanding of God, the Bible, my walk with Christ, life, and relationships. Such was more desirable than continuing under the assumption that everything I had believed for so long was inerrant and that my understanding was infallible. No, I desired to be open to the Spirit's teachings, reproofs, corrections, training, clarifications, redirected emphases, and the like through the Holy Scriptures. My gratitude and humility motivated me to submit my biblical understanding to Christ and to let him correct whatever, however, and whenever he so desired.

Being content with this interpretation of the key scriptures and being fully persuaded of Father's great love for me, I continued to enjoy walking with Jesus. Jettisoning any residual pagan tendencies in my relationship with Father was a work for the Holy Spirit, I realized, and I wanted to be open and yielded to him and the Bible in order to allow him to do this important heart-work. I had no desire for anything detrimental to my walk with Jesus to be a part of my understanding, perspective, or practice; but I also didn't want to be sidetracked by any "introspective traps" either. Therefore, I entrusted this work to Christ and continued being thankful and rejoicing in him. He would correct me, I trusted, wherever correction was needed, and he would do it out of a heart of love and grace for my well-being.

My family and I continued fellowshipping with the brothers and sisters I had first met from the Stone Mountain retreat. We enjoyed the company and encouragement of both them and their families. For a while, in my mind I thought of them as "the Stone Mountain Fellowship," though I never voiced this, not even to Elena. Among ourselves we would often refer to ourselves collectively as "the group" or "the fellowship." There was no desire to organize or to adopt a formal name since our combined experiences tended to demonstrate that too much emphasis on organization for something like this usually ended in disappointment and lifeless routine.

I had even decided in my heart not to approach the other brothers and sisters to discuss the appeasement-based view versus the curative view of the cross. A small part of me was eagerly curious to know especially which perspective Tom espoused, since Father had used him as a vessel to teach me so many significant truths. However, I knew that this was a pointless longing. It would only complicate things if I put too much stock into what he would say about the topic. Either he would express his agreement, much to my delight, inflating my "spiritual ego" or he would verbalize disagreement and possibly a criticism or rebuke, which might profoundly disappoint or wound me and affect my relationship with him. My imagined reaction to this latter scenario would not be right, but it would be human, and in no way edifying to either one of us. Tom would never rebuke me even the least bit harshly, I knew, but I didn't want the chance to take even a slight doctrinal correction the wrong way. Either way, there would be no blessing or benefit to be gained from such a question or discussion, so I considered it a closed book. Nevertheless, I wouldn't shy away from the topic, as I knew that discussions about the cross were inevitable, but neither would I confront anyone concerning it. As much as I respected Tom and as great of an example and encouragement he had always been to me, we both knew that he did not want to take the Spirit's role in my life, approving or disapproving of the many facets and details of my life and beliefs. This was an important lesson to be learned from church history, as it has been a common mistake repeated and taken to the extreme in too many tragic scenarios.

While our fellowship with these brothers and sisters thrived, our involvement in our local congregation became increasingly dull and uninteresting. Even the "church in spite of church" fellowship gatherings were sometimes boring and lifeless. Our times together eventually became routine and perfunctory. Some individuals even became codependent on a few of the others. Problems of proximity ensued, as typically happens with any close group of human beings. Cliques formed, and then both secretive and open criticisms from certain individuals regarding others were voiced. A lot of people no longer enjoyed it as they had in the beginning months, and the attendance and hospitality gradually decreased. It looked like it was dwindling to a halt.

There was to be a wedding! The bride to be was Aletha, Bob

and Linda's second oldest daughter. Most of Bob and Linda's children were either already married and with their own families or away attending college. Only the two youngest teenage daughters still lived at home. My family and I had met all their children on different occasions, but not all in one place. This would be Elena's and my first opportunity to see them all together, a family celebrating this ceremonial union of two hearts and lives. Aletha had graduated from college a few weeks prior to the wedding and was getting married the first Sunday in June of that year. Wedding bells were ringing, and Bob and Linda were content, though feeling a bit nostalgic, at the bittersweet thought of seeing another of their children spread her wings and leave the nest.

All of us in this close-knit fellowship were invited to the wedding, and some of the children would even participate. Aletha's two youngest sisters, Brianna and Charis, and Greg and Kathy's daughter, Katie, were to be junior bridesmaids. From among Walter and Cindy's children, Lynette was to be the flower girl and little Timmy was to be the ring-bearer. Other bridesmaids and groomsmen included Aletha's older siblings and best friend as well as her husband-to-be's siblings and best friend. While we were only acquainted with some of these other family members and friends, the children's participation would make this wedding all the more meaningful and memorable for our group. We were likewise elated to attend and to celebrate the success of Bob and Linda's relationship with their precious daughter Aletha.

Tom had been asked to officiate the wedding, and he was only too delighted to do so. He had cared for Aletha and told her many original children's stories about characters which he had created during her growing-up years as if she were the daughter he never had. The happy couple even met with Tom over a period of months during their engagement for premarital counseling in preparation for their life together. Our fellowship group had many reasons for looking forward to this momentous occasion; it would be joyful and heartwarming for us all!

The ceremony and reception were held one Sunday afternoon at a farm in a little rural community called The Rock, Georgia. It was on a beautiful piece of land with low, sprawling hills and deciduous trees on two sides, a large field and barn on another, and a fourteen-acre lake at the rear. The site for the ceremony was found down a winding, tree-lined, gravel driveway which curved behind the farm house and about one hundred yards preceding the lake. A brick-laced walkway led the wedding party beneath a canopy of two tall oaks, which shaded the whole wedding ceremony. Rows of white, wooden chairs faced the ceremony area, which had a large, decorative iron fountain framed by low shrubs. The reception was to be held in the red-and-white barn off from the bride's side. Purple flowering shrubs, Telstar Dianthus, and other colorful flowers that I couldn't identify, lined both sides of the ceremony area, as did a few smaller oaks and medium-sized elms. The sweet scent of the rich bouquet of flora permeated the slightly humid air.

For a spring wedding, the weather was mild and pleasant. The overcast sky grew darker a quarter before two o'clock, and the concern was that a sudden shower would spoil the outdoor ceremony. We guests all awaited in the rows of white folding chairs for the commencement of the wedding, carefully watching the direction of the clouds. To the amazement and gladness of all, the dark clouds rolled to one side, and apart from a few seconds of sparse raindrops, no other precipitation interrupted the proceedings.

"I bet Aletha's thanking Jesus right now that the rain passed so quickly," Steve said beside us in a voice which was a little louder than necessary.

This time I gave *him* the furrowed-brow look.

"Steve, not now," I whispered.

He chuckled softly, saying, "Don't shame me, Brother."

Then Aby playfully yet firmly elbowed his ribs.

The wedding was truly beautiful. It was a simple, outdoor ceremony with only about sixty or so guests in attendance. Johann Pachelbel's "Canon in D Major" played softly as the wedding party approached and walked down the aisle toward the front. Tom entered the front from the side, wearing a nice gray suit. The grandparents of both families and the groom's parents were escorted down the aisle by ushers. Linda, wearing a flowery, spring dress, was also escorted by an usher. The bridesmaids dressed in lovely, pastel lavender, country dresses, and the groomsmen wore black, country tuxedos with Texas ties, minus the cowboy hats and boots. They entered as couples, as did the maid of honor and the best man. Timmy as the ring bearer in his tiny black tux and Lynette as the flower girl in her frilly, little, lavender dress were oh-so-cute in their wedding attire. The groom, Grant, joined Tom from the side, standing out from the groomsmen in his white tuxedo and goatee. Aletha and Bob approached the aisle arm in arm. She was a pretty bride, dressed in a simple, yet elegant, long-flowing bride's gown with a matching crown and veil.

As Aletha and Bob entered, the music did not change to Wagner's traditional "Wedding March;" therefore, a look of confusion was worn by many of the guests. Elena and I were two of the few who were privy to the changes. What was about to take place was a repeat of what Elena and I did in our wedding. Instead of promenading toward the front, Bob and Aletha stopped at the rear. The wedding director raised his arms, signaling for the guests to stand. Then Grant walked toward Aletha, took her arm in his, and together they approached Tom at the front. The music stopped, and we were motioned to be seated. Tom explained what had just taken place and the symbolism involved.

"As the groom left the wedding party to gather his bride and present her before the minister, so too one day the Lord Jesus Christ—our spiritual Groom—will return from heaven to gather his bride—the body of Christ, the church—and present her before God the Father in heaven."

A gentle expression of "Aww!" was heard among the female guests.

Steve whispered to me. "Was that your idea, Brother?"

I was noticeably beaming. "You could say that. Bob really liked the idea, and Aletha and Grant thought it would bring out the true meaning of a wedding as reflecting our relationship with Christ. We felt the same way about having this in our wedding."

"Shh!" sounded Elena. "Nathaniel is quieter than you two!"

My son looked up at us and giggled quietly.

We remained silent for the rest of the ceremony.

The exchanging of the vows also reminded me of our wedding because they were composed, memorized, and recited by the bride and groom. The whole ceremony was very touching. We were grateful and joyful to have had this opportunity to share in Aletha and Grant's special day.

After the guests were dismissed to the barn for the reception so that photographs of the wedding party could be taken, I commented to Elena. "This is the perfect day for a wedding! The air is just right with very little wind, and the shade trees keep the temperature mild. This feels so open and free having it outside. I wish we had had our wedding outside like this instead of cooped up in a church sanctuary."

"Oh, I know!" she replied blissfully. "It's just perfect! I wish we could have had ours outside too."

A group prayer of thanks for the meal was spoken over the intercom. Then we all formed lines for receiving a plate of barbecue and sides, which was the catered meal for the reception. After getting Nathaniel a plate of food and cutting his food for him, we let him sit at a table with Joey, next to our table. Lynette and Timmy would join them after their few photos were taken with the wedding party. Most of us adults sat at a round table next to the children's table and enjoyed the meal and fellowship. Greg and Kathy sat at Nathaniel and Joey's table.

These children in our group felt like old pals together by then. Elena and I were very thankful that our friends' children were well-behaved and got along so well with our son. Being home-schooled was impacting their lives for the better. Elena and I were also choosing to homeschool Nathaniel formally beginning in the fall of that year.

Just as I sat down, I realized that I had forgotten to get something to drink. I excused myself from the table and walked to the drink line where I encountered Tom. He had just approached the reception after having his photo taken with the wedding party. We spoke for a couple of minutes as we waited in line.

"John, how's the Sunday school fellowship group doing?" he

asked me.

My facial expression must have looked less than positive in reaction to his question.

"It was doing a lot better before," I half sighed. "Now there's not as much genuine love for each other as we had first thought there was. We've become somewhat like porcupines in the cold which try to huddle close together enough for warmth while simultaneously trying to distance themselves just enough to avoid each other's' quills."

Tom grinned at my analogy.

"I'm just not sure what to do about it."

"Who says that you should do anything?" he suggested. "Why don't you stop worrying about it, entrust it to Jesus, and let it run its course?"

Tom picked up a cup of coffee. I grabbed a cup of ice water.

"But then the group will dissolve, and no one will want to meet anymore."

We began walking toward our table.

Tom's tone was comforting. "And that may be for the best. Meeting and socializing because you want your needs met and doing it because you want to encourage others are polar opposites. It's selfishness versus ministry." His eyebrows shot upward as he said, "It sounds to me like the true colors of the fellowship are coming out."

"Yes. That's what concerns me."

"If you were to try to steer it in a different direction, they likely wouldn't want to follow."

"Why do you think that?"

He displayed a knowing grin. "Oh, I've learned a thing or two about human nature in my travels."

"That's right," I said, smiling. "I forgot." I released another sigh. "Truthfully, Elena and I have every intention of keeping our hands off the group. We would like to be an encouragement, of course, but I just don't believe that it's a good idea for us to try to force something on them, even if it's for their good and with pure motives on our part."

400

Tom patted my shoulder. "Now you're thinking like a biblical elder."

The compliment seemed completely out of place. I felt like a failure, not a biblical elder.

"Really? But the group is steering off course. I thought you would share my frustration and disappointment."

"In the final analysis, it's just a fellowship group. Just because people stop fellowshipping together doesn't mean it's the end of the world. Jesus still loves them just as passionately as he always has. Who knows? They may all quit attending the group. Then sometime later a few of them may form a new group, having learned a few lessons. And you will have learned a thing or two that will help you with any future group you're a part of."

"Hmm," I mused aloud. "I never thought of it in those terms. And I certainly never thought of myself as a biblical elder."

"You did say that you didn't want to force them in any way, right?"

"Yes, I did."

"You're respecting their freedom in Christ," he said plainly. "That's how biblical elders function. Remember the rolling tire illustration?"

Suddenly the whole concept came back to me clearly. "Oh, yeah," I realized with pleasant surprise. "It *is* like the rolling tire illustration! I guess I hadn't consciously thought much about that one in a while."

Tom's smile brightened.

"It looks like you're learning a better way to do ministry than what you practiced in Honduras."

Tom and I arrived at our table and took our seats, catching up on the conversation. Cindy had just arrived with Lynette and Timmy, getting them and their plates of food situated at the children's table. Then she took her seat beside Walter. As we all ate at the table, we reflected on the wedding and what we knew of Aletha and this new chapter in her life.

"Wow, these kids are just starting out!" commented Cindy, scooping up a forkful of baked beans. "They have their whole lives ahead of them, walking with the Lord as a new family."

"Yep," added Walter, nodding his head before taking a bite of Brunswick stew. "Life can be quite an adventure, Darlin'."

"It can be a positive one," said Steve, "or a negative one—depending on one's attitude."

"I agree," said Aby. "Life is ten percent what happens to us and ninety percent how we react to it with the attitude we choose. At least that's what Chuck Swindoll says."

"I agree with that. Attitude does play a major part in how things go with us and how we interpret our circumstances and the events that happen to us."

Greg cleared his throat. "A great attitude, a proper perspective founded in a grace-based relationship with Christ, and a vibrant walk with him lead us to view life as having no problems that Jesus can't handle for us by his grace."

"Of course, there will be struggles," Kathy inserted quickly, patting Greg's arm, "but Father's grace is enough to sustain us when we run to him. Truly nothing surprises Father or catches him off guard. He can take even the worst of sorrows and turn them around for his glory and our edification. Well, we've discussed this subject before," she said with a waving motion of her hand. "I know I'm not telling y'all anything you don't already know."

"But those reminders are helpful for us," Tom said. "Sometimes people go through major difficulties, and it's an encouragement to hear a godly testimony like yours and Greg's. Furthermore, we all know that you're not just whistling in the wind either. Sara and I especially are well aware of the stress and pain you folks have gone through, so we know that your testimony is trustworthy. It's good, godly advice backed up by a wonderful example of faith in Jesus."

Kathy smiled affectionately at Tom. "Thanks, Brother Tom. Your kind words really mean a lot to us. You and Sara have been an encouragement to us as well over the years through most of those times. I know that your health didn't always permit you to be at our side through everything, but Jesus has never left us. He has been our faithful, older Brother, consoling us, ministering encouragement to us, and caressing our hearts when we were just so overwhelmed by some of those circumstances."

"Jesus is everything. What we did was nothing," Tom said, shrugging off the compliment. "You'd have done the same thing for me or anyone else. In fact, you all *did* do the same for me during many of my hospital stays. The point for us to take away from this is that Father never leaves us. As believers, and therefore his children, we always have the resources of the whole Trinity—Father, Son, and Spirit—with us at all times. Since God's for us, who or what can be against us?"

"There are some real tragedies in this life," I added slowly in the wake of the silent pause. "Not to sound negative, but I've seen and heard so many heartbreaking stories in Central America and even here in the U.S. Knowing what I know now . . . I mean . . . with everything Father has taught me and walked me through . . ." Then I paused and frowned slightly. "That doesn't sound right either. I don't mean to say that some 'special knowledge' or 'secret insights' have gotten me through everything. I'm not sure how to articulate it."

"Let's see if I can help you some," Tom suggested. "The lessons that Father has taught you have been a great help to you and your family, I'm sure. And it's all been in the context of relationship with Jesus. I wouldn't say that it was just the knowledge you gained—as if just reading about it in a book or having someone tell you these things would have sufficed to break through your walls of bitterness and to change your heart condition in those situations. His presence, his grace, and his love were there too for you all. Even simply reading some Bible verses won't necessarily rescue you from some bad choices and tough situations if your heart is not open to Jesus and what he wants to do for you, in you, and through you."

"That's a lot better way to put it," I said, feeling relieved.

"I'm glad to hear you say that, Brother Tom," inserted Elena. "When we first came back from Honduras, so many of our friends and people at church saw how John was acting so angry and so different. They probably just took one look at him and thought

403

that they knew what his problem was. They would make comments to me like, 'John just needs to trust God. That's what he needs to do.' But just telling us that didn't help us at all."

"I wouldn't expect that kind of advice to work, Elena," offered Walter. "People always want to say, 'Trust in the Lord, Brother. That'll fix things!' But when folks experience some of the harsh moments in life—especially when those moments drag out for years or decades—then telling someone to trust the Lord is one of the last things they need to be told."

"Oh, really?" she asked curiously. "Well, they thought it was a simple fix and the right thing to say because it's in the Bible."

"It *is* in the Bible," Walter agreed. "Sure, it's in there in a lot of places, most notably Proverbs 3:5. 'Trust in the LORD with all your heart, and do not rely on your own understanding.' The next two verses say, 'Acknowledge him in all your ways, and he will make your paths straight. Do not be wise in your own estimation; fear the LORD and turn away from evil.'

"Now, that's some *excellent* advice for someone who's in a close walk with Jesus—someone who has that perspective of looking to him for things and who just needs a reminder and an encouragement to run to Christ. Nevertheless, we must remember that the historical context of the passage was that of a godly father counseling his son. It's likely that the father, whether it was David, Solomon, or someone else, was in close relationship with his son so that he could offer that kind of advice to him. He had the godly character, walk, maturity, and wisdom to make those words really mean something when he said them to his son. Therefore, the son had a close relationship with his father and an exemplary frame of reference through which to interpret and to understand that kind of counsel. He had seen his father trust in Jehovah with all his heart, so he had a pretty good idea of what that looked like. But, you know, just because someone looks at your life and says, 'Trust in the LORD with all your heart, Sister,' and then walks away thinking that they've been a blessing to you by quoting a biblical admonition which they expect to solve your problems, that doesn't mean that they've really done anything to help you. That kind of advice usually just comes off sounding really smug, annoying, or even stupid."

"But you're not saying," I added quickly, "that it's a stupid idea to tell people to trust God, right?"

"Oh, certainly not, John," he replied, shaking his head. "What I'm saying is that—to struggling believers who are really down and stressed at the moment, who more than anything need to be reassured of Father's love for them and need to be open to the grace available to them in Christ—*to those believers*, quoting something like Proverbs 3:5 *will* sound stupid, because it'll most likely *not* encourage them at all. It'll probably just feel like another legalistic rule they can't follow." Suddenly his whole visage changed as if he were fatigued. "'Okay, you told me to trust God, and that's what the Bible says. So, if I don't trust him, then I've committed *another* sin.' You can imagine how that won't help people by loading them up with all that law, guilt, and shame."

"I can imagine it because I've lived through it!" I admitted truthfully. "Okay. So then, what *do* you do to help those discouraged believers?"

"You encourage them by being in close relationship with them, not by laying more law on them. There will be times when you don't know what to say. I don't really know that encouragement is all about having the right words. However, just being there, letting them know that you care and that you're praying for them—all of that can be more encouraging than we often realize. Plus, if you're open to the Spirit, then you might find that he'll give you some encouraging things to say. However, they'll come out of your heart and life and be a byproduct of your relationship with them, not like some legalistic rule of just spitting out Bible verses that they're expected to obey regardless of whatever difficult spot or spiritual condition that they're in."

"John and Elena," Tom said, turning to us, "let me ask you: Did any of those folks who told you to trust the Lord ever spend time with you or try to encourage you in any way like Walter just described?"

We didn't even have to think of how to answer. "No, not at all," we both said, almost in unison.

"The people who said that to us," I explained, "usually just sort of approached us out of the blue, said it, observed my negative reaction, and seconds later went on their way."

"Wasn't that just a blessing for you?" said Steve in his silly, sarcastic voice. "What do they say about you now that Father has graced the bitterness out of your life?"

That I had to think about for a second. "I don't remember any of them really saying much to us since then. Maybe one or two have said something nice about how good or faithful Jesus is, but that's about it. Maybe they just got distracted by all the church politics going on at the time. I don't really know."

"People want to be helpful," Greg offered, "and to feel like they're doing some good, but they don't always care enough to sacrifice their time and effort. I say this as one who's been on *both* sides of that scenario."

Looking at Greg, I knew that he spoke from his heart. *Thank you, Jesus, for such encouraging friends and such wonderful fellowship centered on you and our walk with you.*

Elena looked around the table, speaking to the group. "You know, it's funny, but a lot of people who have met us in the last year or so don't have any idea that John ever went through all that bitterness. I've met some neighbors and made some friends in the homeschool group who sometimes hear part of our story. They're always amazed to hear what we've gone through."

"Elena's right," I added. "When people hear about all the things that she and I have experienced—the various trials and problems—they usually say that we've 'suffered a lot' and had 'such a hard life.' Maybe to some people we have, compared to their life experiences. The truth is that we know that our trials don't even compare to those of so many others. When I look back on everything over the years, it doesn't seem like it was all that bad. Sure, it was rough in those moments going through each trying event and difficult situation that happened. Yet Father was faithful to us every minute of every day. He never forgot about us, and he never left us. He never stopped loving us with all the essence of his being—even

406

though we didn't always recognize him loving us and love him in return. We learned a lot about trusting him in all those situations. He won over our hearts to trust him.

"But don't get me wrong; we're not all that exemplary. Whenever something challenging or unexpected happens to us even now, our knee-jerk reaction isn't always to trust Jesus immediately instead of worrying. We don't always run to Christ, pouring our hearts out before him, and depend on him for his grace and encouragement. I wish we could do that perfectly each time. But even when we panic, eventually he calms us with his grace and peace and lets us reflect on his past faithfulness and love toward us, encouraging us with the Scriptures. That makes it easier not to stress out over the hard times."

"That sounds like Father's still teaching you," observed Tom, "and that you two are still learning to trust him."

"Yeah," I conceded. "I wish we had 'arrived,' but we haven't yet."

"Maybe not," he agreed. "In fact, you may not ever 'arrive' in this life, but that's okay too. As long as you're still running to Christ, abiding in him, and keeping your focus on him, I think you'll find that your walk with him will be much more enjoyable and encouraging. At some point you'll discover that the elusive goal of having 'arrived' is not so important as you once thought it was. And again, even though our use of personal pronouns makes it sound like it's all up to you all and what you do, it's really all up to Jesus working in your hearts and doing what needs to be done in and through you all. You simply yield yourselves to him by his grace and let him do the work. That's what it means to abide in Christ: we allow him, the Vine, to flow through us and to produce his fruit in us as branches in him."

Sara spoke next. "I'm sure we've all been in situations where things didn't turn out as we'd hoped that they would. And *our* reaction to them was not always the most exemplary either." She flashed a grin. "Father's always teaching us, nonetheless, and we're being blessed by his grace. We know that he won't give up on us. Even when our lives end here, we just go to be with Father

407

and get to enjoy him that much more."

"So, other than some suffering and hard times in this life," I concluded, "it's going to end well for us. There's really not anything too bad that can happen to us that we can't endure by Father's grace. Is that what you're saying?"

Sara raised an eyebrow and looked pensively before answering. "That's basically true, although it's not to minimize the genuine heartaches and tragedies that many people experience. Knowing that Jesus endured Calvary for us really speaks infinite volumes of his love for us. That kind of love is just too hard to deny, especially since we have a living relationship with him."

"Like we've said before," Tom added, "as imperfect human beings, we can create some real problems for ourselves and others when we abuse Father's gift of free will. Practically all the world's suffering, in one way or another, is the result of such abuses. Now, I don't mean to infer that Father will rescue us out of our own messes every time we call on him. Remember that this is an intimate relationship with him in which he relates to us as individuals according to who we are, our personalities, our strengths, our weaknesses, our spiritual needs, our level of maturity, and his plans for us individually. Walking with Jesus and relating to him is not a one-size-fits-all dynamic, though we may sometimes like to think that it should be. Therefore, he may not deliver us from our mistakes every time, but that doesn't deny the fact that he knows that the best thing for us is to turn to him and to learn to trust him through everything. Then, as we observe him working in our lives, he *does* win us over to trust him. That's the best scenario in the world to be in."

"Wouldn't you say, Tom," inserted Greg, "that we can generally fall into temptation when we start to think that *we* know what's best for us at any given moment, instead of trusting that Father does? It seems that it's in those times that we are basically saying that we doubt or distrust his motives, similarly to what Adam and Eve did by heeding the serpent's words in the garden."

"That is a common inroad for sin, certainly," Tom agreed. "If we're fully persuaded of Father's love for us, then we are more

408

prone to run to Christ and to trust him to provide what he knows is best for us. However, being sure of Father's love for us is something that most people won't get simply by hearing about it a sermon or reading in a book that it's in their best interests to do. This is another one of those situations where it looks like we're doing the work because of the personal pronouns being used, when it's really *Christ in us* doing the work. So, as I was saying, it's really *Jesus* drawing us by the Spirit to trust him. We have to yield to him willingly, yet he is the one doing all the work. (Again, *we* are the branches, and *he* is the Vine.) We can end up trusting in our own wisdom before we even realize that we're doing it. That's why in Proverbs 3:7, along with being told to trust the Lord with all our hearts, we are also told, 'Be not wise in thine own eyes, but fear the LORD and depart from evil.'* That doesn't mean to fear him as if we should be afraid of him. It's really just another way to say to trust him, but it's more from the Old Covenant perspective."

"Yeah, they probably got that already, Brother Tom," Walter said with a quick grin and a wink toward Elena and me.

"The best demonstration," continued Tom, "or proof of God's love for us is Jesus' suffering and death on the cross for us. That singular act, nearly two thousand years ago, is how we can be assured that Jesus loves us.

"Frequently I hear in the news and on TV how people are always trying to measure their self-worth. It's so important to them that they prove to others and to themselves that they are worthy, that they are valuable. It's usually sought in things like their talents, their skills, or their contributions to society. Many people even feel especially important if they have a lot of money or are attractive-looking.

"However, the Scriptures tell us otherwise. In 1 John 3:1, John said, 'Behold, what manner of love the Father hath bestowed upon us, that we should be called the sons of God!'* When he made us born again as his children through faith in Christ Jesus, he proved his love for us. Ephesians 2:4-7 say, 'But God, who is rich in mercy, for his great love wherewith he loved us, Even when we were dead in sins, hath quickened us together with Christ, (by grace ye

409

are saved;) And hath raised us up together, and made us sit together in heavenly places in Christ Jesus: That in the ages to come he might show the exceeding riches of his grace, in his kindness toward us, through Christ Jesus.'* Beyond those passages, if there were still any lingering doubts about it, Paul states this truth again, but a little differently, in Romans 5. 'But God commendeth his love toward us, in that, while we were yet sinners, Christ died for us. Much more then, being now justified by his blood, we shall be saved from wrath through him. For if, when we were enemies, we were reconciled to God by the death of his Son, much more, being reconciled, we shall be saved by his life.'* He loved us before he even saved us, when we were at our worst. Certainly, his great love continues for us now that we are his children through the new birth. How do we know that we are worthy or valuable? Because of what Jesus did for us on the cross."

"Yes, that's so true, Tom," I agreed. "There's a lady at work who has a bumper sticker which reads, 'Your worth is not measured by your measurements.' While I know that that's true, every time I see it, I want to change it to read, 'Your worth is measured by Jesus Christ's crucifixion for you.'"

"Paul," began Greg, "was fully persuaded of Christ's love for him because he knew it from the start. As you all know, Jesus appeared to Paul on the Road to Damascus as he was traveling to capture and to execute Christians. At the time, he was known as Saul, a Pharisee who hated and persecuted the followers of Jesus. The Lord Jesus didn't appear to him in anger and wrath to harm him; he appeared expressing mercy and love to him—and that was even before Paul repented! According to religion, that's all wrong; it's all backwards. Religion tells us that you don't love the sinner until *after* he repents."

Greg's face emitted an inviting smile. "Nevertheless, that's not what Jesus does. He loves sinners whether they repent or not. It's because of his great love for them that his ultimate desire is to transform them through his love and grace because he knows how damaging sin is. Paul got it then, early on before he became the great apostle and missionary. He was so persuaded of Christ's love

410

for him that ever afterward he could reflect on that loving encounter and say, 'By *this* we know love.' The other apostles could say the same thing about Christ's love for them."

"Amen, Brother Greg," said Steve. "It's hard to doubt or to disprove such a great love for us, no matter that it happened nearly two thousand years ago."

"Steve, it *was* a long time ago," Kathy said with a warm countenance and caring eyes. "Many people think, 'It just doesn't mean much to me, because it happened so long ago, thousands of years before I was even born. To me it's just something you read about in a book. I want to *see* that God loves me and feel the emotion, the compassion. I want God to prove his love to me *now* in my life. I don't just want to read about his love for me in a book; I want it to be real to me *now*.'

"So many people don't understand that Father chose the right time in history to provide salvation for us and for countless others. It was the greatest act of love ever conceived, no matter how long ago it was. Even though we might think that we want a different kind of proof of his love for us, he did what needed to have been done at the appointed time it needed to have happened. What he did through his suffering and death on the cross followed by his resurrection are the real proofs of his love. It's the way he reconciles us to himself so that we can enjoy a relationship with him. Those who trust in what he did for us way back then will begin a real relationship with him and learn to see how he loves us through the multitude of details of our lives. That's what the gospel is all about—it's the story of God's love for us and what he did to make his love effectual in our individual lives. It's that powerful message of love, hope, life, and freedom. It's Father's message of love in which he invites us to know him."

"I agree with you, Kathy," said Cindy. "It *is* powerful. Yet too many people present the gospel as if it's just an escape from hell. Y'know: 'Repeat this prayer and you're in.' They try to cheapen it just to get a lot of 'decisions,' when they're really just deceiving people into thinking they've received something that many probably really didn't. They didn't really understand that this was

411

the beginning of a new life and a grace relationship with Jesus, the Creator, the one who holds their very breath in his hands, the one who loves and accepts them deeply beyond their imaginations. The only thing that a lot of people understand is that they don't want to go to hell and they'll believe or say that they believe anything to avoid it."

"My darlin' speaks the truth," said Walter. "We've seen so much of that kind of thing in missions in so many different countries. It's sad to think of that kind of thing happening, especially when the gospel is so easy to understand that even children can trust Jesus. In fact, children are very good at trusting him, because they understand that it's all about a relationship with God. That's really why Jesus said that we have to be like little children, trusting him unreservedly. It's all about a friendship. It's about becoming a part of his family. Jesus is not just a free ticket to heaven or 'fire insurance,' as I've heard some people call the gospel. He's a real person we can get to know and to trust. However, a lot of people don't try to get to know him personally. Maybe they don't even realize that it's possible to do so. Maybe they just listen to what other people say about him and thereby misunderstand what Jesus is all about. By doing this they miss out on the adventure of walking with him, seeing him work in their lives, and getting to know him better and better. We tend to make this whole walk with Jesus a *lot* harder than it is."

"Hey, Walter," I said excitedly. "I've heard you say that before and wondered what you meant by it. Will you explain how we make it harder?"

Walter sighed slightly. "This isn't so true for those of us sitting at this table, I believe," he said, glancing around at us, "but the body of Christ in general tends to make getting to know Jesus and walking with him day by day a real workout of frustration. As soon as someone trusts Jesus, the religious crowd gathers around and starts loading up the new believer with a lot of rules, requirements, and expectations. They tell them that they have to start reading this really thick book and attending these meetings several times a week and giving away loads of their money and praying in

412

a closet for hours all the time and telling other people about Jesus and how sinful they are so that they'll want the same thing. But it's not really like that at all. It's really just getting to know Jesus and letting him do the heavy work—which he delights to do anyway."

"So," Aby said aloud, reflecting, "a lot of people don't want Jesus because of all the *changes* that they think they'll have to make in their lives: turning from sin, reading the Bible, praying, giving away their money, attending services, and so on."

"To the average Joe, it just sounds like a lot of rules and boring activities," Walter concluded. "If this had nothing to do with growing in a friendship with the Creator of the universe, then it *would* be a lot of boredom, tedium, and drudgery."

"Now, *that* sounds like a lot of the world's religions," chimed in Steve.

"Many people think of trusting Jesus," replied Greg, "as having to meet a lot of requirements or to fulfill a lot of expectations. They especially misunderstand what part repentance plays in salvation. This is really our fault as the church at large in our miscommunication of the gospel. Typically, people hear gospel presentations and think that they have to repent of their sins before they can trust Jesus." He shook his head slowly. "That's not what the New Testament teaches," he added with a grin. "The word 'repent' means to change one's mind. The change of mind or heart is genuine and results in a changed life. However, the gospel doesn't make turning from sin a requirement for salvation. That change of mind that we experience when we hear the message of salvation is an acknowledgment and acceptance of who Jesus is. That means accepting that he is God as the Scriptures teach, not that he's just a mere man. It means realizing that he is the only true God, the only Messiah, and our only hope for salvation. Whatever low, unbiblical view of Jesus we once held, when we are presented with the message of salvation, we change our minds about *him*. We *repent* of what we *used to believe* about him as being anything less than the biblical view of him as God in the flesh and mankind's only Savior, and we accept Christ as God of very God, the only one who can save us eternally, just as the Scriptures present him."

413

"So, then, we *do* repent," I blurted out to clarify, "but it's not that we have to turn from all our sins. We simply repent by believing what the Bible says about Jesus."

"Exactly," answered Greg. "And as far as turning from sin goes, Father will work that into our lives *after* the moment we are saved. We're not required to repent or to turn away from sin *before* trusting Christ. That would make it a salvation based on works. Besides, it would be *impossible* for us to do that in our spiritually weak condition as sinners."

"Wow!" I exclaimed. "Think of all the people who won't even consider the gospel because they think that they have to give up all their sins. And the gospel doesn't even require such!"

"That's a real tragedy," Steve added, looking downward, "believers miscommunicating the message of salvation like that."

"If we sincerely trust in Jesus," Greg continued, "becoming born again in him, then *he* will clean us up and change our lives, just like the father of the prodigal son gave him a new rob, ring, and shoes. It's also like the dad in Tom's story who cleaned his little boy and his muddy shoes. Therefore, the turning from sin is something that only Father can do in us through the indwelling Holy Spirit."

"Others don't want to trust Christ," interjected Sara, "because they don't want to give up control of their lives to someone else. From what I've seen, that's more often the case."

"It's all about control for them?" asked Abby.

"It is," Sara continued, "or rather the *illusion* of having absolute control over their lives."

Aby's expression showed deep concern. "That means that a lot of people would rather *believe* that they're in control of their lives during their few years on earth, missing out on perfect love and eternal life, than begin this wonderful relationship with Jesus and let him do his work and will in them."

"And all their so-called 'control' over their lives only leads them to miss heaven and to settle for hell. That's how cunning and deceitful the enemy is."

"You got it, Sara!" said Walter nodding enthusiastically. "This eternal life in Christ is *all* about him, and it's not to be missed because of some misunderstandings or preconceived notions projected or fostered by some believers. Making it seem so difficult does detour a lot of folks from Jesus, when it's really a lot easier than that.

"This is how I think of getting to know him. I just relate it to real life. I think of it in the same terms of the reality of having a newborn baby. Each time we had a new baby born into our family, we would hold the baby, coddle the baby, feed the baby, change the diapers when they needed changing, and do everything necessary to care for the baby's needs. And what did the baby do? Nothing! Well, that's not entirely true. The baby would look at us, wiggle a little, eat, poop, sleep, and cry when he or she wanted or needed something. Who, then, was responsible for the growth of the relationship? It wasn't the newborn; it was us, the mom and the dad." He motioned to Cindy and then to himself. "*We*, the parents, had to take care of the baby and do everything. The baby didn't do much of anything to get to know us.

"That's kind of how it is with new believers. New believers don't know much of anything beyond the fact that Jesus loves them, and depending on how they heard the gospel, they may even question that sometimes.

"What I tell new believers is, 'Get to know Jesus at your own pace. Let *him* do the hard work. Just talk to him about things going on in your life and be on the lookout for his work in and around your life. And don't think that you have to read the whole Bible from cover to cover. Just read the Gospels. Better yet, just take one book, the Gospel of John. Read it over and over. Read it as much as you can, and simply find out who Jesus is and what he's like. Ask him to teach you, just like Tom did when Jesus came into his heart and life."

"Hey, Brother!" exclaimed Steve with an exuberant grin. "That's what *I* did when I got burned out on all the legalism and performance! I stayed in the Gospels, reading them repeatedly, and just soaked in all I could about Jesus. Put 'er there, Brother!"

Steve stood and extended his hand, and Walter stood and shook it vigorously. They both chuckled lightheartedly. Since they had stood so quickly, people seated at nearby tables looked their way. Aby cringed trying to hide her embarrassed smile behind her hand. Cindy seemed nonplussed at their attention-drawing antics. Both men returned to their seats after a few seconds.

"It's the better way to get to know Jesus," Walter explained as they both returned to their seats, "without all the focus on our work and performance. All the time and effort put into 'The Five-Fold Disciplines' take the focus off Jesus and put it on us and all the effort and work we do 'for God.' This walk with Jesus is not even about what *we* do but about what *he* does in and through us. If we mistakenly think that this walk is all about us *doing* instead of just *being* and letting Christ live through us, then we're not only missing out; we're also hurting ourselves spiritually. Jesus will relate to us and commune with us at some level simply because he loves us, not because we earn it by our behavior, service, or commitment. It doesn't take much to find evidence of him working in our lives. We just tend to make it *seem* really difficult."

"That's what *I* say," chimed in Steve, with his wide-eyed expression. "All those rules and expectations burn people out, and they don't help new believers in the least."

"No, it just frustrates them and heaps on the guilt and shame when they realize that they can't do it all. It makes them think that *that's* what it's all about. Who would be drawn to that kind of life? I know that I wouldn't."

"I've known people," I interjected, "who get all bent out of shape if they miss a day of reading the Bible or a worship service or a Sunday school class. They *really* feel bad if they miss giving a tithe."

"Yes," replied Steve, beginning to interject another voice characterization, "when it comes to keeping all those rules, you just want to say, 'We're doomed! It'll never work, Gulliver!'"

That reference drew a few snickers from around the table.

"Walter," I said toward him, "what you just mentioned—'The Five-Fold Spiritual Disciplines'—that's what I was taught in Bible college as 'The Keys to Spiritual Growth' or 'The Keys to the

416

Victorious Christian Life.' They said that if we pray every day, read the Bible every day, attend every church service, tithe every week, and evangelize weekly, then we'll grow spiritually. But I kinda burned out on those like Steve did because they were so ritualistic, routine, and boring. Next to an exuberant, moment-by-moment relationship with Christ, the spiritual disciplines are just too dull, lifeless, and ineffective.

"I haven't really told anybody this," I said, glancing around a bit sheepishly, "but I no longer do those all the time like I used to do. Instead of following a set routine, I now just try to relate to Jesus in non-legalistic and non-pagan ways like I relate to other people. I don't just complete the list of disciplines and feel like I've earned something, seeing that this is a grace-based relationship with him. Instead of having a scheduled prayer time, I just talk to Jesus throughout the day about anything and everything. When something comes up, be it a problem, a need in someone's life, or a cause for thanksgiving, I just talk to him about it. And I don't always read the Bible everyday either. I read it when I want to so that I enjoy it more and get more out of it. I have enough scriptures memorized that I can meditate on a lot of them throughout the day as well. We're not faithful to every service either, but we don't stress out about it if Father has us doing something else that makes us miss sometimes. Instead of scheduling evangelism with pro-grams and memorized lines, I just wait for Jesus to present the opportunities as I meet people, love them, and relate to them. I trust that he'll open up opportunities for talking to others about him when *he* decides. So, mine is not a life lived by those disciplines, but it *is* a lot more liberating and enjoyable. I don't want my relationship with him to get stagnant like it did in the past."

This was a rambling admission which I offered with a little hesitation. I didn't know how everyone would react. My purpose was not to discourage praying or reading the Bible; it was to express the freedom we have in Christ to relax in him and to allow *him* to teach us and to mature us without all the rituals and traditional practices distracting and shackling us. Nevertheless, I knew that some people might not see it that way. Some might

417

think that I was just being lazy, irresponsible, or apathetic. A reaction was expressed immediately.

Cindy exaggerated a gasp. "You mean you *miss* your quiet time with the Lord?!" she exclaimed with a look of mocked disbelief. "How unchristianly!"

Welcoming grins and cordial chortles from around the table made me feel at ease.

"'Quiet time'!" snickered Steve. "They put some funny labels on it, don't they? 'Quiet time', 'devotion time', 'time with the Lord.' It all refers to the same thing."

"The only 'quiet time' I have," remarked Walter in feigned smugness, "is when I sleep. Right, Darlin'?"

"Honey Bunch," quipped Cindy jovially, "if they were to hear all that *snoring* you do, they wouldn't call *that* 'quiet time.'"

For once Walter was quiet. Apparently, he had no witty comeback because he couldn't deny his snoring. He just had a look of humble resignation on his face.

Cindy leaned her head on his shoulder and rubbed his back. "There, there, my little honey bunch. I still love you anyway."

"Why do they call it 'your time with the Lord'?" I asked. "He's *always* with us no matter what. It's not like you can compartmentalize your walk with Jesus: forty-five minutes of prayer, forty-five minutes of Bible-reading, one hour of the committee meeting, one hour of choir practice, one hour of worship service, and one hour of teacher training class. And if I fulfill all those times, then I reward myself with one hour of watching TV." I glared facetiously at Steve and said, *"Right, Flamen'?"*

Some of the laughter around the table just couldn't be contained.

Steve batted his eyes sheepishly yet playfully. "Brother, I repented of that routine many years ago."

*KJV

418

CHAPTER 17

THE GROWTH OF FAITH

Greg spoke up, diverting attention from Steve. "I guess we've all had our systems for trying to work Father to get him to do what we want. Meeting the requirements of 'The Five-Fold Disciplines' is a pretty popular one among a lot of congregations and Christian schools."

"One of the most essential lessons we learn about this life in Christ," inserted Tom, "is that we earn nothing. Everything is given to us freely. That's what grace is all about. That's what Romans 8:32 and a lot of other scriptures teach."

I smiled to hear Tom contribute once again to the conversation. He once told me that sometimes he likes to listen to the rest of us talk. He said that it gives us a chance to exercise our spiritual gifts and it helps him to evaluate our understanding of what we are discussing. In this way, he can discern how he might help as needed. When it came to the body of Christ and its functioning, he really *did* practice what he preached concerning the rolling tire analogy.

"That's become my new favorite verse in the last year or so," I remarked. "I've even memorized it: 'Indeed, he who did not spare his own Son, but gave him up for us all—how will he not also, along with him, freely give us all things?'"

"Brother," called Steve softly, "I think we've *all* memorized that verse by now."

Unabated by Steve's levity, I continued.

"Brother Tom, Father has taught me so much in the last fifteen months that it just amazes me to no end! He took me from the depths of bitterness where I couldn't care less about walking with Jesus to this amazing space that I'm in now where all I want is to know and to enjoy him with all my heart, soul, mind, and strength. I know that this didn't just happen—this spiritual growth spurt. I've really been wondering lately, now more than ever, how our faith

419

actually grows and how we mature in Christ."

Tom listened carefully; then he took a sip of coffee. By the expression on his face, I couldn't discern if he had just a couple of pithy statements or a long discourse of explanation. However, I knew that whatever he was about to say would be edifying.

"That's an excellent question," he replied contemplatively. "Most believers would benefit from understanding the answer. First of all, let's think about the origin of faith. We know that our faith is in Jesus alone—not in ourselves, our works, our abilities, our background, our resources, or anything else. But, where does this faith of ours originate? Anyone?" He glanced at each of us seated around the table.

Aby spoke up first. "Our faith is given to us from God. Paul told the Philippian saints in Philippians 1:29, 'For it has been granted to you not only to believe in Christ but also to suffer for him.' Father gives us the faith to believe the very moment we choose Christ; that's when he saves us and comes into our hearts and lives."

"Very good, Aby. That's an insightful scripture. As a side note, I'm sure we all noticed from that verse that he also grants us the privilege of suffering persecution for his name's sake." Then he displayed a big grin. "But we won't get into that for the moment. Let's think about this faith, this trust that Father grants us the moment we choose Christ so that he makes us born anew.

"We know from Paul's writings in the New Testament that our faith is expected to grow. He says of the saints in 2 Thessalonians 1:3 that their 'faith groweth exceedingly.'* In 2 Corinthians 10:15, he speaks to those believers of a time in their near future, 'when your faith is increased.'* Therefore, as believers, we are to grow or to mature in Christ. Becoming conformed to his image is the goal of our sanctification, the process of us becoming more and more Christlike."

"There's another verse," added Walter, "about the origin of faith which comes to mind. It's Romans 10:17, which says, 'Consequently faith comes from what is heard, and what is heard comes through the preached word of Christ.' This tells us that the

420

preaching of the gospel is the main vehicle through which Father gives faith."

"Hence, we can say," continued Tom, "that faith or trust in Jesus is a divine gift. It's not something that we can just have apart from him by simply willing it to be or fabricating it by our sheer force of will or desire. He does say, 'whosoever will' may call upon him. Thus, salvation is an open invitation to all humanity, although not everyone will choose him. Yet, for all who do, Father gives them the faith in his Son that they need through which he provides them the new birth and everlasting life in Jesus, among many other blessings.

"There's a parable Jesus presented in Matthew 13 which sort of illustrates this. It's usually called the parable of the sower, but I like to refer to it as the parable of the four soils. It's also presented in Mark 4 and Luke 8. Would anyone like to tell me what you remember from that parable?"

I should have guessed that I would need to bring my Bible, fellowshipping with this group of brothers and sisters—even at a wedding. Although it would be a little frustrating, I would have to do without it for now and make a note to *keep one on me at all times.*

"Yes, Brother Tom," volunteered Steve. "I can give you the gist of it.

"Jesus spoke of a sower who sowed good seed that fell on four different types of soil: along the path, on rocky ground, among the thorns, and on good soil. He said that the good seed was the word or message about the kingdom. The soil along the path where the seed was eaten by birds represents a heart who hears and doesn't understand the gospel. The evil one takes away the word sown in that person's heart. The rocky ground is like a heart who hears the word and is joyful because of it but has no root and does not endure when persecution and problems come. It's the seed which sprang up quickly but withered in the sun because it didn't have enough roots." His eyebrows suddenly furrowed. "And—now I'm drawing a blank. What comes after that one?"

"The thorny ground," offered Walter.

421

"Oh, yeah—the thorny ground. Thank you, Brother. The seed sown on thorny ground is the heart that hears the word but produces nothing because the worldly cares, the seductiveness of wealth, and the pleasures of life act like thorns, choking what sprang up. Finally, the good soil represents a heart who hears and understands, bearing a hundred, sixty, or thirty times the word he received."

"You did it, Babe!" said Aby happily, giving him a hug.

"Thanks, Babe," he replied with a contented grin.

"That's a great memory you have there, Steve," complemented Tom. "I don't know if I could have remembered all that.

"Now that we've reviewed the basics of the parable, what difference led to the four outcomes?"

"Well, the seed was all the same," I observed. "It was the same message about the kingdom. Since there's no fault with God's word, it had to be that the different soils, or hearts, determined the results."

"That's exactly right!" replied Tom encouragingly. "Now, in that day it was the gospel of the coming kingdom being preached, a kingdom which was postponed until a future day, since the nation of Israel as a whole rejected Jesus' offer. But the same principles apply to our generation today with the gospel of salvation. Different people understand or misunderstand, receive or reject the good news about salvation in Jesus due to the condition of their 'soil' or heart.

"Thus, we know that our faith is given to us that it may grow. As you probably already guessed from our discussion just now, we play an active role in affecting the growth or lack of growth of our faith in Christ by the kind of heart we cultivate for ourselves. It's just like a farmer who nurtures and cultivates the soil to prepare it for the seed. Here's another question for you all: What were some things about people's hearts from the parable that *discouraged* faith?"

"Oh!" Cindy blurted out. "I know! The cares of the world, riches, and the pleasures of life."

"That makes three," said Tom. "Are there any more?"

422

"The enemy taking away the word," offered Steve, "persecution, and problems."

"Yes, those also discourage faith for those hearing the word before they trust it. However, for believers in Christ, problems and persecution can strengthen our faith, driving us to depend on Jesus out of necessity. According to this parable, they definitely affect the engendering of faith for those who have not yet trusted Jesus. Now, did you notice any factors that might have led toward a *good* breeding ground for faith?"

"From the problems with the other soils," answered Walter, "it appears that it helped the good soil to have depth, enough space for sufficient roots, and not to be near the side of the road."

"That's some fantastic insight, Walter," said Tom cordially. "Now, how could we understand that in terms of a person's heart?"

"Could we say," suggested Aby slowly, "that a person keeps his distance from the things of the enemy, like anything occultic or fleshly? Perhaps that's like the soil on the path which isn't cared for and nurtured for sowing seeds."

"That's wonderful, Aby! It really does help to keep a distance from the occultic and fleshly things of the enemy. Let's remember also that any works-based understanding or belief, which opposes grace, likewise falls under the category of 'fleshly.' The enemy can use those as tools against people, as well as using shame and other mis-understandings about Father, to take away the gospel presented to them."

"That does make sense," commented Greg, stroking his chin, "about the enemy using shame and misunderstandings to distance unbelievers from Father." He glanced at some of us to ask a question. "Have any of you ever known someone who's not a believer to hear the gospel and say, 'I've done too much wrong in my life,' or, 'I just don't understand it,' and then walk away? I have on several occasions. It happens just like that, probably more often than we're aware of it."

"We have some great observations so far," noted Tom. "Is there anything else we can glean from this parable?"

"The soil depth and space for roots," answered Walter, "might be understood to mean that the person thinks about the scripture or gospel message that he or she has heard and considers it, meditating upon it and letting it sink into his or her understanding, instead of merely brushing it off and ignoring it."

"Renewing the mind," added Tom, "is a significant part of this, just as Romans 12:2 teaches."

"Renewing the mind by meditating on the Scriptures," I concurred, "really can do a lot to help us spiritually."

"You got it, John!" replied Walter, emphasizing with his cup. "The Bible is our spiritual nourishment. When we allow it to penetrate our hearts and refresh our minds, it can transform our perspective on life, on ourselves, and on the world around us. You see, our mental focus and outlook on life can make us either very negative and pessimistic or very positive and optimistic. Having Jesus in our hearts and walking with him makes it easier to have positive thoughts as we renew our minds by meditating on the Scriptures. Yet, even as believers, if we fill our minds with negative thoughts and make that our default focus, then having an optimistic outlook is more of a challenge—hence the importance of renewing our minds with the Scriptures."

"Honey Bunch, I like your use of the word 'outlook,'" said Cindy. "It's used in Romans 8 where Paul talks about a life lived according to the Spirit versus a life lived according to the flesh."

"That's a scripture you've memorized, isn't it, Darlin'?"

Cindy smiled cutely at her husband. "Yes, I have. It begins in Romans 8:5 where Paul says, 'For those who live according to the flesh have their outlook shaped by the things of the flesh, but those who live according to the Spirit have their outlook shaped by the things of the Spirit. For the outlook of the flesh is death, but the outlook of the Spirit is life and peace, because the outlook of the flesh is hostile to God, for it does not submit to the law of God, nor is it able to do so.'"

"Hmm!" began Steve. "I had forgotten about Romans 8 teaching that we shape our outlook or mindset by the way we choose to live—either by the flesh or by the Holy Spirit. That teaches us that we are to *choose* to renew our minds, meditating on the Scriptures and praying as we walk with Jesus daily. By doing so, we live according to the Spirit, which results in a positive outlook or perspective of life. *¡Qué cheque y maquenudo! ¡Qué chequenudo!*"

Steve drew a few puzzled looks for the Spanish. He simply laughed lightheartedly.

"It seems to me," I began slowly, "that the 'positive outlook' talk sounds like some kind of worldly philosophy. Is that what you're promoting?"

"Aw, no, Bro!" Steve replied with his furrowed-brow wince. "The term 'positive outlook' is another way to say what your mind is set on, as some of the other Bible translations phrase it. If your mind is set on the Holy Spirit and seeking to follow his guidance and perspective on things, then your 'perspective' or 'outlook' will be more in line with his, which is a positive thing. I mean—*good night!*—if we set our mind on the flesh and focus on fleshly, worldly things, then it *will* have a negative effect on the way we view life and the world. That's not what we're striving for."

"Maybe I can be of help," Greg suggested plainly. "We know from the Scriptures that we live in a fallen Creation full of depraved people who are driven by selfishness, greed, and other fleshly motives. Likewise, we as believers in Christ contend daily with our own flesh. The enemy is also very active in this world. However, that's the negative side of things."

His serious look was then broken with a smile. "While this is all true, it doesn't tell the full story. As believers in Jesus, we are also the born-again, redeemed, bride of Christ, indwelt by the Spirit of God. Jesus is our Lord, Savior, and King, and he is the ultimate Authority in all Creation. He is active and doing much greater works than the enemy in this life. Christ has endowed us with all the spiritual blessings, grace, and resources we need to live this life in him. Focusing on Christ and the Scriptures and trusting in him and his provision—that's the reality in which we walk. That's the focus on which we set our minds. Therefore our 'mind-set', 'perspective', or 'outlook' is a very positive one, because we don't lose hope. For us, having Jesus is more significant and overcomes all the negativity in this life. Just as 1 John 4:4 states, 'You are from God, little children, and have conquered them,'—by which is meant the false teachers—'because the one who is in you is greater than the one who is in the world.'"

"Amen, Brother Greg!" exclaimed Walter. "It can be a problem with the way we are used to hearing certain words or phrases being used in certain contexts. Sometimes it's hard to shake the denotative meanings from some of these phrases. The way I understand it, the newer Bible translations try to express the concepts using words that will be more readily understood by contemporary readers, even if they don't always employ the exact wording that we've grown up hearing in older translations."

"It all ties together beautifully," concluded Tom. "Getting back to the parable, what else do you all see in it? What makes the shallow soil along the path not ideal for the seed of the word to take proper root and grow when problems and persecutions come?"

"It seems to mean," I offered, "that the person has no real commitment to follow what he or she hears."

"Someone who doesn't want to commit to and follow Jesus," added Steve, "doesn't know him as he truly is. I just can't imagine someone not wanting Jesus! Good night! After getting to know him and learning so much from him for most of my life, I can't imagine living without him."

Walter contributed his thoughts. "It's like I said earlier: Many people in the world hear about religion and what they think Jesus is all about, and then they shrug him off, not even giving him the time of day. Some religious people have done a lot of weird and sinful stuff in Jesus' name, giving our Lord a really bad reputation in the eyes of many people."

"That's heart-breaking, Walter," replied Tom with a quiver in his voice. "There are multitudes of people who don't understand the love and friendship that they are neglecting—all because they are rejecting what they think is Jesus, when none of that has anything to do with him."

"Sad it is indeed, my friend," Walter agreed. "I've said it before, but it bears repeating. Folks mistakenly think that trusting Jesus means that they've got to give up a bunch of things, join a

426

church or a denomination, start giving away a bunch of their money, and so forth. In reality, Jesus doesn't want all that; he just wants *them*. He wants their hearts. He wants that close relationship with them. He wants to be everything to them. They don't have to try to turn from their sins or to 'turn over a new leaf.' Jesus will change their hearts and take care of that for them. He'll give them a new heart with new desires, and they'll see the folly of the old, sinful ways and not long for them anymore. They'll be so in love with Jesus that gradually those things won't have the same kind of pull on them that they used to have."

"You know, Walter," offered Greg, "a lot of times the thing that really drives people to do what they do is their personal need to feel loved and accepted. So many lifestyles and deeds done apart from Christ are really just the acting out of people trying to deal with their need to feel loved and accepted. If they only understood that the one who matters most in all Creation *already loves them beyond their wildest dreams*, then they wouldn't have to live like they weren't loved by an incredible Father with his unfathomable love. Nevertheless, it goes beyond just people of the world. As believers in Jesus, we can get pulled into that 'trying-to-feel-loved' trap too if we don't trust in the fact as the Scriptures teach it or if we don't live based on his incomparable love for us rather than something the world promotes."

"I agree, Greg," said Steve. "Some believers try to earn Father's love, either through the spiritual disciplines or something else, not realizing that they don't *have* to earn it, because he's already *giving* it to them every moment of every day. *He's already pleased with us believers* because we are in Christ. When Father considers us, he sees Jesus."

Walter shook his head slowly. "Trying to earn what we couldn't possibly merit with our own efforts, despite that it's given to us freely all the while—if that doesn't sound ridiculous, then I don't know what does. However, the enemy is crafty, and he has a lot of folks convinced that that's what they have to do. All the while, Father still loves us all, no matter what we may believe."

"Yes," said Greg, "many people think that they have to earn it.

I can't imagine how frustrating it must be to live that way."

"It's almost," began Steve, "like those who think that they can lose or forfeit their salvation by committing certain sins. Christ bore *all* our sins on the cross. He didn't just take care of some sins and not others."

"As regenerated yet frail beings still struggling with the flesh," Greg added, "we can't be certain that we'll always walk in a way to avoid what some think of as 'big ticket' sins. But we do have the assurance of 2 Timothy 2:13, which tells us, 'If we are unfaithful, he remains faithful, since he cannot deny himself.'"

"It's definitely a package deal, that's for sure," said Walter. "In Ephesians 1:13 and 14, Paul wrote, 'And when you heard the word of truth (the gospel of your salvation)—when you believed in Christ—you were marked with the seal of the promised Holy Spirit, who is the down payment of our inheritance, until the redemption of God's own possession, to the praise of his glory.' Now, how could Father possibly give us his Spirit as a promise of our future home with him just to take him back because of some sin we commit? Jesus himself bore all our sins, even the 'really big sins,' on the cross long ago when they were all in the future from that point in time. Besides that, we didn't do anything to earn or merit our salvation. How could we possibly do anything to forfeit or to lose it either?"

"In Galatians 3:3," said Tom, "Paul told those believers, 'Are ye so foolish? Having begun in the Spirit, are ye now made perfect by the flesh?'* Therefore, it's evident from the Scriptures that we grow and are perfected in Christ in the Holy Spirit, not by our own efforts."

Steve made a further observation. "John and I have talked before about this idea that some believers have of losing their salvation. It must be a control issue that some denominational leaders use in order to keep people in check—y'know, by stringing together a few scriptures and slanting them to make them sound like they teach that we could lose our salvation if we don't put all our efforts into avoiding certain sins. It's a system of doctrine that works against both our freedom *and* our security in Christ. It's definitely not a healthy way to view Father and our relationship with him."

"Brother Tom," I called out, "I know that this discussion has taken a few interesting turns, but I really want to hear about how we grow in Jesus. Could we get back to that topic please?"

"Certainly, John," answered Tom. "Now, we looked at the parable of the four soils and saw that there are some factors which discourage the growth of faith and some which encourage our growth in Christ. Let's think about some of the believers in the Scriptures and what encouraged their faith to grow. Can anyone think of some pertinent examples?"

"Generally speaking," said Greg, "anytime a scripture or a word from the Lord was heard and followed, those who believed and practiced what they heard tended to grow spiritually. This is true of the prophets in the Old Testament and those who obeyed the word of the Lord spoken through them and the apostles in the New Testament. Furthermore, there were usually immediate results from their obedience, which made it easier for them to trust the Lord the next time.

"There's the account in 1 Kings 17 of the widow of Zarephath. By faith she prepared a meal for the prophet Elijah before cooking for her son and herself. The Lord didn't let their oil and flour run out during some three years of drought. In 2 Kings 5, Naaman the Aramean was healed of his leprosy by obeying the word of the Lord spoken through the prophet Elisha. Then there's also the account of the royal official in John 4 believing Jesus when he said that the man's son was healed even though the boy was sick at home many miles away. Also in John 4, the Samaritan woman at the well believed the words of Jesus, and many in that town of Sychar believed in him as well. In John 9, Jesus healed a man born blind by making mud, smearing it on the man's eyes, and telling him to wash his eyes in the pool of Siloam. Shall I continue?"

"Sounds like someone knows the Gospel of John pretty well there, huh, Brother Greg?" asked Steve in his friendly announcer voice.

Greg smiled. "It's my favorite New Testament book."

"Those examples are wonderful, Greg," said Tom, "because

they hit close to the next factor that encourages our faith. What is closely associated with the Scriptures or the word of the Lord in the examples that Greg mentioned?"

For a few seconds, no one spoke. We had long since finished our meal, so I knew that the food wasn't distracting any of us. Perhaps the noises and conversations of those seated at nearby tables were diverting our concentration. I also presumed that a few of them could have easily answered this but decided to give the rest of us an opportunity. Then Cindy spoke.

"Each account," she began a bit timidly, "had the *word* of the Lord followed closely by a *work* of the Lord. Is that what you mean?"

"Yes, Cindy! That's exactly it!" Tom chortled softly. "You and Aby are outshining these brothers here.

"Often in the Scriptures, God demonstrates his love toward people first and declares it later. In the Old Testament God showed his love for different ones—people like Abraham, Isaac, Jacob, the children of Israel as a nation—by providing for them and protecting them. Sometime later he stated that he loved them. One well-known example is how he cared for the Israelites for over four hundred years in Egypt and delivered them from their slavery under the Pharaoh. Yet he didn't state that he loved them until he manifested his presence on Mt. Horeb.

"These accounts which Greg mentioned have a word from the Lord and someone's obedience to it immediately followed by a miracle or work of God. The Gospel accounts of Jesus' ministry are simply full of these kinds of examples in which Jesus spoke, performed a miracle, and people believed. You can imagine how the apostles grew in their faith, being so close to Jesus and witnessing his miracles right before their eyes. Now, it's true that they scattered in fear the night that Jesus was arrested. However, the growth of their faith from all that they had witnessed first-hand as they walked with him during those years, as well as the Spirit working through them after they were baptized with the Holy Spirit in Acts 2, is evident in the book of Acts. Jesus' resurrection and his ascension into heaven are further examples of works of

God which encouraged the growth of people's faith. We know that the primary purpose for the miracles of Jesus was to engender faith in him—that is, to encourage the people to trust Christ."

"It's interesting," said Greg, moving his now empty plate to clear the table space before him, "how his words and his works are so closely associated. This is seen in a couple of statements in the Gospel of John in which the works encourage faith because they validate Jesus' words. In John 13 on the night before his crucifixion, Jesus spoke with his disciples and told them of things that were about to happen. Then in verse nineteen Jesus said, 'I am telling you this now, before it happens, so that when it happens you may believe that I am he.' When those things that Jesus predicted took place, then the disciples remembered that he had said that they would happen. It not only proved to them his trustworthiness and prophetic ability but also encouraged their faith in him to grow."

"And I'm sure I can guess another of those statements in John," interrupted Steve. "It's near the end of the book and serves as the purpose for which John wrote his long account. John 20:30-31 states, 'Now Jesus performed many other miraculous signs in the presence of the disciples, which are not recorded in this book. But these are recorded so that you may believe that Jesus is the Christ, the Son of God, and that by believing you may have life in his name.' Jesus performed the miraculous works, and later they were put into writing. Now we read the accounts nearly two thousand years later and have faith in Christ as a result." Steve leaned a little toward Greg and said, "You're not the only one who considers John to be his favorite New Testament book, Brother."

Greg chuckled a little. "That's okay, Brother Steve. I don't mind sharing."

"While we're all considering John's Gospel for the moment," added Walter, "let's remember that in John 12 after Jesus resurrected Lazarus from the dead, there's a verse there that says that the chief priests were planning to kill both Jesus *and* Lazarus, since so many were believing in Jesus because of Lazarus being raised from the dead by Christ. He literally stood as an example of the power of Jesus to perform the miraculous. That's another account

431

of a work of God engendering others' faith in him."

"C'mon, Brother Walter," Steve boomed in his baritone announcer voice, "join The Gospel of John Bandwagon!"

"Oh, I've been on that one for many years now, Brother. In fact, I usually ride shotgun."

"Here's a question for you all," continued Tom, picking up where he was earlier. "Can anyone tell me about an account in the Gospels of a man who struggled with doubt even while Christ stood before him and what Jesus did to encourage his faith to grow stronger?"

"Tom, that's too easy," said Steve plainly. "We all know that in Mark 9 the father of the demon-possessed boy approached Jesus, wanting to believe that he could heal his son, yet struggling with doubt since the disciples failed to do any good. When he asked for Jesus' help, he said, 'if you are able.' Jesus then said, '"If you are able?" All things are possible for the one who believes.' The man said, 'I believe; help my unbelief.' Immediately, Jesus helped him by casting out the demon from the man's son. So, Jesus encouraged his faith by performing a miraculous work before his eyes."

"That's it," nodded Tom with an impish grin. "That's the one I had in mind."

"That's an encouraging one," said Walter with a twinkle in his eye. "I also thought of a *different* account that shares a few similarities. It's the one in Luke 8 about Jairus the synagogue ruler and his daughter who was dying at home. He pressed through the crowd to beg Jesus to come heal his daughter. On their way to Jairus' house, a woman with a twelve-year hemorrhage touched Jesus' cloak and was healed immediately. Jesus performed *one* miracle on his way to perform *another* miracle. You would think that Jairus would be *encouraged* to trust in Jesus' healing power after seeing this miraculous healing before his eyes. Instead, Jairus was *discouraged* when someone immediately approached him and gave him the news that his daughter had already died. Jesus told him, 'Do not be afraid; just believe, and she will be healed.'

"When they finally reached Jairus' house, Jesus took only the girl's parents and Peter, James, and John into the room where the girl's body was. More than just healing her, Jesus raised her from the dead. He encouraged Jairus to have faith both with the miraculous healing of the hemorrhaging woman and with his words of exhortation, in addition to him raising the daughter back to life. Imagine how Jairus and his wife must have trusted Jesus after that miracle! Sometimes I wonder if they just might have expected Jesus to rise from the dead after his crucifixion even more than the disciples did, having seen him resurrect their little girl."

"You know," said Aby, "the beginning of 1 Peter 2 also makes the point about focusing on the Bible for growth in salvation. It reads, 'So get rid of all evil and all deceit and hypocrisy and envy and all slander. And yearn like newborn infants for pure, spiritual milk, so that by it you may grow up to salvation.' I've heard that there's something there that points to the Scriptures, but I'm not sure what it is."

"If I may, Aby," offered Greg. "There's a play on words there in the original text whereby the Greek words for 'spiritual' and 'word' are very close in spelling and pronunciation. Since the two preceding verses speak of 'the living and enduring word of God' through which the original recipients of the epistle were born anew, it's a hint that the nourishment for their spiritual growth was the word of God. Some Bible translators bring this out in their translation by translating it as the 'spiritual milk of the word,' since the play on words doesn't come across in English."

"Oh," replied Aby happily. "I always wondered why this Bible translation didn't have that. Thanks for the info."

"You're quite welcome."

"Hey, Brothers," said Walter, "we might be patting ourselves on the back seeing as how we know the Scriptures well enough to quote all these verses about how faith grows when people observe Jesus' works in the world, but there's still a problem. I'm sure you've noticed that most people don't see much of the miraculous being worked out in their daily lives. What do we say to those folks who don't see much if any of God's works to encourage the growth of their faith in Jesus?"

"Thank you, Walter, for that important point," responded Tom.

"It's quite often the case that in the daily walk of believers in general—as well as in our own personal walk—that we *don't* frequently see much of the hand of Father actively working miracles in our lives. What, then, do we say to those individuals who would point that out to us? How can their faith grow if they don't have the works of God close by to observe? If you haven't heard that question from someone before, then I'm sure that you will sooner or later."

I glanced around the table, eager to see who would respond as well as what the answer to this question would be. To my surprise, Sara replied.

"It isn't *that* difficult to answer," she began nonchalantly. "While we walk with Father daily, he relates to each one of us individually as one of his children. As we commune with him throughout the day, he hears us. In his sovereignty, he chooses how to direct us and to impact our lives and the lives of others around us. We'll each see him work in the details of our lives whether it's in the way he provides things for us which wouldn't otherwise occur apart from our relationship with him or in the way he answers our prayers as we intercede for different needs in our lives and in the lives of others.

"Mind you, I'm not saying that you'll *necessarily* see him raise the dead or heal folks in mighty ways before your eyes. Nevertheless, the child who walks with him usually looks with expectancy for Father to work in, through, and around him or her, be they actual miracles or just things that can't be explained away apart from Father's intervention in some way."

"You're right, Sara," I added, inspired by her answer. "I've been in some tough situations that seemed to have no workable solutions, yet in time Father worked behind the scenes and in people's hearts so that I've seen and experienced some amazing things. They may not qualify as crowd-drawing miracles, but they're definitely evidences of his hand in a lot of situations."

"What are some of those examples, Brother?" asked Steve.

"For starters, I'll never forget the way everything happened for us to get Elena's residence visa. Despite the fact that some of the documentation arrived after our appointment at the U.S. Embassy in Honduras, Father gave us favor with individuals there so that everything worked out and her visa was approved."

"It's true!" Elena exclaimed, flashing her grand, heart-winning smile. "We prayed without ceasing during that whole time, asking Father to give us favor with the different people we had to meet and to submit the paperwork throughout the whole process and to make a way for it to be approved. And he *did* make everything work together for good. So, here I am with you all today! Thank you, Jesus!"

"Fla-*men!*" said Steve, almost shouting.

"There have been countless other times," I continued, "when Father completely turned a negative situation into a positive one. I've seen him work in the hearts of individuals so that they came to me and apologized for wrongs which they had done toward me without any coercion or input on my part. Also, we've had times as a family when Father's provision came just at the right time or the last minute for us to pay a bill or to have a need filled. There have been times when he's given us some impressions in our spirits to make choices about matters concerning which we simply had no clue or wisdom at all. Later we discovered that we were led to the wisest and best options. Really, the list is practically endless!"

"I have to agree with Elena and John," said Kathy. "Greg and I have our own testimonies of how Father has walked us through some very trying times, both with finances and with little Katie's health. No matter what anyone may say to the contrary, I know in my heart that Father was guiding us every step of the way. To look at Katie now," she said, as she gazed gratefully at her child seated nearby, "to see how healthy she is and to see all that she can do now after so much pain and so many hospital visits, surgeries—she's a miracle to us!" Tears were visible in Kathy's eyes. "She's Father's workmanship, and she encourages and strengthens our faith every time we look at her. Katie's just such a blessing!"

Greg put his arm around his wife as she spoke and wiped away a few tears. He smiled at her warmly.

"That she certainly is, Kathy," said Tom, nodding with

agreement. "Every believer in Jesus who searches with the eyes of faith can see Father's handiwork evident in a multitude of ways around him or her. *That's* one of the ways that our faith can be encouraged to grow and to strengthen in him."

"A lot of folks," began Walter with a smidgen of sarcasm, "would say, 'Yeah, but those kinds of things would have happened anyway. You *still* would have been approved for a residence visa had you not prayed so fervently. Those people *still* would have apologized and reconciled with you whether or not you trusted Jesus to work behind the scenes. You *still* would have received those needed funds whether or not you prayed. You would have made those same decisions whether or not you believed that the Holy Spirit guided you. Katie would have made it through all those surgeries and sufferings whether or not y'all had sought the Lord and trusted him for each need'—and on and on and on. Some people call it luck or just things working out to our advantages, but they wouldn't interpret the results of these situations the same way *we* do."

"That being said," replied Greg, looking directly at him, "the Scriptures still teach us in James 1:17 that 'All generous giving and every perfect gift is from above, coming down from the Father of lights, with whom there is no variation or the slightest hint of change.' If some people choose to believe that these blessings and gifts are just part of some 'delusional perspective' on our part, then *they* will be the ones to miss out on all that Father is doing and could be doing in their lives and in the world around them. We, however, choose to view these situations and outcomes from the biblical perspective."

Walter nodded contentedly. "That's a good comeback, Greg. I was just presenting the secular perspective to see how you'd answer."

Greg gave him a cordial grin. "Walter, I know you too well, my brother. That's exactly what I thought you were doing."

"We have to keep things interesting, right, Brother?"

"If you say so, Walter," he said with a twinkle in his eye.

"I'll always stick with Jesus and the way the Scriptures present things. No doubt about it."

"Brother Tom," Steve called out, "isn't there a pitfall to avoid in all this? Some people might get the impression that they can pump up or energize their faith to will Father to grant us something he doesn't want us to have."

"You're right, Steve. I wouldn't expect anyone at this table to fall into that pit, but it is a concern to discuss so that we'll know how to explain it to others.

"The Scriptures teach us that God does all things after the counsel of his own will. That is to say that we can't twist his arm with our 'great faith' just because we believe strongly enough for something that he has decided is not our best. God is absolutely sovereign, and we have absolute free will. We've discussed this before, but a reminder won't hurt us. It may seem strange how a sovereign God and a free-willed humanity can exist in the same universe apart from any contradictions. Nevertheless, that is the reality in which we live.

"We can mistakenly convince ourselves that a particular outcome or course of action is his will and fall flat on our faces if we try to conjure up the 'necessary' faith and will to try to force his hand. Sometimes we might even enlist masses of prayer warriors to pray that things will turn out according to our agendas. In fact, some believers pray certain scriptures back to Father as if to say, 'You promised you'd do this for us, so you have to do it!' Many believers have fallen into those presumptuous traps, resulting in a lot of unwanted disappointment and bitterness."

"You're right, Tom," said Steve. "I've known people who have been drawn into the prayer warrior movement. They read dozens of books and attend countless workshops and prayer sessions—all designed to train them how to pray, to fast, and to do whatever else is deemed necessary to try to force Father to submit to *their* wills for whatever agendas they have. They're praying for some great things, but they don't always come to pass. Then when they learn the hard way that God doesn't want prayer and a relationship with him to become another system and strategy to get Father to do what they want him to do, it's a crushing blow to their faith. And the

437

pendulum can often swing them to the opposite direction with Jesus, so that they no longer trust him as before or walk closely with him."

"That just goes to show you how serious of a pitfall these presumptuous expectations can really be. Father loves us and wants us to walk with him, enjoying the relationship. However, when we try to work him and to manipulate him to our advantage, then we no longer submit to him as his children. We miss out on a lot of blessings and biblical understanding.

"Also worth mentioning is the way a few things are presented in the Scriptures, especially in the Old Testament. There's some debate over a few situations in the Bible where it appears to some that Father granted things which he never wanted for his children, such as allowing Israel to have a king like all the other nations. I may not be able to articulate a satisfying answer for those scenarios to the naysayers and contrary folks, but it's not really my responsibility to do so. Father can and does answer for himself in the Scriptures, though not necessarily for mankind's benefit and to his satisfaction. And that's okay. He has proven his love for us all, and he continues to do so daily. That's good enough for me. As one among us has pointed out, Father's not the type to pace back and forth in heaven, wringing his hands with worry about being misunderstood. His love for us endures despite our comprehension or misunderstanding of him. Right, Walter?"

"You got it, Tom!" replied Walter with a big grin. "Father's trustworthy. With him we have nothing to worry about."

"This is great!" I said excitedly. "Okay, so we can further our spiritual growth by meditating on the Scriptures and by recognizing Father's work in our lives and also in the lives of others. I like this point that we just discussed, because it's always fun to see Father's activity in my life. It's always so encouraging to me! What else will help our faith to grow?"

"There's another factor," Tom said casually, "but this one may seem a little tricky, although that's not the intention."

I blinked twice as if to brace myself mentally for something difficult to understand. "Okay. What is it?"

438

"It's this: Obey Jesus and follow him wherever he leads you." He then slowly took a sip of his coffee, probably to allow us a moment for his words to sink into our comprehension.

This one hit me like a feather.

"*That's* difficult to understand?"

"Not exactly," he replied light-heartedly, "but it may sound tricky, because we've talked so much about walking with Jesus as 'being' more than 'doing' and that it's more about us yielding our wills and agendas to him and letting him live and minister through us. Telling someone to obey and to follow Jesus sounds like we might be emphasizing less grace and dying to self for growth and more works and effort for growth. It might be misinterpreted as contradicting most of what we've been saying about walking with Jesus. All I really mean by the phrase is that when the Holy Spirit inclines you to do something, don't look for excuses not to obey him. Just do it. Don't try to explain away what the Spirit is leading you to do; just follow his leading. Obey what you know that he wants you to do, just like the examples we mentioned of people in the Scriptures who obeyed the word of the Lord."

"You have a point there, Tom," said Steve. "It's hard for our faith to grow when we disobey even the little things that the Spirit leads us to do."

"That's really what we're trying to say."

"Sometimes we might disobey the Holy Spirit in the small things," Steve observed, "thinking that they're insignificant. When a thought hits me about saying a kind word to someone, calling or visiting a friend to see how he's doing, praying for someone, or simply doing chores around the house like cleaning out the gutters, it may well be the Spirit putting the idea in my head because he has something planned."

Aby giggled openly. "I especially like the part about you doing household chores."

"Thanks, Babe. The point is that listening to his still, small voice is one of the things that we're learning to do as his children. Obviously, we'll miss out on his leading many, many times without even trying. Therefore, when it looks like he's pointing us in a

439

certain direction or course of action, we might as well follow him whether or not it makes sense to us or seems important. It's part of our spiritual 'training in righteousness' spoken about in 2 Timothy 3:16 and even Hebrews 5:14."

Walter leaned toward me and said to me with a wide grin, "As frail human beings, we're not battin' a thousand. Right, John?" He patted my shoulder.

"So, then," Steve continued, "when we recognize his leading and follow him, it helps us to sense the Spirit's guidance more easily in the future."

"Yeah, I agree, Steve," said Walter. "If we choose to reject the Spirit's leading, telling him 'no' over and over again—even when it's for what we consider to be 'little things'—then we shouldn't be surprised if our faith begins to feel stagnant."

"Amen, Brother Walter," said Tom. "This is not to be taken as heaping law on your backs, either. That's another misunderstanding that some could derive from the statement. In fact, *none of these points* is to be considered as a rule to follow. I would rather sacrifice my own freedom in Christ than to take away someone else's. So, no, this isn't a law or rule of any kind. It's just a reminder to us all that as we walk with Jesus and we sense him leading us to do something, we should just do as he asks. It will avoid problems for us later."

"In other words," inserted Walter, "we don't want to get into the realm of grieving, quenching, or insulting the Spirit."

"Yes, Walter," Tom replied with a casual nod. "That's a succinct and biblical way to put it."

"Obedience brings blessings, according to James 1:25," chimed in Steve. "But don't just obey with the motivation that you're only doing so to be blessed. The blessing is a byproduct, not the end goal in itself."

Just then Tom had a far-off, almost starry look in his eyes. I was sure that he was about to say something profound, so I gave him my full attention.

"This walk with Jesus was intended to be very simple," he began quietly. "By that I don't mean that it's to be free of suffering.

We live in a fallen world full of sinners and imperfect saints, so that's obviously not going to be the case. My point is that this whole walk—this life in Jesus—is about enjoying a relationship with God. It isn't to be fraught with systems and rules and performance. It's meant to be as simple as a little child enjoying the time he spends with his or her daddy. It's an affectionate, grace-based, love relationship.

"Think of when your children were very small. When your little boy or little girl spent a whole day with you, perhaps at a park or visiting some place or in a garden or just in your own backyard, didn't it feel special?" An affecting grin radiated on his countenance. "Didn't it seem like nothing else in the world mattered except your child? That's somewhat the way it is from Father's perspective, although it's without any sin on his part in parenting.

"Now picture yourself as that little child, walking with your heavenly Father, holding his hand as you take him to show him some of your toys to play with or some craft or creation you made just for him. He focuses all his attention on you because he loves you so and delights in spending time with you. He wants you to get to know him and to enjoy looking to him for all your needs. When you fall down and scrape your knee, he's the one you run to crying. When you have a question about something you don't understand, he's the one you talk to. And you don't have to be pretentious with him; just talk to him like a four-year-old talks with his or her dad. Don't be so self-conscious about trying to say everything the right way; just share your heart with him. He loves you—*he loves you!*—and he will listen to you and encourage you with all his heart. The Bible shows us this.

"Now, I know we can't see him, hear him, or touch him—though we all wish that we could," Tom said, emitting a slight chuckle. "He's with us nonetheless, in all our moments and throughout all our days. When you're stressed or confused or sad or angry or hurt—even when you're in sin—he wants you to know that he's here to help you. When you sin, don't hide from him in shame or cower before him. Go to him and tell him what you've done so that he can step in and love on you. He wants to meet you

441

in the midst of that sin so that he can clean you up, heal your hurts, and pull you out of that sin. He died to break the power of sin in our lives, and he still abides with us and helps us even when we slip up. Just remember: he's your loving Father, and he wants you to enjoy walking with him."

As I listened, I reflected on my moments with Nathaniel as his dad. My heart soared, thinking of my love for him and enjoying just being with him. Then I pondered what it must be like to have the kind of exemplary father Tom described, knowing that I didn't have my father as I was growing up. Then I was suddenly overwhelmed with the thought that I *did* have that kind of Father, that I *still* had that kind of Father with me every second of every day! He has always been with me, and he has always reached out to me. I've not always appreciated his presence in my life, but he has only and always loved me with his perfect love. As a loving Father, he only relates to me from a heart of perfect love. I couldn't fear or dread him as if he were some impatient, merciless, rule master who's relentlessly peering over my shoulder, trying to catch me disappointing him. I could only love him, which was mostly my feeble attempts to reciprocate his heart for me. Mine was not a perfect love back to him, but that was okay, because he would love me to make me more and more like Jesus. Whether or not one day in this life I would grow to have a heart very similar to Christ's, I was persuaded from the Scriptures that once I see him face to face, then I will be like him. He will never let me go.

"It sounds to me," I said with my eyes now moistened, "like walking with Father, walking with Jesus, is worth it just because of who he is and just for the sheer joy of his fellowship. It's not that we should do it so as to get something selfish from him."

"That's exactly it, John," said Tom amiably. "You've hit the bull's eye! None of this walking with Jesus is intended to be a selfish grab for whatever we want from him on our part. If we're walking with him just because we want something out of the relationship, then we won't enjoy this walk much. It will feel like drudgery, like duty, and we'll be disappointed continuously. Who would want that? We simply walk with him for the sheer delight of

442

enjoying his company. He loves us more than anyone else can, for crying out loud! Why would anyone *not* want to know him and to walk with him? (Those who don't, show that they don't know him as he really is. That's why we want to share him with others.) As we enjoy him and follow him, he will bless his children just as he always has."

These things that Tom was sharing with us were so edifying! Realizing who Father was and gleaning truths about him from the Bible and from the walk of this faithful brother in Jesus were a blessing to my heart. I sensed that I could truly trust Father, now more than ever. My heart soared with gratitude and love for my Savior!

There was a pause in the conversation. It seemed that we were all ruminating on the things which Tom just spoke to us about Father. The soft music, conversations, and laughter surrounding us were reminders of life and people important to us all. This wedding—this union of hearts and lives—seemed so appropriate to celebrate our mutual life in Christ, this relationship that we, the bride of Christ, share with him, our Groom and the Lover of our souls.

After a moment, Steve drew our attention back to the main topic of conversation—that being things which facilitate spiritual growth.

"Would you also say, Brother Tom," he began, "that we can add 'focusing on the person of Christ' as a fourth element which encourages our faith to grow? That has helped me innumerable times as I've walked with him through the years. Noticing his heart in the Gospels as he ministers to others and even recognizing his passion, mercy, love, and grace reflected through individual believers around me have strengthened *my* faith."

Tom blinked and set down his coffee cup. "I've always thought of that as a 'given,' but if it helps you to remember, then add it to the list."

"You mean," Steve began with his announcer voice, "'The List of Non-Rules for Spiritual Growth'?"

Tom chuckled. "If that's what you want to call it, then that's the

443

one."

"Flamen', I don't even *want* a list," I admitted. "I just want *Jesus*. I just want to fellowship with him all the time. No matter what trials and difficulties I'm experiencing, I just want to know him better and to see him work in people's lives."

"Then maybe it's better that we had this discussion at a wedding reception where you didn't bring your Bible and paper to jot down tons of notes."

A sigh came over me then at that realization.

"This may sound crazy after what I said earlier, but I really do miss reading the Bible right now. This whole discussion has made me crave delving into the Scriptures. I'll have to do some studying on these passages at home."

Steve suddenly displayed a goofy facial expression, and I just knew that he was going to pull out another voice characterization. "Brother, are you sure it's not just the guilt and shame you feel from not keeping 'The Five-Fold Spiritual Disciplines'?"

The facetious smirk I displayed probably communicated something to Steve. I was about to speak, but then the announcement was made over the speakers that the wedding party was making their grand entrance.

"The photos must have taken a lot longer than expected," Steve commented over the entrance music.

"Or maybe they sneaked a meal while we were waiting," offered Kathy with a grin. "Earlier I noticed someone taking plates of food around to the back of the barn."

It was only then that I realized that Cindy had already taken Lynette and Timmy to prepare them for the wedding party's grand entrance into the reception. Katie had also left since she was a junior bridesmaid.

The wedding party arrived as a line of couples: Bob and Linda, Grant's parents, the bridesmaids and groomsmen, Lynette as the flower girl and Timmy as the ring bearer, the maid of honor and the best man, and finally the newlyweds. They looked so happy together! A glow of joy emanated from their faces. Their first dance as husband and wife was announced, and they took to the center of the barn floor for a slow waltz. As I looked at them both, I asked Father to bless their union and to remind them to run to Christ daily, both individually and as a family.

Before long, the announcement was made that the bride was going to dance with her father.

"Well, *this* is surprising!" said Walter with raised eyebrows. "I didn't know that Bob could cut a rug."

Cindy, now back at his side, waved him off with a flick of her wrist.

"Oh, Honey Bunch, give it a rest. Bob's going to miss her dearly." Then she leered toward him with a half-smirk. "Don't forget that that will be *you and Lynette* in a few years."

Walter's joviality was quickly reduced to somberness. He didn't say much for a while after that.

We watched Bob and his daughter waltzing in the middle of the floor. He smiled with sheer delight, gazing into her eyes as a loving father. Aletha looked up at him with such joy and affection glistening on her face. No one could hear what Bob was saying to her, but I'm sure that it was words of love and affection for his child who was leaving the nest.

The recent discussion at the table left me thrilled and ever grateful for Father's past and present work in my heart and family. It also encouraged me to look forward to the future work that Father would perform in and through us. I reviewed parts of the conversation in my mind as we watched the two ballroom-dance around in wide circles.

"Brother Tom," I said, leaning toward him, "this walk with Jesus as you described it is simply wonderful! I don't think I've ever pictured it quite the way you described it just now. It's so encouraging, and I'd like to hear more. Is there some kind of illustration or analogy for cooperating with Jesus as we exercise our free will and he works sovereignly in our lives to mature us in him? Maybe there's something like the rolling tire illustration that you use to describe the function of elders in a local body."

As he listened, Tom kept his gaze on Bob and Aletha, who were dancing in sweeping motions as they glided on the dance floor. He

445

seemed to have a far off look in his eyes. I wasn't sure if he had heard my question. Wanting to be respectful, I looked from him to the father and daughter waltzing before us.

"I think that it can be compared to a dance," he finally said slowly. "We—the body of Christ—are the bride, and Jesus is the Groom. Individually in our own lives, he takes each one of us by the hand and the small of our back and leads us in a dance called 'My Life in Christ.' Those moments when we surrender to him and yield to his leading, it's a beautiful thing. It's majestic; it's breathtaking. Under his guidance, we can achieve such graceful movements that we never knew we were capable of. It's in those moments when we truly soar as we were created to do, delighting in oneness and in fellowship with him.

"But when we resist his touch, his hold on us, his movements in our lives, then it is *we* who are trying to lead *him* as we navigate our lives. This is something that simply can't be done." He turned to face me with an inviting grin. "Have you ever seen a couple try to waltz where each one tries to lead? It's not graceful; it's messy. It's in those moments that we step on his toes, fumble, and even trip over our own feet, getting out of time with the music. No, *he* must lead, and *we* must let him lead. We must follow his leading, yielding to his touch and movements. Dancing in this way is cooperating with what he wants to do in and through us. And if we let him lead as is proper for the dance, then it'll be obvious that he's leading, and our relationship with him will be delightful."

It was then that we noticed Elena, Steve, and Aby listening intently to what he was saying.

"By the way," he said, turning to them, "this isn't meant to be a performance issue, even though dancing sounds like a performance-based analogy with all the time invested, effort exerted, and routines learned. In truth, that's where the analogy breaks down. No—in this dance, its being light on your feet because Christ is carrying you and moving you as you yield to him. As little children growing in him, we start out standing on his feet, craning our necks to look up at his tall frame, letting him carry us through the steps, and letting him teach us how to cooperate with

446

him. And sure, we'll make plenty of mistakes. But that's okay, because Jesus is patient with us. Remember that the Scriptures teach that love is patient, so he is patient. He never gives up on us. He's always waiting for us to yield to his leading so that our lives can become a thing of beauty once more. And all the while, he's teaching us to relax in his arms and to let him do all the work."

Our walk with Christ is like a dance! It seemed to be such a fitting illustration. At that moment, it reminded me of Matthew 11:28-30, one of the "run to Christ" passages on the list in my note-book. I had memorized it since it was so uplifting. In it, Jesus extended an invitation to all in need: "Come to me, all you who are weary and burdened, and I will give you rest. Take my yoke on you and learn from me, because I am gentle and humble in heart, and you will find rest for your souls. For my yoke is easy to bear, and my load is not hard to carry."

*KJV

EPILOGUE

This walk with Jesus has definitely been an adventure! It continues to be so because our last chapter is not yet written. When I trusted Jesus as a seventeen-year-old, I couldn't have imagined all the things that my Lord and Savior would walk me through, accompanying me and showering me with his grace upon grace through every moment and in every situation. Granted, it hasn't always been joyful. There have been a fair share of sufferings, worries, doubts, and tears through it all. Nevertheless, knowing Jesus—and Father through him together with the Holy Spirit—has more than made this life worth every moment.

The best part of this relationship is yet to come, as we eagerly await the day when Jesus will take us home. For many, this has happened sooner than we expected. In the intervening years since the preceding detailed events occurred, we have grieved the passing of my mom, Elena's dad, Tom, and many others who are dear to us. For some, death came suddenly and unexpectedly; for others it was a release of relentless pain and agony which they had borne over months or years. We can't adequately articulate our sorrow over the loved ones who have proceeded to heaven before us. We love them and miss them dearly! However, we have this sure hope in Christ that we will be reunited with these believers again. I've always longed for heaven, knowing that once we arrive we will forever be in the manifest presence of Jesus; nothing outshines his love and affection for us. Now that so many family members and friends have gone ahead of us, I also anticipate seeing them as well, along with the Jesus they loved and who shone through their hearts and lives in this life.

For Elena and me, we have never accepted as true the idea that some repeat, that "Father took them on to heaven because he wanted them to be with him" or "he needed another angel in his choir." That's a sentiment that I've never understood. The only explanation I have for people repeating this is that they want to console others in their time of grief. For us, the reality is quite different.

449

We are imperfect people living in a fallen world, and the sin which began in the garden in Eden has permeated Father's Creation. Physical death is a natural consequence of sin, and though we experience it at the end of our lives, it does not have to have the final word. The Lord Jesus Christ conquered sin, death, and shame on our behalf; he also fulfilled the Law in our place. His love and grace are real and available to everyone who will trust him through a childlike faith.

Some of us do succumb to death prematurely as a result of our own poor choices, be they related to our health, our diet, our activities, or other such factors influenced or directed by our wills. Some of us come to the end of our lives as a result of events in this fallen Creation. Still others fall prey to the poor choices of those who abuse Father's gift of free will given to them. Nevertheless, Father does not end our lives simply because "he wants us to be with him."

A new chapter began in my life completely unexpectedly. Through the connections of social media, my father's three brothers and their families found me and made contact with me. My parents divorced when I was a baby; I have not seen my father since I was six-years-old. Neither of my parents ever mentioned that my father had any brothers, so until recently I had no idea that any of them even existed. My father had passed away just a few months before they found me; thus, I missed reconnecting with him and introducing him to my wife and son. However, my new uncles, aunts, and cousins have been such a delight and a blessing to come to know. We are deeply grateful to Father for bringing them into our lives. *Thank you, Jesus!*

The grace of Jesus is far greater than we realize. His grace is more than enough to free us from the enslavement of sin, to transform our hearts and lives, and to restore his beauty in our lives. Walking with him is such a privilege and an honor. It surpasses anything that we may attempt or achieve in our personal lives or careers. I am persuaded that the rest of my life will be spent getting to know him better and that, when the time comes for that to be over—whether anticipated or not—then I'll be ushered into his manifest presence to enjoy him for eternity. In the meantime, many in this world still need to know him.

When we returned from Honduras, I thought that we would never have the opportunity to go there again to live and to minister. We have visited Elena's family many times over the years since moving back to the States; however, relocating overseas again seemed to be an elusive dream. This is no longer simply a dream. Since our return from Honduras, I have held different jobs of one kind or another, but I've never settled on any career for too long. Nothing else fulfilled my lifelong dream of loving people and sharing Jesus in Honduras and then watching them grow in him. I especially yearned to disciple and to train some of the nationals there to reach their own people for Jesus. Now that looks like it will soon become a dream come true.

Father has worked behind the scenes to bless us in our finances all along the way. After a couple of years of trying to pay down what began as our growing tax debt on credit cards, we took the opportunity to transfer the debt into a home equity loan, which would not grow with rising interest rates and be on a reasonable payment schedule. We are now in the final stages of paying off this debt and being free of it once and for all. *Thank you, Jesus!* Father has also provided for us in another way.

When Steve returned from Honduras, he did so looking for a wife. He found one in Aby, his true love. Throughout many years of their marriage, they have enjoyed a career together working in real estate and managing other investments. They have both continued with their business investments, eventually attaining a sustainable stream of residual income. In recent years, Steve has even helped me and taught me how to do some of the same. As a result, Elena and I will have enough income along with jobs we will acquire in Honduras (bilinguals are much sought after in that job market) to allow us to live permanently in Elena's hometown close to her mom and sisters. We'll have the joy of sharing Jesus and ministering to individuals and small groups in our spare time.

In this way, we will not be dependent on local congregations or mission organizations in the United States to fund our living expenses. Elena and I will serve alongside Steve and Aby, allowing Jesus to minister his grace and love through us to as many people as possible. *Thank you, Jesus!*

As Nathaniel has grown up over the years in the Unites States, he has always delighted in visiting Elena's family with us. He has long enjoyed the life in Honduras with his grandparents, cousins, aunts, and uncles. Nathaniel has already graduated from high school and is eagerly anticipating moving to Honduras with us. He will continue studying on-line to further his education. Then he'll see what Jesus has in store for him. *Thank you, Jesus!*

It never dawned on me that Father would take someone like me, "a bitter, washed-up, disgruntled, ex-missionary" who looked like he was down for the count due to his bitterness and callousness, and break through that wall of hardheartedness with Father's grace and love to make something wonderful of his life. Nevertheless, that is exactly what he did with me! Father has transformed my heart and life so incredibly—something that I never could have deserved or anticipated—and blessed my family and me beyond my imagination. His grace could never be deserved; that's why it's called "grace." Financially, I'm not as well off as are others, and I'm not as gifted and talented as are many, but I am loved and accepted by the one who matters most in all Creation. Walking with Jesus in this truth makes all the difference. *Thank you, Jesus!*

Once I asked Tom about all the grace that I received during those years of bitterness which I endured. "Brother Tom, a few people have told me that all this talk of Father's grace is just my opinion or perspective. They say, 'Just because you started looking at things differently or suddenly had a change of heart doesn't mean it's because of something you call "the grace of God." You're attributing your improvement in attitude to an intangible thing. How do you know for sure that there even *is* such a thing as grace?' Walter once told me that, during my whole ordeal with bitterness, as a believer, I always had Father's grace and love,

Jesus' enabling and wisdom, the Holy Spirit's guidance and ministry, and the Bible. He said that what made the difference was that, during my bitterness, I didn't appropriate or avail myself of these resources. And, okay, so these spiritual resources are not tangible so as to allow me to identify when, where, and how they became active in my life. I guess my question is this: How am I to understand or to explain that, as a believer, I *already* had all this grace all along and that I just didn't believe it or appropriate it during my period of bitterness?"

Tom's reply to me was simple. "We know from the Scriptures that the grace of God is real. The Bible is the story of God's loving pursuit of mankind to redeem him; it reveals the unfolding of his glory throughout parts of history as he relates to us by his grace. Therefore, for us as believers in Jesus, there's no doubt about it being true. If you don't believe it and trust it—even at times as a believer—then it feels the same as if you didn't have it. Besides, if our perspective is marred by bitterness or some other sin, then it's hard to view or to sense his grace as evident in our lives. Living your life out of fellowship with him makes it most difficult to enjoy his grace. However, not believing in it doesn't mean that Father isn't constantly showering you, as a believer, with his grace upon grace. Remember that he always showers his grace upon grace to us believers and to whomsoever will accept by faith his offer of salvation and relationship with him, thereby becoming a believer in Jesus. He really does love us, and he wants to heal our hurts and to clean us up. He wants to free us from sin so that we can enjoy fellowshipping and walking with him. Through Jesus, Father has already made that possible. Therefore, he really leaves the choice to each one of us. And whatever our choice is, the consequences go with them."

At the time, I held my gaze on him with wonder.

"Father's grace is accessed by faith, then," I surmised. "This really *is* a walk of faith by grace!"

"It really is," he agreed, with a twinkle in his eye and a grin from ear to ear.

Although for a time I completely misunderstood Father and his grace and love for me, they have now been clear and undeniable to me for these many years. Throughout this period, I've learned that Father wants to meet us in the midst of our sin, pain, doubt, and the mess we may have made of our lives. He doesn't desire to scold us or to punish us; he longs to restore our relationship with him. He wants to free us from all the sin, shame, self, law, and misunderstanding in which we find ourselves so entrapped. Jesus made a way for this to become a reality in our lives through his work on the cross and his resurrection. His grace and love can make the difference in *anyone's* heart and life. Even though I haven't experienced all the sorrowful scenarios that many have, nevertheless I stand as proof of and as a recipient of the grace and love of Jesus. Anyone can have his or her own personal break-through of Father's grace and love. This becomes our reality once we allow him to enter our hearts and lives by faith in what Jesus did for us all so long ago.

Every time I tell the story of that night at Tom and Sara's when Father's grace and love broke through my wall of bitterness, I still weep like a baby—even after all these years. I'll never forget how Father used my son to communicate his abiding love and affection for me. His grace and love broke through my bitterness, and I'll always be grateful to Father for it.

APPENDIX: "RUN TO CHRIST"

Tom had asked me a very profound question: "When you sin, do you find yourself running toward Jesus or away from him?" After he shared with me some of the "refuge" passages from the Psalms and Father broke through my bitterness, Tom then said, "Remember: always run to Jesus, even when it doesn't make sense." This led me to ask a very different question: "If he wants me to seek him when I'm at my worst, then when would he *not* want me to run to him?" The following scripture passages and biblical examples are presented to help in answering this question.

This is the collection of scriptures which I compiled during my search after that night at Tom and Sara's house when Father's grace and love broke through my hardheartedness. This list is not intended to be exhaustive, but it will serve to help you, the reader, to understand some of God's heart of grace, love, and compassion. Concerning the biblical narratives, since Father's heart was like this to those individuals in the past, then he is the same toward you now, because he is immutable and not given to change. Keep in mind that some of the Old Testament scriptures reflect features of that covenant and do not necessarily apply to believers today under the New Covenant in Christ. Please read these in their respective biblical passages to gain an understanding of the context of each selection.

"May your walk with Jesus make you ever aware of and ever a vessel of his grace, love, gratitude, peace, and joy." – John

DRAW NEAR TO GOD

16 Answer me, O LORD, for your loyal love is good!
　　Because of your great compassion, turn toward me!
17 Do not ignore your servant,
　　for I am in trouble! Answer me right away!
18 Come near me and redeem me!
　　Because of my enemies, rescue me!
　　　　　　　　　　　　～ PSALM 69:16-18

455

The LORD is near all who cry out to him,
all who cry out to him sincerely.
~ PSALM 145:18

28 "Come to me, all you who are weary and burdened, and I will give you rest. **29** Take my yoke on you and learn from me, because I am gentle and humble in heart, and you will find rest for your souls. **30** For my yoke is easy to bear, and my load is not hard to carry."
~ MATTHEW 11:28-30

14 Therefore since we have a great high priest who has passed through the heavens, Jesus the Son of God, let us hold fast to our confession. **15** For we do not have a high priest incapable of sympathizing with our weaknesses, but one who has been tempted in every way just as we are, yet without sin. **16** Therefore let us confidently approach the throne of grace to receive mercy and find grace whenever we need help.
~ HEBREWS 4:14-16

Draw near to God and he will draw near to you. Cleanse your hands, you sinners, and make your hearts pure, you double-minded.
~ JAMES 4:8

Everyone whom the Father gives me will come to me, and the one who comes to me I will never send away.
~ JOHN 6:37

1 God's Spirit came upon Azariah son of Oded. **2** He met Asa and told him, 'Listen to me, Asa and all Judah and Benjamin! The LORD is with you when you are loyal to him. If you seek him, he will respond to you, but if you reject him, he will reject you. '"
~ 2 CHRONICLES 15:1, 2

Therefore say to the people: The LORD who rules over all says,

"Turn to me," says the LORD who rules over all, "and I will turn to you," says the LORD who rules over all.

~ ZECHARIAH 1:3

From the days of your ancestors you have ignored my command-ments and have not kept them! Return to me, and I will return to you," says the LORD who rules over all. "But you say, 'How should we return?'"

~ MALACHI 3:7

18 On the one hand a former command is set aside because it is weak and useless, **19** for the law made nothing perfect. On the other hand a better hope is introduced, through which we draw near to God.

~ HEBREWS 7:18, 19

5 Your conduct must be free from the love of money and you must be content with what you have, for he has said, *"I will never leave you and I will never abandon you."* **6** So we can say with confi-dence, *"The Lord is my helper, and I will not be afraid. What can people do to me?"*

~ HEBREWS 13:5, 6

THE ONLY SOURCE

For you are the one who gives
and sustains life.

~ PSALM 36:9

"Do so because my people have committed a double wrong:
they have rejected me,
the fountain of life-giving water,
and they have dug cisterns for themselves,
cracked cisterns which cannot even hold water."

~ JEREMIAH 2:13

37 On the last day of the feast, the greatest day, Jesus stood up and shouted out, "If anyone is thirsty, let him come to me, and **38** let the one who believes in me drink. Just as the scripture says, *'From within him will flow rivers of living water.'"* **39** (Now he said this about the Spirit, whom those who believed in him were going to receive, for the Spirit had not yet been given, because Jesus was not yet glorified.)

~ JOHN 7:37-39

66 After this many of his disciples quit following him and did not accompany him any longer. **67** So Jesus said to the twelve, "You don't want to go away too, do you?" **68** Simon Peter answered him, "Lord, to whom would we go? You have the words of eternal life. **69** We have come to believe and to know that you are the Holy One of God!" **70** Jesus replied, "Didn't I choose you, the twelve, and yet one of you is the devil?" **71** (Now he said this about Judas son of Simon Iscariot, for Judas, one of the twelve, was going to betray him.)

~ JOHN 6:66-71

The fear of the LORD is like a life-giving fountain,
to turn people from deadly snares.
~ PROVERBS 14:27

You are the one in whom Israel may find hope.
All who leave you will suffer shame.
Those who turn away from you will be consigned to the
 netherworld.
For they have rejected you, the Lord, the fountain of life.
~ JEREMIAH 17:13

9 And by being perfected in this way, he became the source of eternal salvation to all who obey him, **10** and he was designated by God as high priest *in the order of Melchizedek.*

~ HEBREWS 5:9, 10

THE WORD OF GOD LIBERATES

31 Then Jesus said to those Judeans who had believed him, "If you continue to follow my teaching, you are really my disciples **32** and you will know the truth, and the truth will set you free.

33 "We are descendants of Abraham," they replied, "and have never been anyone's slaves! How can you say, 'You will become free'?" **34** Jesus answered them, "I tell you the solemn truth, everyone who practices sin is a slave of sin. **35** The slave does not remain in the family forever, but the son remains forever.

36 So if the son sets you free, you will be really free. **37** I know that you are Abraham's descendants. But you want to kill me, because my teaching makes no progress among you. **38** I am telling you the things I have seen while with the Father; as for you, practice the things you have heard from the Father!"

~ JOHN 8:31-38

Every word of God is purified;
he is like a shield for those who take refuge in him.

~ PROVERBS 30:5

GOD SEEKS US OUT WHEN WE SIN

1 Now the serpent was more shrewd than any of the wild animals that the LORD God had made. He said to the woman, "Is it really true that God said, 'You must not eat from any tree of the orchard'?" **2** The woman said to the serpent, "We may eat of the fruit from the trees of the orchard; **3** but concerning the fruit of the tree that is in the middle of the orchard God said, 'You must not eat from it, and you must not touch it, or else you will die.'"

4 The serpent said to the woman, "Surely you will not die, **5** for God knows that when you eat from it your eyes will open and you will be like divine beings who know good and evil."

6 When the woman saw that the tree produced fruit that was good for food, was attractive to the eye, and was desirable for making one wise, she took some of its fruit and ate it. She also gave some of it to her husband who was with her, and he ate it.

7 Then the eyes of both of them opened, and they knew they were naked; so they sewed fig leaves together and made coverings for themselves.

8 Then the man and his wife heard the sound of the LORD God moving about in the orchard at the breezy time of the day, and they hid from the LORD God among the trees of the orchard.

9 But the LORD God called to the man and said to him, "Where are you?" 10 The man replied, "I heard you moving about in the or-chard, and I was afraid because I was naked, so I hid." 11 And the LORD God said, "Who told you that you were naked? Did you eat from the tree that I commanded you not to eat from?" 12 The man said, "The woman whom you gave me, she gave me some fruit from the tree and I ate it." 13 So the LORD God said to the woman, "What is this you have done?" And the woman replied, "The serpent tricked me, and I ate."

~ GENESIS 3:1-13

3 At the designated time Cain brought some of the fruit of the ground for an offering to the LORD. 4 But Abel brought some of the firstborn of his flock—even the fattest of them. And the LORD was pleased with Abel and his offering, 5 but with Cain and his offering he was not pleased. So Cain became very angry, and his expression was downcast.

6 Then the LORD said to Cain, "Why are you angry, and why is your expression downcast? 7 Is it not true that if you do what is right, you will be fine? But if you do not do what is right, sin is crouching at the door. It desires to dominate you, but you must subdue it."

8 Cain said to his brother Abel, "Let's go out to the field." While they were in the field, Cain attacked his brother Abel and killed him

9 Then the LORD said to Cain, "Where is your brother Abel?" And he replied, "I don't know! Am I my brother's guardian?"

10 But the LORD said, "What have you done? The voice of your

brother's blood is crying out to me from the ground! **11** So now, you are banished from the ground, which has opened its mouth to receive your brother's blood from your hand. **12** When you try to cultivate the ground it will no longer yield its best for you. You will be a homeless wanderer on the earth." **13** Then Cain said to the LORD, "My punishment is too great to endure! **14** Look! You are driving me off the land today, and I must hide from your presence. I will be a homeless wanderer on the earth; whoever finds me will kill me." **15** But the LORD said to him, "All right then, if anyone kills Cain, Cain will be avenged seven times as much." Then the LORD put a special mark on Cain so that no one who found him would strike him down. **16** So Cain went out from the presence of the LORD and lived in the land of Nod, east of Eden.

~ GENESIS 4:3-16

GOD IS NEAR TO THE CONTRITE HEART

The sacrifices God desires are a humble spirit—
O God, a humble and repentant heart you will not reject.
~ PSALM 51:17

For this is what the high and exalted one says,
the one who rules forever, whose name is holy:
"I dwell in an exalted and holy place,
but also with the discouraged and humiliated,
in order to cheer up the humiliated
and to encourage the discouraged.
~ ISAIAH 57:15

"My hand made them;
that is how they came to be," says the LORD.
I show special favor to the humble and contrite,
who respect what I have to say.
~ ISAIAH 66:2

461

GOD IS NEAR TO THE BROKENHEARTED

The LORD is near the brokenhearted;
he delivers those who are discouraged.
~ PSALM 34:18

He heals the brokenhearted,
and bandages their wounds.
~ PSALM 147:3

The spirit of the sovereign LORD is upon me,
because the LORD has chosen me.
He has commissioned me to encourage the poor,
to help the brokenhearted,
to decree the release of captives,
and the freeing of prisoners,
~ ISAIAH 61:1

GOD REJOICES WHEN WE SEEK HIM HUMBLY

1 Now all the tax collectors and sinners were coming to hear him. **2** But the Pharisees and the experts in the law were complaining, "This man welcomes sinners and eats with them."

3 So Jesus told them this parable: **4** "Which one of you, if he has a hundred sheep and loses one of them, would not leave the ninety-nine in the open pasture and go look for the one that is lost until he finds it? **5** Then when he has found it, he places it on his shoulders, rejoicing. **6** Returning home, he calls together his friends and neighbors, telling them, 'Rejoice with me, because I have found my sheep that was lost.' **7** I tell you, in the same way there will be more joy in heaven over one sinner who repents than over ninety-nine righteous people who have no need to repent.

8 "Or what woman, if she has ten silver coins and loses one of them, does not light a lamp, sweep the house, and search thoroughly until she finds it? **9** Then when she has found it, she calls together her friends and neighbors, saying, 'Rejoice with me, for I have found the coin that I had lost.' **10** In the same way, I tell you, there is joy in the presence of God's angels over one sinner who repents."

11 Then Jesus said, "A man had two sons. **12** The younger of them said to his father, 'Father, give me the share of the estate that will belong to me.' So he divided his assets between them.

13 After a few days, the younger son gathered together all he had and left on a journey to a distant country, and there he squandered his wealth with a wild lifestyle. **14** Then after he had spent everything, a severe famine took place in that country, and he began to be in need. **15** So he went and worked for one of the citizens of that country, who sent him to his fields to feed pigs. **16** He was longing to eat the carob pods the pigs were eating, but no one gave him anything. **17** But when he came to his senses he said, 'How many of my father's hired workers have food enough to spare, but here I am dying from hunger! **18** I will get up and go to my father and say to him, "Father, I have sinned against heaven and against you. **19** I am no longer worthy to be called your son; treat me like one of your hired workers."' **20** So he got up and went to his father. But while he was still a long way from home his father saw him, and his heart went out to him; he ran and hugged his son and kissed him. **21** Then his son said to him, 'Father, I have sinned against heaven and against you; I am no longer worthy to be called your son.' **22** But the father said to his slaves, 'Hurry! Bring the best robe, and put it on him! Put a ring on his finger and sandals on his feet! **23** Bring the fattened calf and kill it! Let us eat and celebrate, **24** because this son of mine was dead, and is alive again—he was lost and is found!' So they began to celebrate.

25 "Now his older son was in the field. As he came and approached the house, he heard music and dancing. **26** So he called one of the slaves and asked what was happening. **27** The slave replied, 'Your brother has returned, and your father has killed the fattened calf because he got his son back safe and sound.'

28 But the older son became angry and refused to go in. His father came out and appealed to him, **29** but he answered his father,

'Look! These many years I have worked like a slave for you, and I never disobeyed your commands. Yet you never gave me even a goat so that I could celebrate with my friends! **30** But when this son of yours came back, who has devoured your assets with prostitutes, you killed the fattened calf for him!' **31** Then the father said to him, 'Son, you are always with me, and everything that belongs to me is yours. **32** It was appropriate to celebrate and be glad, for your brother was dead, and is alive; he was lost and is found.'"
~ LUKE 15:1-32

GOD IS MY HIDING PLACE

You are my hiding place;
you protect me from distress.
You surround me with shouts of joy from those celebrating
deliverance. (Selah)
~ PSALM 32:7

You are my hiding place and my shield.
I find hope in your word.
~ PSALM 119:114

GOD IS MY REFUGE

But may all who take shelter in you be happy!
May they continually shout for joy!
Shelter them so that those who are loyal to you may rejoice!
~ PSALM 5:11

Protect me, O God, for I have taken shelter in you.
~ PSALM 16:1

The LORD rescues his servants;
all who take shelter in him escape punishment.
~ PSALM 34:22

The LORD helps them and rescues them;
he rescues them from evil men and delivers them,
for they seek his protection.
~ PSALM 37:40

Have mercy on me, O God! Have mercy on me!
For in you I have taken shelter.
In the shadow of your wings I take shelter
until trouble passes.
~ PSALM 57:1

The godly will rejoice in the LORD
and take shelter in him.
All the morally upright will boast.
~ PSALM 64:10

But as for me, God's presence is all I need.
I have made the sovereign LORD my shelter,
as I declare all the things you have done.
~ PSALM 73:28

8 It is better to take shelter in the LORD
   than to trust in people.
9 It is better to take shelter in the LORD
   than to trust in princes.
~ PSALM 118:8, 9

17 In the same way God wanted to demonstrate more clearly to the heirs of the promise that his purpose was unchangeable, and so he intervened with an oath, 18 so that we who have found refuge in him may find strong encouragement to hold fast to the hope set before us through two unchangeable things, since it is impossible for God to lie. 19 We have this hope as an anchor for the soul, sure and steadfast, which reaches inside behind the curtain,
20 where Jesus our forerunner entered on our behalf, since he became *a priest forever in the order of Melchizedek.*
~HEBREWS 6:17-20

www.ingramcontent.com/pod-product-compliance
Lightning Source LLC
Chambersburg PA
CBHW031943090426
42739CB00006B/59